M000072911

CALIFORNIA WATERFALLS

ANN MARIE BROWN

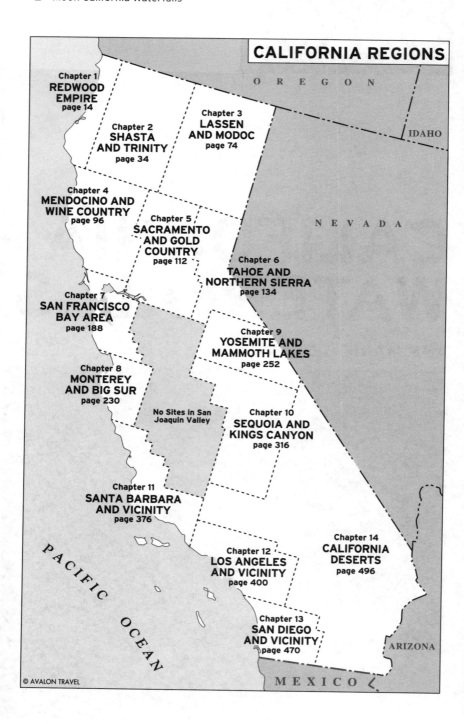

CALIFORNIA REGIONS

O R E G O N

IDAHO

Chapter 1
REDWOOD EMPIRE
page 14

Chapter 2
SHASTA AND TRINITY
page 34

Chapter 3
LASSEN AND MODOC
page 74

Chapter 4
MENDOCINO AND WINE COUNTRY
page 96

Chapter 5
SACRAMENTO AND GOLD COUNTRY
page 112

N E V A D A

Chapter 6
TAHOE AND NORTHERN SIERRA
page 134

Chapter 7
SAN FRANCISCO BAY AREA
page 188

Chapter 9
YOSEMITE AND MAMMOTH LAKES
page 252

Chapter 8
MONTEREY AND BIG SUR
page 230

No Sites in San Joaquin Valley

Chapter 10
SEQUOIA AND KINGS CANYON
page 316

Chapter 11
SANTA BARBARA AND VICINITY
page 376

Chapter 14
CALIFORNIA DESERTS
page 496

P A C I F I C

Chapter 12
LOS ANGELES AND VICINITY
page 400

O C E A N

Chapter 13
SAN DIEGO AND VICINITY
page 470

ARIZONA

© AVALON TRAVEL

M E X I C O

Contents

How to Use This Book

ABOUT THE MAPS

This book is divided into chapters based on regions within the state; an overview map of these regions precedes the table of contents. Each chapter begins with a region map that shows the locations and numbers of the trails listed in that chapter.

Each trail profile is also accompanied by a detailed trail map that shows the hike route.

Map Symbols

– – – – – ·	Featured Trail	(80)	Interstate Freeway	○	City/Town
– – – – – ·	Other Trail	(101)	U.S. Highway	↘	Waterfall
▓▓▓▓▓	Expressway	(21)	State Highway	✕✈	Airfield/Airport
═══════	Primary Road	66	County Highway	⚲	Golf Course
▬▬▬▬▬	Secondary Road	★	Point of Interest	▲	Mountain
▫ ▫ ▫ ▫ ▫ ▫	Unpaved Road	P	Parking Area	⚑	Park
··············	Ferry	T	Trailhead	)(	Pass
───·──·─	National Border	A	Campground	▱	Swamp
───··──	State Border	▪	Other Location	✦	Unique Natural Feature

ABOUT THE TRAIL PROFILES

Each profile includes a narrative description of the trail's setting and terrain. This description also typically includes mile-by-mile hiking directions, as well as information about the trail's highlights and unique attributes.

The trails marked by the **BEST** ◖ symbol are highlighted in the author's Best list.

Directions

This section provides detailed driving directions to the trailhead from the city center or from the intersection of major highways. When public transportation is available, instructions will be noted here.

Information and Contact

This section provides information on fees, facilities, and access restrictions for the trail. It also includes the name of the land management agency or organization that oversees the trail, as well as an address, phone number, and website if available.

ABOUT THE ICONS

The icons in this book are designed to provide at-a-glance information on special features for each trail.

- Access is by day hiking on an established trail.
- Access may require extensive travel or an overnight trip.
- Access may be slippery, including wading and stream crossings.
- The trail is accessible by mountain bike.

- The waterfall is accessible by car and is suitable for families.
- The waterfall has a swimming hole.
- The trail is wheelchair accessible.
- Dogs are allowed.
- Tent sites are available nearby.

Author's Note

There's magic in waterfalls. In the space where rock meets water, resulting in the steep descent of a river or stream, something occurs that is far richer than just a geologic irregularity. You can see it in the faces of people watching a waterfall. A star-filled sky can be compelling, a snow-capped mountain range can be awe-inspiring, an after-storm rainbow can stop you in your tracks, but only a waterfall can make you feel like you've fallen in love.

Some scientists explain this phenomenon by pointing out that fast-flowing water ejects ionized particles into the air, supercharging the atmosphere with energy. Others say that because our human bodies are mostly water, and water is the lifeblood of the earth, we have a natural affinity with free-flowing rivers and streams. I take a less systematic approach. I believe that humans are innately drawn to natural beauty, and that despite our efforts to control the goings-on of every inch of our planet, we are still thrilled to see beauty that is created without, or in spite of, human intervention . . . beauty that is caused by elements as random (and fickle) as rainfall, snowmelt, and the meandering course of water over rock.

It seems we cannot contain our delight at finding a river or stream that appears to fall from the sky. Perfectly responsible adults get downright giddy at the base of a plummeting cataract. When face-to-face with a shimmering cascade, children forget about the miles of trail they were forced to walk. Or, as my friend said when I took her on a particularly successful waterfall hunt, "Oh, now I see. We get to visit all of God's art museums."

I've spent several years wandering around the state of California, following the courses of rivers and streams in mountainous areas and praying for rain. The results of my research are found in this book, including all the facts you need to visit California's finest falls, whether you go by car, by bicycle, or on foot, and whether you carry a 40-pound backpack or a diaper bag for your newborn baby. Inside these pages, you'll find waterfalls from the beaches to the mountains to the desert. You'll find falls ranging in height from 15 feet to 2,425 feet, and falls that are easy, moderate, and difficult to reach. Some are world-famous, and others are secret, hidden spots, far from the madding crowd. Some have luscious swimming holes; others occur in streams and rivers that are laden with hungry trout. All of them are places you'll want to visit again and again.

In your travels, please remember to take care of this beautiful land. I wish all of us many inspiring days in the outdoors.

Best Waterfalls

Can't decide which waterfall to visit this weekend? Here are my picks of the best falls in California:

❰ Best Short Backpacking Trips
Maple Falls (8.0 miles), Shasta and Trinity, page 37
Little Jamison Falls (3.0 miles), Tahoe and Northern Sierra, page 137
South Fork Kaweah Falls (3.4 miles), Sequoia and Kings Canyon, page 348
Potrero John Falls (5.4 miles), Santa Barbara and Vicinity, page 394
Santa Ynez Canyon Falls (6.0 miles), Los Angeles and Vicinity, page 416
Switzer Falls (2.5 miles), Los Angeles and Vicinity, page 423

❰ Best Long Backpacking Trips
Wilderness Falls (13.0 or 19.0 miles), Redwood Empire, page 22
Canyon Creek Falls (15.0 miles), Shasta and Trinity, page 49
Alamere Falls (10.5 miles), San Francisco Bay Area, page 192
Pine Falls (10.6 miles), Monterey and Big Sur, page 244
Seven Falls and Mission Falls (12.0 or 38.0 miles), Santa Barbara and Vicinity, page 386

❰ Best by Bicycle
Gold Bluffs Beach Falls, Redwood Empire, page 25
Russian Gulch Falls, Mendocino and Wine Country, page 98
Feather Falls, Sacramento and Gold Country, page 121
Berry Creek Falls, San Francisco Bay Area, page 218
Los Peñasquitos Falls, San Diego and Vicinity, page 481

❰ Best by Car
Devil's Falls, Tahoe and Northern Sierra, page 160
Leavitt Falls, Tahoe and Northern Sierra, page 184
Whiskey Falls, Sequoia and Kings Canyon, page 324
Grizzly Falls, Sequoia and Kings Canyon, page 336
South Creek Falls, Sequoia and Kings Canyon, page 369

❰ Best Easy Waterfall Walks
McCloud Falls, Shasta and Trinity, page 64
Burney Falls, Lassen and Modoc, page 77

Big Falls, Santa Barbara and Vicinity, page 379
Seven Falls and Mission Falls, Santa Barbara and Vicinity, page 386
Santa Ynez Canyon Falls, Los Angeles and Vicinity, page 416

◖ Best Wheelchair-Accessible Waterfalls
Rush Creek Falls, Sacramento and Gold Country, page 124
Frazier Falls, Tahoe and Northern Sierra, page 140
Bear River Falls, Tahoe and Northern Sierra, page 152
McWay Falls, Monterey and Big Sur, page 240
Bridalveil Fall, Yosemite and Mammoth Lakes, page 286
Yosemite Falls, Yosemite and Mammoth Lakes, page 289
Roaring River Falls, Sequoia and Kings Canyon, page 337

REDWOOD EMPIRE

© ANN MARIE BROWN

BEST WATERFALLS

【 Long Backpacking Trips
Wilderness Falls, **page 22**

【 Bicycle
Gold Bluffs Beach Falls, **page 25**

【 Most Unusual
Gold Bluffs Beach Falls, **page 25**

【 State Parks
Gold Bluffs Beach Falls, **page 25**

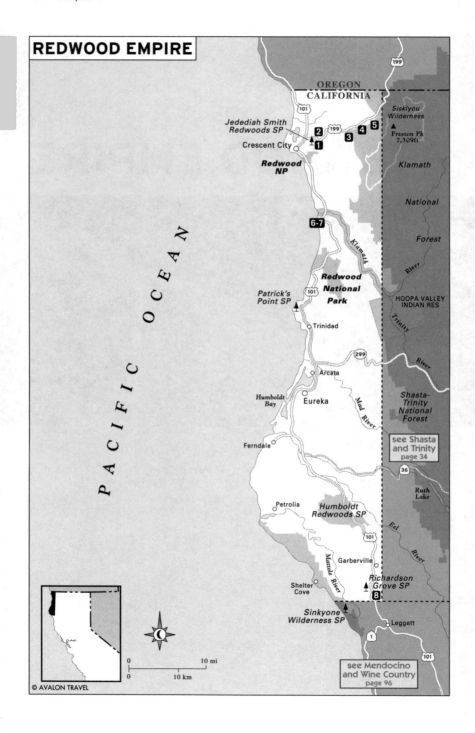

TRAIL NAME	LEVEL	DISTANCE	ELEVATION	SEASON	FEATURES	PAGE
1 Fern Falls	Moderate	6.0 mi rt	200 ft	Dec.–June		16
2 Myrtle Creek Falls	Strenuous	5.0 mi rt	400 ft	Dec.–June		17
3 Highway 199 Falls	Easy	Negligible	500 ft	Dec.–June		19
4 Middle Fork Falls	Strenuous	0.25 mile rt	150 ft	Dec.–June		20
5 Wilderness Falls	Moderate	13.0–19.0 mi rt	1,200 ft	June–Sept.		22
6 Gold Bluffs Beach Falls	Easy	3.0 mi rt	Negligible	Dec.–June		25
7 James Irvine Trail Falls	Easy	2.0 mi rt	200 ft	Dec.–June		27
8 Dora Falls	Easy	0.25 mile rt	20 ft	Dec.–May		30

❶ FERN FALLS
Jedediah Smith Redwoods State Park

Level: Moderate   **Distance:** 6.0 miles round-trip

Best Season: December–June   **Elevation Change:** Total gain 200 feet

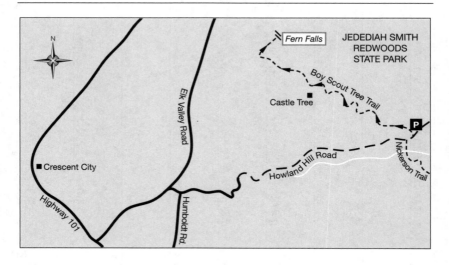

At only 35 feet tall, Fern Falls may not be the largest waterfall around, but it's one of the prettiest in the Redwood National and State Parks. It's hard to look big when you're surrounded on all sides by 300-foot-tall coastal redwood trees with trunks large enough to build a room in.

   The drive to the trailhead alone is worth the trip; a narrow dirt road leads through superb old-growth redwoods. Next comes the hike through drop-dead gorgeous scenery along the Boy Scout Tree Trail. It's three sublime miles of old-growth redwood trees, giant sword ferns, and cloverlike sorrel with its deep green topsides and purple undersides. If you feel a little light-headed as you hike, it's probably because you're not accustomed to such an abundance of plant life and all the oxygen it produces. Or maybe you're just feeling dizzy from spending so much time with your neck craned, gazing up toward the sky to see the tops of the big trees.

   The Boy Scout Tree Trail is a gentle up-and-down route that never gains or loses more than 200 feet in elevation. Despite the minimal grade, the going is slow because there's so much to see, photograph, and remark on. On my last trip, I passed a hiker coming out of the forest. He grinned and said, "Turn back! We're outnumbered by the trees!" I knew exactly how he felt; it's downright humbling walking among these giants. At 2.5 miles, an obvious spur trail leads to the Boy Scout Tree, a huge double redwood. It seems more appropriate to call this magnificent specimen the Eagle Scout rather than merely the Boy Scout.

At the trail's end at 3.0 miles, you're rewarded by the sight of Fern Falls, a 35-foot cascade on a tributary of Jordan Creek. The path ends at an overlook next to the waterfall, but if you wish, you can scramble a few feet down to its base. From either viewpoint, it's easy to admire the waterfall's graceful S-curve as it rushes down the canyon wall, forming a twisting rope of whitewater amidst deep green ferns and redwoods.

Fern Falls

Directions

From U.S. 101 in Crescent City, turn east on Elk Valley Road and drive 1.1 miles, then turn right on Howland Hill Road. Drive 3.5 miles to the Boy Scout Tree Trailhead on the left.

Information and Contact

There is no fee. Park brochures and maps are available for free by download at www.parks.ca.gov. For more information, contact Jedediah Smith Redwoods State Park, 707/458-3018 or 707/464-6101, www.parks.ca.gov.

2 MYRTLE CREEK FALLS
Smith River National Recreation Area

Level: Strenuous   **Distance:** 5.0 miles round-trip

Best Season: December–June   **Elevation Change:** Total gain 400 feet

The trip to Myrtle Creek Falls starts as a blissfully easy romp on an interpretive trail, but before long, it turns into a treacherous, muddy scramble along the streambanks, up and over rock slides, and against an advancing army of waist-high sword ferns. Depending on the season, you can slip in the mud on steep slopes, get scratched by thimbleberry bushes, or be soaked to the skin from heavy dew on the streamside plants. Even if you make it to the falls, you still have to endure the return trip.

Is it worth it, you ask? Maybe. If your footing is sure when there is no trail to follow, if you know how to travel on steep, rough streamside routes—then yes, Myrtle Creek Falls is worth it. This 60-foot waterfall drops on a roaring stream that feeds directly into the Middle Fork of the Smith River. If you reach it, you're likely to have this beauty all to yourself.

Even if you're not willing to make the rough cross-country trip to the falls, the Myrtle Creek Trail is worth a gander for its first mile. In this initial stretch, the trail is well-maintained, and the Gasquet Ranger Station provides an interpretive brochure that corresponds with numbered posts on the trail, so you can learn about the streamside flora and the area's gold-mining history. For instance, can you guess the size of the largest gold nugget ever taken out of Myrtle Creek? Forty-seven ounces. That must have bought the miners a few dinners out.

The first mile of trail is built on an old mining ditch, high above the creek, so it's virtually flat. After signpost 15 and the end of the interpretive trail, the route continues, but it is quickly overgrown. In minutes you reach the first of several landslides, which you must navigate around.

And so it goes. There are three main slides to get past, plus numerous other obstacles, such as very wet, unstable soil and thick forests of ferns on steep slopes. (The good news is that because Myrtle Creek is fed by springs and feeder streams, you cross paths with many small cascades along the way. You could be content with these and turn around at any point.)

After an hour of slow off-trail travel (try to keep high above the creek on the rough, hard-to-discern route), you'll come upon the first of several small cascades and falls on Myrtle Creek. From there, you have 0.5 mile to go, and if the creek is low, it's advisable to descend to the creekbed and follow it. If Myrtle Creek is running hard, as it was on my trip, you'll have no choice but to stay high, fighting for footholds amid the downed trees, tangled branches, and ubiquitous ferns. Are we having fun yet?

If all goes well, you should reach Myrtle Creek Falls in an hour and a half of scrambling, during which you will have covered only 1.5 miles from the end of the one-mile, maintained Myrtle Creek Trail. Don't say I didn't warn you.

By the way, one more hazard exists on the Myrtle Creek Trail. It's the carnivorous (actually insectivorous) pitcher plant, a distant cousin of the Venus flytrap plant. You'll see its two-foot-high stems with cobralike heads growing along the trail. The hungry plants won't bother you, but make sure you keep your pet beetle on a short leash.

Directions

From Crescent City, drive north on U.S. 101 for four miles to the Highway 199 exit. Turn east on Highway 199 and drive 6.5 miles to the Myrtle Creek Trailhead, west of the Myrtle Creek bridge and the South Fork Road turnoff. Park on the south side of Highway 199, then cross the road to reach the trailhead.

Information and Contact

There is no fee. Maps of Six Rivers National Forest, which include Smith River National Recreation Area, are available for a fee from the National Forest Store (406/329-3024, www.nationalforeststore.com), or can be downloaded for free from www.fs.fed.us/r5/maps/. For more information, contact the Gasquet Ranger Station of Six Rivers National Forest, 707/457-3131, www.fs.fed.us/r5/sixrivers.

3 HIGHWAY 199 FALLS
Smith River National Recreation Area

Level: Easy   **Distance:** Negligible

Best Season: December–June   **Elevation Change:** Total gain 500 feet

In the rainy season, so many waterfalls cascade alongside Highway 199 and the Smith River that it seems there are too many to count. But if it's quality you want, not quantity, the tallest waterfalls along this stretch of Highway 199 are in the proximity of Grassy Flat Campground. Across the river from the camp, an unnamed creek drops 80 feet along the steep slope leading down to the Middle Fork Smith River. And less than a mile east of the camp, another 80-foot fall drops over a rockslide just off the highway, accessible by a gravel spur road.

The best way to see the fall across from Grassy Flat is to take the camp access road, then follow it past the camp, down to the river's edge. At the end of the road, you're directly across from the big fall, which often has a sibling waterfall running 50 yards distant from it. The two of them make quite a sight, racing down the hillside to join the Smith River. Of course, the river itself also makes quite a sight, running fast and green in winter and spring, dropping through rapids and into deep pools, and passing swiftly through granite gorges. It's the largest wild and undammed river still flowing in California.

You can get closer to this waterfall by driving 0.25 mile farther east on Highway 199, to the river-access turnoff just past Grassy Flat Campground. Leave your car at the end of the access road, near the river, and scramble downstream a few hundred feet to the falls. If the weather is dry, this is easily accomplished, but if it's wet, scrambling over the jumbled base of a rockslide is slippery and difficult. Use your judgment.

Just down the road from the Grassy Flat Camp waterfall is another 80-foot cascade, spilling down a giant landslide and plainly visible from the highway. To reach it from Grassy Flat, drive east on Highway 199 for 0.75 mile. There's a gravel turnoff on the right, where you can pull off the highway, park, and walk to the base of the falls.

Directions
From Crescent City, drive north on U.S. 101 for four miles to the Highway 199 exit. Turn east on Highway 199 and drive 14 miles to Gasquet, then continue east for 4.5 miles more to the Grassy Flat Campground turnoff on the right. (The campground is often closed in winter, but you can still enter.)

Information and Contact
There is no fee. Maps of Six Rivers National Forest, which include Smith River National Recreation Area, are available for a fee from the National Forest Store (406/329-3024, www.nationalforeststore.com), or can be downloaded for free from www.fs.fed.us/r5/maps/. For more information, contact the Gasquet Ranger Station of Six Rivers National Forest, 707/457-3131, www.fs.fed.us/r5/sixrivers.

◢ MIDDLE FORK FALLS
Smith River National Recreation Area

Level: Strenuous   **Distance:** 0.25 mile round-trip

Best Season: December–June   **Elevation Change:** Total loss 150 feet

I almost didn't bother to go see Middle Fork Falls, on the Middle Fork Smith River east of Gasquet and Patrick Creek. The ranger told me the waterfall was only 25 feet high, and because I knew it was a river fall, I expected a wide, rocky cascade and lots of white water, but not much drama. But when a rainy day cancelled my plans for a longer hike, I took the drive down Knopki Road off Highway 199 to see what Middle Fork Falls was all about.

© ANN MARIE BROWN

Middle Fork Falls

The rain was lucky for me. Middle Fork Falls, which some call Knopki Falls, turns out to be a sensational drop of churning river over a 25-foot vertical cliff. Rather than pouring wide and evenly over its lip, the river has channeled a V-shape into the granite, funneling itself into a narrow stream. This makes the flow of water at the falls double or triple what it is elsewhere on the river. The Middle Fork Smith was running high on the day I visited, and the waterfall ran in two streams—one big drop on the left and an overflow drop on the right, creating a tremendous rush of water. The crashing fall has incredible impact, both on its viewers and where it strikes its wide pool below.

The unmarked route to the waterfall is not easy to find. Make sure you travel exactly 2.2 miles on Knopki Road, then start looking for the point where the Middle Fork Smith River separates from the road and heads south. If Knopki Road starts to follow Knopki Creek instead of the Smith River, you've gone past the trailhead. (A map of the Smith River National Recreation Area is immensely helpful.)

On my trip, the start of the route to the falls was marked with an odd, hand-lettered sign hanging high on a tree: "Hope is Eternal." It got my hopes up, and so did the noise of falling water, which was surprisingly loud at the road. One hundred feet of travel down a well-worn route over a rockslide brought me to a cluster of moss-covered oak trees. Some waterfall-lover had tied a strong rope to the largest oak, which I used to safely lower myself down to a rock outcrop with a wide-open view of the falls, on the far side of its giant pool. In wet weather, the outcrop is no place for the unsure-footed, since it has very little surface area and can be slippery.

Another rope leads down from the rock to the fall's pool, a perfect place for swimming on some fair summer day.

Directions

From Crescent City, drive north on U.S. 101 for four miles to the Highway 199 exit. Turn east on Highway 199 and drive 14 miles to Gasquet, then continue east for 15.5 more miles to the Knopki Road turnoff on the right. Turn right on

Knopki Road/Forest Service Road 18N07 and drive 2.2 miles to the unmarked trailhead on the right. Park alongside the road, and look for a route leading from the south side of the road down to the river.

Information and Contact

There is no fee. Maps of Six Rivers National Forest, which include Smith River National Recreation Area, are available for a fee from the National Forest Store (406/329-3024, www.nationalforeststore.com), or can be downloaded for free from www.fs.fed.us/r5/maps/. For more information, contact the Gasquet Ranger Station of Six Rivers National Forest, 707/457-3131, www.fs.fed.us/r5/sixrivers.

5 WILDERNESS FALLS
Siskiyou Wilderness

Level: Moderate

Distance: 13 miles round-trip (Doe Flat) or 19 miles round-trip (Young's Valley)

Best Season: June-September

Elevation Change: Total loss 1,200 feet

If you're planning to make the trek to Wilderness Falls, you have some soul-searching to do. Two different trails can take you there, each with its individual challenges. You need to know the details of both itineraries, consider your options, then decide which path suits you best. Once that's accomplished, the hard work is over and the fun begins, because Wilderness Falls is the most spectacular cataract in the northwest corner of California.

The route from the Young's Valley Trailhead is the longest and most scenic route to Wilderness Falls. It requires a long, winding drive to reach the trailhead—at least an hour from Gasquet—then a 9.5-mile hike to the falls. If you have the time and don't mind the

Wilderness Falls

mileage, this is the way to make the trip. The first two miles of trail are a closed road, but after that, you drop into the canyon of Clear Creek—a 600-foot elevation loss—and it's smooth sailing the rest of the way. The trail strolls pleasantly along the east side of the stream, mostly out in the sun, covering a gentle and gradual descent from the headwaters of Clear Creek at 4,600 feet to Wilderness Falls at 3,000 feet. The elevation loss is spread out over seven miles, so it makes for an easy climb on the return trip.

The alternative is to come in from the Doe Flat Trailhead at Siskiyou Pass, a shorter drive from Gasquet and a much shorter hike to the falls—only 6.5 miles one-way, with a 1,200-foot elevation loss. As with the Young's Valley Trail, here again you walk on a closed road for

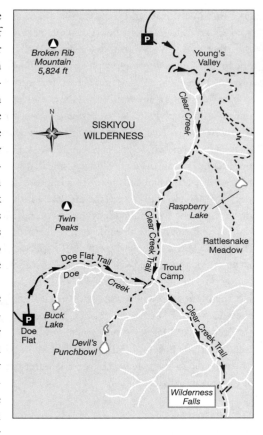

1.5 miles before you reach the real trail, which is an old mining path along Doe Creek. You pass an old mine site on your way to Trout Camp at 3.5 miles, where the Doe Flat Trail ends and joins with the Clear Creek Trail out of Young's Valley. (There's also a turnoff here for the trail to Devil's Punchbowl, an area of stunning glacial beauty.) Then it's an easy three miles on the Clear Creek Trail to Wilderness Falls.

If the Doe Flat Trail seems like the obvious choice for the trip, be forewarned about the junction at Trout Camp where the trail ends and connects with the Clear Creek Trail. The problem? The Doe Flat Trail is on the west side of Clear Creek and the Clear Creek Trail is on the east side, and never the twain shall meet unless you ford the stream. Clear Creek is not a narrow, babbling brook. Especially early in the summer, when Clear Creek runs full with snowmelt and is freezing cold, the crossing can be difficult. You can't make the ford with your shoes off; your toes will go numb in no time, and the streambed is too slick. The only choice is to take off your socks and wear your boots on your naked feet, then grit it out till you get to the other side. Those warm, dry socks will feel heavenly when you put them back on. In late summer, some people walk up and down the stream near Trout Camp till they find a way to rock-hop across, but most hikers just give up and wade.

Consider your route options, make a choice, then one way or another get yourself to Wilderness Falls. What can you expect when get there? An excellent camp, for starters, just five minutes from the waterfall. It's located at a small clearing near the stream, where you can watch the stars all night. Then, just around a few boulders lies magnificent Wilderness Falls, where Clear Creek drops 50 feet in perfect free fall, then collides with a big rock and cascades downward. Although the Clear Creek Trail crosses the creek at a ford right above the falls, you need not do so to see the waterfall. There are two excellent overlook points on big boulders on the east side of the stream, just 50 feet from the falls. If you choose to make the ford, you can descend to the fall's spectacular 100-foot-wide pool, which is clear, deep, and white with foam from the continual pounding of water.

Keep in mind that because you've driven so far east on Highway 199, you've left the giant redwood forests and the cool, foggy coast far behind. That means they have "real" summer here, and because the forest is a mixed bag of Douglas firs, cedars, and Jeffrey pines, you're not protected by impenetrable shade all day long. It can be hot, especially when hiking back out and heading uphill on either of the trails. Make sure you have your water filter with you, and fill your bottles at every opportunity.

Directions

For the Young's Valley Trailhead: from Crescent City, drive north on U.S. 101 for four miles to the Highway 199 exit. Turn east on Highway 199 and drive 14 miles to Gasquet; then continue east for 15.5 more miles to the Knopki Road turnoff on the right. Turn right on Knopki Road/Forest Service Road 18N07 and drive approximately 14 miles, passing Sanger Lake. The trailhead is at the end of the road.

For the Doe Flat Trailhead: follow the directions above to Gasquet. From Gasquet, continue east on Highway 199 for 11 miles to the Little Jones Creek Road/Jawbone Road turnoff on the right, shortly past Patrick Creek Lodge. Turn right and drive about 10 miles to the Bear Basin junction. Turn left and follow the road to Siskiyou Pass. The trailhead is at the end of the road.

Information and Contact

There is no fee. A free wilderness permit is required for overnight stays; they are available at the Gasquet Ranger Station of Six Rivers National Forest, 707/457-3131. Maps of the Siskiyou Wilderness are available for a fee from the National Forest Store (406/329-3024, www.nationalforeststore.com), or can be downloaded for free from www.fs.fed.us/r5/maps/. For more information, contact the Gasquet Ranger Station of Six Rivers National Forest, 707/457-3131, www.fs.fed.us/r5/sixrivers.

6 GOLD BLUFFS BEACH FALLS
Prairie Creek Redwoods State Park

Level: Easy

Best Season: December–June

Distance: 3.0 miles round-trip

Elevation Change: Negligible

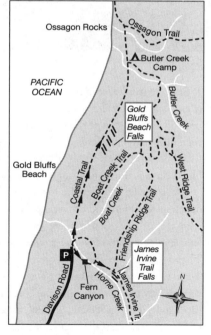

The only thing that keeps Fern Canyon, Gold Bluffs Beach, and the Coastal Trail's waterfalls from being completely overrun with tourists is the long, unpaved road to reach them. No trailers or RVs are allowed on gravel-lined Davison Road, so that eliminates plenty of visitors right there. In addition, the road has different moods in different weather: sometimes it's smoothly graded, almost like glass, and sometimes it's full of potholes, or has a foot-deep stream running across it. You just never know.

If your vehicle is able to make the seven-mile drive from U.S. 101, you're in luck, because there are many hidden treasures at the end of Davison Road. Probably the most famous is Fern Canyon, a secluded, rocky grotto on Home Creek that is a veritable paradise of ferns growing on 50-foot-high canyon walls. (See the James Irvine Trail Falls listing in this chapter.) There's also an excellent chance of seeing magnificent Roosevelt elk, perhaps even looking eye-to-eye with some of these resident deer on steroids. Plus there's Gold Bluffs Beach, a pristine, windswept stretch of sand along the Pacific, where you can beachcomb and walk for miles.

© ANN MARIE BROWN

Gold Bluffs Beach Falls

And last but certainly not least, there is the Coastal Trail, with three sweet waterfalls that drop alongside it. The trail traverses a flat route from the end of Davison Road to a backpacking camp 2.2 miles out, then it continues for another 2.2 miles along the coast before it climbs back out to the highway. If you just want to see its three falls along Gold Bluffs Beach, you need only walk (or ride your bike) 1.5 miles out from the parking lot.

The waterfalls are just slightly off the trail; you must listen for the gentle sound of splashing water, and keep looking to your right for spur trails leading into the trees. Each of these spurs is your ticket to one of three tall, narrow cataracts, all of them hidden in grottos carved from a canopy of spruce and alders.

Start your hike from the Fern Canyon parking lot by negotiating the sometimes tricky crossing of Home Creek. Coastal Trail starts due north of the lot, at a signpost on the far side of the creek. After the stream crossing, the rest of the trail is incredibly easy and level and it stays fairly dry even in the wettest weather. That's why bikes are allowed on this section of the Coastal Trail; the flat, windswept bluffs have soil tough enough to withstand their weight and speed.

After a brief stint in the forest, the scenery opens up and you walk with the ocean on your left and tall, vertical bluffs on your right. Be prepared to see big elk, who are usually grazing somewhere along the trail. It's not uncommon to see at least a dozen of the big males, who bear impressive antler racks most of the year. They tend to completely ignore hikers, but hikers rarely ignore them.

At 1.1 miles, start listening for the sound of falling water and look for an unsigned spur trail penetrating the alder and spruce forest on your right. Follow the short spur and you'll find the first cascade, an 80-foot narrow free fall reminiscent of Hawaiian waterfalls—tall, slender, and delicate, and surrounded by a myriad of ferns. On one visit here, I spotted hundreds of three-inch-wide mushrooms growing on a log near the fall's base, forming a thick forest of fungus.

Walk 0.25 mile farther, listen again for the sound of water, and watch again for a spur trail. You'll find yourself holding court with Gold Dust Falls, which is even taller and more mystical looking than the first fall. (The park has put up a sign on Coastal Trail denoting the spur to Gold Dust Falls, but each time I've visited, the sign was lying on the ground or hidden in the bushes.) Gold Dust Falls has a wooden bench near its base for waterfall watching, but it is often soaking wet and covered with moss.

Gold Dust is the only fall of the three that is named. It is dubbed for the short-lived 1850s gold rush along Gold Bluffs Beach, when five prospectors discovered gold dust in the sand and staked a claim. Thousands of others flocked to this beach and set up a tent city, but alas, extracting the gold turned out to be hard work that produced little profit. The mining boom ended almost as quickly as it began. Too bad they weren't looking for waterfalls instead.

The third waterfall is very close to Gold Dust Falls; another couple hundred feet on the Coastal Trail brings you to its spur trail. It, too, is a tall, narrow cataract, hidden in the deep shade of forest and ferns. Pay a visit, and then turn around and head back, or continue hiking on the Coastal Trail. Your options include an out-and-back trip of up to nine miles along the coast, or a seven-mile loop: you can turn right on the West Ridge Trail at 2.2 miles, then connect to the Friendship Ridge Trail, and follow it back to Fern Canyon and the parking area.

Directions

From Eureka, drive north on U.S. 101 for 41 miles to Orick. Continue north for 2.5 more miles to Davison Road, then turn left (west) and drive 6.5 miles to the Fern Canyon Trailhead. No trailers or RVs are permitted on unpaved Davison Road.

Information and Contact

An $8 day-use fee is charged per vehicle. Park brochures/maps are available for free by download at www.parks.ca.gov, or for a small fee at the park entrance kiosk or visitor center. For more information, contact Prairie Creek Redwoods State Park, 707/458-3018 or 707/464-6101, www.parks.ca.gov.

7 JAMES IRVINE TRAIL FALLS
Prairie Creek Redwoods State Park

Level: Easy	**Distance:** 2.0 miles round-trip
Best Season: December–June	**Elevation Change:** Total loss 200 feet

The wetter it is, the better it is. That's not always the case with hiking trails, but it's true if you're going to see the waterfalls in Fern Canyon and along the neighboring

James Irvine Trail in Prairie Creek Redwoods State Park. It can rain cats and dogs all day long and you'll still have a fine time on your trip. It's a convenient truth, because the area gets an average of 70 inches of rain a year.

Although the waterfalls benefit from the rain as much as anything else, they are really only a sideshow here. The falls in and around Fern Canyon are small and delicate. They are pretty to look at but unlikely to be the highlight of your trip. Instead, the foliage is the headliner—an overflowing cornucopia of ferns, redwood trees, Sitka spruces, alders, and moss. The more it rains, the more these plants like it.

James Irvine Trail Falls

Start your trip at the trailhead at the end of Davison Road. If it's winter or spring, the first thing to do is survey the level of Home Creek, which crosses just to the north of the trailhead parking lot. In summer and early fall, the creek level drops, and park rangers put up little bridges and walkways in Fern Canyon, making travel easy. In winter and spring, the stream often floods the canyon, wiping out any semblance of a trail. Although much of the time you can wear good hiking boots and rock-hop your way around, sometimes the stream level is too high even for that. Then you have a choice: put on your waterproof boots, and wade the 0.5 mile to the back of the canyon, or skip the Fern Canyon section of the trip and proceed directly to the James Irvine Trail. The latter has two entry points, one at the back of Fern Canyon and one at the entrance to it. You'll still need to cross Home Creek to access it.

Let's assume you can travel the entire route on both trails. Start by heading to your right into the canyon, passing through a corridor of ferns. Keep walking up the streambed, observing as the canyon walls grow taller and squeeze tighter. Try to identify all the fern types—sword ferns, lady ferns, five-finger ferns, chain ferns, and bracken ferns. You're completely surrounded by greenery, rocks, and water. Stay alert for the rare Pacific giant salamander, as well as more common frogs, salamanders, and newts.

Near the back of Fern Canyon, be sure to enter the small side canyon that harbors a narrow 12-foot waterfall. Then pick up the well-signed James Irvine Trail on the left, and climb upward. You'll enter a lush mixed forest of Sitka spruces, redwoods, alders, ferns, and vines. Like in Fern Canyon, every inch is covered in green. You'll see some very large and old examples of "octopus" trees: Western hemlocks that have sprouted on the tops of redwood stumps, then grown over and around them, clutching the stumps in their roots, or "legs."

A half mile after leaving the back of Fern Canyon (or one mile from the parking area, if you started hiking on the James Irvine Trail from there), you cross a bridge with two small benches where a 25-foot-tall, delicate waterfall drops into a remarkably narrow and deep canyon, eventually flowing to Home Creek and Fern Canyon. A sign denotes that the bridge and benches are dedicated to John Baldwin, and bears this lovely verse: "You shall walk where only the wind has walked before, and when all music is stilled, you shall hear the singing of the stream, and enter the living shelter of the forest."

You can turn around here and head back to the parking lot, either by following the James Irvine Trail the entire way or returning to Fern Canyon, but most likely you will want to walk farther. The trail continues onward for 3.5 miles before it ends at the park visitor center. The entire distance makes a terrific out-and-back walk.

While you are visiting Prairie Creek Redwoods State Park, you might want to take another short hike to see a diminutive waterfall near Elk Meadow, near the start of Davison Road. Lovely, 10-foot-high Trillium Falls cascades over mossy rocks beneath a canopy of big-leaf maples. A delightful 2.5-mile loop trail visits the falls, starting at the Trillium Falls Trailhead at Elk Meadow.

Directions
From Eureka, drive north on U.S. 101 for 41 miles to Orick. Continue north for 2.5 more miles to Davison Road, then turn left (west) and drive 6.5 miles to the Fern Canyon Trailhead. No trailers or RVs are permitted on unpaved Davison Road. For a trail map, see the listing for Gold Bluffs Beach Falls in this chapter.

Information and Contact
An $8 day-use fee is charged per vehicle. Park brochures/maps are available for free by download at www.parks.ca.gov, or for a small fee at the park entrance kiosk or visitor center. For more information, contact Prairie Creek Redwoods State Park, 707/458-3018 or 707/464-6101, www.parks.ca.gov.

8 DORA FALLS
Smithe Redwoods State Natural Reserve

🏃 🐕

Level: Easy   **Distance:** 0.25 mile round-trip

Best Season: December–May   **Elevation Change:** Total gain 20 feet

The truth of the matter: no one comes to Smithe Redwoods State Natural Reserve just to see Dora Falls. They come because the tiny park is a good leg-stretcher, a place to pull off the highway among big coastal redwoods. It's a roadside stop for walking the dog, or taking a look at the Eel River running by.

Dora Falls

Only an elite few know that right across the highway from the big trees and the river is a hidden waterfall, accessible by a five-minute walk. Unfortunately, seeing it means crossing U.S. 101 on foot, which you must do with care. Then it's an easy 100-yard stroll behind the highway bridge guardrail back into the canyon where Dora Falls drops, then pours under the highway and into the Eel River.

Poor Dora Falls has lost much of its original splendor. A huge landslide in 1978 filled in the lower portion of the falls, so its one-time 60-foot length is now only half that. The filled-in area at the fall's base is now overgrown with brush. It's easy to imagine what this canyon and waterfall looked like before the slide.

The grounds now known as Smithe Redwoods State Natural Reserve were once the site of Lane's Redwood Flat, a popular 1920s resort with a museum, restaurant, and 18 cabins. Right next to the present-day parking lot is a wide redwood tree with a walk-through tunnel, which used to serve as the entrance to the resort's restaurant. Lane's was destroyed in a 1930s fire, and eventually the state obtained the land and preserved it as a State Natural Reserve.

Dora Falls runs only after winter rains, so forget visiting it in summer or autumn. From December to May, it can put on quite a show. That's also when the

Eel River is most spectacular—high, green, and full of vigor. The reserve's redwoods are a marvel in any season.

Directions
From Willitts, drive north on U.S. 101 for 47 miles. Smithe Redwoods State Natural Reserve is 2.4 miles north of Standish-Hickey State Recreation Area, on the west side of the road. Dora Falls is across the highway on the east side of the road.

Information and Contact
There is no fee. For more information, contact the rangers at nearby Richardson Grove State Park at 1600 Highway 101, Garberville, CA 95440, 707/247-3318, www.parks.ca.gov.

MORE WATERFALLS IN THE REDWOOD EMPIRE
Usal Beach Waterfall on the Lost Coast. Walk 4.5 miles round-trip along the beach from the end of the road near Usal Campground. A low or minus tide is required to reach the waterfall. To reach Usal Beach, watch for the 90.88 mile marker on Highway 1 (about one hour north of Fort Bragg), where you turn north on Usal Road (it is often unsigned). Drive six miles to the road's end at the campground. The access road may be impassable in the rainy season, and is slow-going even when it is open and dry (plan on about one hour to travel the six miles of steep, narrow dirt road). Four-wheel-drive is recommended, but not necessary. For more information, phone Sinkyone Wilderness State Park at 707/986-7711, www.parks.ca.gov.

SHASTA
AND TRINITY

© ANN MARIE BROWN

BEST WATERFALLS

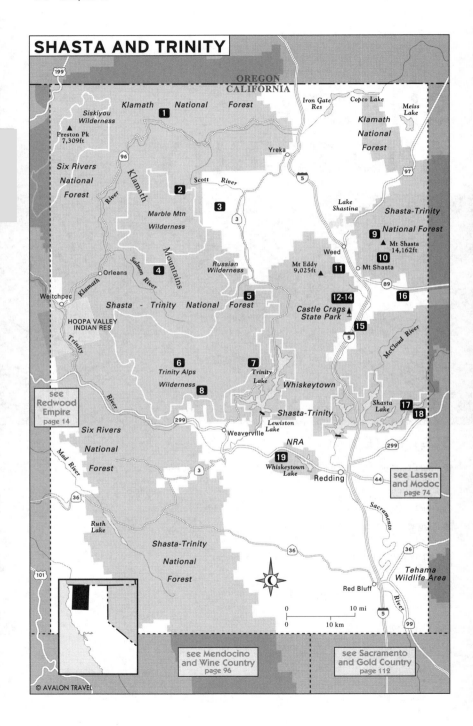

SHASTA AND TRINITY

OREGON
CALIFORNIA

Klamath National Forest

Siskiyou
Wilderness

▲ Preston Pk
7,309ft

Six Rivers
National
Forest

Klamath
National
Forest

Iron Gate
Res

Copco Lake

Meiss
Lake

Yreka

Scott River

Lake
Shastina

Shasta-Trinity
National Forest

Weed

▲ Mt Shasta
14,162ft

Mt Eddy
9,025ft ▲

Mt Shasta

Marble Mtn
Wilderness

Salmon River

Mountains

Klamath River

Orleans

Russian
Wilderness

Shasta - Trinity National Forest

Weitchpec

Castle Crags
State Park

McCloud River

HOOPA VALLEY
INDIAN RES

Trinity River

Trinity Alps

Wilderness

Trinity
Lake

Whiskeytown

Shasta
Lake

see
Redwood
Empire
page 14

Six Rivers

National

Forest

Mad River

Weaverville

Lewiston
Lake

Shasta-Trinity

NRA

Whiskeytown
Lake

Redding

see Lassen
and Modoc
page 74

Sacramento

Ruth
Lake

Shasta-Trinity

National

Forest

Tehama
Wildlife Area

Red Bluff

0   10 mi
0   10 km

see Mendocino
and Wine Country
page 96

see Sacramento
and Gold Country
page 112

© AVALON TRAVEL

TRAIL NAME	LEVEL	DISTANCE	ELEVATION	SEASON	FEATURES	PAGE
1 Horsetail Falls	Easy	Negligible	5,500 ft	Apr.-July		36
2 Maple Falls	Moderate	8.0 mi rt	1,800 ft	Apr.-Sept.		37
3 Shackleford Falls	Easy	0.5 mile rt	Negligible	June-Sept.		39
4 Sur Cree Falls	Moderate	6.5 mi rt	900 ft	Apr.-Sept.		40
5 East Boulder Lake Falls	Moderate	4.0 mi rt	800 ft	June-Sept.		42
6 Grizzly Lake Falls	Strenuous	12.0-38.0 mi rt	4,500-5,000 ft	July-Sept.		44
7 Swift Creek Falls	Moderate	2.5 mi rt	200 ft	June-Sept.		47
8 Canyon Creek Falls	Moderate	8.0-15.0 mi rt	2,500 ft	June-Sept.		49
9 Whitney Falls	Easy	3.5 mi rt	800 ft	May-July		52
10 Mud Creek Falls	Easy	2.0 mi rt	600 ft	June-Sept.		54
11 Faery Falls	Easy	2.0 mi rt	100 ft	Apr.-July		56
12 Burstarse Falls	Strenuous	6.0 mi rt	900 ft	Apr.-June		57
13 Hedge Creek Falls	Easy	0.25 mile rt	100 ft	Apr.-July		59
14 Mossbrae Falls	Easy	2.8 mi rt	Negligible	May-Aug.		61
15 Sweetbriar Falls	Easy	0.25 mile rt	Negligible	Feb.-June		63
16 McCloud Falls	Easy	3.6 mi rt	400 ft	Apr.-Aug.		64
17 Potem Falls	Easy	0.5 mile rt	50 ft	Apr.-Aug.		66
18 Hatchet Creek Falls	Easy	0.5 mile rt	50 ft	year-round		68
19 Whiskeytown Falls	Moderate	3.4 mi rt	700 ft	Mar.-June		69

1 HORSETAIL FALLS
Klamath National Forest

Level: Easy	**Distance:** Negligible
Best Season: April–July	**Elevation Change:** 5,500 feet

You're so far north in California at Horsetail Falls that you're almost in Oregon. The fall is just below Cook and Green Pass, a mere five miles from the state border as the crow flies.

And waterfalls don't come much easier than this: you can drive right up to Horsetail, which drops on the East Fork of Seiad Creek, right next to the road. About 50 feet of the falls are visible above the road, on the east side, where the stream cuts down through a notch in the rock face. But Horsetail Falls also continues below the road in a long, white-water cascade, heading far downhill to Seiad Valley.

You must visit this fall in springtime. Although Horsetail Falls still runs in late summer and fall, it isn't much to see. Be sure to call the Forest Service to check on road conditions before you head out in spring; although ordinary passenger cars can drive the dirt road some of the year, high-clearance vehicles may be necessary when it's wet.

Of course, once you drive up the long hill and take a few photos of the falls, you probably won't want to get back in your car immediately and drive home. The best option for a day hike? Drive 1.7 miles north on Road 48N20 to Cook and Green Pass. Park there and walk up the gated road on the left, heading out on the Boundary National Recreation Trail. Look for the trail signed for Elk Lake on your right, about three miles out. It's another half mile to the scenic lake, with great views along the way—both north into Oregon and south into California.

Directions
From I-5 north of Yreka, drive west on Highway 96 for approximately 50 miles to Seiad Valley. Turn north on Seiad Creek Road and drive 10 miles to the falls on the right side of the road. At 3.8 miles, Seiad Creek Road becomes 48N20, a gravel road; be sure to take the left fork to continue on 48N20. (Or, from Cook and Green Pass, drive south on 48N20 for 1.7 miles to the falls.)

Information and Contact
There is no fee. Maps of Klamath National Forest are available for a fee from the National Forest Store (406/329-3024, www.nationalforeststore.com), or can be

downloaded for free from www.fs.fed.us/r5/maps/. For more information, contact Klamath National Forest, Happy Camp Ranger District, 530/493-2243, www.fs.fed.us/r5/klamath.

2 MAPLE FALLS   BEST (
Marble Mountain Wilderness

Level: Moderate   **Distance:** 8.0 miles round-trip

Best Season: April–September   **Elevation Change:** Total gain 1,800 feet

A trip to Maple Falls in the Marble Mountain Wilderness is a walk through history on the Kelsey National Recreation Trail, an 1850s supply route that once ran all the way from Fort Jones to Crescent City. It's a long uphill walk through history, so make sure your boots are strapped on tight and your lunch is packed.

The trail starts to climb at the trailhead, and uphill is the status quo for… well, actually, all four miles to the waterfall. While you're hoofing it, think of the early travelers on this route who brought supplies to the U.S. Army military post at Fort Jones and settlers in Scott Valley, and carried gold and local commodities back to the coast at Crescent City. Whatever your pack weighs, it's gotta be lighter than gold.

Maple Falls

© ANN MARIE BROWN

Trailhead elevation is 2,400 feet, which means that the Kelsey Trail is open year-round to Maple Falls. (The upper part of the trail that accesses the Paradise Lake Basin can get snowed on, but that's another three miles past the waterfall.) Although Maple Falls is at its peak in the spring, I visited in September and found its flow was still full and lovely. An incentive for hiking here in autumn is that the trail's many maple trees, for which the falls are named, turn a brilliant gold in late September and October.

You have 1,800 feet to gain in four miles, but the trail is well-graded and the surroundings are inspiring. Kelsey Creek roars along below you, creating a ruckus even late in the year. Shade is abundant for most of the trip, offered by oaks, maples, Douglas firs, and ponderosa pines. A dense army of low-elevation foliage surrounds your feet.

Hike upstream, and also up and above the stream, on the Kelsey Trail, which is cut into the steep canyon slopes. Most of the time, you're at least 100 feet above the stream, but two miles out, the trail drops down, and you'll see a couple of primitive campsites on Kelsey Creek's bank. Another set of falls, about 25 feet high and tucked in behind a big boulder, drops below the camp. You can glimpse the waterfall from the trail just before you reach the camp. A short spur trail will take you closer.

As a matter of fact, you hear and occasionally behold dozens of water chutes, slides, and falls along most of the length of the Kelsey Trail. But because the trail is so high above the creek and the banks are so steep, most of these water drops are inaccessible. At any rate, none compare to Maple Falls, which dives 60 feet, mostly in free fall over clifflike boulders, before cascading and running level again. Still, Maple Falls can be a bit tricky to spot late in the summer, in low flow. The Kelsey Trail passes about 50 yards from it, and dense foliage obscures all except the top of the fall. Trust your ears to guide you. After four miles of fairly relentless uphill, you'll be searching anxiously for your destination.

Watch for these landmarks: at 2.6 miles, you'll pass a worn Marble Mountain Wilderness sign. Then, between miles 3.0 and 3.8, the trail crosses two good-size creeks, which run even in autumn. At 4.0 miles (about two hours of hiking time), you'll spy the falls across the canyon. Walk past them for a minute or so until you see a spur trail on your left. (The Kelsey Trail continues to climb, heading for Paradise Lake.) Take the spur, an excellent route that leads to the top of the falls, where a perfect makeshift campsite is located, complete with a crude table and fire grill. From the campsite, you can cross the creek by rock-hopping (at low water), then scramble another 50 feet to get a good side view of the falls. As this is your first opportunity to see Maple Falls' full height, it may surprise you.

If you like rock scrambling, you can descend all the way to the base of the falls, where in summer and autumn a small rocky beach awaits. Have a seat on a log and cast admiring glances at the wonderful watery scene before you.

Directions

From I-5 at Yreka, take the Highway 3 exit and drive west for 16.5 miles to Fort Jones. Turn right on Scott River Road and drive 16.8 miles to the Scott River Bridge. Cross the bridge and turn left immediately onto a dirt road. Drive 0.3 mile and bear right on another dirt road. (Don't continue to a second bridge, which leads to some spawning ponds.) Drive 0.25 mile farther to the Kelsey Creek Trailhead.

Information and Contact

There is no fee. Maps of the Marble Mountain Wilderness or Klamath National Forest are available for a fee from the National Forest Store (406/329-3024, www.nationalforeststore.com), or can be downloaded for free from www.fs.fed.us/r5/maps/. For more information, contact Klamath National Forest, Scott and Salmon River Ranger District, 530/468-5351, www.fs.fed.us/r5/klamath.

3 SHACKLEFORD FALLS

Klamath National Forest

Level: Easy

Best Season: June-September

Distance: 0.5 mile round-trip

Elevation Change: Negligible

Shackleford Falls is one of those locals-only waterfalls, a rocky cataract and swimming hole that you'd never find unless somebody told you about it. Luckily, somebody told me. Actually, they had to tell me twice, because the first time I drove off, I got completely lost, and had to go back for a repeat on the directions.

© LEON TURNBULL/WATERFALLSWEST.COM

Shackleford Falls

The waterfall is technically on private property within Klamath National Forest, so be on your best behavior here. It's owned by the Fruit Growers Supply Company, and although they allow people to use the area, they don't have to. It's a use-at-your-own-risk kind of deal.

Reaching the waterfall is an easy drive from Fort Jones (provided you have the right directions, of course). After parking in the pullouts near the Shackleford Creek bridge, just walk up the dirt road next to the bridge, heading upstream. Stay to the left, as close to the creek as possible, and in just a few minutes, you're at a clearing just above the falls. People sometimes camp here.

The 15-foot-high waterfall is a rush of white water that flows so heavily even late in the year, it's difficult to make out the details of its shape. It drops over a large boulder and forms a pool for swimming—a great spot on a hot day.

Directions

From I-5 at Yreka, take the Highway 3 exit and drive west for 16.5 miles to Fort Jones. Turn right on Scott River Road and drive seven miles, then take the left fork, which is Quartz Valley Road. Drive 3.9 miles on Quartz Valley Road and turn right on Road 43N21, signed for the Shackleford Trailhead. Drive 1.2 miles on 43N21 until you cross the bridge over Shackleford Creek. Park near the bridge in any pullout, then walk up the dirt road on the far side of the bridge, heading upstream.

Information and Contact

There is no fee. Maps of Klamath National Forest are available for a fee from the National Forest Store (406/329-3024, www.nationalforeststore.com), or can be downloaded for free from www.fs.fed.us/r5/maps/. For more information, contact Klamath National Forest, Scott and Salmon River Ranger District, 530/468-5351, www.fs.fed.us/r5/klamath.

4 SUR CREE FALLS
Marble Mountain Wilderness

Level: Moderate

Best Season: April–September

Distance: 6.5 miles round-trip

Elevation Change: Total gain 900 feet

Sur Cree Falls may not be a star-quality waterfall, but one thing is for sure: if you've driven all the way out here to the Little North Fork Trailhead, you're not going to see a whole lot of other people. In fact, if your idea of a top-notch waterfall is one that you can have all to yourself, you should sign up for this trip immediately.

The Little North Fork Trail is where I managed to escape on the opening day of deer season in Trinity and Siskiyou counties. My hiking trip to the Trinity Alps and Marble Mountain Wildernesses was, shall we say, badly timed, because I had forgotten about the hunting opener. There were crowds at virtually every trailhead. Some were hunters, and others were hikers trying to get away from the hunters. But way out here at the Little North Fork, everything was peaceful and quiet. You could hear a bear drop a pin.

Off I went on the trail, which was signed for Specimen Gulch, English Peak, and Hancock Lake. In the first 0.5 mile, I reached an unmarked trail fork, but after much deliberation decided that this was one of those high-road/low-road trails, where you could take the route either way and end up at the same place. I took the high trail, although the low trail takes you closer to the rushing Little North Fork. If you've brought your fishing rod, take the lower trail.

The mostly level path follows a retired aqueduct ditch for a distance, crossing two creeks in the first mile. The trail tunnels through a mix of hardwoods, conifers, ferns, and vines. This is low-elevation hiking, which means you're surrounded by tons of foliage in all shapes and sizes. It also means plenty of shade, so the route is pleasant even on a warm summer day.

At 2.25 miles, the trail passes through a small burned area where the lower trail rejoins the upper trail. From there, the trail starts to climb. After the basic flatness of the first two miles, this comes as a bit of a surprise. I spotted a bear along this stretch, and as she ran off, I warned her to look out for anybody wearing camouflage.

At 2.7 miles, a gravel road crosses the trail, leading down to Specimen Gulch. Cross the road, and continue straight ahead on the trail. It's about 20 minutes of hiking from Specimen Gulch to the falls, all uphill. The Little North Fork Trail crosses right in the middle of Sur Cree Falls, which empties into the Little North Fork, so it's impossible to miss. Unfortunately, most of the fall's drop is below the trail, with virtually no way to view it because the canyon is so steep. The total cascade is about 200 feet, but with only 30 feet above the trail and visible. Huge elephant ears, bigger than dinner plates, grow out of the nooks and crannies of the cascade. Rocks around the edges of the fall supply places where you can sit down, take off your pack, and soak your feet.

And guess what? Most likely, nobody else is going to show up. Sur Cree Falls is all yours.

Directions

From I-5 at Yreka, take the Highway 3 exit and drive west for 25 miles to Etna. At Etna, drive west on Etna-Sawyers Bar Road for 25 miles to Sawyers Bar. From Sawyers Bar, continue 4.2 miles west to Road 40N51 on the right. Drive 0.5 mile on 40N51 to the signed Little North Fork Trailhead.

Information and Contact

There is no fee. Maps of the Marble Mountain Wilderness or Klamath National Forest are available for a fee from the National Forest Store (406/329-3024, www.nationalforeststore.com), or can be downloaded for free from www.fs.fed.us/r5/maps/. For more information, contact Klamath National Forest, Scott and Salmon River Ranger District, 530/468-5351, www.fs.fed.us/r5/klamath.

5 EAST BOULDER LAKE FALLS
Marble Mountain Wilderness

Level: Moderate

Best Season: June-September

Distance: 4.0 miles round-trip

Elevation Change: Total gain 800 feet

Pack up your family in the car for the long drive to Callahan. Stop at the Callahan Emporium, pick up some picnic supplies (don't expect anything too gourmet), then head out to the East Boulder Lake Trailhead. You're about to take a day hike that will make your spouse and kids think you are the greatest outdoor trip planner on earth.

You have to climb a bit, but the rewards are great. In fact, this is probably one of the greatest short hikes to an alpine lake in all of the Trinity Alps and Marble Mountain Wildernesses. Using up only one hour of your allotted time on the planet, you will arrive aerobically fit and fully oxygenated at a deep blue lake with a waterfall on its outlet stream.

East Boulder Lake Falls

© ANN MARIE BROWN

The hike up to the lake leads through meadows mixed with fir and pine groves, plus some great sections of knee-high fern fields. You follow East Boulder Creek for the whole route, but won't get close enough to see it until you're at its waterfall. The climb is fairly moderate, with a few level sections interspersed. The only minus on this trail is the possible presence of bovines, because grazing is permitted here. I saw a dozen or so, but they ran away from me with their cowbells tinkling.

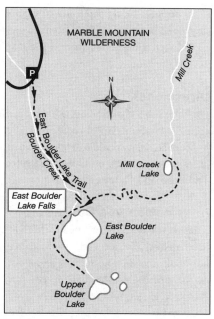

At 1.5 miles, you exit from the forest to a clearing and get a head-on view of the waterfall on East Boulder Creek. The fall is delicate and lacy in late summer and autumn, and a downright downpour in spring. It's a 30-foot free fall over volcanic black rock, and similar in appearance to Black Wolf Falls in Sequoia National Park or Sardine Falls in Toiyabe National Forest. Another 30-foot cascade continues below the free fall. Try to see East Boulder Falls in the morning, as it is north-facing and will be shaded by midafternoon.

The trail has its steepest pitch in the last 0.5 mile from the waterfall to the lake, where you have to get up and over the fall. Fortunately, looking at the cascading water keeps you somewhat distracted from the work of your fast-pumping heart. Once you reach the waterfall's crest, it's only five minutes farther on flat trail to the lake. You'll see evidence of a small avalanche above the falls—lots of downed trees. Some of them have been used to build a log walkway across the meadow. Follow it, then continue on the path alongside East Boulder Creek above the fall. When you top the ridge, check out the incredible view behind you, looking a few thousand feet down into Scott Valley.

Your first eyeful of the deep blue of the lake will knock your socks off. On a sunny day, East Boulder Lake is like a rare and expensive sapphire, shimmering within the walls of a barren cirque. Little grows around the lake's near side except sagebrush, manzanita, and the occasional pine. The far edge has a more substantial stand of pines. Even the lake bottom looks bare and sandy.

There are a few campsites around the lake, although it can be windy because of a lack of tree cover. A couple trails branch out from East Boulder Lake, the most popular being the route to Upper Boulder Lake in one mile. Most people stop right here, however, content to gaze out over 32 acres of azure water and eat a sandwich, or wander around the lake's circumference, marveling at the blueness of the blue.

Directions

For the Hobo Gulch Trailhead: From Redding, drive west on Highway 299 for approximately 50 miles to Weaverville. Continue west on Highway 299 for 14 miles past Weaverville to Helena. Turn north on East Fork Road and drive four miles, then turn left on Hobo Gulch Road and drive 13 miles to the Hobo Gulch Trailhead and Campground.

Information and Contact

There is no fee. Maps of the Marble Mountain Wilderness or Trinity Alps Wilderness are available for a fee from the National Forest Store (406/329-3024, www. nationalforeststore.com), or can be downloaded for free from www.fs.fed.us/r5/ maps/. For more information, contact Shasta-Trinity National Forest, Big Bar Ranger District, 530/623-6106, www.fs.fed.us/shastatrinity. Or contact Klamath National Forest, Scott and Salmon River Ranger District, 530/468-5351, www. fs.fed.us/r5/klamath.

6 GRIZZLY LAKE FALLS
Trinity Alps Wilderness

Level: Strenuous

Best Season: July–September

Distance: 12 miles round-trip (China Creek) or 38.0 miles round-trip (Hobo Gulch)

Elevation Change: Total gain/loss 4,500–5,000 feet

At least once in your life, you should backpack to Grizzly Lake and its waterfall in the Trinity Alps Wilderness. Like climbing Half Dome in Yosemite or making the long trek to the top of Mount Whitney, this is an epic wilderness trip that you'll tell your grandchildren about.

If you have nearly a week's vacation time, you can take a long, 19-mile one-way backpack trip to the lake and its waterfall, traveling along beautiful Grizzly Creek on a moderate-grade trail. If you're short on time, you can make a grueling, six-mile one-way trip to Grizzly, but the route is such a butt-kicker that you should plan on at least two days for the round-trip. Some people go out and back in a day, but that leaves little time and energy for enjoying the waterfall and the lake.

Alas, despite the fact that the long route is far more enjoyable, most people opt for the short route. Even with its extreme changes in elevation, the six-mile trail from China Creek has become incredibly popular, sometimes even getting crowded on summer weekends. It seems that most people are willing to pay the price to get to Grizzly Lake and Grizzly Falls as quickly as possible.

If you decide to join that club, start your trip at the China Creek Trailhead near Cecilville. Be forewarned of the facts: The trail gains 1,500 feet in the first mile. Then, unbelievably,

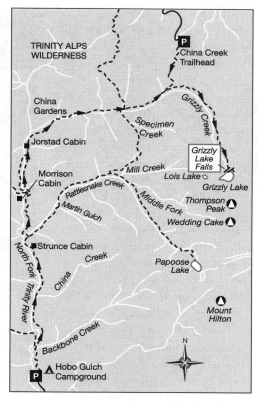

it drops 1,000 feet in the second mile. Are we having fun yet? The next three miles are the "easy" ones; their total gain is only 1,500 feet. The final, brutal mile rises nearly 1,000 feet.

What's good about the trail from China Creek? It isn't easy to think of something positive, but let's see: the first mile is shaded and dense with fir trees. In the second mile, you start to get some good views of the peaks and canyon ahead. At 2.5 miles, when you reach the junction with Grizzly Creek Trail, you can rejoice because much of the worst is over. Bear left on the Grizzly Creek Trail, passing several campsites along the way. You'll begin to feel extremely envious of hikers coming from the other trailhead on the Grizzly Creek Trail, because even though they've been hiking longer, they haven't suffered like you have.

At 1.5 miles from the junction of the two trails, you get your first look at stunning Thompson Peak, elevation 9,002 feet. Your destination is located below the snowfield-lined mountain, the most impressive peak in Switzerland, I mean, the

Trinity Alps. The scenery is so evocative of the European Alps, it's easy to forget where you are.

Next you pass Grizzly Meadows, laden with corn lilies in early summer. Then comes a series of unbelievable mountain vistas, with every color and hue you can imagine of granite, sky, snow, and sunlight. As you draw nearer, Grizzly Falls completes the scene, a vista that's as epic as any in Yosemite Valley. Grizzly is an 80-foot-high, near-perfect free fall, tumbling off the perpendicular cliff that supports Grizzly Lake. The waterfall is formed as the lake's outlet creek drops over a square lip of stacked granite blocks, then hits a less vertical surface and cascades hundreds of feet farther.

Grizzly Lake Falls

The Grizzly Lake Trail officially ends after a series of stone steps that ascend a boulder field. From there to the lake, you're basically on your own, scrambling up the often vertical route. Since this is such a popular destination, the route is extremely well-marked, and you're likely to see other people using it, but do not expect a real trail. Your hands will need to assist your feet in keeping you connected to the bare rock. If you have any doubts about your ability to make the final ascent to the lake, just park yourself in Grizzly Meadows and drink in the unbelievable view. One could hardly call this second best.

If you decide to trek the final mile, your reward is a close-up look at one of the largest alpine lakes in the Trinity Alps. Grizzly has 42 surface acres and is 170 feet deep. Situated at the base of Thompson Peak, it mirrors the peak's pure white snowfields and the hardy groves of firs and pines below them. Needless to say, it's gorgeous.

If you can possibly spare the time to take the long route to Grizzly Lake and Falls, you'll have a much better time. Not only is the trail grade far more sensible, but fishing prospects are excellent along the entire route. The trail starts at Hobo Gulch (access is from Highway 299 near Weaverville), then heads north about five miles along the North Fork Trinity River to Rattlesnake Camp, a large flat where the trail junctions with the Rattlesnake Creek Trail.

Ford Rattlesnake Creek and keep hiking northward. Get this: the first 10 miles of trail have only a 1,200-foot elevation gain. There are mixed conifers almost all the way. From Rattlesnake Camp, hike another three miles, passing Morrison Cabin and various mining relics, to Pfeiffer Flat and another mining cabin. A half mile farther, the North Fork Trinity is joined by Grizzly Creek. The trail to Grizzly Lake follows Grizzly Creek eastward from this point on, meeting up with the China Creek Trail at 14.5 miles from the trailhead. The rest of the trip is the same as on the shorter route, but you should be much better rested and prepared for the final climb to Grizzly Lake.

Directions

For the Hobo Gulch Trailhead: From Redding, drive west on Highway 299 for approximately 50 miles to Weaverville. Continue west on Highway 299 for 14 miles past Weaverville to Helena. Turn north on East Fork Road and drive four miles, then turn left on Hobo Gulch Road and drive 13 miles to the Hobo Gulch Trailhead and Campground.

For the China Creek Trailhead: From I-5 at Yreka, take the Highway 3 exit and drive southwest for 35 miles to Callahan. At Callahan, turn west on Callahan/ Cecilville Road 93, and drive 27 miles to Road 37N24. (If you reach Cecilville, you've gone two miles too far.) Turn south and drive 3.8 miles to the intersection with Road 37N07 for China Creek Trailhead. Take Road 37N07, and drive six miles to the trailhead (the route is well-signed). Park alongside the road.

Information and Contact

There is no fee. Maps of the Trinity Alps Wilderness are available for a fee from the National Forest Store (406/329-3024, www.nationalforeststore.com), or can be downloaded for free from www.fs.fed.us/r5/maps/. For more information, contact Shasta-Trinity National Forest, Big Bar Ranger District, 530/623-6106, www. fs.fed.us/shastatrinity. Or contact Klamath National Forest, Scott and Salmon River Ranger District, 530/468-5351, www.fs.fed.us/r5/klamath.

7 SWIFT CREEK FALLS
Trinity Alps Wilderness

Level: Moderate	**Distance:** 2.5 miles round-trip
Best Season: June-September	**Elevation Change:** Total loss 200 feet

A short walk in the Trinity Alps takes you to a dramatic rocky gorge with four waterfalls, but the stream keeps its watery treasures well-hidden from the average passerby. The walk alone won't give you the rewards you seek; it's only with a short but steep off-trail scramble that you get a good look at the falls.

First, be forewarned that the trailhead parking lot can be loaded with horse trailers, and the first section of trail is somewhat beaten down by the continual weight of hooves. Other destinations from this trailhead are popular with horse packers and hunters in the fall.

Swift Creek Falls are only one mile in on the Swift Creek Trail, a few hundred yards before a trail junction for the Granite Lake Trail. The hike to the falls' general location is easy, but you're unlikely to be satisfied with the trail's long-distance, peek-a-boo view of it. The hard part is finding the best place to scramble down for a closer look, because the canyon slope is dauntingly steep.

Swift Creek Falls

The falls are encased in a 200-yard-long rock gorge, which you see only fleetingly from the trail. Their location is given away by the continual roar of water. Although you can glimpse falling white water from one point on the trail, this is not the best place to try to scramble downslope; it's too steep and slick with fallen leaves. Instead, backtrack a few hundred feet to where the slope is gentler, then make your way down to the stream. You'll wind up looking upstream at the falls, which is the best view of them. If you don't want to descend all the way to the streambed, look for some rock outcrops about halfway down the canyon wall, where the waterfall views are also good. Be wary of slippery leaf litter, though.

Four main falls drop in this 200-yard-long area, plunging as white-water chutes over and through the smoothed granite. All of them are between 20 and 35 feet in height. If you look carefully, you'll see that many small trout swim in their rocky pools.

If scrambling isn't your bag, and you prefer to hike on a "real" trail, continue past the falls to the junction of Swift Creek Trail and Granite Lake Trail. The left fork stays along Swift Creek for 0.2 mile, then crosses a picturesque footbridge on its way to Granite Lake in five miles. (Once you pass this junction, you're free of pack animals sharing the trail.) Granite Lake makes a great day hike or backpacking destination, but be prepared to climb.

Directions

From Redding, drive west on Highway 299 for approximately 50 miles to Weaverville. At Weaverville, turn north on Highway 3 and drive 28 miles to Trinity Center. Turn west on Swift Creek Road and drive 6.8 miles to the trailhead.

Information and Contact

There is no fee. Maps of the Trinity Alps Wilderness are available for a fee from the National Forest Store (406/329-3024, www.nationalforeststore.com), or can be downloaded for free from www.fs.fed.us/r5/maps/. For more information, contact Shasta-Trinity National Forest, Weaverville Ranger District, 530/623-2121, www.fs.fed.us/r5/shastatrinity.

8 CANYON CREEK FALLS   BEST (
Trinity Alps Wilderness

Level: Moderate   **Distance:** 8.0-15.0 miles round-trip
Best Season: June-September   **Elevation Change:** Total gain 2,500 feet

The Canyon Creek Trail is the "glamour" trail of the Trinity Alps Wilderness, the route that everybody takes if they can only hike one trail in the area. Like similarly famous trails at Tuolumne Meadows in Yosemite or Desolation Wilderness by Lake Tahoe, the Canyon Creek Trail earns its popularity for good reasons: it

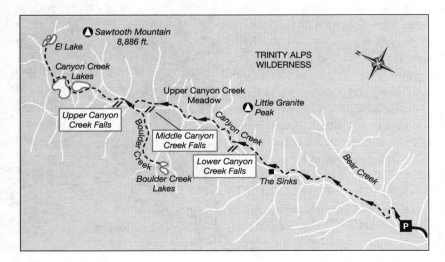

has drop-dead gorgeous scenery, including waterfalls, lakes, and old-growth forest; and it follows a mellow grade.

Don't be scared off by the potential of crowds along the trail. This place is worth seeing no matter how much company you have. Take your pick between a hike of 8.0 miles round-trip to Lower Canyon Creek Falls, a hike or backpack of 11.0 miles round-trip to Middle Canyon Creek Falls, or a 15-mile round-trip backpack to Upper Canyon Creek Falls and the Canyon Creek Lakes.

It's an easy trip, because the trail climbs only moderately and is mostly shaded for the first few miles. As the route gradually becomes more exposed, hikers are rewarded with increasingly better views of surrounding peaks and ridges. Even most beginning backpackers can hike the 7.5 miles into the lakes on the first day.

The 13-mile-long paved road to the trailhead, and the giant-sized parking lot at its end, give you an idea of how well-loved and well-used Canyon Creek is. From the trailhead sign, hike to your left on the Canyon Creek Trail. In about 10 minutes of walking, you cross Bear Creek, not Canyon Creek, but then the trail winds around to meet Canyon Creek, and parallels it continually from there. The trail gets better and better the farther upstream you go, with the scent of Douglas firs and incense cedars intoxicating you along the way. At 2.0 miles in, a campsite is located beside the creek at a tiny waterfall. At 3.0 miles in, a short

but steep spur trail on your left is signed for The Sinks, a boulders-and-pools section of Canyon Creek near a large rockslide. More campsites are found along the creek here.

At 4.0 miles, you reach a clearing across from a 20-foot waterfall, with still more campsites. This fall is attractive enough in its own right, tumbling over a granite ledge into a perfectly rounded aquamarine pool, but don't finish your trip here: this is not Lower Canyon Creek Falls, although some people call it that. Actually, it is best described as the upper cascade of Lower Canyon Creek Falls, because if you scramble downstream for 100 yards, you'll find a much larger fall below it, the true Lower Canyon Creek Falls. The trail was once routed alongside the 100-foot lower fall,

© ANN MARIE BROWN

Middle Canyon Creek Falls

but now bypasses it and reaches only its upper cascade. But why quibble? Either fall makes a great day-hike destination, with both possessing marvelous turquoise pools for swimming on summer days.

From this 4.0-mile point onward, the trail runs very close to the creek and has a more level grade. Pass a meadow on your left as the path continues for another mile. At 5.5 miles, while under the magic spell of an old-growth Douglas fir forest, listen for the roar of Middle Canyon Creek Falls, just off the trail to your left. A short cutoff trail will take you to the base of the 150-foot cascade, a series of 25–40-foot drops over granite. This is probably the most beautiful of all the falls on Canyon Creek, and ironically, it's on the cutoff trail that most hikers miss. If you reach the trail junction for Boulder Creek Lakes, you have missed the cutoff trail.

While day hikers will probably choose to make Middle Canyon Creek Falls their destination and then head back for an 11-mile round-trip, backpackers should either start looking for a campsite or push on to the upper falls and the lakes. Dozens of established campsites are found along Canyon Creek, so despite the popularity of the trail, there should be plenty of room to find a private spot for the night. (Remember: no camping in the fragile meadow areas near Canyon Creek. Also, camping is limited at the lakes, and may eventually be forbidden to protect their fragile shores, so you're better off choosing a spot below them.)

From Middle Canyon Creek Falls, it's only one mile to 50-foot Upper Canyon Creek Falls. This fall is smaller than both the lower and middle falls, and it has a vastly different shape—more of a classic river fall at the top, but smooth and sloping at the bottom, like a water slide. Because it is set right alongside the trail, this is the waterfall that everybody sees, and the campsites near it are coveted.

Less than a mile of trail, a few switchbacks, and several thousand tons of granite separate Upper Canyon Creek Falls from Lower Canyon Creek Lake. You're so close, you might as well continue. Follow the trail up and above the falls and then to the west side of the deep blue lake to check out the eastward views of Sawtooth Mountain, elevation 8,880 feet. Should you wish to press on, rock cairns lead the way to Upper Canyon Creek Lake, where there are a few campsites and even better vistas. You'll be rewarded for the climb with long looks at towering granite crags, ages-old snowfields on Thompson Peak, tumbling streams of snowmelt, and stands of red fir and Jeffrey pine encircling the lake.

Directions

From Redding, drive west on Highway 299 for approximately 50 miles to Weaverville. Continue west on Highway 299 for 8.1 miles past Weaverville to Junction City and Canyon Creek Road. Turn right on Canyon Creek Road and drive 13 miles to the trailhead. (It's paved all the way.)

Information and Contact

There is no fee. Maps of the Trinity Alps Wilderness are available for a fee from the National Forest Store (406/329-3024, www.nationalforeststore.com), or can be downloaded for free from www.fs.fed.us/r5/maps/. For more information, contact Shasta-Trinity National Forest, Weaverville Ranger District, 530/623-2121, www.fs.fed.us/r5/shastatrinity.

9 WHITNEY FALLS   BEST ℂ
Mount Shasta Wilderness

🥾 🐕

Level: Easy   **Distance:** 3.5 miles round-trip

Best Season: May–July   **Elevation Change:** Total gain 800 feet

You like drama? You came to the right place. You like to see water in your waterfalls? You better come early in the year, because Whitney Falls usually disappears by the Fourth of July.

But even when Whitney Creek is dry, this hike and its destination are still first-rate. That's because Whitney Falls is set in an incredible canyon on the back side of Mount Shasta, accessible by one of the few trails that enter Shasta's northern wilderness.

You get an idea of what's ahead right at the trailhead sign. While you fill out your self-serve day-hiking permit, check out the views of Mount Shasta and smaller Shastina on its right flank. Snowy Whitney Glacier sits between them, the source of Whitney Falls' flow.

Head right and cross the often-dry Bolam Creek, then follow a wide trail for about a mile along Bolam Creek canyon. It's a bit desert-like out here, with only a few pines and lots of brush and manzanita, but the route gets more forested as you walk. The trail veers away from the creek twice, and the second time provides sweeping views of the Shasta Valley, plus a peek at Lake Shastina. It's so quiet up here, you can hear a train 15 miles away. One and a half miles from the trailhead, look carefully for an unsigned path that veers right.

Turn right on the Whitney Falls Trail and follow it for 0.25 mile through a forest of pines and firs to an incredible overlook and picnic site. Incredible? Yes. You are standing on the rim of Whitney Creek's canyon, staring up at the peaks of Shasta and Shastina, Whitney Glacier, and if you time it right, Whitney Falls. The fall drops 200 dramatic feet over a jagged rock face, then hits boulders and continues to cascade downcanyon. Unlike at the viewing spot for Mud Creek Falls on the southeast side of Mount Shasta, here you're only a few hundred feet from the fall. Everything—even the peak of Mount Shasta—seems within arm's reach across the great chasm.

A few words on timing: probably the best time to see Whitney Falls is when a little snow still covers the trail, usually in early May. But when the trail has snow patches, the Whitney Falls turnoff can be very difficult to discern. Be on the lookout for it.

If you miss the early season, you can also see the waterfall run just after a spring or summer storm. And don't worry if Whitney Creek is dry when you cross it on Highway 97; there can still be water in the fall, far upstream.

Directions

From I-5 at Weed, take the Highway 97 exit and drive north through Weed for 0.75 mile. Turn north on Highway 97 and drive eight miles, then turn right on unsigned Forest Service Road 43N21. (If you reach Road A12, you've gone 0.2 mile too far.) Continue four miles to the Bolam Creek Trailhead at the end of the road. A high-clearance vehicle is necessary.

Information and Contact

There is no fee. Day hikers must fill out a self-serve wilderness permit at the trailhead. Maps of the Shasta-Trinity National Forest are available for a fee from the National Forest Store (406/329-3024, www.nationalforeststore.com), or can be downloaded for free from www.fs.fed.us/r5/maps/. A more detailed map of the Mount Shasta Wilderness is available from Tom Harrison Maps, 415/456-7940, www.tomharrisonmaps.com. For more information, contact Shasta-Trinity National Forest, Mount Shasta Ranger District, 530/926-4511, www.fs.fed.us/r5/shastatrinity.

10 MUD CREEK FALLS
Mount Shasta Wilderness

Level: Easy

Distance: 2.0 miles round-trip

Best Season: June–September

Elevation Change: Total gain 600 feet

Some waterfalls are found in settings so grand and dramatic that they dwarf the fall itself, even though its size and flow may be tremendous. Such is the story with Mud Creek Falls, a geologic wonder that pours hundreds of feet from Mud Creek Glacier down the side of 14,162-foot Mount Shasta. When you're dealing with a background that tall, it tends to minimize things.

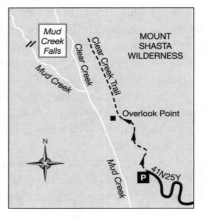

You know you're in for an unusual trip right from the Clear Creek Trailhead sign. While you're filling out your free day hiker's permit to enter the Mount Shasta Wilderness, be sure to read the sign. In addition to the usual cautionary statements about carrying plenty of water and letting someone know where you're going, the sign bears an interesting quote from Carlos Castaneda: "All paths lead to nowhere. You might as well choose a path with a heart." It goes on to warn that people who go into the Mount Shasta Wilderness unprepared can get lost, die, or just plain "go crazy." Hmm. Well, you're only heading out for about an hour's walk, so you should be all right.

The Clear Creek Trail is a steady uphill walk through Shasta red firs, just steep enough to make you feel like you're getting aerobic exercise. It's a bit odd knowing that you're so close to magnificent Mount Shasta, but not seeing anything but trees, trees, trees. Have patience. First you must climb high enough to get over a ridge, one mile distant from the trailhead. Once there, you reach a clearing, and with an off-trail walk of 30 feet, your view opens wide: you look directly at the southeast side of Mount Shasta and down and across 1,000-foot-deep Mud Creek Canyon, with Mud Creek Falls billowing down its long crevice.

Your view also includes Konwakiton and Mud Creek Glaciers, the Thumb Rock climbing route to Shasta's peak, distinctive Thumb Rock itself at 12,923 feet, and the edge of the Shasta ski bowl, far above the falls. A giant rockslide has left an

© ANN MARIE BROWN

Mud Creek Falls

untidy pile of talus across the canyon, which makes you think twice about sitting too close to the edge for long.

Although you're about a mile from Mud Creek Falls, its roar is carried across the canyon in a steady stream of sound. If you bring binoculars with you, you can get a better look at the waterfall and see that it drops over an intricate rock cliff. Of course, the close-up view is just an extra blessing, because the long view is so extraordinary.

The trail continues for another mile or so uphill, mostly through trees, then peters out. This clearing is by far the best destination on the route. In addition to the world-class view, the ground is sprinkled with clumps of mountain pride and Indian paintbrush.

If you drive Highway 89 east of McCloud and happen to notice where the highway crosses Mud Creek (there is a small sign), you'll see that the stream is, indeed, mud-colored. From the Clear Creek Trail, it's more difficult to see Mud Creek's color, because so much snow surrounds the creek from the permanent snowfields and glaciers. (The white snow looks a lot like white water.) The creek's brown tint is glacial change in action: the east side of Mount Shasta is being slowly carried away in Mud Creek. Not only water is flowing though the creek, but also rock and debris from the remaining glaciers chewing up the mountain. At this rate, Mount Shasta will virtually disappear in about five million years. What a pity.

Directions

From Redding, drive 65 miles north on I-5. Take the Highway 89/McCloud/Reno exit and drive east on Highway 89. Pass the town of McCloud in nine miles, then continue three miles farther east to Pilgrim Creek Road (Road 13). Turn left and drive five miles, then turn left on Road 41N15 and follow it for another five miles. Continue straight on 41N61, then bear left on Road 41N25Y and follow it 2.8 miles to the signed trailhead for the Clear Creek Trail. The last few junctions are well-signed. A high-clearance vehicle is recommended.

Information and Contact

There is no fee. Day hikers must fill out a self-serve wilderness permit at the trailhead. Maps of the Shasta-Trinity National Forest are available for a fee from the National Forest Store (406/329-3024, www.nationalforeststore.com), or can be downloaded for free from www.fs.fed.us/r5/maps/. A more detailed map of the Mount Shasta Wilderness is available from Tom Harrison Maps, 415/456-7940, www.tomharrisonmaps.com. For more information, contact Shasta-Trinity National Forest, Mount Shasta Ranger District, 530/926-4511, www.fs.fed.us/r5/shastatrinity.

11 FAERY FALLS
Shasta-Trinity National Forest

🚶 🐕

Level: Easy

Best Season: April–July

Distance: 2.0 miles round-trip

Elevation Change: 100 feet

The Shasta-Dunsmuir-Siskiyou area is a mecca for waterfall-lovers, with several relatively easy trails leading to beautiful cataracts. Water is in plentiful supply in this part of California, and that's a happy situation.

Faery Falls

If you would enjoy a little history lesson with your easy waterfall hike, the trip to Faery Falls and Ney Springs near Lake Siskiyou is for you. This one-mile stroll up an old road passes tall leopard lilies in early summer, a sure sign that water is in the ground below your feet. As you travel the road, take the short side trails you see on the left and right, which lead to the meager ruins of John Ney's mineral springs resort, built in 1889. You'll need to use your imagination to picture it, but Ney built a 30-room hotel and bathhouse here. Guests came by horse-drawn carriage. Ney even tried bottling the water, which he called "Aqua de Ney," and selling it for medicinal purposes. The water was indeed special: it has a pH of 11.6 and a silica content of 4,000 parts per million—the highest values known to occur in natural ground waters. All that remains here is an old stone wall with the words "Ney Springs A.D. 1889" etched above a pipe and a trough, and the concrete foundations of a bathhouse containing stairsteps, a retaining wall, and a pool of cold mineral water.

Return to the main trail after visiting the resort ruins and travel another 100 yards to a side trail on the left. This one will take you steeply uphill to 50-foot Faery Falls, which forms a bright white fan against dark granite rock. The fall is best seen in spring when it is running full, but it's also lovely to visit in autumn, when the vine maples in this area turn bright gold. Flat rocks below the falls edge its clear pool and make perfect spots for lingering and munching on sandwiches.

Directions

From I-5 in Mount Shasta City, take the Central Mount Shasta exit and drive west on Hatchery Lane. Turn left on South Old Stage Road. In 0.2 mile, bear right and continue on W. A. Barr Road. Drive 2.3 miles on W. A. Barr Road to the dam at Lake Siskiyou. Cross the dam, then turn left on Castle Lake Road and left again almost immediately on gravel Ney Springs Road. Drive 1.4 miles, passing a turn-off for Cantara/Ney Springs (stay to the right at all forks), to a dirt road that heads uphill on the right just before a gate. Park off the road in any clearing or or turn-out. Start walking on the dirt road just before the gate.

Information and Contact

There is no fee. Maps of the Shasta-Trinity National Forest are available for a fee from the National Forest Store (406/329-3024, www.nationalforeststore.com), or downloaded for free from www.fs.fed.us/r5/maps/. For more information, contact Shasta-Trinity National Forest, Shasta Lake Ranger District, 530/275-1587, www.fs.fed.us/r5/shastatrinity.

12 BURSTARSE FALLS
Castle Crags Wilderness

Level: Strenuous   **Distance:** 6.0 miles round-trip

Best Season: April–June   **Elevation Change:** Total gain 900 feet

There may be some whining on the first stretch of trail to Burstarse Falls. Worse than that, if you don't time your trip for the wet season, there will surely be some whining when you reach Burstarse Falls and find it dry.

So listen up: visit Burstarse as soon as the snow has melted off the trails in the Castle Crags Wilderness, when the creeks are running full and the temperatures on the steep hillsides are still cool and comfortable. We're talking mid-June at the latest; April and May are usually the best months.

Burstarse Falls

Once you have your calendar set, be prepared for a short but steep climb from the parking lot on the strangely named Dog Trail. Why Dog Trail? It's a mystery. Maybe because you're panting like a tired puppy by the time Dog Trail reaches a junction with the Pacific Crest Trail (PCT), where your ascent is largely finished. It's only 0.6 mile from the parking lot to the PCT intersection, but it's a steep grade on loose rocks and exposed to the sun all day long.

When you reach the PCT, turn left, breathe a sigh of relief, and cruise for a much gentler 2.2 miles along on the shady route that laterals across the mountainside. You're accompanied by manzanita, Douglas fir, ponderosa pine, incense cedar, and black oak, plus what seems like a million lizards scurrying along the trail. Some interesting views of the tops of Castle Crags come into view. The crags are hauntingly beautiful granite spires, 200-million-year-old rocks that rise as high as 6,544 feet. The best view of them comes shortly after your first crossing of Burstarse Creek.

Look for small wooden signs posted on trees as you cross Popcorn Spring, then Burstarse Creek, and Ugly Creek. Don't expect to see the falls at your first crossing of Burstarse Creek; they are higher up on the stream. Don't expect Ugly Creek to be ugly, either; it's a cascading clear-water stream in a bed of granite lined with ferns and Indian rhubarb.

Start paying close attention after you cross Ugly Creek. Follow the trail for only 100 yards farther, to the next switchback where the trail curves tightly around to your left and continues uphill. Don't take that switchback; instead, head straight and downhill, cutting off the trail. If the fall is running, you'll hear it loud and clear, although you can't see it from here.

Descend off-trail about 50 feet to Burstarse Creek, taking careful measures on the steep hillside. Many rocks are unstable and the oak leaves can be deadly slippery. Look for a fairly defined route made by others who have gone before; you will head roughly downhill to the creek. When you reach the water's edge, walk upstream for about 100 yards. If the water is too high and you can't walk up the creekbed, follow the rough route along the far side of the creek, safely above water level. Don't try to head uphill immediately from where you've cut off the PCT; this route is treacherous.

Fifty yards upstream, Burstarse Falls plunges 40 feet off a rock ledge. Its lower reaches are a series of small pools and cascades. Stay for a while, enjoy the spring wildflowers near the falls, and then carefully scramble your way back to the PCT.

Directions

From Redding, drive 50 miles north on I-5 and take the Castle Crags/Castella exit, which is four miles south of Dunsmuir. Turn west and follow Castle Creek Road for 3.2 miles. Turn right into the unsigned parking area. The trail is on your left as you drive in, although it's hard to see from the parking lot.

Information and Contact

There is no fee. Maps of the Shasta-Trinity National Forest are available for a fee from the National Forest Store (406/329-3024, www.nationalforeststore.com), or can be downloaded for free from www.fs.fed.us/r5/maps/. For more information, contact Shasta-Trinity National Forest, Mount Shasta Ranger District, 530/926-4511, www.fs.fed.us/r5/shastatrinity.

13 HEDGE CREEK FALLS
City of Dunsmuir

Level: Easy	**Distance:** 0.25 mile round-trip
Best Season: April-July	**Elevation Change:** Total loss 100 feet

Imagine you're hightailing it up I-5 with the kids, on your way to visit Grandma in Portland. They are going berserk from being locked in the car for hours, and you're about to lose it if you see any more concrete, guardrails, or fast-food restaurants. But then you reach the town of Dunsmuir, 57 miles north of Redding, and you remember a freeway antidote: Hedge Creek Falls.

Get off the highway and head to Dunsmuir Avenue. Park in the small picnic-area parking lot, do a few warm-up stretches, and then hike down the path. Blink and you'll miss it—not the waterfall but the walk to it. You'll reach the falls in about five minutes of downhill cruising.

Hedge Creek Falls drops 30 feet over a sheer granite slab into a shallow pool and a babbling stream. The cliff that creates the fall is so sheer that it makes the water chute appear much grander than it really is. A large indentation in the bottom of the cliff, near where the fall hits the pool, creates a small cave. When the water flow is somewhat diminished in summer, you can sneak behind the falls and pretend you are a water ouzel, that funny bird that makes its home behind waterfalls.

Prolong your visit to this paradise just off the freeway by settling in on the

Hedge Creek Falls

bench by the falls. Consider the history of this pastoral spot: a small cave behind the waterfall is said to have been a secret hideout of the notorious 1850s stagecoach robber Black Bart. In this century, it was saved from the bulldozers when I-5 was built through Dunsmuir. Local citizens rallied to move the freeway a few yards to the east, just far enough to preserve Hedge Creek Falls.

More benches are positioned up and down the trail, which may come in handy on the return climb. When you hike back uphill, be sure to turn around a few times for parting glances at the falling water. At a few spots, about 20–30 feet from the waterfall, you can peer through the lush canopy of leaves and see another cataract directly above this one, set back in the canyon about 50 feet.

When you return to the trailhead, make sure you take a long drink out of the water fountain at the picnic area. This is Dunsmuir's pride and joy, what they call "The Best Water on Earth."

Directions

From Redding, drive 57 miles north on I-5 to Dunsmuir and take the Dunsmuir Avenue/Siskiyou Avenue exit. Turn left at the stop sign and cross under the freeway, then turn right (north) on Dunsmuir Avenue, travel about 20 yards, and turn left into the small parking area at Hedge Creek Park.

Information and Contact

There is no fee. For more information, contact the Dunsmuir Chamber of Commerce, 800/386-7684 or 530/235-2177, www.dunsmuir.com.

14 MOSSBRAE FALLS   BEST ☾

City of Dunsmuir

🚶 🏊 🐕

Level: Easy   **Distance:** 2.8 miles round-trip

Best Season: May-August   **Elevation Change:** Negligible

Getting to Mossbrae Falls required the most unusual walk of all the waterfalls in this book. It's a weird trek—even a little spooky—but it has never kept the crowds away from one of the most unique waterfalls in California. However, as of 2011, that may soon change, since plans are in place to create a new trail to Mossbrae Falls.

First, the back story. For decades, the only way to access Mossbrae Falls has been to walk 1.4 miles along the railroad tracks upstream from Shasta Retreat in Dunsmuir. There's no room for a foot trail alongside the Sacramento River, so everybody—anglers, swimmers, dog-walkers, and waterfall enthusiasts alike—walks alongside the tracks, or sometimes even inside the tracks, for a stretch that lasts about 30–40 minutes. During this

Mossbrae Falls

time, many visitors have said a prayer or two in the hope that a train doesn't roll by. Even if there isn't a train, walking on a railroad bed is nowhere near as pleasant as strolling on a pine needle–covered path in the woods.

After completing this rather unpleasant stretch, hikers followed an obvious cutoff trail just before a steel railroad trestle that leads 30 yards down to Mossbrae Falls as it pours into the wide Sacramento River. (The falls can be seen and heard from the railroad trail, so it's impossible to miss the cutoff.)

Waterfall-lovers aren't the only ones who have been unhappy with this strange route to Mossbrae Falls. The Union Pacific Railroad doesn't like it either, and insists that people who hike this route are trespassing on private property. As of August 2010, they closed the railroad right-of-way to public use by putting up No Trespassing signs and blocking off parking areas.

This hasn't made the city of Dunsmuir very happy, since Mossbrae Falls is their pride and joy and a prime tourist attraction. Dunsmuir plans to build a separate trail to Mossbrae Falls from nearby Hedge Creek Falls (see listing in this chapter). The trail, which would most likely be wheelchair-accessible and would require a bridge across the river, will cost upwards of $1.5 million. As of December 2010, that trail hasn't been built, but city officials say it may be completed as early as summer 2011. Phone the Dunsmuir Chamber of Commerce for an update (530/235-2177).

However you get there, you've never seen a waterfall quite like Mossbrae. It's only about 50 feet tall at its highest point, but it's about 150 feet wide, creating an entire wall of delicate spray pouring out of the moss-covered canyon wall and into the river. It looks more like a water sculpture than a waterfall, with more than 100 separate rivulets and thousands of tiny holes shooting water out of the cliff. Yes, that's *out* of the cliff, rather than over the top, as with most waterfalls. The fall's source is natural springs, so the water flows from underground. It is freezing cold, even in summer. The waterfall's many cascading streams create a gorgeous effect, like a symphony of lawn sprinklers spraying in unison. Mossbrae Falls looks and feels like hundreds of waterfalls, not just one.

It's not just the water that creates the beauty. Mossbrae Falls is gracefully framed by elephant ears, maidenhair ferns, and bracken ferns. Dense mosses grow underneath the spring water flow, making Mossbrae one of the few waterfalls in California that has been rightfully named. The fall is so photogenic that it has appeared in magazines, travel brochures, and even on the cover of the local phone book. Every photographer in the area has hundreds of pictures of Mossbrae. Its charm is irresistible.

Earlier in this century, passenger trains would stop at Mossbrae Falls so travelers could get out and admire it. Today, your best bet for admiring Mossbrae Falls is to pick a spot on the little rocky beach along the river. When the flow is low enough, you can rock-hop halfway out into the stream and stand just a few feet from the falls. Of course, most people who do this bring along a fishing rod, because the Upper Sacramento is an angler's paradise. It all depends on where your interest lies.

Directions

From Redding, drive 57 miles north on I-5 to Dunsmuir and take the Dunsmuir Avenue/Siskiyou Avenue exit. Turn left and cross under the freeway, then turn left again (south) and head into the town of Dunsmuir. In 0.6 mile, make a sharp right turn on Scarlett Way (drive under the arch that is signed "Shasta Retreat.") Bear right at the fork and cross the bridge over the Sacramento River, then cross the railroad tracks and park on the far side, alongside the tracks. (Total distance on Scarlett Way is 0.25 mile.) Start walking upstream (to your right as you drive in) along the tracks.

Special note: before you visit, contact the Dunsmuir Chamber of Commerce to make sure that this route is still accessible to the public, or if a new trail to Mossbrae Falls from Hedge Creek Falls has been completed.

Information and Contact

There is no fee. For more information, contact the Dunsmuir Chamber of Commerce, 800/386-7684 or 530/235-2177, www.dunsmuir.com.

15 SWEETBRIAR FALLS
Sacramento River and Sweetbriar Creek

Level: Easy

Best Season: February–June

Distance: 0.25 mile round-trip

Elevation Change: Negligible

The truth is, nobody comes to Sweetbriar Falls just to see the waterfall. It's only about 20 feet tall, and the trek to reach it is little more than 100 yards, so it doesn't exactly make for a great outdoor adventure. The falls probably wouldn't even have made it into this book if it weren't for two significant nearby features: mighty Mount Shasta and the Sacramento River. At Sweetbriar Falls, you get great views of the former and access to the latter.

Still, Sweetbriar Falls is sweet. Its only failing is that a road was built right above it, so a metal guard rail above its lip mars your view somewhat. It's a pint-sized cataract, best seen as early in the spring as

© ANN MARIE BROWN

Sweetbriar Falls

possible. Because the elevation here is only 2,300 feet, snow is rarely an obstacle to visiting.

To reach the falls, leave your car on the west side of the railroad tracks in the community of Sweetbriar. Cross the tracks and walk up Sweetbriar Road toward the Sacramento River, passing several cozy-looking cabins. Many of the cabins originally were summer homes built for Redding residents who wanted to get away from the intense summer heat. As you cross the river bridge, look upstream for a perfectly framed view of Mount Shasta. You get a head-on look at the huge, snowy volcano, glistening white even in summer, one of the greatest sights in all of Northern California.

At the far side of the bridge, walk 50 feet to your right (downstream) on the trail along the river. This puts you smack in front of small Sweetbriar Falls. A wooden footbridge crosses the creek near the fall's base, giving you the option to continue your hike along the river. On a warm day, you can combine a visit to Sweetbriar Falls with a few hours of fishing or swimming in the Sacramento River.

Directions

From Redding, drive 49 miles north on I-5 to two miles south of Castle Crags State Park. Take the Sweetbriar exit, drive east for 0.5 mile, and park alongside the train tracks (just before crossing them, on their west side).

Information and Contact

There is no fee. For more information, contact the Shasta Cascade Wonderland Association, 530/365-7500, www.shastacascade.org.

16 McCLOUD FALLS   BEST C
Shasta-Trinity National Forest

Level: Easy   **Distance:** 3.6 miles round-trip

Best Season: April–August   **Elevation Change:** Total gain 400 feet

The McCloud River has three falls within two river miles of each other, each with its own distinct personality. Lower Falls is a busy family swimming hole, complete with a metal ladder to assist jumpers and divers as they exit the chilly water. Middle Falls is one of the most spectacular river falls in Northern California—wide, powerful, and commanding—and lures photographers and the hardiest of swimmers. Upper Falls is exotic looking—a narrow funnel of water that drops

© ANN MARIE BROWN

McCloud Falls

into a circular turquoise pool—but it's difficult to view. One hiking trail links all of the McCloud Falls, so you can visit them all in about an hour.

Start hiking at Lower Falls, located just below Fowlers Camp. Lower Falls is the smallest of the McCloud Falls, a 12-foot plunge into a giant pool. In the spring, it's a popular put-in spot for kayakers heading down the McCloud River. In summer, it's crowded with people who want to jump in and cool off. Usually there is someone trying to catch a fish or two amid all the chaos.

Check out the action at Lower Falls, then walk the 0.5-mile paved trail along the river that leads through Fowlers Camp. On the camp's east side, near the restrooms, you'll find the start of the trail to Middle Falls, signed only with a wildlife-viewing marker. Take the flat, Douglas fir–lined route along the McCloud River, and in 20 minutes you'll find yourself face-to-face with Middle McCloud Falls. Tall, wide, and regal-looking, Middle McCloud Falls drops 50 feet over a cliff and then forms a deep pool at its base before continuing downstream.

Bold teenagers sometimes jump off the basalt cliffs on the fall's left side, diving into the chilly waters. Plenty of boulders downstream make good perches for watching the scene. Elephant ears grow in and around the falls, and water ouzels somehow manage to build their homes behind the fall's tremendous flow of water.

As is common with river waterfalls, Middle McCloud is at least twice as wide as it is tall, adding breadth to its grandeur. The resulting flow is lavish, especially in spring.

Pay homage and then get ready for an easy ascent to Upper Falls. A series of long, graded switchbacks take you gently up to the top of Middle Falls, where a classic photo opportunity awaits: a breathtaking view of the fall's brink and the creek above it. The trail then levels out and continues upriver, clinging to the edge of the canyon wall. Views of the coursing stream below capture and hold your attention.

Keep your eyes peeled for the first sight of Upper Falls. This waterfall is more secretive than the two downriver; rarely do you get a look at its entire length. At a few scattered points along the trail, you can see five tiers of Upper Falls, but only in fleeting glimpses. When you reach an exposed outcrop of basalt boulders across from the fall, you can see only the two lowest tiers where they plunge into a rocky bowl. They are gorgeous, with circular pools colored a remarkable shade of aquamarine. Although the trail continues to the top of the fall, the best place for viewing is here, on the rock outcrop.

You'd think three waterfalls would be about all the excitement you could take on one trail, but another surprise awaits on your return trip: an extraordinary view of Mount Shasta, which was hiding behind your back on the way in. It appears to be so close, you could reach out and touch it.

Directions
From Redding, drive 65 miles north on I-5. Take the Highway 89/McCloud exit and drive east on Highway 89. Pass the town of McCloud in nine miles, then continue 4.5 miles farther east to a small Forest Service sign for Fowlers Camp/McCloud Falls/River Access. Turn right and follow the signs to the McCloud River Picnic Area and Lower McCloud Falls. (Bear right when the road forks, driving 0.7 mile past Fowlers Camp.) Park in the day-use parking area at Lower Falls.

Information and Contact
There is no fee. Maps of the Shasta-Trinity National Forest are available for a fee from the National Forest Store (406/329-3024, www.nationalforeststore.com), or can be downloaded for free from www.fs.fed.us/r5/maps/. For more information, contact Shasta-Trinity National Forest, McCloud Ranger District, 530/964-2184, www.fs.fed.us/r5/shastatrinity.

17 POTEM FALLS
Shasta-Trinity National Forest

Level: Easy	**Distance:** 0.5 mile round-trip
Best Season: April–August, but good year-round	**Elevation Change:** Total loss 50 feet

When you're in the waterfall-watching business, every now and then a beautiful fall gets handed to you on a silver platter, and you can't believe your good luck. Potem Falls, on the Pit River Arm of Lake Shasta, is such a place. It's a pristine

© ANN MARIE BROWN

Potem Falls

and beautiful waterfall, with a perfect swimming hole, that you can reach with little effort.

It takes a long but simple drive, plus a short and easy hike, to reach Potem Falls. Located 30-plus miles east of Redding, the waterfall never gets visited by anyone who just happens to be passing by. Those who show up are mostly locals who consider the place a secret swimming hole, or lovers looking for a spot to hold hands and gaze at something inspiring.

Once you make the drive on paved and dirt roads to the unmarked parking pullout above the fall, you have only a 10-minute walk ahead of you. Potem Falls drops into the Pit River arm of Lake Shasta, but this spot doesn't look anything like the overcrowded reservoir you see while driving I-5.

A well-built trail leads from the dirt road and parking pullout, descending to the stream canyon in four switchbacks, straight to the waterfall's pool. Along the way, you'll have to stop to *ooh* and *aah,* because the view of the falls from a distance is just as stunning as from up close.

Potem Falls is 70 feet high, plunging in a single, compact stream over a rock cliff, surrounded by thick and leafy oak trees. It's a perfect free fall, like a miniature Yosemite Falls, but beautifully framed by a plethora of foliage. An ideal swimming pool lies at its base—circular, wide, and reasonably warm—with a gravel beach large enough to lay a towel or two at its edge. For those who prefer picnicking or hand-holding to swimming, there are plenty of big rocks to sit on and admire the scene, as well as a bench situated near the foot of the falls.

Directions

From Redding, take Highway 299 East and drive 29 miles. Turn left on Fenders Ferry Road and drive nine miles (the pavement ends at 3.5 miles and the road turns to dirt). Look for a large unmarked parking pullout on the left side of the road. You can hear the falls from the road. High-clearance vehicles are recommended.

Information and Contact

There is no fee. Maps of the Shasta-Trinity National Forest are available for a fee from the National Forest Store (406/329-3024, www.nationalforeststore.com), or can be downloaded for free from www.fs.fed.us/r5/maps/. For more information, contact Shasta-Trinity National Forest, Shasta Lake Ranger District, 530/275-1587, www.fs.fed.us/r5/shastatrinity.

18 HATCHET CREEK FALLS   BEST ☾
Shasta-Trinity National Forest

Level: Easy   **Distance:** 0.5 mile round-trip

Best Season: Year-round   **Elevation Change:** Total gain 50 feet

© ANN MARIE BROWN

Hatchet Creek Falls

Sure, Hatchet Creek Falls is a lovely sight to behold. But people who make the long drive east of Redding to Hatchet Creek aren't usually visiting for the scenery; they are looking for a place to swim. Hatchet Creek Falls has a deep, clear pool at its base that must be considered one of the finest swimming holes in the Redding and Shasta area. Some refer to the falls and swimming hole as Lions Slide, but since the waterfall is on Hatchet Creek, the proper name should be Hatchet Creek Falls.

Getting to the waterfall is simple. After the pleasant drive out of Redding, you park in a pullout by the highway bridge over Hatchet Creek, jump out of your car, and follow the obvious path upstream. In about 150 yards, you'll have to cut down the steep bank to the creek, then wade across and rock-hop your way up to the fall's base. When I visited in August, this was fairly easy, but it could be much more difficult soon after the rainy season. Hatchet Creek's current is strong and its rocks are slippery. Use caution and good judgment if the water is high.

The waterfall is 25 feet high and its flow is almost 20 feet wide, even in late summer. A large fir tree trunk has toppled over its lip and bisects the cataract. Most impressive is the spectacular pool at its base, which is at least 40 yards wide and round. Although the pool is shallow around its edges and lined with smooth, rounded rocks, it's surprisingly deep in the center near the falls. If you swim, you'll find it's hard to get close to where the waterfall hits the pool because its current is so forceful. Also, the temperature drops several degrees in the deeper areas. The pool is continually refreshed by the waterfall's constant rushing flow, creating beautifully clear water. On a warm day, you'll have to drag yourself out of the swimming hole and back out to your car.

Directions

From Redding, take Highway 299 east for 35 miles. Turn left on Big Bend Road and drive 0.8 mile to the bridge over Hatchet Creek. Park in the dirt parking area on the right, just before the bridge. An unsigned trail begins from this parking area; hike upstream.

Information and Contact

There is no fee. Maps of the Shasta-Trinity National Forest are available for a fee from the National Forest Store (406/329-3024, www.nationalforeststore.com), or can be downloaded for free from www.fs.fed.us/r5/maps/. For more information, contact Shasta-Trinity National Forest, Shasta Lake Ranger District, 530/275-1587, www.fs.fed.us/r5/shastatrinity.

19 WHISKEYTOWN FALLS
Whiskeytown National Recreation Area

Level: Moderate

Best Season: March–June

Distance: 3.4 miles round-trip

Elevation Change: 700 feet

The rangers at Whiskeytown National Recreation Area are proud of their "new" waterfall—so proud that they lead guided hikes to Whiskeytown Falls almost every weekend. You can also hike on your own to see the falls almost any day of the year, and if you do so, you might as well go see Whiskeytown's other falls, too: Brandy, Boulder, and Crystal Falls.

Whiskeytown Falls isn't actually new; it was rediscovered in 2004 and a lovely trail was built to access it. Now it's one of the most popular destinations in the park, especially during the spring months when the 220-foot cataract flows with vigor.

How the waterfall got "lost" is an interesting story. In 1965, when the National Park Service took over the 42,000 acres of what is now Whiskeytown National Recreation Area, the park rangers thought that it was best to keep the falls a secret, so that the "hippies and beatniks" of that era wouldn't trash the place. The waterfall had never appeared on any map—not even a U.S. Geological Survey topo—and no maintained trail was cut through the steep, heavily forested terrain to the falls, so it was pretty easy for everyone to keep their lips zipped. Eventually, all the park staff who knew about

Whiskeytown Falls

the falls had either quit or retired. So it wasn't until a park biologist, who had heard rumors of the waterfall's existence from old-timers who lived in the area, went on a bushwhacking hunt for it that it was rediscovered (although surely a few hunters or loggers had come upon the falls sometime in the last half decade).

To see the falls, follow Mill Creek Trail downhill, then cross over the west fork of Crystal Creek and continue walking until you come to the James K. Carr Trail on the right. The trail was named for one of Redding's most famous residents. (Carr was Undersecretary of the Interior during the Kennedy Administration in the early 1960s and instrumental in the protection of Whiskeytown.) Follow the trail as it leads steadily uphill (ignore the side trails that are old logging roads). Eventually the path levels out and reaches a picnic area; there is a hitching post and bike rack for horses and bikes. Everyone must walk from here; the trail follows the creek for 0.25 mile until it reaches the base of the falls. From here, you can see only the bottom 35 feet of the cascade; in fact, there is no vantage point from which you can see all 220 feet of flowing whitewater. On the fall's left side, stone stairsteps with a metal handrail lead up the waterfall's cliff to two vista points from which you can see the upper sections of the falls. During peak runoff in spring, it's a glorious sight to behold.

In November 2010, a surprising sight at Whiskeytown Falls was the presence of a trail register box at the fall's base. Here, visitors could use the rubbing plates to make an impression on their park-supplied "waterfall stamp card." Those who got three stamps or impressions on their cards after visiting Whiskeytown, Boulder Creek, and Brandy Creek Falls could win a small prize from the Whiskeytown Visitor Center. Even if the stamp cards are no longer in use when you visit, you should certainly go see these other lovely falls.

The hike to Boulder Creek Falls is an easy two miles round-trip. The trailhead is two miles up Mill Creek Road, off Carr Powerhouse Road (Mill Creek Road is usually closed in winter, but during closures you can take a longer hike to Boulder Creek Falls from the trailhead on South Shore Drive). At over 138 feet high, the three cascades of Boulder Creek Falls are tucked into a dark, shaded box canyon filled with moss and ferns. The trail that accesses them is an old logging road.

Brandy Creek Falls is a moderate three miles round-trip. Find the trailhead at the end of Shasta Bally Road off Kennedy Memorial Drive. The trail is a steady uphill ascent and crosses several small streams. Brandy Creek Falls is a series of five cascades that drop over polished granite in a box canyon. The upper falls is the most beautiful of the lot; follow the trail all the way to its end at the base of the upper falls.

While you are visiting waterfalls, you might as well go see Crystal Creek Falls, which is a mere 200 yards' walk from Crystal Creek picnic area, two miles down Crystal Creek Road from Highway 299 (on the way to Whiskeytown Falls).

Directions

From the Whiskeytown Visitor Center on Highway 299, drive eight miles west on Highway 299 and turn left on Crystal Creek Road. Drive 3.6 miles and turn left into the gravel parking area and trailhead. Parking is limited; the lot may be full on weekends.

Information and Contact

There is a $5 entrance fee per vehicle at Whiskeytown National Recreation Area, good for seven days (it's payable at the visitor center, not at the trailheads). Park maps are available for free at the entrance stations and visitor center, or by free download at www.nps.gov/whis. For more information, contact the Whiskeytown Visitor Center at 530/246-1225 or park headquarters at 530/242-3400, www.nps.gov/whis.

MORE WATERFALLS IN SHASTA AND TRINITY

•**Kickapoo Falls, Trinity Alps Wilderness.** Seeing Kickapoo Falls requires a long backpacking trip along the North Fork Coffee Creek. For more information, phone Klamath National Forest, Salmon and Scott River Ranger District (530/468-5351).

•**Root Creek Falls, near Castle Crags State Park.** This newly discovered, 300-foot-high waterfall in Shasta-Trinity National Forest can only be accessed via a made-by-use trail that cuts off the maintained Root Creek Trail in Castle Crags State Park. Rangers intend to build an "official" trail to access the falls in the near future; check with Castle Crags State Park (530/235-2684) for an update.

•**Ukonom Falls, near Happy Camp.** Seeing the falls requires a boat ride and a hike, but it's gorgeous. For more information, phone Klamath National Forest, Orleans Ranger District (530/627-3291).

•**Whitmore Falls, near Millville (Redding area).** This 15-foot-high waterfall won't amaze you because of its height, but rather because of its shape, which is a near-perfect horseshoe. A popular swimming hole in the summer months, Whitmore Falls is accessible via a one-mile hike. From Highway 44 in Millville, take Old Highway 44 one mile to Whitmore Road. Turn right and drive almost 11 miles to an old bridge on the right side of the road. Follow the trail alongside the right side of the creek to the falls and swimming hole.

LASSEN
AND MODOC

BEST WATERFALLS

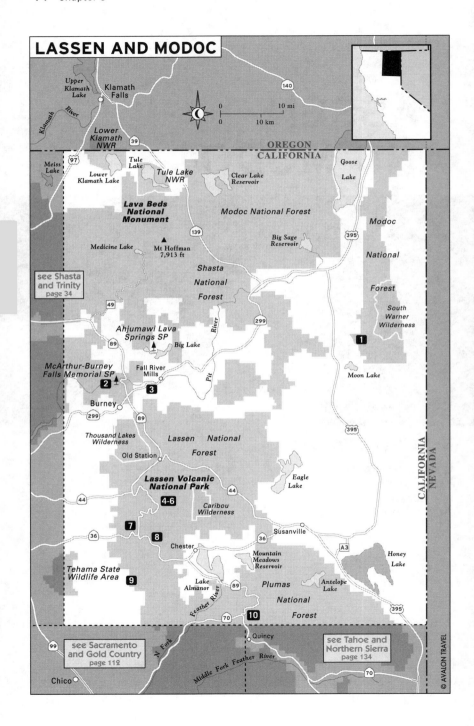

TRAIL NAME	LEVEL	DISTANCE	ELEVATION	SEASON	FEATURES	PAGE
1 Mill Creek Falls	Easy	0.5 mile rt	50 ft	May-Sept.		76
2 Burney Falls	Easy	1.0–4.0 mi rt	150 ft	year-round		77
3 Pit River Falls	Easy/Moderate	2.5 mi rt	400 ft	Apr.-Sept.		80
4 West Fork Hat Creek Falls	Easy	2.8 mi rt	600 ft	June-Sept.		81
5 Kings Creek Falls	Easy	2.4 mi rt	700 ft	June-Sept.		83
6 Mill Creek Falls	Moderate	3.2 mi rt	300 ft	June-Sept.		85
7 Bluff Falls	Easy	0.25 mile rt	40 ft	June-Sept.		87
8 Canyon Creek Falls	Strenuous	11.6 mi rt	2,000 ft	June-Sept.		88
9 Deer Creek Falls	Easy	3.5 mi rt	300 ft	Apr.-Aug.		90
10 Indian Falls	Easy	0.5 mile rt	50 ft	Apr.-Aug.		92

1 MILL CREEK FALLS
Modoc National Forest

🚶 🏊 🦌 ⛰️

Level: Easy

Best Season: May–September

Distance: 0.5 mile round-trip

Elevation Change: Total gain 50 feet

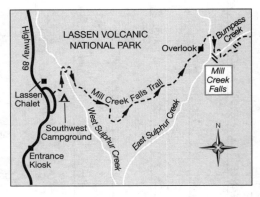

Most people need a good reason to travel all the way to Modoc County in the remote northeastern corner of California. Here's a good reason: Mill Creek Falls in the Warner Mountains.

You can leave your hiking boots in your tent for this trip. Mill Creek Falls are a mere quarter mile from the Forest Service campground that bears the same name. To see the waterfall, take the trail out of camp and bear left at the fork. The right fork goes to Clear Lake and then deep into the South Warner Wilderness, a rugged land that ranges from sagebrush and grasslands to high alpine lakes and peaks. The wilderness, within which Mill Creek Falls sits just inside the boundary, is well-known for having snowstorms in every month of the year. It bears repeating: it's a rugged land.

After just a few minutes of walking through a forest of white firs, you're at an overlook area for the 100-foot falls, watching Mill Creek make a vertical plummet over a narrow sandstone cliff. A railing keeps eager waterfall enthusiasts from falling into the creek.

You're only about 200 feet from the falls at the overlook, an ideal spot for taking pictures. Don't try to go any closer by scrambling off-trail, especially in spring and early summer when the creek level is high, because many slippery rocks line the edge of Mill Creek Falls.

Later in the summer, you can swim in Mill Creek, although not right by the falls—the current is too strong. Head downstream, between the falls and the camp, to any of numerous swimming holes. It's usually not hard to find a secluded pool to call your own.

While you're out moseying around, be sure to take the 0.25-mile hike to Clear Lake, elevation 5,900 feet. From the campground, just continue past the waterfall fork and bear right, following the clearly marked signs. Clear Lake is a decent-sized lake with big fish, both brown and rainbow trout. The catch is so dependably good, people even come here in the winter to ice fish. A trail follows along the right side of the lake.

Directions

From Alturas, drive south on U.S. 395 for 18 miles to Likely. Turn east on Jess Valley Road (County Road 64) and drive nine miles. At the fork in the road, bear left on Forest Service Road 5 and drive 2.5 miles, then turn right on Forest Service Road 40N46 and continue two miles to the campground and trailhead.

Information and Contact

There is no fee. Maps of Modoc National Forest and/or the South Warner Wilderness are available for a fee from the

Mill Creek Falls

National Forest Store (406/329-3024, www.nationalforeststore.com), or can be downloaded for free from www.fs.fed.us/r5/maps/. For more information, contact the Warner Mountain Ranger District of Modoc National Forest, 530/279-6116, www.fs.fed.us/r5/modoc.

2 BURNEY FALLS   BEST (

McArthur-Burney Falls Memorial State Park

Level: Easy   **Distance:** 1.0–4.0 miles round-trip

Best Season: Year-round   **Elevation Change:** Total gain 150 feet

It's a fact that Burney Falls is more of a tourist attraction than a mountain sanctuary. It's true that they made the falls too easy to see—just pay your five bucks and drive right up to the overlook. But when you visit the towering 129-foot waterfall at McArthur-Burney Falls Memorial State Park, you understand why it's worth the trip even just to sightsee.

Watching 100 million gallons of water pour over a cliff, rain or shine, snowmelt or no snowmelt, is an experience you don't forget. President Theodore Roosevelt, a devout naturelover, went so far as to call Burney Falls the eighth wonder of the world.

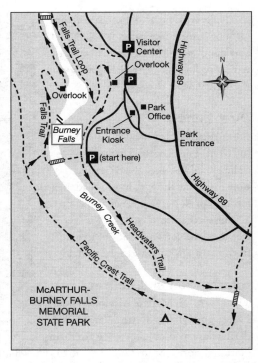

The good news is that you have options for viewing Burney Falls. There's the drive-up-and-peer-over-the-railing routine, two different one-mile loop trips, or longer hikes along Burney Creek. The most peaceful waterfall-watching route is via the Headwaters Trail, which starts from the parking area to the left of the entrance kiosk (not the main lot on the right). You walk upstream, heading away from the falls. With this approach, you get a pretty hike through the forest with much less company than on the main Falls Loop Trail, and you save your waterfall visit for last.

Headwaters Trail's woodland is filled with ponderosa pines, big Douglas firs, and white and black oaks. A half mile out, you reach a long footbridge over Burney Creek and an intersection with the Pacific Crest Trail (PCT). Cross the bridge and follow the PCT downstream, now heading in the direction of Burney Falls. In another half mile, exit the PCT and turn right on Falls Loop Trail, which was regraded and improved during the summer of 2010. A few switchbacks lead you downhill to a sign for the Burney Falls overlook and a small clearing, where the view of the huge waterfall is framed by trees. This perspective is different from most photographs you've seen of the falls; they are usually taken from the overlook on the east side of the creek.

Burney Falls' height, at 129 feet, doesn't tell the whole story of its splendor. Many waterfalls in this book are far taller, yet few have the grandeur to match Burney Falls. It is unique because it flows at basically the same rate all year, making it one of the few waterfalls in California that you can visit in every month of the calendar. That's because the water from Burney Creek comes from underground springs and stored snowmelt in the basalt rock layers that

Burney Falls

make up the falls. If you look closely, you can see that much of the fall's flow actually pours out of the face of the cliff, rather than over the top of its lip. Due to its underground source, the fall's water temperature, even on warm summer days, is a chilly 42°F.

To make a loop back to the parking area, backtrack up Falls Loop Trail for a few hundred yards, then turn left on another footbridge that will take you back to your car in 100 yards. Or you can continue past the overlook, heading farther downstream on Falls Trail, to yet another footbridge that returns you via the most popular route in the park. This is the Falls Loop Trail proper, a one-mile trail that begins and ends by the eastern falls overlook and crosses two different footbridges over Burney Creek. The best feature of this trail is that it's routed near the base of the falls, where you can admire its huge sapphire pool and be doused with spray and mist. The bad news is that the path is paved and crowds are a problem, especially on summer weekends. Some visitors don't follow the whole loop; they just walk from the main overlook to the base of the falls and back.

You're likely to see fly fishers working the waters in the deep, cold pool of Burney Falls, or farther upstream along the Headwaters Trail. Burney Creek is a well-loved trout stream, although novices don't fare well here.

If you want to hike farther, you can make a terrific loop by heading out on the Falls Loop Trail from the main overlook, continuing straight on the Burney Creek Trail rather than crossing the creek, then looping back on the Rim Trail for a three-mile loop. Or combine this loop with the loop on the Headwaters Trail and Pacific Crest Trail for a 4.5-mile hike.

Directions

From I-5 at Redding, turn east on Highway 299 and drive 50 miles to Burney. At Burney, continue five miles east on Highway 299 to its junction with Highway 89. Turn left (north) on Highway 89 and drive 5.5 miles to the park entrance. Park at the main lot and follow the signs to the overlook and Falls Trail, or park at the lot to the left of the entrance kiosk and begin hiking on the Headwaters Trail.

Information and Contact

An $8 day-use fee is charged per vehicle. Park brochures/maps are available for free by download at www.parks.ca.gov, or for a small fee at the park entrance kiosk or visitor center. For more information, contact McArthur-Burney Falls Memorial State Park, 530/335-2777, www.parks.ca.gov or www.burney-falls.com.

3 PIT RIVER FALLS
Bureau of Land Management lands

Level: Easy/Moderate

Best Season: April-September

Distance: 2.5 miles round-trip

Elevation Change: Total loss 400 feet

Pit River Falls is an "easy way" or "hard way" waterfall. You can take the easy way, which is to simply drive up to the overlook, preferably with a pair of binoculars and a picnic. Or you can take the hard way, which is to descend steeply through scratchy brush to the bottom of the deeply cut canyon where the falls spill. It's your choice.

The overlook is a bit of a disappointment, partly because you are too distant from the waterfall, but mostly because people party here at night and leave trash around. In the daytime, you'll probably have the place to yourself, and it's a good spot to get a view of the impressively steep Pit River canyon. Surrounded by basalt cliffs and boulders, this deep canyon was formed by volcanic activity.

Pit River Falls

© ROGER HOOPER

If you decide to make the scramble to the falls, take note of how steep the canyon is, because if you go down, you have to come back up. Two rough routes lead from the overlook, but neither of these are good trails. Instead, drive down the road another 0.5 mile, toward Fall River Mills, to a parking area on the right. Follow the dirt road, which leads toward the river. When you reach the canyon rim, put on your long pants and long-sleeve shirt and follow any of the rough routes downhill. After you touch bottom, head downstream on an old dirt road, which leads to a broken-down metal bridge just below Pit River Falls. Stay off the dilapidated bridge; instead, clamber below it to the waterfall's base. You may be surprised at the fall's height and velocity, which can't be discerned from the drive-to overlook. Pit River Falls drops 40 feet over a basalt cliff. If it's a hot day, you can swim a short distance downstream, where the current is milder. Enjoy the Pit River, then get mentally prepared for the breath-taking, brushy scramble back uphill.

Directions

From Redding, take Highway 299 east for 58 miles to the junction of Highways 299 and 89. Continue east on Highway 299 for 10 more miles to one mile west of Fall River Mills. Watch for the blue "Vista Point" sign and then turn into the parking area on the right side of the road.

Information and Contact

There is no fee. For more information, contact the Bureau of Land Management, Alturas Field Office, 530/233-4666, www.ca.blm.gov/alturas/.

4 WEST FORK HAT CREEK FALLS
Lassen Volcanic National Park

Level: Easy	**Distance:** 2.8 miles round-trip
Best Season: June–September	**Elevation Change:** Total gain 600 feet

Let's call a spade a spade and say that the waterfall on Hat Creek by Paradise Meadows in Lassen Park is really only a cascade, and not even a big one at that. But the rangers told us to go see it anyway, because there were secret rewards to be found on the hike to Paradise Meadows. Rewards that would make a 20-foot cascade seem like an excellent excuse for a hike.

Those rangers know their stuff. There are actually two good-size cascades in the last quarter mile of trail to Paradise Meadows, and both are great spots for a picnic or for shooting a few pictures. But the route wowed us in other ways as well. First, it's only a 1.4-mile walk to Paradise Meadows, but it's uphill the whole way until the last 100 yards, and at this 6,300-foot elevation, my heart was pumping aerobically in no time. Second, the area's wildflowers are tremendous. In July, there was truly a heart-stopping display of color along the trail and stream. Third, there's Paradise Meadows itself, a large green expanse that's the size of a couple of football fields, strewn with lavender wandering daisies. I wandered, too, among the daisies, and resisted the temptation to roll around in them, fearing I might squash too many.

Of the two Hat Creek cascades, the upper one is the most impressive, especially if you cut down off the trail and sit close to its base. It has more of a free fall to its flow, and makes a startling show of white against the green of the grasses surrounding it.

West Fork Hat Creek Falls

Few people stop at the falls, though, because it's only 10 more minutes of walking to reach Paradise Meadows. When they reach the meadow, hikers tend to stand respectfully at its edge, staring out at the wonder of Paradise, afraid to tread on even one precious blade of grass. It's that pristine-looking.

Along the trail, I counted more than a dozen kinds of wildflowers, even in midsummer when most places in California have lost their bloom. I saw both blue and yellow lupines, shooting stars, corn lilies, columbines, daisies, gentian, and wallflowers. So much color, so little time.

To cover a little more distance, you can continue beyond the meadow to Terrace and Shadow Lakes, another two miles farther. And if you need one more reason to make the trip to Hat Creek's cascades and Paradise Meadows, the trail's abundant views of glistening, snow-capped Lassen Peak should do it.

Directions

From I-5 at Redding, turn east on Highway 44 and drive 46 miles to the park's northern entrance. Continue southeast on Lassen Park Road for 10 miles to the Paradise Meadows Trailhead on the right (south) side of the road. Park near the sign for Hat Lake.

Information and Contact

There is a $10 entrance fee per vehicle at Lassen Volcanic National Park, which is good for seven days. Park maps are available for free at the entrance stations, or by download at www.nps.gov/lavo. For more information, contact Lassen Volcanic National Park, 530/595-4480, www.nps.gov/lavo.

5 KINGS CREEK FALLS
Lassen Volcanic National Park

Level: Easy   **Distance:** 2.4 miles round-trip

Best Season: June–September   **Elevation Change:** Total loss 700 feet

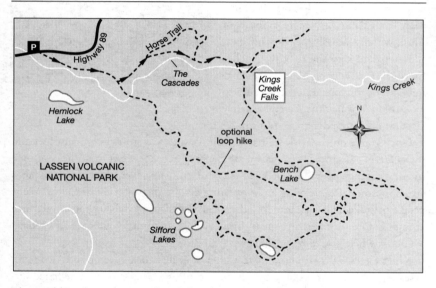

It's possible to be momentarily confused. Are you walking on the granite stairsteps of the Mist Trail in Yosemite National Park, on your way downstream to Vernal Fall? Of course not. Here you are in Lassen Volcanic National Park, following the rocky stairway to Kings Creek Falls. But the two trails share so many similarities, you might think the two parks hired the same trail builders. Sections of the stairstepped walkway to Kings Creek Falls are just as scenic, and just as treacherous, as the world-famous Mist Trail in Yosemite. Of course, the Kings Creek Trail sees only a fraction of the number of hikers that the Mist Trail sees.

The waterfall is rated only an 8 but the trail is a 10. The route follows Kings

Creek all the way, is frequently shaded by big fir trees, and descends from the parking lot for 1.1 miles to the falls. An especially pleasant, level stretch near the halfway mark follows alongside Lower Meadow. Dark green and teeming with corn lilies in summer, the meadow makes a perfect place to rest on the uphill hike back.

Kings Creek Falls

Beyond Lower Meadow, you have two options: follow the Foot Trail or the Horse Trail. The Horse Trail is more level and less treacherous, but it's nowhere near as scenic, because it moves away from Kings Creek. Take the Foot Trail, which leads steeply downhill on stairsteps cut into the rock just inches from The Cascades on Kings Creek. Before you begin your descent, be sure to look ahead of you at the incredible valley vista far off in the distance. You can see for miles.

Once you're on the rock stairsteps, you must keep your eyes on your feet and their careful placement because you are stepping only a few feet from the continual rushing cascade of white water. This is difficult, however, since The Cascades are so mesmerizing, serving as an opening act for the waterfall to follow. Some people mistake The Cascades for Kings Creek Falls, and they unknowingly turn around before they reach the real thing. Keep going until you come to a fenced overlook, where you're witness to a vertical drop.

Kings Creek Falls are about 50 feet high, split by a rock outcrop into two main cascades, which make a steep and narrow drop into the canyon. The fence surrounding the waterfall keeps people out of trouble on the unstable slopes. A picnic lunch at the overlook and a turnaround there make a lovely 2.4-mile round-trip. If you wish to hike farther, you can make a five-mile loop by crossing the foot-bridge just 100 yards before the falls and following the trail to Bench Lake and beyond. Be sure to take the spur off the loop to the Sifford Lakes.

Directions

From I-5 at Red Bluff, turn east on Highway 36 and drive 47 miles. Turn north on Highway 89 and drive 4.5 miles to the park's southwest entrance. Continue

12 miles on Lassen Park Road to the parking area and the trailhead on the right, near milepost 32. Park along the road.

Or, from I-5 at Redding, turn east on Highway 44 and drive 46 miles to the park's northern entrance. Continue southeast on Lassen Park Road for 17 miles to the trailhead on the left side of the road at milepost 32. Park in the pullouts on either side of the road.

Information and Contact

There is a $10 entrance fee per vehicle at Lassen Volcanic National Park, which is good for seven days. Park maps are available for free at the entrance stations, or by download at www.nps.gov/lavo. For more information, contact Lassen Volcanic National Park, 530/595-4480, www.nps.gov/lavo.

6 MILL CREEK FALLS
Lassen Volcanic National Park

Level: Moderate **Distance:** 3.2 miles round-trip
Best Season: June-September **Elevation Change:** Total loss/gain 300 feet

The woman working at the entrance gate said Mill Creek Falls was the highest waterfall in Lassen Volcanic National Park, but she forgot to mention that it's also the prettiest, despite some serious contenders.

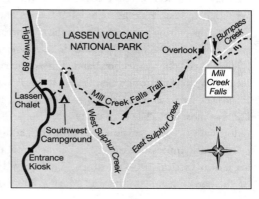

The trail to the falls is only 3.2 miles round-trip and has a constant up-and-down undulation, so you're never sure if you're losing elevation or gaining it. The trailhead is on the south side of Lassen Park, at Southwest Campground. A brief stint on pavement takes you through the campground, but after you pass the tents and picnic tables, things start to look a whole lot better.

"Better" begins at a log bridge over West Sulphur Creek, just beyond the campground. Acres and acres of mule's ears grow on the far side of the bridge, and a postcard-perfect view of Lassen Peak lies straight ahead. A memorable vista awaits here, encompassing the lush, emerald-green valley that lies between Sulphur Creek and the old, snowy volcano.

The trail laterals across hillsides and over feeder streams for two miles. Most of the time, you walk under a canopy of red firs, white firs, and pines, many of them covered with bright green staghorn moss, but occasionally the trail leads to small, open meadows rife with corn lilies and grassy wildflowers.

After a while, you begin to wonder where you're going and if you'll ever get there, as the trail heads steadily eastward through the trees. But then comes the magic moment when you hear the sound of water plummeting—and in moments, you are standing at an overlook, peering across the canyon at Mill Creek Falls.

Mill Creek Falls

A 75-foot, plunging free fall, Mill Creek makes a solid impression. It's not only big, it's also quite graceful. Two creeks join together at its lip, then spill as one through a very deep and narrow canyon. Sulphur Creek contributes to Mill Creek Falls' greatness; it's the pairing and funneling of the two streams that results in the tremendous water flow. The outcome is a classic double waterfall; the upper section drops about 25 feet, then collects in a bowl and gathers force to drop again, this time about 50 feet, in one long chute of water. Perhaps what is most spectacular about the waterfall is the rock face over which it pours—it's a rather knobby-looking cliff with multiple layers of moss and algae in colors ranging from rust and orange to deep green. Huge old-growth fir trees grow on top of the cliff, adding to the majesty.

It's nearly impossible to access the bottom of the fall because the canyon walls are a near-vertical 100-foot drop. The waterfall view is best from this overlook, or you can continue on the trail another 200 yards to the fall's brink.

Directions

From I-5 at Red Bluff, turn east on Highway 36 and drive 47 miles. Turn north on Highway 89 and drive 4.5 miles to the park's southern entrance. Continue 100 yards past the entrance station to the parking area on the right, near the restroom at Southwest Campground. Begin walking on the paved trail by the restroom, heading through the camp to its north side.

Information and Contact

There is a $10 entrance fee per vehicle at Lassen Volcanic National Park, which is good for seven days. Park maps are available for free at the entrance stations, or by download at www.nps.gov/lavo. For more information, contact Lassen Volcanic National Park, 530/595-4480, www.nps.gov/lavo.

7 BLUFF FALLS
Lassen National Forest

Level: Easy

Best Season: June–September

Distance: 0.25 mile round-trip

Elevation Change: Total gain 40 feet

Bluff Falls may not be worth a special trip all the way out to this remote corner of Northern California, but if you happen to be in Lassen Volcanic National Park and it's crawling with tourists, you might just want to stop by. You can probably get yourself your own private waterfall.

The 50-foot cataract is just outside of the park's southern border, visible from the road if you're watching carefully. Gaining access to it is no mystery—just follow the rough route from the closest parking pullout (across the road), which winds around to near the fall's base. You'll have to walk over quite a few boulders, not all of which were made by nature. Bits of concrete, cables, and other evidence of mining activity remain here; Bluff Falls was once the site of a quarry. Even the waterfall's cliff has been excavated. When you see it, it's clear how Bluff Falls got its name.

It's critical to see this fall in the morning, and as soon after snowmelt or rainfall as possible. By late afternoon, the sun goes behind the bluff of Bluff Falls, putting the waterfall in shadow.

Directions

From I-5 at Red Bluff, turn east on Highway 36 and drive 47 miles. Turn north on Highway 89 and drive 3.5 miles. The waterfall is visible on the left (west) side of the road. If you're coming from Lassen Volcanic National Park, Bluff Falls is 1.5 miles south of the park's southern entrance.

Information and Contact

There is no fee. Maps of Lassen National Forest are available for a fee from the National Forest Store (406/329-3024, www.nationalforeststore.com), or can be downloaded for free from www.fs.fed.us/r5/maps/. For more information, contact the Almanor Ranger District of Lassen National Forest, 530/258-2141, www.fs.fed.us/r5/lassen.

8 CANYON CREEK FALLS
Lassen National Forest

🚶 🚗 🐕

Level: Strenuous

Distance: 11.6 miles round-trip

Best Season: June-September

Elevation Change: Total gain 2,000 feet

Canyon Creek Falls at low flow in autumn

© ANN MARIE BROWN

If you want to see Canyon Creek Falls, you must be willing to sign up for a long day hike or backpacking trip. Is it worth it? Yes. Just pack along a good lunch and prepare to make a day of it, or load up your backpack for a longer trip beyond the falls.

The path to the waterfall is the Spencer Meadow National Recreation Trail, which begins just outside of Childs Meadows, only a few miles from the southern entrance to Lassen Volcanic National Park. While the national park may be crowded on summer weekends, things are sure to be quieter out here in the neighboring national forest. From the trailhead, the trail begins a long climb up a ridge. The good news is that it is shaded by pine and fir trees all the way; the bad news is that both the forest and the ascent seem relentless. At the trail's one and only fork, bear left. At 2.4 miles you break out of the trees to some fine views of wide, green Childs Meadows. The continuing ascent provides you with even wider vistas, now looking northwest to Brokeoff Mountain, Mount Diller, and Lassen Peak.

Your final views before you head back into dense forest are down into the valley of Canyon Creek. From your perch on the trail, you are high above it.

At 4.0 miles, the trail levels out along a ridgeline, curving in and out of small

ravines. You'll cross several of these, including a sizeable one lined with large boulders, in the last mile before the falls. Don't be alarmed if the small streams are dry. Canyon Creek has a dependable year-round flow.

Finding the fall isn't easy, however, because it doesn't drop right along the trail. Use your ears to guide you to the sound of rushing water. Watch carefully for an informal spur heading left at approximately 5.8 miles from the trailhead. It's only a 75-yard walk to the edge of the narrow stream canyon, then a steep descent down to the creek below the falls. If Canyon Creek's water level is low enough, you can pick your way up and around boulders to reach the base of the waterfall, which drops 50 feet over a steep, rock-lined cliff.

Note that if you choose to backpack the Spencer Meadow Trail, you can continue another 1.3 miles to Spencer Meadow, spend the night, then make a loop back to the trailhead.

Directions

From I-5 at Red Bluff, turn east on Highway 36 and drive 47 miles. At the junction of Highways 36 and 89, continue east on Highway 36 for another five miles, or 0.3 mile past Childs Meadows Resort. The signed trailhead and parking lot are on the north side of Highway 36.

Information and Contact

There is no fee. Maps of Lassen National Forest are available for a fee from the National Forest Store (406/329-3024, www.nationalforeststore.com), or can be downloaded for free from www.fs.fed.us/r5/maps/. For more information, contact the Almanor Ranger District of Lassen National Forest, 530/258-2141, www.fs.fed.us/r5/lassen.

9 DEER CREEK FALLS
Lassen National Forest

Level: Easy

Distance: 3.5 miles round-trip

Best Season: April–August

Elevation Change: Total gain 300 feet

Lower Deer Creek Falls

© ANN MARIE BROWN

When most people come to Deer Creek in Lassen National Forest, they have only one thing in mind: trout fishing. While I think angling is a fine pursuit, I came with a different goal: to cast a discerning eye on Deer Creek Falls and its sibling, Lower Deer Creek Falls, and determine if they were worthy of this book.

They didn't disappoint me. Not only were both waterfalls running full even in late July, the lower fall provided me with a 3.5-mile hike through a forest canopy and some of the quickest skinny-dipping I've ever done. Deer Creek is frigid, even late in the season.

From the parking area, the trail is routed downstream along the river through dense firs, pines, and live oaks. Lower Deer Creek Falls is 1.7 miles from the trailhead. I'd like to say it was a nice walk, but the truth is that the gnats were driving me crazy. If you have the bad luck to visit during the few weeks of gnat season, you have to wear sunglasses to keep them out of your eyes or keep fanning yourself continually. Otherwise, they relentlessly hover around your face.

The trail is mostly flat and pleasantly shaded till the last quarter mile before the falls; then the route climbs a bit and is more exposed. The good news is that the gnats leave you alone when you are in the sun—a blessed reprieve.

Two left spur trails cut off from the Deer Creek Trail to go down to the falls. When you descend to the creek, you see that a fish ladder has been built around the main waterfall, consisting of a series of four stairstepped concrete dams with notches cut into them, creating one-foot-high falls that the fish can easily jump over, and a tunnel in the rock for them to swim through. If you take the second of the two spur trails, it leads you right to the fish ladder. Your view of the falls is partially blocked by the huge boulder housing the fish tunnel, but you can sit on a small rocky beach and watch the 15-foot cascade, hoping that a fish will come by and climb the ladder. (The first spur trail gives you a view of the entire height of the fall and its powerful, churning white water.)

If you like to fish, don't forget your tackle box on this trip. Deer Creek is stocked with rainbow and brook trout almost every week near the two upstream campgrounds, Potato Patch and Alder Creek. Plenty of those fish make it downstream. However, don't get any ideas about fishing near the fish ladder, because it is clearly posted as a big no-no within 250 yards.

Now that you've seen Lower Deer Creek Falls, you should take the shorter trip to the upper falls as well. They are four miles upstream, so you can't get there from here. Walk back to the trailhead parking area, then drive northeast on Highway 32 to 1.5 miles east of Potato Patch Campground, where there are some springs on the side of the road and a parking pullout. Park there and look for an unmarked route that leads from the road down to the waterfall. It's steep, but only about 100 yards long. You'll find that Upper Deer Creek Falls is about the same size as the lower one, and it provides more swimming and fishing holes nearby.

Directions
From the intersection of Highways 32 and 99 in Chico, drive 40.2 miles northeast on Highway 32. Cross the Deer Creek bridge and park in a dirt pullout on the right. Cross the road to reach the trailhead on the northeast side of the bridge. Or, coming from the east, drive 14 miles west of Chester on Highway 36. Turn south on Highway 32 and drive 14 miles to the Deer Creek bridge and trailhead. (The trailhead is also 1.5 miles southwest of Potato Patch Campground on Highway 32.)

Information and Contact
There is no fee. Maps of Lassen National Forest are available for a fee from the National Forest Store (406/329-3024, www.nationalforeststore.com), or can be downloaded for free from www.fs.fed.us/r5/maps/. For more information, contact the Almanor Ranger District of Lassen National Forest, 530/258-2141, www.fs.fed.us/r5/lassen.

🔟 INDIAN FALLS   BEST 🅒
Plumas National Forest

Level: Easy   **Distance:** 0.5 mile round-trip

Best Season: April–August   **Elevation Change:** Total loss 50 feet

Indian Falls

The farther northeast from Oroville you travel, the better the Feather River canyon gets. Highway 70, which parallels it for 60 miles, gives you an up-close look at the river's sculptured rock formations, granite cascades, and thickly forested banks, all the way to the road's intersection with Highway 89. And what do you see when you get there? A waterfall, of course.

That's Indian Falls on Indian Creek, a major offshoot of the North Fork Feather River, with a backyard swimming hole and a waterfall that is well-loved by locals and visitors alike. The fall is in a beautiful rock gorge setting not far off the road, and it's accessible by an easy walk through the trees.

On summer afternoons, it's no sweat to find the trailhead because cars are always parked there. The trail is maintained by the volunteer group Friends of Indian Falls, who are clearly a fine group of human beings. In five minutes of walking, you'll reach a picnic table and wooden fence, and from there you can continue hiking to your right to reach a calm swimming beach across from the falls. Or, you can scramble downhill to your left and come out on jagged rocks closer to the falls, the best place for taking photographs or just watching the action. You'll probably find several families and groups swimming, picnicking, and playing at the falls.

Strong swimmers play in the spray at the base of Indian Falls, while small children and dogs seem to prefer the calmer beach area. If you want to swim, you should enter the water at the beach, then paddle 50 yards upstream to the falls. Although Indian Falls is only about 20 feet tall, it runs with a forceful flow even in late summer. Many people wear lifejackets here; it's recommended because the current is strong.

Directions

From Quincy, drive approximately 10 miles north on Highway 70/89 to the right turnoff for Highway 89 North to Greenville and Lake Almanor. Drive three miles north on Highway 89, watching for Indian Falls Road. Drive 0.2 mile farther north on Highway 89, past the Indian Falls Road turnoff, to a dirt road on the right (east). Park alongside the dirt road, then walk down it for about 100 yards. Look for the single-track trail on the left. (If you are coming from Oroville, drive northeast on Highway 70 for 65 miles to the Highway 89 turnoff.)

Information and Contact

There is no fee. Maps of Plumas National Forest are available for a fee from the National Forest Store (406/329-3024, www.nationalforeststore.com), or can be downloaded for free from www.fs.fed.us/r5/maps/. For more information, contact the Mount Hough Ranger District of Plumas National Forest, 530/283-0555, www.fs.fed.us/r5/plumas.

MORE WATERFALLS IN LASSEN AND MODOC

•**The Cascades, on the Feather River near Keddie.** A half-mile hike from Highway 70 leads to the falls. For more information, phone Plumas National Forest, Greenville Ranger District, 530/284-7126.

•**Jackass Falls, near Tobin Resort.** From Oroville, drive about 35 miles north on Highway 70 until you reach the Tobin Resort. Park here or continue a bit farther to a turnout before the Tobin Bridge. Look across the Feather River to see Jackass Falls.

•**Rock Creek Cascades.** From Oroville, drive about 30 miles north on Highway 70. You'll pass through a tunnel and cross over the North Fork of the Feather River. Watch for a railroad trestle, where you pull over to the left and park. Walk up the road from the trestle, then bear right and follow the unmarked trail that parallels Rock Creek. There are lots of big granite rocks where you can sit and watch the cascading falls.

MENDOCINO AND WINE COUNTRY

© ANN MARIE BROWN

BEST WATERFALLS

◖ **Bicycle**
Russian Gulch Falls, **page 98**

MENDOCINO AND WINE COUNTRY

see Redwood Empire page 14

see Shasta and Trinity page 34

Yolla Bolly Middle Eel Wilderness

Red Bluff

Garberville

Leggett

Coast Ranges

Mendocino

National

Forest

Black Butte Lake

Stony Gorge Reservoir

see Sacramento and Gold Country page 112

Laytonville

Eel River

Lake Pillsbury

East Park Reservoir

MacKerricher SP

Fort Bragg

Willits

2

Jackson State Forest

3

Snow Mtn Wilderness

1

Mendocino

Lake Mendocino

Indian Valley Reservoir

Navarro River

Ukiah

Clear Lake

128

Russian River

Boonville

Clearlake

Manchester State Park

Manchester

Garcia R.

Clear Lake SP

Cobb

Cache Creek

Middletown

4

Gualala

Lake Sonoma

Geyserville

Mt St Helena 4,343ft

Lake Berryessa

Armstrong Redwoods State Reserve

Healdsburg

Bothe-Napa Valley SP

Santa Rosa

5

Napa

Sonoma

6

PACIFIC

Point Reyes National Seashore

Petaluma

see San Francisco Bay Area page 188

Vallejo

San Rafael

Oakland

SAN FRANCISCO

OCEAN

0   10 mi
0   10 km

© AVALON TRAVEL

TRAIL NAME	LEVEL	DISTANCE	ELEVATION	SEASON	FEATURES	PAGE
1 Russian Gulch Falls	Easy/Moderate	4.5-7.5 mi rt	200 ft	Dec.-June	🚶🚲◀	98
2 Chamberlain Falls	Easy	0.5 mile rt	150 ft	Dec.-June	🚶🧗	100
3 Stony Creek Falls	Moderate	5.0-13.0 mi rt	700-1,200 ft	Apr.-Nov.	🚶🏃🧗	102
4 Zim Zim Falls	Moderate	7.4 mi rt	750 ft	Jan.-Apr.	🚶🏊🧗	104
5 Sonoma Creek Falls	Easy	1.0 mi rt	300 ft	Dec.-May	🚶	106
6 Devil's Well Falls	Moderate	2.0-6.0 mi rt	500 ft	Dec.-May	🚶	108

1 RUSSIAN GULCH FALLS

BEST C

Russian Gulch State Park

Level: Easy/Moderate

Distance: 4.5-7.5 miles round-trip

Best Season: December–June

Elevation Change: Total gain 200 feet

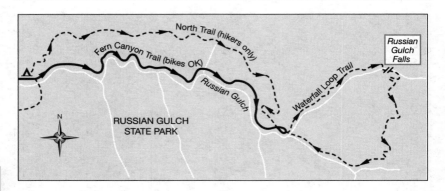

If you head to Russian Gulch Falls, you'll have to choose between many great options for getting there. You can hike on luscious single-track through dense forest for a 6.5-mile out-and-back trek. You can increase or decrease that distance by taking different routes. Or you can ride your bike on the level, paved trail through the canyon, then lock it up at a bike rack and hike the remaining 0.75 mile to the falls.

No matter how you get there, visiting Russian Gulch Falls is a high-quality outdoors experience. This is an excellent place to introduce children to nature, or convince a reluctant friend or spouse that the outdoors is not just tough uphill ascents, mosquitoes, and poison oak.

Make your way to the Fern Canyon Trailhead at Russian Gulch State Park's campground, then choose your route. The paved 1.5-mile Fern Canyon Trail heads straight into the canyon, paralleling Russian Gulch, and it's the only choice for bike riders. Some hikers also prefer it, because it is the shortest route. The unpaved North Trail is for hikers only, and because it winds and meanders through the forest, it's one mile longer than the paved Fern Canyon Trail. Both trails end before the falls at a junction with the Waterfall Loop Trail. There bikers must dismount and lock up their bikes, and all trail users continue on foot to the falls.

But you still have choices. Because the waterfall is situated along a loop trail, you can take the loop's left fork for the shortest trip to the falls (0.75 mile), then

© ANN MARIE BROWN

Russian Gulch Falls

simply turn around and head back. Or you can take the right fork and make a 2.5-mile circle around to the falls and back to the junction.

Which route you take depends on your time and energy, because they are all equally good. The paved trail parallels the stream and is rife with vines, ferns, alders, and willows. The single-track North Trail has more ups and downs, and travels through a mixed forest of big trees—tan oaks, redwoods, and Douglas firs. It's not until both trails join at the Waterfall Loop that the path starts to climb more seriously. The ascent is made easy by well-placed wooden stairsteps.

If you take the short end of the loop to Russian Gulch Falls, you'll climb gently most of the way, then make a brief descent to the fall's base (although some of the best views are from up above). Russian Gulch Falls is 35 feet high, with an abundance of fallen redwood trees gathered in its hollow, dividing the waterfall's flow into several streams. It's fascinating to observe from different angles, noting how the water bobs and weaves its way around logs and branches before making its way to the waterfall's pool. Many of these fallen trees have been here so long that other plants have grown on their trunks, creating a lush green frame for the falling water. Although the entire length of Fern Canyon is lavish with foliage, here at the waterfall, the flora is most extravagant. The result is a scene you won't forget. Best time to see it? Unquestionably, it's just after a few days of rain.

Directions

From Mendocino, drive two miles north on Highway 1 to the entrance for Russian Gulch State Park on the left. Turn left, then left again immediately to reach the entrance kiosk. Continue past the kiosk and turn left again to cross under the highway. Drive through the campground to the Fern Canyon Trail parking area. (If the campground is closed for the winter, you must park near the recreation hall and walk in to the trailhead.)

Information and Contact

An $8 day-use fee is charged per vehicle. Park brochures/maps are available for free by download at www.parks.ca.gov, or for a small fee at the entrance kiosk. For more information, contact Russian Gulch State Park, 707/937-5804, www.parks.ca.gov.

2 CHAMBERLAIN FALLS
Jackson Demonstration State Forest

🏃 🐕

Level: Easy

Best Season: December–June

Distance: 0.5 mile round-trip

Elevation Change: Total loss 150 feet

Chamberlain Falls

Although most people come to Mendocino to savor its spectacular coast, there's another Mendocino that is less well-known, yet equally beautiful. A drive inland on Highway 20 unveils the "other" Mendocino, a land of big conifers, roaring streams, and you guessed it—waterfalls.

A dozen miles from the windswept beaches, Mendocino's Jackson Demonstration State Forest is composed of 50,000 acres of big trees, mostly redwoods and Douglas firs, that line the Big River and Noyo River watersheds. Much of the land has been used for logging, but plenty more is available for public recreation, including the lovely trail to 50-foot Chamberlain Falls.

The route to the trailhead includes nearly five miles of narrow dirt roads, with the possibility of logging trucks bearing down on you at any time, so drive with caution. In good weather, passenger cars can handle the roads without a problem, but when the roads are wet, four-wheel drive is more than a good idea.

After parking your car alongside the road at the trailhead, descend the steep wooden steps into the canyon, then continue downhill on the dirt trail. If the weather is wet when you visit, be wary both on the steps and on the trail, as the fallen oak leaves underfoot can be slippery.

The canyon is dense with foliage, including oaks, Douglas firs, redwoods, sword ferns, and sorrel. After 10–15 minutes of downhill walking, you'll catch sight of Chamberlain Falls and then walk right to its base. Its setting is stunningly simple— just a massive black cliff jutting out of the forest wall, forcing Chamberlain Creek to tumble 50 feet over its bulk before cascading downcanyon. Look for white three-leaf trilliums in early spring, growing amidst the ferns in the fall's grotto. In winter, the entire rock face is covered with rushing water; in summer, the stream is reduced to less than a foot wide. By July, the water is usually warm and tame enough that you can take a shower in the waterfall, or at least dip your head in.

There are many fallen logs on which you can sit and admire Chamberlain Falls, or you can continue hiking on the Chamberlain Creek Trail by crossing the waterfall's stream. Just around the canyon corner is a pristine stand of old-growth redwoods that escaped the loggers' saws. It's a good place to ponder your relatively short existence on the planet. From there, the trail begins to climb steadily out of the canyon, heading northward and eventually joining back up with the road, about 0.3 mile north of where you left your car. You can make a loop, if you wish, but it's easiest and most enjoyable just to return the way you came.

Directions
From Fort Bragg, drive south on Highway 1 for one mile to the turnoff for Highway 20. Turn east on Highway 20 and drive 17 miles to the Dunlap Conservation Camp (mile marker 17.4). Turn left on Road 200, an unsigned dirt road immediately past (east of) the Chamberlain Creek bridge. Drive 1.2 miles on Road 200 to a fork, then bear left and drive another 3.5 miles. (This dirt road is fairly well-maintained and usually suitable for passenger cars, although high clearance might be necessary immediately after big storms.) At exactly 4.7 miles from Highway 20, you'll reach a parking pullout area on the left by a set of stairs. Park in the pullout and descend the stairs to access the trail. (Note: Road 200 can also be reached from Willits by driving 17 miles west on Highway 20 to just before the Chamberlain Creek bridge.)

Information and Contact
There is no fee. Maps are available for $5 from the Jackson Demonstration State Forest (CalFIRE) office at 408 N. Main Street in Fort Bragg. Maps are also available by free download at www.jacksonforest.com. For more information, contact Jackson Demonstration State Forest, 707/964-5674, www.fire.ca.gov or www.jacksonforest.com.

3 STONY CREEK FALLS

Snow Mountain Wilderness

Level: Moderate   **Distance:** 5.0-13.0 miles round-trip

Best Season: April-November **Elevation Change:** Total gain 700-1,200 feet

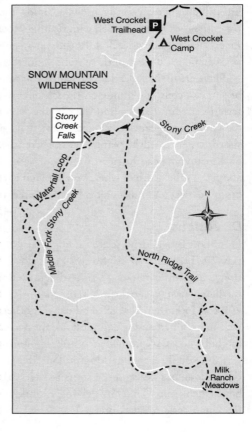

Snow Mountain Wilderness is a long way from everywhere. From I-5, it's a 50-mile drive to the wilderness trailhead. From U.S. 101, it's 60 miles. Tucked into that never-never land west of the Central Valley and east of the Mendocino coast, Snow Mountain Wilderness is a place you must earn with a drive.

Its spectacular waterfall, on the other hand, is easy to reach. Located only 2.5 miles from West Crockett, the main Snow Mountain Wilderness Trailhead, Stony Creek Falls can be seen in an easy afternoon of hiking. Or, if you want to make an overnight trip out of it, you can backpack the 13-mile Waterfall Loop Trail from West Crockett to Milk Ranch Meadows and back.

California waterfalls are not supposed to be this good in November. When it's autumn in Yosemite, everything is bone dry. In the harvest months, even the coastal falls are sadly lacking in H2O. But Stony Creek Falls runs as vigorously as if it was the first of April. Middle Fork Stony Creek is fed by underground springs and drains a vast, vegetation-filled area, so it stays full of water year-round.

The countryside surrounding Stony Creek is as lush and lovely as the waterfall itself. Although you drive through endless farmlands, foothills, and oak woodlands

© ANN MARIE BROWN

Stony Creek Falls

to reach it, the Snow Mountain Wilderness is made up of giant Douglas fir trees, Jeffrey pines, incense cedars, rushing creeks, steep hillsides, and quite often, plenty of snow. They've logged Mendocino National Forest very close to the wilderness boundary, but once your feet step inside that magic line, there's plenty of old growth, especially firs. Sadly, a human-caused wildfire in 2001 torched a large swath of this virgin forest, but there is plenty of vigorous new growth among the charred stumps and snags in the first mile or so of trail.

At the trailhead, a large sign marks the start of the Waterfall Trail. The path travels a level course for a few hundred yards, then parallels a tiny stream as it descends to Middle Fork Stony Creek. Look for the variety of colors in the rocks at your feet. In autumn, vine maples and ferns turn yellow along the creek, and willows turn rosy. In spring, the stream cultivates a multitude of wildflowers. This trail starts out good and stays good the whole way.

At 1.3 miles, you meet up with Middle Fork Stony Creek and must ford or rock-hop, depending on the season. Once on the other side, prepare to switchback uphill, gaining back all the elevation you just lost, but on a steeper grade. At two miles, you top the ridge. The trail continues 100 yards to a fork, where you turn right on the Crooked Tree Trail. (The left fork is the return loop for backpackers making the Milk Ranch Meadows trip.)

About 200 yards from this junction, you'll reach another junction where a hairpin right turn leads to the waterfall, and the left fork leads to Milk Ranch. Go right and, after descending for a few hundred feet, you'll hear the roar of the falls. Keep walking until the spur trail ends, just 100 yards downstream of the fall, on a rise with a perfect view of the 50-foot plunge. Pull up a log and enjoy the view from here, or follow a rough route to your left along the canyon wall. In a few minutes, you'll drop to the foot of the waterfall, where a large pool awaits, plus very chilly air and water.

Stony Creek Falls drops in a free fall over a rock cliff, set in the back of a forested canyon surrounded by steep walls. The fall spills over a mossy, rounded rock lip, then drops gracefully in one long plume to meet its pool and cascade downstream.

A few campsites are found on the canyon wall above the creek. This is an ideal spot to spend the night. After all, it's not a place you'll want to leave quickly. Backpackers opting for the 13-mile loop must retrace their steps to the last junction, then head right for Milk Ranch Meadows. Once at the privately owned meadows, they can choose to add on a couple of short loop hikes. The return to the trailhead is on the steeper North Ridge Trail, but it's mostly downhill. Day hikers simply head left at the junction and walk back to the trailhead, getting the opportunity to enjoy the forest all over again.

Directions

From I-5 at Willows, take Highway 162 west for 20 miles, then turn left and drive 1.3 miles through Elk Creek. Turn right on Road 308 and drive five miles. Bear right on Ivory Mill Road (Road 20N01), signed for the Snow Mountain Wilderness, and drive 9.8 miles. Turn left on Road M3 and drive 15.5 miles to the West Crockett Trailhead sign (Road 18N66). Turn left and drive 0.4 mile to the trailhead parking area. High-clearance vehicles are recommended. (You can also access the trailhead via Road 18N02 out of Stonyford, but this is a much rougher dirt road.)

Information and Contact

There is no fee. Maps of Mendocino National Forest and/or Snow Mountain Wilderness are available for a fee from the National Forest Store (406/329-3024, www.nationalforeststore.com), or can be downloaded for free from www.fs.fed. us/r5/maps/. For more information, contact Mendocino National Forest, Stonyford Work Center, 530/963-3128, www.fs.fed.us/r5/mendocino.

4 ZIM ZIM FALLS
Knoxville Wildlife Area

Level: Moderate

Distance: 7.4 miles round-trip

Best Season: January–April

Elevation Change: 750 feet

Zim Zim Falls is pretty far *out there* in the lonely Napa County backcountry, accessed by a long, winding road that leads 10 miles north of Lake Berryessa to the Knoxville Wildlife Area. The drive to the trailhead is slow and somewhat tedious, but waterfall-lovers who go to this extra effort soon after a period of substantial rain will be well-rewarded. Cascading just over 100 feet, Zim Zim Falls is an impressive sight to behold during the winter and early spring months. By mid-May, however, the show is usually over, or severely diminished.

The waterfall is just one of the highlights of this wildlife preserve managed by the California Department of Fish and Game. Popular with hunters in the autumn, and far too hot to be popular with anyone in the summer, Knoxville Wildlife Area is a land of rugged hills and canyons, with elevations ranging from 1,000–2,000 feet.

Zim Zim Falls

© ANDREW SAWADISAVI

This landscape is more special than it may appear at first glance. Knoxville is one of only a handful of sites in California that protects unusual serpentine habitats. Serpentine soils are chemically hostile to most plant species, so only highly unusual types of plants can tolerate them—often rare and endemic species. The wildlife area provides important breeding grounds and feeding areas for black-tailed deer, quail, Rio Grande wild turkeys, hawks, harriers, falcons, and owls.

The trail to Zim Zim Falls starts at a green gate and follows an old dirt road along the Zim Zim Creek canyon. It is mostly level along the entire route and fairly easy to follow, as long as you remember to stay close to the creek. (Ignore all the side trails that spur off this main road.) You'll cross the stream nearly a dozen times before you get to the falls, and if you don't get your feet wet, there won't be a strong flow at the falls. Hope for wet feet.

For most of the hike, it's hard to believe you are approaching a waterfall. There's nothing about these rolling, oak-studded, chaparral-clad hills that says "sudden vertical drop of falling water." Just have faith and keep walking.

Shortly after the last stream crossing, as you near the end of the valley, there's a trail fork near a prominent, pink-colored boulder. Go right and head up the hill, then at a second junction, go left. The trail cuts back to a high viewpoint of Zim Zim Falls from about 150 yards away. This lovely overlook makes a great spot for lunch.

Many hikers aren't content with the long-distance view and insist on scrambling down the steep, chaparral-covered slopes to the base of the falls, but a somewhat easier way to get there is to simply backtrack to the boulder-marked fork and head straight up the creek.

If you're wondering about this waterfall's name, Zim Zim is actually a misspelling of Zem Zem, which was the name given to a sulphur spring and hotel located near here in the 1860s. The story goes that a visitor to the spring tasted the water and exclaimed, "This water tastes like it's from the sacred well of Zem Zem!" He was referring to a term from the Islamic religion. Zem Zem is a sacred stop along the way for pilgrims traveling to Mecca; a goal of all pilgrims is to drink the water of Zem Zem.

Unless you've brought a filter or purifier with you, you probably shouldn't taste the water of Zim Zim, but you might want to hang out for a while and soak in its surprising beauty.

Directions

From Napa, take Highway 128 east through Rutherford to Berryessa-Knoxville Road, a distance of about 25 miles. Turn north on Berryessa Knoxville Road and drive 23.9 miles to the trailhead at a green gate on the left side of the road (just before mile marker 24). During the wet season, you will have to drive through the shallow waters of Eticuera Creek several times to get to the trailhead, so a high-clearance vehicle is a good idea. Immediately following the heaviest storms, the road may be impassable.

Information and Contact

There is no fee. Free maps are available by download at www.dfg.ca.gov/lands/wa/region3/knoxville.html. For more information, contact the Department of Fish and Game Bay-Delta Regional Office, 707/944-5531 or 707/944-5537, www.dfg.ca.gov.

5 SONOMA CREEK FALLS
Sugarloaf Ridge State Park

Level: Easy

Best Season: December-May

Distance: 1.0 mile round-trip

Elevation Change: Total loss 300 feet

You want a short, pretty trail in a redwood forest? You got it. You want to see a 25-foot waterfall cascading down over rocks, surrounded by big-leaf maples and ferns? Here it is. You want to walk downhill all the way to reach it? No problem. You get all of this on the Canyon Trail in Sugarloaf Ridge State Park when you pay a visit to Sonoma Creek's tumbling waterfall.

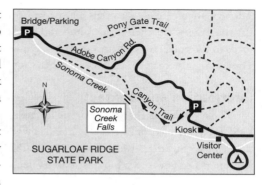

The fall is surprising not just because it runs in notoriously dry and warm Sonoma County, but also because it's hidden just off the road, less than a half-mile walk from where you leave your car. Start walking downhill at the Canyon Trail sign from near the entrance kiosk, dropping a steep 300 feet in 0.4 mile. Descend through a dense and shady forest of hardwoods—oaks, bays, madrones, and alders.

When you reach the falls after about 15 minutes of walking, you enter a lush, wet grotto that is piled with huge, rounded, moss-covered boulders. Many of them are more slippery than they look, so use caution. The trail runs along the edge of the creek. You can climb on the rocks and explore quite close to the cascading water.

Huge boulders have tumbled down the canyon to create Sonoma Creek Falls, a stairstepped cascade about 25 feet high. Big-leaf maple vines and plentiful ferns thrive at the water's edge, providing a leafy green contrast to the dark, jagged rock. Although Sonoma Creek Falls is best seen right after a period of rain, this shady glen remains a cool respite even in the summer heat, when the waterfall is nearly dry.

If you want to hike a little more, continue downstream from the falls into a grove of redwoods along Sonoma Creek. When the trail meets up with Adobe Canyon Road, cross the road and follow Pony Gate Trail back to the parking lot where you left your car. This makes a 3.5-mile loop.

Directions

From U.S. 101 in Santa Rosa, turn east on Highway 12 and drive 11 miles to

Sonoma Creek Falls

Adobe Canyon Road. Turn left and drive 3.5 miles to the park entrance kiosk. Pay the day-use fee, then turn around and head back down the road for about 100 yards to the gravel parking area on your right and the trailhead for the Pony Gate Trail. Cross the road to reach the trailhead for the Canyon Trail.

Information and Contact

An $8 day-use fee is charged per vehicle. A park map is available at the entrance kiosk for a small fee, or by free download at www.parks.ca.gov. For more information, contact Sugarloaf Ridge State Park, 707/833-5712 or 707/938-1519, websites: www.parks.ca.gov or www.parks.sonoma.net.

6 DEVIL'S WELL FALLS
Archer Taylor Preserve, Napa Land Trust

Level: Moderate   **Distance:** 2.0-6.0 miles round-trip

Best Season: December-May   **Elevation Change:** 500 feet

Devil's Well Falls

This is Napa County like you've never seen it before. Here there are no grapevines, or tasting rooms, or shops selling *fromage* and fancy bottle openers. Devil's Well Falls is a little slice of watery paradise tucked into the back of a redwood-studded canyon, and a hike here may make you forget the "other" Napa even exists.

First, the downside: if you are a first-timer, you can't hike here on your own. This series of falls is located on private property, and you can only see them by taking a guided hike with The Land Trust of Napa County. But guided hikes are offered several weekends in winter and spring, so you'll have plenty of chances. Once you've taken a guided hike, or have helped out at one of the Saturday workdays on the preserve, you can usually get permission from the caretakers to hike here without a guide. If you live anywhere nearby, this is a place you will want to come to repeatedly.

The hike begins at Archer Taylor Preserve, west of the town of Napa, and roughly follows Redwood Creek to the falls. There are several possible routes; the shortest is the Tin Cabin Trail (built in 2007), which is about four miles round-trip. If you just want to see the lower falls, the hike can be as short as two miles round-trip. However, this redwood-studded preserve is so beautiful, I highly recommend signing up for the longest hike possible. There's much to see here besides just the lovely falls.

Devil's Well (also called Trinity Falls) consists of three cataracts: the lower 25-foot fall, the slightly taller middle fall, and the tallest upper fall (which is also the most difficult to see in its full glory). The name "Devil's Well" refers to the deep pool at the base of the upper falls, where it is customary to rest and soak your feet.

The Land Trust of Napa County also manages the property around another spectacular Napa waterfall, 31-foot Linda Falls on Conn Creek, near Angwin. The trust offers guided hikes each winter and spring to Linda Falls, as well. If you want to do something good with a few of your hard-earned dollars, make a $40 (or greater) donation to the Land Trust and become a card-carrying member.

Directions

From Highway 29 in Napa, take Redwood Road west for nine miles to the entrance to Archer Taylor Preserve.

Information and Contact

If it's your first visit to Archer Taylor Preserve, you must sign up for a guided hike with the Land Trust of Napa County (707/252-3270, www.napalandtrust.org). If you have hiked here in the past, you may be able to get permission to hike on your own from the preserve caretakers. Phone them 24 hours in advance of your trip at 707/254-0996.

MORE WATERFALLS IN MENDOCINO
AND WINE COUNTRY

•**Stornetta Falls, Point Arena.** Stornetta Ranch is a 1,400-acre preserve located within view of the Point Arena Lighthouse. An easy trail across the coastal bluffs leads to a 40-foot waterfall that descends to the ocean. To reach it, from Highway 1 in Point Arena drive west on Lighthouse Road for 1.4 miles. Park at the turnout on the left by the gate and follow the trail south along the coast.

•**Linda Falls, Angwin, Napa County.** Like Devil's Well Falls, Linda Falls is also on land managed by the Land Trust of Napa County. Linda Falls is a unique waterfall that formed where Conn Creek cascades over angular volcanic boulders; the trip is a three-mile hike. Contact the Napa Land Trust (707/252-3270, www. napalandtrust.org) to take part in a guided hike to the falls.

SACRAMENTO AND GOLD COUNTRY

© ANN MARIE BROWN

BEST WATERFALLS

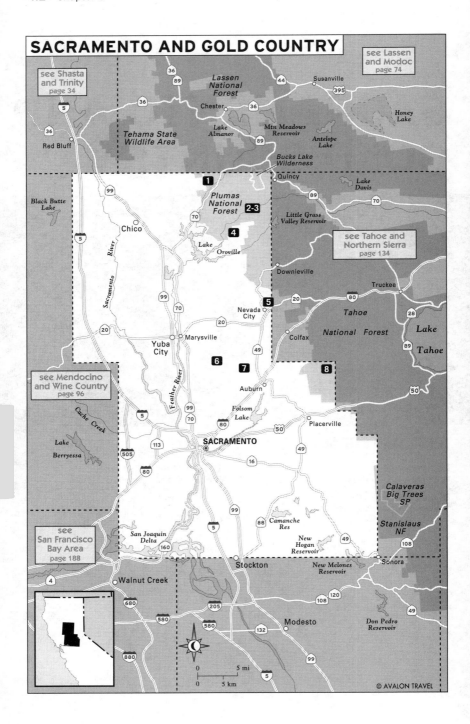

SACRAMENTO AND GOLD COUNTRY

see Shasta and Trinity
page 34

see Lassen and Modoc
page 74

Lassen National Forest

Susanville

Honey Lake

Chester

Tehama State Wildlife Area

Lake Almanor

Mtn Meadows Reservoir

Antelope Lake

Red Bluff

Bucks Lake Wilderness

Black Butte Lake

1

Quincy

Lake Davis

Plumas National Forest

2-3

Little Grass Valley Reservoir

Chico

4

Lake Oroville

see Tahoe and Northern Sierra
page 134

Sacramento River

Downieville

Truckee

5

Nevada City

Tahoe National Forest

Lake Tahoe

Colfax

Marysville

Yuba City

6

7

8

see Mendocino and Wine Country
page 96

Auburn

Cache Creek

Folsom Lake

Placerville

Lake Berryessa

Feather River

SACRAMENTO

Calaveras Big Trees SP

Stanislaus NF

see San Francisco Bay Area
page 188

Camanche Res

New Hogan Reservoir

San Joaquin Delta

Stockton

New Melones Reservoir

Sonora

Walnut Creek

Modesto

Don Pedro Reservoir

0   5 mi

0   5 km

© AVALON TRAVEL

TRAIL NAME	LEVEL	DISTANCE	ELEVATION	SEASON	FEATURES	PAGE
1 Chambers Creek Falls	Strenuous	4.0 mi rt	1,800 ft	Apr.-June	🥾 🧗	114
2 Seven Falls	Strenuous	1.0 mile rt	1,200 ft	Apr.-Aug.	🥾 🏊	116
3 Curtain Falls	Strenuous	5.0 mi rt	1,800 ft	July-Aug.	🥾 🏊 🧗	118
4 Feather Falls	Moderate	7.4-9.8 mi rt	1,000 ft	Apr.-Oct.	🥾 🚴 🧗	121
5 Rush Creek Falls	Easy	2.0 mi rt	Negligible	Apr.-July	🥾 ♿	124
6 Dry Creek Falls	Easy	5.0 mi rt	100 ft	Nov.-May	🥾 🚴 🧗	126
7 Hidden Falls	Easy	3.0 mi rt	350 ft	Nov.-May	🥾 🚴	128
8 Grouse Falls	Easy	1.0 mile rt	100 ft	Mar.-July	🥾 🧗	130

1 CHAMBERS CREEK FALLS
Plumas National Forest

🏃 🏊 🐴

Level: Strenuous   **Distance:** 4.0 miles round-trip

Best Season: April–June   **Elevation Change:** Total gain 1,800 feet

---

Do you like hearing the sound of yourself panting hard on a hot summer day? If so, this is your trail. The Chambers Creek Trail leads four miles uphill from Highway 70 and the North Fork Feather River Canyon to Chambers Peak, elevation 5,800 feet. Halfway there, it crosses Chambers Creek at a set of picture-perfect waterfalls and a historic 1932 Conservation Corps footbridge. If you enjoy hard work, you'll hike the two miles and 1,800-foot elevation gain to the falls. If you're somewhat masochistic, you'll do it at high noon on a hot July day. If you're totally out of your mind, you'll go all the way to the peak, for a 4,000-foot elevation gain and the feeling that you can survive anything.

Chambers Creek Falls

Take your pick. Just remember that this trail is almost entirely out in the sun, especially for the first two miles, so you must have plenty of water with you. You can filter more water at Chambers Creek Falls, but from the trailhead to the falls, there's not a drop to be found. Oh yeah, and if you're having a particularly bad day, expect the gnats to show up.

Begin by hiking 100 yards on an old dirt road, then turn off the road onto a single-track trail on the right. Cross a creek and parallel Highway 70, ignoring all trail spurs and heading upward, ever upward. Here's what you have to look forward to: Half a dozen brutal, exposed, sunny, manzanita-lined switchbacks, which take more than 30 minutes to assault. Whenever you hit a tiny patch of shade, stop and watch the sweat drip off your nose. Say a few choice words. Look down at the road far, far below you and feel jealous of people in their air-conditioned cars.

Finally, after almost an hour of hiking, there's a change in the action—a left bend in the trail, which leads you up and along the edge of the Chambers Creek canyon. It's blissfully shady here, and soon you will be able to hear the creek, although it's too far down below for you to be able to see it. The forest gets thicker and more interesting, with dogwoods and more varied conifers. The sound of water spurs you on, and voila! Shortly, you round a curve and come out to Chambers Creek Falls and the quaint wooden footbridge that crosses it. The bridge is painted a bright aquamarine, which seems a little strange way up here in the middle of nowhere, but you'll be so happy to see the water that you won't worry about aesthetics.

The fall cascades about 250 feet, and one of the nicest drops and pools is right below the bridge. The granite that forms this drop makes it slippery and inaccessible, so scramble upstream for about 50 yards above the bridge, climbing over boulders to another cascade. Pick a spot hidden from the trail, throw off your clothes, and go wading. You deserve it.

You can't scramble any farther upstream because you're blocked by the cliff of this waterfall. You have two choices: continue hiking beyond the bridge, heading farther uphill toward Chambers Peak for more ascent and greater views, or turn around and head back down, this time with enough oxygen to enjoy the vistas of the valley, the river below, and its forested canyon. And if you're in a hurry, don't fret: while it took me 70 minutes to climb up to the falls, it took me only 40 minutes to return.

Directions

From Oroville, drive northeast on Highway 70 for 42.5 miles to the Chambers Creek Trailhead, which is on the north side of Highway 70, across from a school and a closed campground. There is a dirt parking pullout by the trailhead sign. (Coming from the east at Quincy, it's 40 miles northwest on Highway 70.)

Information and Contact

There is no fee. Maps of Plumas National Forest are available for a fee from the National Forest Store (406/329-3024, www.nationalforeststore.com), or can be downloaded for free from www.fs.fed.us/r5/maps/. For more information, contact Plumas National Forest, Mount Hough Ranger District, 530/283-0555, www.fs.fed.us/r5/plumas.

2 SEVEN FALLS

Plumas National Forest

Level: Strenuous

Best Season: April-August

Distance: 1.0 mile round-trip

Elevation Change: Total loss 1,200 feet

© DEE RANDOLPH

Seven Falls

Let's say straight off that there are two ways to make the trek to spectacular Seven Falls in Feather Falls Scenic Area near Lake Oroville. One is to fire up your high-clearance, four-wheel-drive vehicle, tie down anything that might fly loose, then make the slow, jolting, rock-strewn drive to the unmarked, inconspicuous trailhead off Milsap Bar Road—all the while praying that you find it.

The other way is to take your regular old car, pack up some food and maybe your passport and toothbrush for the long journey ahead, and drive 20 long miles to reach Seven Falls via the back route around Feather Falls, requiring only 2.5 miles of bumpy, dirt-road travel—all the while still praying that you can find the darn trailhead.

No matter which way you choose, this trek will cost you some driving time and energy, but Seven Falls is worth any price. The falls are a series of free falls—some as tall as 100 feet high—set in a hidden, pristine canyon that's hard to reach by car and by foot. But they are so spectacular that the Forest Service has long considered building an overlook platform with an official trail to reach it, and possibly even paving the road to make the area more accessible. Since Seven Falls are so close to popular Feather Falls, it just seems logical to open them up for greater recreational use.

Not everybody is in favor of this idea, of course, so while it's being debated, Seven Falls remains a secluded, special place that only those willing to labor can visit. The long, rocky drive and the unmarked, nearly invisible trailhead scare off many potential visitors. The steep descent on a rough route, not a real trail, keeps away plenty more. The route is slippery; it drops 1,200 feet in 0.5 mile;

and if you think going down is tricky, wait till you have to come back up. It's not for the faint of heart.

But the falls...ahhh the falls. Once called Pompy's Falls, for a Maidu shaman who used to worship above the falls at Pompy's Point, Seven Falls are actually seven-plus falls along the South Branch Middle Fork of the Feather River (hence the alternate name, South Branch Falls). It depends on whom you talk to, but many folks claim that Seven Falls is really nine or 11 falls. You can explore as many or as few of them as you like, but remember, this is not hiking, it's more like rock scrambling or climbing.

The rough route from Milsap Bar Road brings you right to the middle of this series of cataracts, to the fourth fall in the series. Head upstream or downstream and you'll find the rest, although many people tire out from this steep off-trail scrambling long before they see all seven. Even if you see only two or three, you'll be suitably awed: each of the Seven Falls is between 50 and 100 feet high, and each is a showering white-water wall that runs wide and forceful even as late as August. In springtime, the power of these falls can be downright frightening. It's worth seeing at least once in your life.

Directions

There are two possible routes. The first is routed around Feather Falls and is mostly paved, although the final 2.5-mile dirt section can sometimes be rough enough to require a high-clearance vehicle: From Highway 70 in Oroville, take the Oroville Dam Boulevard exit (Highway 162) east and drive 1.6 miles to Olive Highway/Highway 162. Turn right and drive 6.5 miles on Highway 162. Turn right on Forbestown Road and drive six miles. Turn left on Lumpkin Road and drive 10.8 miles to the left turnoff for Feather Falls. Reset your odometer here and continue on Lumpkin Road, past the Feather Falls turnoff. At 1.2 miles past the Feather Falls turnoff, take the right fork onto Forest Service Road 27. At 7.9 miles, stay straight at the junction; this puts you on Road 94. At 14.5 miles, reach a major fork and turn right. At 16.2 miles, bear left. At 19.0 miles, take the left fork off pavement and onto dirt. At 19.4 miles, take the left fork onto Road 22N62, Milsap Bar Road. At 21.7 miles, you'll see a good-size clearing on the left before the dirt road curves to the right. Park here and walk back down the road (in the direction you came) for about one-third mile to a spot that has small pullout spaces on both sides of the road. Listen for the falls, which you will not be able to see because of the deep, forested canyon, and look for an unmarked route by the small pullout that leads downcanyon in the direction of the roaring falls. A fallen log obscures the start of the route. Good luck!

The second route is through Brush Creek on an extremely rough four-wheel-drive route via Milsap Bar Camp. Follow the directions above, but drive 25 miles on Highway 162 to the Brush Creek Ranger Station. Turn right (south) on the eastern end of Bald Rock Road and drive 0.5 mile to Forest Service Road 22N62, Milsap Bar Road. Turn left and drive 7.4 miles to the campground. The road gets progressively rockier. Continue 4.6 miles past the campground on Milsap Bar Road to the unmarked route to Seven Falls. Look for the dirt clearing and pullouts along the road, as in the above directions.

Information and Contact
There is no fee. Maps of Plumas National Forest are available for a fee from the National Forest Store (406/329-3024, www.nationalforeststore.com), or can be downloaded for free from www.fs.fed.us/r5/maps/. For more information, contact Plumas National Forest, Feather River Ranger District, 530/534-6500, www.fs.fed.us/r5/plumas.

3 CURTAIN FALLS
Plumas National Forest

Level: Strenuous

Best Season: July–August

Distance: 5.0 miles round-trip

Elevation Change: Total loss 1,800 feet

If you've hiked the well-maintained national recreation trail to Feather Falls, scrambled your way down steep slopes to Seven Falls, and still haven't had your fill of waterfalls in the Feather Falls Scenic Area, well...you have one more trip to take. And unless you're an ace kayaker willing to make the run down the Middle Fork of the Feather River, you have a long hike and an interesting river trek ahead of you.

The first time I tried to reach Curtain Falls, I was told by the Forest Service that the best way to get there was to rent a boat, motor it up the Middle Fork Feather River arm as far as possible, then tie it up and hike along the riverbank to the falls. What they didn't tell me is that the bank is steep granite—sometimes vertical granite—and that hiking it is treacherous and nearly impossible.

After that attempt, I got in touch with Dee Randolph, who used to be an adventure guide in the Feather Falls Scenic Area. Randolph said he never heard of anyone getting to Curtain Falls that way, and added that the 40-foot fall is best seen by kayaking in high water. But Randolph used to take hiking groups to Curtain Falls every summer. He did it by leading them on a two-mile hike on the

© DEE RANDOLPH

Curtain Falls

Dome Trail, descending 1,800 feet to the river canyon. It's a steep, scenic trek, skirting under the soaring heights of 3,200-foot Bald Rock Dome.

From the trailhead, you begin walking on an old skid trail that barrels down the ridge. In about 200 yards, it leads to the actual start of the Dome Trail, which cuts off to your left. Then you simply follow the main trail, with no junctions or intersections to bother with, for two miles downhill. Views of both the river canyon below and the granite of Bald Rock Dome above are spectacular the whole way. In the spring, buckeye trees are in full bloom; their sweet scent wafts along the path with you. Keep an eye out for rattlesnakes, which are commonly seen on this trail. Poison oak is also prevalent, so watch out for that, too.

The second mile of the Dome Trail is for those who are unafraid of heights. The Forest Service blasted the trail out of the canyon's granite wall, then installed railings to keep people from falling off the edge. In one section where blasting was impossible, the trail makers built a steep, 75-foot-tall staircase and bolted it into the rock to bridge the trail.

Where the Dome Trail ends at the river's edge, you can glimpse Curtain Falls, but you are still 0.5 mile away. Some people try to walk from here, but the granite walls are sheer and footing is dicey. Accidents happen every year. Instead, you must wade to the far side, but the river current is strong even as late in the year as August. Don't attempt this unless you are sure the flow is low enough that you can get across. The safest method is to cross using an inner tube. Tie it to a rope secured to the bank to ensure you don't float too far downstream.

If you make it to the far side, a rough route leads upcanyon, via some boulder scrambling and possibly some inner-tubing down granite waterslides. It's great fun, but you must be prepared to get wet. A half mile of this partly by land, partly by water trekking brings you to the pool in front of Curtain Falls. At 40 feet high and at least 100 feet wide, Curtain is a formidable river fall. Top-notch kayakers make the run over its lip in springtime, but they are the brave and the few. Curtain's pool is almost as impressive as the fall itself, with a depth of at least 50 feet and an intense aquamarine hue. Some people have tried scuba diving in the crystalline pool, but alas, no secret treasures have been found.

Randolph believes the waterfall is called Curtain Falls because its cliff is divided by a rock tongue. During heavy rain, when the river level rises, the tongue disappears and the curtains of water seem to close. Then when the rain stops and the river level drops, the tongue re-emerges and divides Curtain Falls' flow, giving the appearance of curtains opening.

A dynamited staircase on the fall's right side, probably left from ambitious miners in the late 1800s, runs up and over Curtain Falls. Ledges above the falls make perfect jumping platforms. While the sun is high, you can hang out and swim here in your own private paradise. Just be sure to save some energy for the return trip. It's easy to forget that after scrambling back downstream to the end of the Dome Trail, you have a two-mile hike and a 1,800-foot elevation gain ahead of you. Most important of all: save some water for this part of the hike. It's completely exposed, and can be hot and dry in the afternoon.

Directions

From Highway 70 in Oroville, take the Oroville Dam Boulevard exit (Highway 162) east and drive 1.6 miles to Olive Highway/Highway 162. Turn right and drive 17 miles on Highway 162 to Bald Rock Road on the right. (This is the western end of Bald Rock Road.) Turn right and drive five miles, then turn left on Zink Road. Drive three more miles until you reach a four-way intersection; continue straight across on Forest Service Road 21N51Y. Drive three miles to a fork in the road; take the left spur. In a few hundred feet, take the left spur to the Dome Trail Trailhead.

Information and Contact

There is no fee. Maps of Plumas National Forest are available for a fee from the National Forest Store (406/329-3024, www.nationalforeststore.com), or can be downloaded for free from www.fs.fed.us/r5/maps/. For more information, contact Plumas National Forest, Feather River Ranger District, 530/534-6500, www.fs.fed.us/r5/plumas.

4 FEATHER FALLS

Plumas National Forest

BEST

Level: Moderate

Distance: 7.4-9.8 miles round-trip

Best Season: April-October

Elevation Change: Total gain 1,000 feet

Let's get the tricky part out of the way first. What river does Feather Falls fall on? Feather Falls falls on the Fall River, near Fall River's confluence with the Middle Fork of the Feather River. Despite its name, it doesn't fall on the Feather River.

It's easy to see why it's hard to get this right. So, all together now: Feather Falls falls on the Fall River.

Of course, few people concern themselves with river nomenclature while they are hiking the Feather Falls National Recreation Trail, because they are too busy having the time of their lives. Feather Falls is one of the most famous waterfalls in California outside of Yosemite, and that's because it has status: it's the sixth highest free-falling waterfall in the

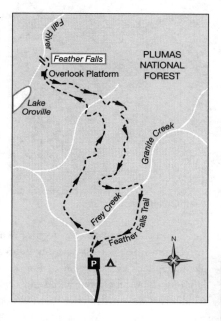

continental United States and the fourth highest in California. Its flow drops 640 feet, then continues for another half mile till it joins the Middle Fork Feather River, which is dammed as Lake Oroville in these parts. (Dammed or damned, depending on how you look at it.)

The waterfall is so spectacular, it has a whole recreation area named after it—the 15,000-acre Feather Falls Scenic Area in Plumas National Forest. The land includes part of the Middle Fork Feather River canyon and three of the river's tributaries: Fall River, Little North Fork, and South Branch. Within its reaches are three other record-class waterfalls: Seven (or South Branch) Falls, Curtain Falls, and Brush Creek Falls. But Feather Falls outdoes them all.

A few options exist for hiking to the fall, all of them good. The trail is a loop: one side is short and steep; the other side is longer and more flat. After your first 0.25 mile of walking, you reach a fork and it's decision time: do you want to get to

© DEE RANDOLPH

Feather Falls

the falls faster but with a tougher climb, or slower and more gradually? The two routes join again a few hundred yards before the falls, so you have to ask yourself a similar question on the return trip.

My suggestion is to take the short way up (the left fork) and return on the longer trail. That makes a 9.8-mile round-trip, which, combined with a couple hours of waterfall-watching, swimming, and picnicking with someone you love makes a perfect day. If you need to shave a little time off, you can take the short route out and back, for a 7.4-mile round-trip.

You can visit any time; the Feather Falls Trail is accessible in all seasons. Although the waterfall and wildflowers are most dramatic in spring, the autumn colors make October an excellent time to visit. Summertime can be hot, but if you start early in the morning, you can beat the 95-degree afternoon heat and be rewarded with swimming holes above the fall. In late winter, a wondrous event happens every year near Frey Creek, about 1.7 miles from the trailhead: ladybugs who have hibernated near the creek from November to January will suddenly wake up and take flight. Thousands of them can fill the air in a single day as they prepare to travel back to the Central Valley to feed. In the process, they alight on the arms and legs of passing hikers. It's an amazing and delightful scene to experience.

Although Feather Falls is in the northern Sierra Nevada foothills and the elevation is low, its trail is surprisingly shaded and lush. A great feature of this 2,400-foot elevation is the incredible speciation of plant life. Along the trail, you pass 17 species of trees, including ponderosa pine, incense cedar, Douglas fir, black oak, canyon oak, madrone, big-leaf maple, white alder, bay, dogwood, and digger pine. They are joined by 20 kinds of shrubs, 11 types of vines, and 10 different ferns. If wildflowers are your bag, visit in March or April, when more than 180 species have been identified. These include purple shooting stars, scarlet Indian pinks, star tulips, Indian paintbrush, starflowers, western bleeding hearts, violets, wild ginger, bush monkeyflowers, wild roses, and red clarkia.

Because it's a designated National Recreation Trail, the Feather Falls route is incredibly well-maintained, with posted trail markers every half mile, letting you know exactly where you are. Bikes are allowed on the trail with a 10-mile-per-hour speed limit, but the route is far more popular with hikers. (If you're on a bike, you should take the easier side of the loop in both directions.)

Start walking from the parking lot trailhead and reach the start of the loop in an easy 0.25 mile. Take the left fork (the short way), and drop elevation for the first two miles, crossing a bridge over Frey Creek. Be sure to look for ladybugs. Then parallel the creek, and come out to a stunning view of the Middle Fork Feather canyon and Bald Rock Dome. The granite dome rises 2,000 feet above the river canyon. It's a sacred meditation place for Maidu Native Americans.

After the dome vista, the trail starts to climb, and it continues to do so steadily between the two- and three-mile markers. Just after three miles, you reach a wooden bench and the junction where the two legs of the loop connect. They become one for the final half-mile ascent to the falls overlook. A couple of easy switchbacks bring you to a fenced viewpoint above the Middle Fork Feather; after a few more minutes of walking, you're at the left turnoff for the falls overlook.

Walk to the overlook before continuing uphill to the top of the falls. The trail is an elaborate series of short walkways that leads to the top of a granite outcrop jutting out into the middle of the canyon. There you get a straight-on view of Feather Falls and the Fall River canyon that is guaranteed to take your breath away.

Feather is a horsetail-shaped fall. The first 100 feet are slightly slanted, somewhat like a cascade, then the whole thing dumps into free fall for 500 magnificent feet. Because the overlook platform situates you at nearly the same height as the top of the fall, you get an exciting vista of its entire length. Downstream from the fall, you can see the confluence of the Fall River with the Middle Fork Feather River, where boaters sometimes cruise up from Lake Oroville to get a look at Feather Falls.

When you're ready for a different view, head back to the main trail and continue toward the fall. A few hundred paces put you above Feather's crest, where several routes lead to terrific pools for swimming. Make sure you choose one that is back far enough so that you can't get swept into the current. The water is cold, but it feels incredibly refreshing after the climb.

If you choose the longer but easier trail for your return trip, be prepared for a smoothed-out grade, more like a serpentine. The trail-makers added a few curves and lengthened the route, making it suitable for mountain bikers and hikers with bad knees. Hiking the entire loop with the steep side up and the easy side down makes for a perfect 9.8-mile day hike, with plenty of extra time for photography, skinny-dipping, berry-picking, picnicking, or just standing at the overlook and grinning a lot.

Directions

From Highway 70 in Oroville, take the Oroville Dam Boulevard exit (Highway 162) east and drive 1.6 miles to Olive Highway/Highway 162. Turn right and drive 6.5 miles on Highway 162. Turn right on Forbestown Road and drive six miles. Turn left on Lumpkin Road and drive 10.8 miles. Turn left at the sign for the Feather Falls Trail and drive 1.6 miles to the trailhead.

Information and Contact

There is no fee. Maps of Plumas National Forest are available for a fee from the National Forest Store (406/329-3024, www.nationalforeststore.com), or can be downloaded for free from www.fs.fed.us/r5/maps/. For more information, contact Plumas National Forest, Feather River Ranger District, 530/534-6500, www. fs.fed.us/r5/plumas.

5 RUSH CREEK FALLS   BEST (

South Yuba River State Park

🏃 ♿

Level: Easy   **Distance:** 2.0 miles round-trip

Best Season: April–July   **Elevation Change:** Negligible

The problem with most wheelchair-accessible trails is simple: they are paved. Although this may seem necessary, trail users often say that paving the ground takes away from the nature experience. After all, most people get outdoors to get away from artificial materials like pavement.

So for wheelchair users, the South Yuba Independence Trail is a stroke of genius and a blessing. It's the first identified wheelchair wilderness trail in the United States, and it leads a total of six miles on hard-packed dirt and over wooden flumes along the Yuba River canyon. The trail is a beauty, and it travels right past a fast-flowing waterfall on Rush Creek.

Everything about this trail has been done right. A nonprofit group called Sequoya Challenge maintains the trail in partnership with California State Parks. It was originally built in 1859, not as a hiking trail but as a canal to carry water from the South Yuba River to a hydraulic mining site in Smartville, 25 miles downstream. Consisting of rock-lined ditches with adjacent paths for ditch tenders, plus wooden flumes (bridges) allowing passage over creeks, the canal followed a nearly level contour along the steep hillsides above the South Yuba River.

Since 1970, the abandoned water canal has undergone a transformation, with the old flumes being upgraded and re-built, and new sections of trail being opened up for all-access hiking. In many places, two trails run parallel, one for wheelchairs and one for hiking legs. Outhouses built for wheelchair users are positioned along the trail, as well as accessible platforms for picnicking and fishing on Rush Creek.

At the trailhead, you have a choice of hiking east or west. (The trail does not loop; if you want to walk the whole route, you must go out-and-back in both directions.) To see the waterfall, head to the right (west). In the first 100 yards from the parking area, you must duck your head and pass through a tunnel under Highway 49. Rush Creek Falls is exactly one mile away. The route travels through a densely wooded area and pass-

Rush Creek Falls

es a roofed platform with a scenic overlook of the South Yuba River canyon.

Shortly, you leave the forest and come out to an amazing cliff-hanging flume, its wooden boards making a horseshoe-shaped turn around the back of a canyon. Above and below it, Rush Creek Falls flows over polished granite. The waterfall has many tiers. The best place to see its lower cascades is from the eastern edge of the flume, before you reach the creek itself. The flume forms a bridge just above the tallest drop of the falls, a double tier that is 50 feet high.

This area is known as the Rush Creek Ramp at Flume 28, where volunteers built an intricate wooden ramp that circles down from the flume to the edge of Rush Creek, above the fall's main drop. Several smaller cascades tumble upstream of the ramp, near a picnicking and fishing platform that's in place in summer months.

If you choose to continue beyond the falls, you can go another mile to Jones Bar Road, but then you must turn around and hike back, making a four-mile round-trip. You can also hike the eastern section of trail from the parking area, a five-mile round-trip that includes more flumes, views of the river and foothills, and springtime wildflowers.

Directions

From I-80 at Auburn, drive north on Highway 49 for 27 miles to Nevada City.

Continue on Highway 49 for eight miles past Nevada City to the trailhead parking area along the highway (just before the South Yuba River bridge). Park at the large paved pullout—it is well-signed but comes up fast.

Information and Contact

There is no fee. A map of South Yuba River State Park is available by free download at www.parks.ca.gov. A trail brochure is available at the trailhead. For more information, contact South Yuba River State Park, Bridgeport Visitor Center and Ranger Station, 530/432-2546, www.parks.ca.gov or www.southyubariver-statepark.org. Or contact Sequoya Challenge, 530/477-4788.

6 DRY CREEK FALLS
Spenceville Wildlife Area

Level: Easy

Distance: 5.0 miles round-trip

Best Season: November–May

Elevation Change: Total gain 100 feet

© ANN MARIE BROWN

Dry Creek Falls

From the first autumn rain till midsummer, Dry Creek is anything but dry. Because the creek is located in the middle of arid oak-and-grassland country in the Central Valley, it's surprising that Dry Creek keeps a steady flow of water year-round, but Dry Creek is fed by perennial springs. An even greater surprise is that although the terrain it traverses is mostly level, the creek possesses a steep and narrow rock gorge, which forms two sizable cataracts.

Dry Creek Falls is known by two other names, Shingle Falls or Fairy Falls. The source of the latter name is unknown, but may be related to the wildflowers commonly called fairy lanterns that bloom in the grasslands near the falls. Shingle was the name of a retired military officer from nearby Beale Air Force Base.

Access to Dry Creek Falls is through Spenceville Wildlife Area, an 11,000-acre wildlife preserve that is seldom visited by hikers but frequently visited by hunters and equestrians. Leashed dogs are allowed in the refuge, and horses and bikes are allowed on the fire roads. A small campground is located near the end of Spenceville Road, shortly before the start of the trail to the falls.

Don't be put off by Dry Creek Falls' trailhead, which is a blocked-off, old concrete bridge at the end of Spenceville Road. Although it's only an eyesore now, at one time, you could drive across this bridge over Dry Creek. When you walk across it, watch out for gaping holes that have been burned through some of the planks.

Turn right on the dirt road immediately following the bridge (Old Spenceville Road Trail) and hike eastward. Dry Creek is on your right, gurgling over rounded rocks. The route is wide, level, and easy, winding through open grasslands and stands of white, valley, and canyon oaks. When the white oaks' leaves drop in winter, you see that their branches are completely shrouded with lime-colored lichens. Spring wildflowers can be fantastic in these oak grasslands. April and early May are usually the best months to see California poppies, blue gilias, Chinese houses, many species of brodiaea, and other colorful blooms.

Keep on the lookout for wild turkeys. I saw a large flock of them, as well as a couple of handsome ring-necked pheasants, scurrying across the trail. The plentiful turkeys invite plentiful hunters during turkey season; you would be wise to avoid this trail during the weekends of turkey season (late March and April). Deer season in the fall also brings in the hunters, but most waterfall-seekers will want to visit Spenceville in the winter or spring.

Stay on this main road, ignoring any side trails, for just shy of a mile, then turn right and hike south where the left fork is gated off. Shortly beyond a cattle-guard, two trails take off on your left, the Upper and Lower Loop Trails, open to hikers only. Either of these will take you to the falls, but a better choice is to stay on the main path, which becomes Fairy Falls Trail. This trail brings you alongside Dry Creek, then heads upstream to Dry Creek Falls (or Fairy Falls, Shingle Falls, or whatever you prefer to call it). The first waterfall you reach is about 30 feet tall, pouring through a notch in the rounded rock. It's somewhat difficult to get a full-length view of it. If you scramble around, you can find some good picnicking spots on the rocky, serpentine outcrops above the creek.

A more impressive fall awaits about 100 yards upstream, this one dropping 50 feet into an immense pool. It free falls, then hits a slanted ledge, then free falls again, creating an interesting angular shape. The trail side of the cliff is barricaded with a 50-yard-long chain-link fence, so you can view the fall without plummeting over the edge. A sign warns against diving off the cliffs, but it's hard to believe that anyone would do so. It's a long, scary drop to the pool.

From the upper fall, you can choose to simply backtrack for your homeward trip, or follow the Upper or Lower Loop Trails back to the cattle-guard and Old Spenceville Road Trail.

Directions

From Marysville, drive east on Highway 20 for approximately 14 miles, then turn right (south) on Smartville Road. Drive 0.9 mile and bear left at the fork to stay on Smartville Road. Continue another 3.8 miles to Waldo Road and bear left on the gravel road. Follow Waldo Road 1.9 miles to the Waldo Bridge. Cross it and turn left on Spenceville Road, then drive 2.2 miles to the end of the road at an old blocked-off bridge. Park by the bridge and walk across.

If you are coming from Grass Valley, drive 12.5 miles west on Highway 20 to Smartville Road, then turn left (south) and continue as above.

Information and Contact

There is no fee. Free maps of Spenceville Wildlife Area are available at information signposts in the refuge. For more information, contact the California Department of Fish and Game, 530/538-2236, www.dfg.ca.gov. Or contact Friends of Spenceville, www.spenceville.org.

7 HIDDEN FALLS
Hidden Falls Regional Park

Level: Easy

Best Season: November–May

Distance: 3.0 miles round-trip

Elevation Change: Total gain 350 feet

There's a brand new waterfall in the foothills between Auburn and Lincoln, and Gold Country hikers are thronging to see it. Well, okay, it's not really a new waterfall—the 30-foot cascade has been around for a substantial amount of geologic time—but the park that encompasses it is new as of 2006, and it's a beautiful, well-managed chunk of public land.

Hidden Falls Regional Park is tucked into the foothill country, accessible by driving a series of winding back roads through the oak woodlands. This land was previously known as the Didion Ranch before its owners donated the land to Placer County. As of 2011, 221 acres of the ranch are open to the public, but the long-term plan is to increase that to 1,200 acres. Crisscrossed by two creeks, Coon and Deadman, the park is a lush, shady oasis in a region that is notoriously hot and dry in the summer months. The predominant tree species in the park is the blue oak, but you'll also notice canyon oaks, foothill pines, bay laurel, and even a few ponderosa pines.

Hidden Falls

The park's large parking lot has two separate trailheads. For this trip, head for the trailhead next to the restrooms, where three trails begin. Walk just a few feet past the signboard and then immediately turn right and hike down a few stairsteps to the lower (right-hand) trail, which is Poppy Trail. (The upper trail is a wheelchair-accessible path that circles back to the parking lot; the middle trail is a wide gravel road called Pond Turtle Road, which will eventually join up with your path.)

Once on Poppy Trail, you'll switchback gently downhill to roughly parallel the babbling course of the Whiskey Diggins Canal. In one mile, Poppy Trail meets up with Pond Turtle Road at a sturdy footbridge; turn right and cross the bridge. On the far side, a few more footsteps bring you to another junction of trails. Bear left on Blue Oaks Loop, and then almost immediately, bear left again on Hidden Falls Access Trail. (Yes, there are a ton of trail junctions in this park, but each one is so well signed it is virtually impossible to get lost.)

A half-mile of walking on the Hidden Falls Access Trail under a shady canopy brings you to a final switchback leading down to an overlook platform across from the 30-foot falls. During the rainy season, this waterfall can put out some serious hydropower, and the large wooden platform is the best place to view it safely. Enjoy this special spot, then head back the way you came, or continue onward to explore more of this lovely new park.

Directions

From Sacramento, drive east on I-80 for 30 miles to Auburn. Take the Highway 49 North exit and drive 2.7 miles to Atwood Road. Turn left (west) on Atwood Road and follow it for 1.7 miles until it turns into Mount Vernon Road. Continue straight on Mount Vernon Road for 2.7 miles to Mears Road. Turn right on Mears Road and drive 0.5 mile. Turn right on Mears Place and drive 0.2 mile to the trailhead parking area.

Information and Contact

There is no fee. Maps of Hidden Falls Regional Park can be downloaded for free from www.placer.ca.gov. For more information, contact Placer County Parks, 530/886-4901, www.placer.ca.gov.

8 GROUSE FALLS   BEST ◖

Tahoe National Forest

Level: Easy

Best Season: March–July

Distance: 1.0 mile round-trip

Elevation Change: Total loss 100 feet

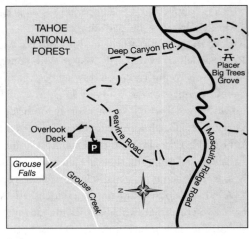

Are you willing to drive 25 miles out of your way just to see a waterfall? No? Okay, what if the waterfall is several hundred feet high, so tall that even the Forest Service doesn't know exactly how tall it is? What if you get a spectacular, short, and easy walk through a forest of big trees in the process? What if your destination is a wooden deck overlooking the falls, with a canyon vista that is so sensational you'll want to pitch a tent on the spot and spend the rest of your days here?

The drive is worth it. The hike is worth it. Grouse Falls is definitely worth it.

To get there, first you must get to the town of Foresthill. Stop at the grocery store and pack a picnic because you'll be gone for several hours. Then head east on Mosquito Ridge Road through a rocky, rugged canyon. Before you drop down too far, watch for a glimpse of the snowy peaks of the Sierra, which you can see from the ridge near the start of the road. The route is paved and winding, and curves its way through big trees and steep hillsides, with good views all the way.

After 19 miles, turn left on Peavine Road, a well-graded gravel road, drive 5.5

miles, then turn left again for a short 0.5 mile on dirt. Finally you're at the trailhead. Passenger cars can easily handle the trip.

The trail leads downhill, deep into the woods, and at first, it's hard to get a bead on where you're heading. You're surrounded by dense conifers, and huge pine cones litter the trail. In 15 minutes you hear the sound of roaring water, then you suddenly come out to a beautiful wooden deck with a wide-open view of the canyon. On your right is Grouse Falls, one of the finest waterfalls in Northern California, especially at peak flow.

Grouse Creek drains into the North Fork of the Middle Fork American River, and it earns its 10 rating for sheer grandeur alone. Early in the year, the fall

Grouse Falls

doesn't stream, cascade, or drop, but rather it hurtles itself down the mountainside. Grouse Falls is a half mile away from your perch on the overlook, yet it's so large, it's majestic even from a distance. Two main cascades tumble down the forested slope; the one on the right is larger. It has a visible drop of about 250 feet, then it disappears into the trees and reappears 100 feet below. Be sure to visit this fall soon after snowmelt to get the full effect.

The scene is made even more impressive because the waterfall's canyon is steep, thickly forested, and completely uninhabited. There isn't a glimpse of a building, road, or trail anywhere.

Luckily, the overlook has a bench, because you won't want to leave too quickly. If nobody else is around, which is often the case, you might want to spread out a picnic. If you plan to photograph the falls, midday is the best time to visit, when the sun is directly overhead. The rest of the time, the waterfall is shaded by the canyon walls.

Oh, and one more reminder. Mosquito Ridge gets its name from...you guessed it. Pack along the bug spray.

Directions

From I-80 at Auburn, take the Foresthill/Auburn Ravine Road exit, then drive 16 miles east to Foresthill. In Foresthill, turn right (east) on Mosquito Ridge Road, across from the Foresthill post office. Drive 19 miles to Peavine Road (Road 33). Turn left on Peavine Road and drive 5.5 miles to the Grouse Falls turnoff on the left. Turn left and drive 0.5 mile to the trailhead.

Information and Contact

There is no fee. Maps of Tahoe National Forest are available for a fee from the National Forest Store (406/329-3024, www.nationalforeststore.com), or can be downloaded for free from www.fs.fed.us/r5/maps/. For more information and a map/brochure on the Foresthill Divide, contact Tahoe National Forest, American River Ranger District, 530/367-2224, www.fs.fed.us/r5/tahoe.

TAHOE AND NORTHERN SIERRA

© ANN MARIE BROWN

BEST WATERFALLS

❰ Short Backpacking Trips
Little Jamison Falls, page 137

❰ Car
Devil's Falls, page 160
Leavitt Falls, page 184

❰ Easy Waterfall Walks
Frazier Falls, page 140

❰ Swimming Holes
Spring Creek Falls, page 150

❰ Wheelchair-Accessible
Frazier Falls, page 140
Bear River Falls, page 152

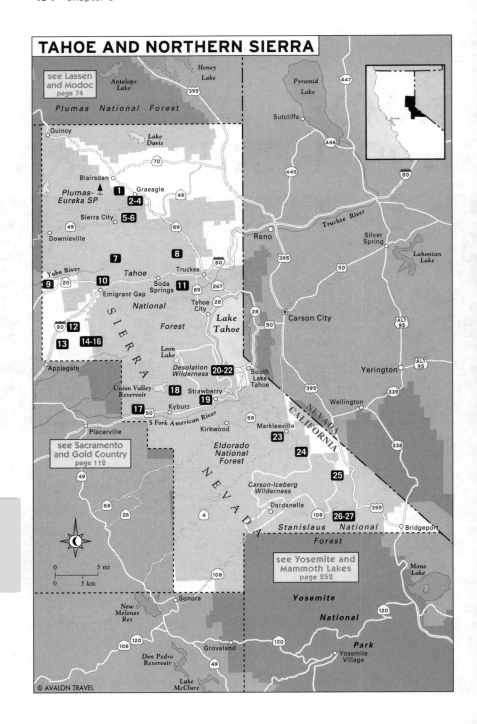

TAHOE AND NORTHERN SIERRA

see Lassen and Modoc page 74

Plumas National Forest

Antelope Lake
Honey Lake
Pyramid Lake
Sutcliffe

Quincy

Lake Davis

Blairsden
Plumas-Eureka SP
1
Graeagle
2-4

Sierra City
5-6

Downieville

Reno

Silver Spring

Lahontan Lake

Truckee River

7
8

Truckee

Yuba River
Tahoe
9
10
Emigrant Gap
Soda Springs
11

Tahoe City

National

12
13
14-16

Lake Tahoe

Carson City

Loon Lake

Desolation Wilderness
20-22
South Lake Tahoe

Union Valley Reservoir
18
Strawberry
19

Applegate

17
Kyburz

Placerville
S Fork American River
Kirkwood

Markleeville
23

NEVADA
CALIFORNIA

Yerington

Eldorado National Forest
24

see Sacramento and Gold Country page 112

Carson-Iceberg Wilderness
25

Dardanelle
26-27
Stanislaus National

Bridgeport

Forest

see Yosemite and Mammoth Lakes page 252

Mono Lake

New Melones Res
Sonora

Yosemite

National

Don Pedro Reservoir
Groveland
Lake McClure

Park
Yosemite Village

0   5 mi
0   5 km

© AVALON TRAVEL

TRAIL NAME	LEVEL	DISTANCE	ELEVATION	SEASON	FEATURES	PAGE
1 Little Jamison Falls	Easy	3.0 mi rt	500 ft	May–July	(icons)	137
2 Halsey Falls	Easy	2.0 mi rt	100 ft	May–July	(icons)	138
3 Frazier Falls	Easy	1.0 mile rt	50 ft	May–July	(icons)	140
4 Fern Falls	Easy	0.25 mile rt	Negligible	May–July	(icons)	141
5 Love's Falls	Easy/Moderate	0.5–4.5 mi rt	600 ft	May–Aug.	(icons)	143
6 Great Eastern Ravine Falls	Moderate	6.0 mi rt	1,500 ft	May–July	(icons)	145
7 Bowman Lake Falls	Moderate	0.8 mile rt	500 ft	June–Oct.	(icons)	146
8 Webber Falls	Easy	0.25 mile rt	Negligible	May–Sept.	(icons)	148
9 Spring Creek Falls	Moderate	1.2 mi rt	200 ft	May–Sept.	(icons)	150
10 Bear River Falls	Easy	1.0 mile rt	20 ft	Apr.–July	(icons)	152
11 Heath Falls and Palisade Falls	Strenuous	12.0–17.0 mi rt	1,700 ft	May–July	(icons)	153
12 Stevens Creek Falls	Easy	3.0 mi rt	600 ft	Apr.–July	(icons)	156
13 Codfish Creek Falls	Easy	3.0 mi rt	50 ft	Apr.–Sept.	(icons)	158
14 Devil's Falls	Easy	Negligible	1,500 ft	Apr.–July	(icons)	160

TRAIL NAME	LEVEL	DISTANCE	ELEVATION	SEASON	FEATURES	PAGE
15 Indian Creek Falls	Moderate	3.0 mi rt	50 ft	Late May-early July		161
16 Chamberlain Falls	Strenuous	3.0 mi rt	200 ft	Mar.-May		163
17 Bridal Veil Falls	Easy	Negligible	3,500 ft	Apr.-June		165
18 Bassi Falls	Easy	1.0 mile rt	50 ft	Apr.-June		166
19 Horsetail Falls	Easy	2.0 mi rt	200 ft	Apr.-Sept.		167
20 Eagle Falls	Easy	0.5-2.0 mi rt	50-400 ft	Apr.-July		170
21 Cascade Falls	Easy	2.0 mi rt	100 ft	Apr.-July		172
22 Glen Alpine Falls and Modjeska Falls	Easy	1.0 mile rt	50 ft	May-Aug.		174
23 Hot Springs Creek Waterfall	Easy	3.0 mi rt	200 ft	Apr.-July		176
24 Wolf Creek Falls	Moderate	10.0 mi rt	800 ft	June-Oct.		178
25 Llewellyn Falls	Strenuous	13.0 mi rt	1,000 ft	June-Sept.		180
26 Sardine Falls	Easy	2.5 mi rt	300 ft	June-Sept.		182
27 Leavitt Falls	Easy	Negligible	7,000 ft	June-Sept.		184

1 LITTLE JAMISON FALLS   BEST ◖

Plumas National Forest and Plumas-Eureka State Park

🚶 🚐 ⛵ 🐕

Level: Easy

Best Season: May–July

Distance: 3.0 miles round-trip

Elevation Change: Total gain 500 feet

Sometimes when you go looking for one thing, you wind up finding something even better. That's how it was for me at Plumas-Eureka State Park, when I set off on the Grass Lake Trail in search of lakes with trout. While I didn't catch any fish, I did find Little Jamison Falls, a free-falling cataract that in early season has the size and flow of a river fall.

The trail begins in the state park, then leaves its boundary and enters Plumas National Forest. For that reason, you don't have to pay a day-use fee to hike here. That's one bonus, and more await at the trailhead. Like the fact that the trail begins at the old Jamison gold mine, and some of its buildings are still standing in decent repair. You get an interesting glimpse into California mining history:

© ANDREW SAWADISAVI

Little Jamison Falls

the mine was in operation from 1887 to 1919, producing gold for the Sierra Buttes Mining Company.

Bear left at the buildings, head uphill on the steep and rocky path, and follow Little Jamison Creek for the entire route. Pass a left fork for Smith Lake (a steep trail but worth the trip another time), then continue straight through a canopy of firs and pines till you leave the state park boundary. Ironically, as soon as you pass a sign noting that you are now in national forest, you enter an area of logged trees. Bummer.

Just 0.2 mile farther, you hear the sound of roaring water. Look for an unsigned trail spur on your right, which takes you to Little Jamison Creek's edge and 40-foot-high Little Jamison Falls. It's a surprisingly wide, dramatic drop, especially early in the year.

Since you've climbed up here, you might as well continue on for another five minutes to Grass Lake, elevation 5,842 feet, a scenic alpine lake surrounded by Jeffrey pine, lodgepole pine, and red fir. It has a few excellent campsites and many good picnic spots. Hike around to the west side of the lake for a stunning view of the water backed by surrounding craggy peaks. The trail also extends another one–two miles to Rock Lake, Jamison Lake, and Wades Lake, all excellent destinations for fishing, camping, and swimming.

Directions

From Truckee, head north on Highway 89 for about 50 miles to Graeagle. At Graeagle, drive west on County Road A-14 for 4.5 miles to the Jamison Mine/ Grass Lake access road on the left. Turn left and drive one mile, past Camp Lisa, to the trailhead parking area. The trailhead is on the far side of the lot, signed for Grass, Smith, Rock, Wades, and Jamison Lakes.

Information and Contact

There is no fee. A Plumas-Eureka State Park map is available by free download at www.parks.ca.gov or for $1 at the park office, 0.5 mile past the trailhead access road on County Road A-14. Maps of Plumas National Forest are available for a fee from the National Forest Store (406/329-3024, www.nationalforeststore.com), or can be downloaded for free from www.fs.fed.us/r5/maps/. For more information, contact Plumas-Eureka State Park, 530/836-2380, www.parks.ca.gov.

2 HALSEY FALLS
Plumas National Forest

Level: Easy | **Distance:** 2.0 miles round-trip
Best Season: May–July | **Elevation Change:** Total gain 100 feet

Staying at Gray Eagle Lodge is my idea of the perfect vacation. The lodge has cozy cabins, a good restaurant, and access to all the hiking and fishing that anybody could want. But whether you stay there or just use the excellent trailhead a quarter mile from the lodge, your first trip should be to Halsey Falls (on some maps, it is spelled "Hawlsey Falls.")

Find the Halsey Falls Trail marker on the left side of the trailhead parking lot, and start walking upstream, following Gray Eagle Creek for your entire route. Shady conifer forest alternates with open areas and views of surrounding ridgelines along the way. One small climb takes you to the top of a low ridge directly

© ANN MARIE BROWN

Halsey Falls

behind Gray Eagle Lodge, but the rest of the hike is flat. You'll cross two small feeder streams, which empty into Gray Eagle Creek.

Although the trail markers can be a little confusing along this trail, sometimes greatly exaggerating the mileage, just follow the creek and you'll be fine. As you near one mile, your ears guide you to the sound of rushing water and the fall.

The roar of water grows louder and the air cooler as you come nearer. Standing close to 20-foot Halsey Falls, you can feel the breeze from its billowy cascade. If you want to cool off from your hike, climb on the rocks and fallen trees until you're underneath the spray.

The Gray Eagle Trailhead offers many other hiking options, and you'll want to try them all. Although the trip to Halsey Falls is the easiest hike, a separate trail leads to Smith Lake in one steep mile, and the Halsey Falls Trail continues to Long Lake and Grassy Lake, each about one mile beyond the falls.

Directions

From Truckee, drive north on Highway 89 for about 50 miles to Forest Service Road 24 (Gold Lake Highway) and turn left. (Forest Service Road 24 is 1.3 miles south of Graeagle on Highway 89.) Drive five miles south on Road 24 to the sign for Gray Eagle Lodge. Turn right and drive 0.3 mile to the trailhead for Smith Lake and Halsey Falls, which is 0.2 mile before the lodge. The Halsey Falls Trail starts on the left side of the parking lot.

Information and Contact

There is no fee. Maps of Plumas National Forest are available for a fee from the National Forest Store (406/329-3024, www.nationalforeststore.com), or can be downloaded for free from www.fs.fed.us/r5/maps/. For more information, contact Plumas National Forest, Beckwourth Ranger District, 530/836-2575, www.fs.fed.us/r5/plumas.

3 FRAZIER FALLS   BEST 🄲
Plumas National Forest

🚶 🐎

Level: Easy   **Distance:** 1.0 mile round-trip
Best Season: May–July   **Elevation Change:** Total gain 50 feet

Frazier Falls

Frazier Falls is one of the most famous landmarks in all of the Lakes Basin area, and deservedly so. In spring and early summer, the waterfall is a showstopper. It doesn't matter how jaded you are, Frazier Falls will give you a thrill.

Reached via an easy, paved, wheelchair-accessible trail, Frazier is a 178-foot free fall with a total height of 248 feet if you include its lower cascade. The fall is big, but more importantly, it's dramatic. It has style. Frazier Creek is incredibly mild and tranquil both above and below the falls. As you hike along the trail, Frazier Creek seems like just an average-sized stream channeling around and through granite. Then all of a sudden, its flow hits a big cliff and *whoosh!*—over it goes, creating a tremendous free fall.

In springtime, millions of gallons of water hurtle over Frazier Falls' granite lip, producing a convincing display of the power of melting snow. But by the Fourth of July, Frazier Falls appears almost tame.

The walk to the fall's observation point is as delightful as the fall itself. The easy path is popular with campers, and especially families, staying in the Lakes Basin. The trail is almost completely level, and even restless toddlers are momentarily impressed by the sight of the giant waterfall.

From the parking lot, head east on the well-marked trail, surrounded by shiny, polished granite, ponderosa and Jeffrey pines, and bunches of lupine and Indian paintbrush. Cross a footbridge over Frazier Creek, and gaze downstream. You'll notice the water seems to disappear over the edge—you can't hear it yet, but you're on top of the waterfall. The trail continues around to Frazier Falls' overlook, a fenced-in platform across the creek canyon and 200 yards from the fall. This is the best possible view of the waterfall's entire length. Check out the visitors' sign-in register to see how many people made the trek to Frazier that day, or write in a few comments yourself. When I visited in May, an earlier visitor had simply scribbled, "Holy snowmelt."

Directions

From Truckee, drive north on Highway 89 for about 50 miles to Forest Road 24 (Gold Lake Highway) and turn left. (Gold Lake Highway is 1.5 miles south of Graeagle on Highway 89, signed as Lakes Basin Recreation Area.) Drive 8.4 miles south on Road 24 and turn left at the sign for Frazier Falls (on Old Gold Lake Road, directly across Road 24 from Gold Lake). Drive 1.8 miles north to the trailhead parking lot.

Information and Contact

There is no fee. Maps of Plumas National Forest are available for a fee from the National Forest Store (406/329-3024, www.nationalforeststore.com), or can be downloaded for free from www.fs.fed.us/r5/maps/. For more information, contact Plumas National Forest, Beckwourth Ranger District, 530/836-2575, www.fs.fed.us/r5/plumas.

4 FERN FALLS
Plumas National Forest

Level: Easy
Best Season: May–July

Distance: 0.25 mile round-trip
Elevation Change: Negligible

In an area as waterfall-laden as Plumas National Forest, Fern Falls isn't exactly an award-winner. On the other hand, if Fern Falls was in some other place in the state, it might be the centerpiece of its own park.

It's all relative. If you want splash and melodrama in Plumas, visit nearby Frazier Falls (see previous listing in this chapter). If you want a quiet, watery place to have a picnic, with little chance of anybody else showing up, a trip to Fern Falls might suit you fine.

Take the drive down Gold Lake Highway and decide for yourself. The waterfall is marked by a sign noting "Fern Falls Picnic Area and Vista Trail," which is a bit of an exaggeration. The picnic area consists of merely two picnic tables, one near the road and one above the falls. But hey, who needs a picnic table to have a picnic? And the Vista Trail is not much of a trail, more like a footpath a few hundred feet long. But never mind.

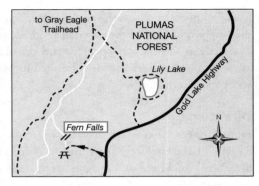

Vista Trail takes you through big conifers, across a footbridge, and up to a granite knoll where you can view Fern Falls. From there, you can wander around on the rock slabs to get closer to the water. Fern Falls drops 15 feet over big boulders on the outlet creek from Grassy Lake, one mile upstream. From the waterfall, the bustling creek tumbles downstream till it joins with larger Gray Eagle Creek, which in turn flows downstream all the way to Graeagle and the Middle Fork of the Feather River. That gives you something to think about while you watch the cascading water.

If you're in the mood for a little more walking, you can get in your car and drive 0.5 mile up the road to the Lily Lake Trailhead. A short jaunt of about 10 minutes will bring you to the edge of the lily pad–covered lake. A path circles the lake, connecting with a trail from the Gray Eagle Trailhead, from which you can hike to Halsey Falls (see listing in this chapter). You might as well make a day of it.

Directions

From Truckee, drive north on Highway 89 for about 50 miles to Forest Service Road 24 (Gold Lake Highway) and turn left. (Forest Service Road 24 is 1.3 miles south of Graeagle on Highway 89.) Drive six miles south on Road 24 to a pullout marked "Fern Falls Picnic Area and Vista Trail."

Information and Contact

There is no fee. Maps of Plumas National Forest are available for a fee from the National Forest Store (406/329-3024, www.nationalforeststore.com), or can be downloaded for free from www.fs.fed.us/r5/maps/. For more information, contact Plumas National Forest, Beckwourth Ranger District, 530/836-2575, www.fs.fed.us/r5/plumas.

5 LOVE'S FALLS
Tahoe National Forest

Level: Easy/Moderate   **Distance:** 0.5-4.5 miles round-trip

Best Season: May-August   **Elevation Change:** Total gain 600 feet

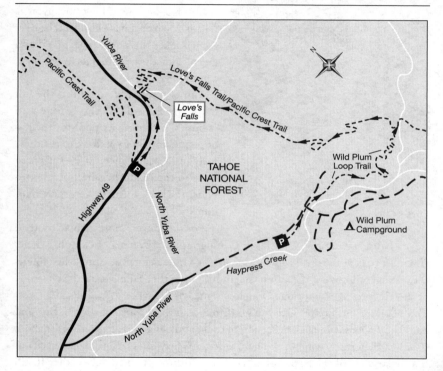

You have a choice. Do you wanna take the easy way or the not-so-easy way to Love's Falls? Both routes are good, and the destination is terrific, so you can't miss however you go. The easy way requires only a 10-minute walk on a nearly level trail. The not-so-easy way is a two-mile up-and-down route that will wake up your cardiovascular system. Both routes lead to a great waterfall vista with terrific fishing and picnicking spots. It's your call.

For the easy way, look for the Pacific Crest Trail (PCT) signs on Highway 49, just east of Sierra City. (There are small markers on both sides of the highway, where the trail crosses.) Start walking on the PCT as it parallels Highway 49, heading southeast. In a few minutes of easy walking, you're at the PCT bridge over the North Yuba River, perched right on top of the best cascade of Love's Falls.

© ANN MARIE BROWN

Love's Falls

Love's is a typical river waterfall, wide and full of white water, but its biggest drop is only about 20 feet high. It's surrounded by huge boulders and a narrow gorge cut through volcanic rock, which forms deep pools. While you're still on the bridge, be sure to look upcanyon as well as downstream at the falls. The river gorge makes the water appear gold and green from all the minerals in the rock, a gloriously colorful sight.

You can scramble down to the fall from the far side of the bridge and choose a spot near its pool for fishing or picnicking, but you have to get there early in the day. Since Love's Falls is so close to the road, the small beach area under the bridge usually gets spoken for quickly.

For the longer, more aerobic route to Love's Falls, start at the Wild Plum Campground. If you're not camping there, you must park at the trailhead parking lot 0.25 mile before the camp, then follow the access trail toward the camp. Begin hiking at the trailhead on the west side of the Haypress Creek bridge, which is signed as "Haypress Trail, Pacific Crest Trail, Wild Plum Loop." Off you go through a mixed forest of cedars, firs, and hardwoods. Walk along a flat section of trail paralleling Haypress Creek for about 0.5 mile, then start switchbacking up a ridge. When you reach the top, check out the stellar view of the back side of the Sierra Buttes. If you're lucky, they'll still be crowned with snow.

Meet up with the PCT, also signed for Love's Falls, and turn left. One-and-a-half miles of well-graded trail, with some downhill switchbacks at its end, lead you to the bridge over the falls.

Directions

From Truckee, drive north on Highway 89 for about 30 miles to Highway 49 at Sattley. Drive west on Highway 49 for 15 miles toward Sierra City. For the shorter hike, watch for the Pacific Crest Trail signs along Highway 49, 0.5 mile east of Nevada Drive in Sierra City. Park along the road in any of the nearby pullouts. For the longer hike, drive to the trailhead at Wild Plum Campground in Sierra City (see directions for Great Eastern Ravine Falls in the following waterfall description).

Information and Contact

There is no fee. Maps of Tahoe National Forest are available for a fee from the National Forest Store (406/329-3024, www.nationalforeststore.com), or can be downloaded for free from www.fs.fed.us/r5/maps/. For more information, contact Tahoe National Forest, Yuba River Ranger District, 530/288-3231, www.fs.fed.us/r5/tahoe.

6 GREAT EASTERN RAVINE FALLS

Tahoe National Forest

Level: Moderate

Best Season: May–July

Distance: 6.0 miles round-trip

Elevation Change: Total gain 1,500 feet

Great Eastern Ravine is a waterfall to see if you like to hike. Hike uphill, that is. The trail that takes you there doesn't fool around—it just climbs nonstop from Wild Plum Campground for three miles, then levels out just before the fall. Luckily, the trail is good, the scenery is beautiful, and the sound of Haypress Creek accompanies you the whole way.

You can reach the fall in about an hour and a half of climbing. Start by finding the Haypress Creek Trailhead in Wild Plum Camp; there are two, but the best one for this hike is on the east side of the camp. It climbs more gradually at the start. Walk into Wild Plum, crossing a road bridge over Haypress Creek. Then walk to your left, through the upper campground loop, until you reach a forked dirt road. Take the upper road, which leads uphill and out of camp. Watch carefully for a left turnoff onto single-track in 0.5 mile. (There's a trail sign posted high on a tree, but it's easy to miss.) Follow the single-track through forest for 0.5 mile, crossing a footbridge over Haypress Creek. (Parts of this route are signed as the "Pacific Crest Trail and Wild Plum Loop.") Check out the incredible view of the back of the Sierra Buttes.

Shortly after the bridge, take the right fork, which is signed as the Haypress Creek Trail. There are no more junctions after this point. Just climb, first through a rocky, open area, then a mixed conifer forest, then on an old logging road through some private property. The fragrant scent of white- and blue-flowered ceanothus bushes envelopes you in early season. Haypress Creek Trail has some very sunny, open areas, so bring plenty of water with you. You're too high above the creek to be able to access it for water.

The route veers right on a dirt road, then eventually leaves the private property and re-enters National Forest land, becoming single-track again. Haypress Creek Trail's only drawback is that it's routed on logging roads too much of the time. When the trail becomes single-track again, life suddenly seems better.

The route finally goes flat at 2.8 miles, just before you reach the fall. The cascade on Great Eastern Ravine is easy to spot because your trail crosses right over it. It's 20 feet tall and narrow, a tumbling stream of white. A big, flat rock a few yards in front is the perfect place to sit and have a snack.

An award-winner? No, but you have one near-certain guarantee: if you've climbed all the way up here, you're probably going to have the waterfall all to yourself.

Directions

From Truckee, drive north on Highway 89 for about 30 miles to Highway 49 at Sattley. Drive west on Highway 49 for 15 miles toward Sierra City. Turn left on Wild Plum Road, one mile east of Sierra City. Drive 1.2 miles on Wild Plum Road to the trailhead parking area, 0.25 mile before Wild Plum Campground. Begin hiking at the trail marker on the left side of the lot. This access trail leads to the camp in 0.25 mile.

Information and Contact

There is no fee. Maps of Tahoe National Forest are available for a fee from the National Forest Store (406/329-3024, www.nationalforeststore.com), or can be downloaded for free from www.fs.fed.us/r5/maps/. For more information, contact Tahoe National Forest, Yuba River Ranger District, 530/288-3231, www.fs.fed.us/r5/tahoe.

7 BOWMAN LAKE FALLS
Tahoe National Forest

Level: Moderate   **Distance:** 0.8 mile round-trip

Best Season: June–October   **Elevation Change:** Total gain 500 feet

Everybody has their own name for the waterfall that drops into Bowman Lake. Although the waterfall falls on Canyon Creek, almost nobody calls it Canyon Creek

© ANN MARIE BROWN

Bowman Lake Falls

Falls. Instead, it's usually called Bowman Lake Falls, or sometimes Sawmill Falls after nearby Sawmill Lake. Canyon Creek is Sawmill Lake's outlet stream and Bowman Lake's inlet stream.

Call it what you like, this is a spectacular 80-foot cascade that carves its way down a granite cliff. Although it forms some gorgeous, clear pools, the water is bitter cold for swimming, even in late summer and autumn.

You first glimpse the falls as you drive the dirt road that runs alongside huge, deep-blue Bowman Lake, a popular reservoir for camping and fishing. The dirt road starts out smooth but gets rougher as you go, although passenger cars can frequently make the trip in good weather. As you drive along Bowman's shoreline, look to the lake's eastern end to spot the cascade tumbling down the granite slope. (You won't see it until you're about two-thirds of the way along the lakeshore.) At the far end of the lake, park your car near the sandy wash where the lake peters out and a feeder stream pours in. (This area is often used for camping or as a put-in spot for car-top boats.)

Don't try to follow the lakeshore to reach the falls; although this seems logical, it's actually longer and more difficult. (The waterfall is set back about 200 yards from the lakeshore. After the main cascade, the stream runs fairly level for the last 200 yards to the lake.) Instead, walk across the wash, rock-hopping across one of the lake's inlet streams, Jackson Creek. Then make a beeline due south through the forest, passing a primitive campsite and heading up and over a small ridge. You should be able to discern a primitive-use trail to keep you on track. If not, just keep heading for the sound of the falls. You'll cross an area with heavy deadfall and reach a small 15- by 15-foot meadow. Before you know it, you'll come out about 100 feet below the main cascade. The entire walk should take only about 15 minutes from the wash where you left your car.

Hike upstream to get closer to the fall. You can follow the granite slabs along the streambed or take the use trail higher up on the slope. If you do the latter, you'll have to fight your way through some scratchy manzanita. From any standpoint, your main view is of the last 50 feet of the cascade; another 30 feet of white water is obscured above it. More aggressive climbing will take you to the upper cascade, but be sure to exercise caution on the slick granite. Downstream are many smaller cascades and good swimming holes where the water is more placid.

Directions

From Auburn, drive east on I-80 for 40 miles to the Highway 20 exit. Drive west on Highway 20 for 4.3 miles to Bowman Lake Road. Turn right and drive 15 miles to the western edge of Bowman Lake (the road turns to dirt after the first 10 miles and may require a high-clearance vehicle). Continue driving along the edge of the lake to its eastern end; you'll see the falls flowing down into the lake. Park just off the road in the sandy wash area at the east end of the reservoir. (People launch kayaks and car-top boats in this area.) Walk across the rocky wash, heading south, to access the falls.

Information and Contact

There is no fee. Maps of Tahoe National Forest are available for a fee from the National Forest Store (406/329-3024, www.nationalforeststore.com), or can be downloaded for free from www.fs.fed.us/r5/maps/. For more information, contact Tahoe National Forest, Nevada City Ranger District, 530/265-4531, www. fs.fed.us/r5/tahoe.

8 WEBBER FALLS
Tahoe National Forest

Level: Easy

Distance: 0.25 mile round-trip

Best Season: May–September

Elevation Change: Negligible

A thousand thanks to the Louisiana Pacific Lumber Company for allowing day-use on their private property at Webber Falls. Their rules are clearly posted at the informal dirt parking lot: no camping and no fires. Fair enough. But swimming and jumping in the waterfall pool are okay, and on any summer weekend, you're bound to see plenty of people doing just that.

Webber Falls is a beautiful double waterfall with two big drops and a deep pool in between. The top fall is 25 feet tall and 35 feet wide; the second drop is more dramatic—about 80 feet tall and 25 feet wide. While the top fall and its big pool can be easily seen from the edge of the creek, a few feet from the parking area, it takes some careful footing along steep canyon walls to get a good look at the bigger, lower fall. It can be done from both sides of the creek, although the ground is very unstable. Use good judgment.

Most folks just walk the few yards downhill from the parking area to the near side of the big pool. Some folks rock-hop over the top of the waterfall and make their way to the far side, where the best rocks for diving are; others just jump in and swim around on the near side. On the Saturday I visited, there were about 30 people, mostly kids of various ages, taking turns diving into the big pool in between the upper and lower fall. And everybody I saw, every single person, was smiling. Thanks again, Louisiana Pacific.

Webber Falls

Directions
From Truckee, drive north on Highway 89 for 14 miles, then turn west on Road 07, signed for Independence Lake and Webber Lake, and drive 6.6 miles. Watch for the Lake of the Woods turnoff on the right, then turn left just beyond it on an unsigned dirt road. Turn left again on another unsigned dirt road, drive about 50 feet, then turn right into the dirt parking area. (You will travel about 200 yards off Road 07.)

Information and Contact
There is no fee. Maps of Tahoe National Forest are available for a fee from the National Forest Store (406/329-3024, www.nationalforeststore.com), or can be downloaded for free from www.fs.fed.us/r5/maps/. For more information, contact Tahoe National Forest, Sierraville Ranger District, 530/994-3401, www.fs.fed.us/r5/tahoe.

9 SPRING CREEK FALLS

BEST

South Yuba River State Park

Level: Moderate

Distance: 1.2 miles round-trip

Best Season: May-September

Elevation Change: Total gain 200 feet

The Yuba River is one of the most beautiful rivers in Northern California. It's set in a steep, rugged canyon filled with oaks, bays, and gray pines. Water-polished rock creates pool after pool of liquid-emerald water interrupted by flowing cascades. The remarkable color of the water is what sticks in your mind long after you've left the riverbanks; it's an alluring, gem-like green you can see clear through.

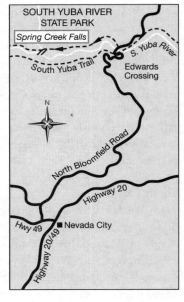

Fly fishers comb these river pools for trout and gold prospectors ply the waters for their prize. But the river may be best loved by swimmers, who seek out its deep stretches and smooth granite banks for long days in the sun. If you happen to enjoy a good waterfall with your swimming hole, you're in luck.

The adventure begins at Edwards Crossing, where North Bloomfield Road out of Nevada City crosses the South Yuba River. This stretch of land is managed by South Yuba River State Park, so signs are posted for gold diggers stating "Pans and Hands" only. No mechanized dredging is allowed, which keeps the river pure.

Park at the wide pullouts on the south side of the bridge, then walk across the bridge to the north side and take the trail to the left, leading west. Follow the path along the river's north side, heading upriver. The footpath is a little rough in places and it has some steep drop-offs. Watch your footing and you'll be fine. The worst problem is not the rough trail but rather the spectacular color of the Yuba River, which makes it impossible to keep your eyes on the path.

In a little more than 0.5 mile, Spring Creek cascades down across the trail and into the river. The trail leads up the creek (away from the river) to a suitable place where you can cross Spring Creek by rock-hopping. As soon as you land on the other side, leave the trail and cut down to the river.

© ANN MARIE BROWN

Spring Creek Falls

Somewhat hidden by the clifflike riverbank, Spring Creek forms a 20-foot, free-falling waterfall that plunges into the Yuba River. Imagine the coldest shower you've ever taken. Even on the hottest summer day, that's what this waterfall feels like. Most visitors wade into its pool, dunk their heads under the cascading flow, then yell like hell when they feel how cold the water is.

Right alongside the waterfall is a deep, clear, 40-yard-long pool in the Yuba River, where medium-sized trout and water-loving bathers while away their afternoons. Bring a picnic and your towel. One thing to consider: on my trip, I found that this pool's bathers were evenly divided between those wearing bathing suits and those wearing birthday suits. Just a warning, in case you have strong opinions about such things.

Directions

From Highway 20 in Nevada City, take the Highway 49 exit. Drive 0.3 mile and turn right on North Bloomfield Road. Drive 0.5 mile and turn right again, staying on North Bloomfield Road. Drive seven miles to Edwards Crossing, a long bridge over the Yuba River. Take the footpath on the northwest side, leading west.

Information and Contact

There is no fee. There is no fee. A map of South Yuba River State Park is available by free download at www.parks.ca.gov. For more information, contact South Yuba River State Park, Bridgeport Visitor Center and Ranger Station, 530/432-2546, www.parks.ca.gov or www.southyubariverstatepark.org.

10 BEAR RIVER FALLS   BEST ☾

PG&E Bear Valley Recreation Area

🚶 🏊 ♿ 🐕

Level: Easy   **Distance:** 1.0 mile round-trip

Best Season: April–July   **Elevation Change:** Total gain 20 feet

Bear River Falls

The Pacific Gas and Electric Company has done a good deed in the form of the PG&E Sierra Discovery Trail at Bear Valley, where everyone, regardless of hiking ability, can take a pleasant loop trip that culminates at Bear River's waterfall.

Although the fall is only rated a 6, mostly due to its small size, the trail is a 10. The surface is pavement and gravel with some boardwalk sections, all of which are suitable for wheelchairs and baby strollers. The one-mile loop packs in a lot of information about Bear Valley's ecosystems, wildlife, geology, and cultural history. It offers far more than a typical "this is a sugar pine; this is a Jeffrey pine" interpretive trail, although you will learn to identify some trees here—various pines, as well as willows, white alders, and incense cedars.

The walk begins at the parking lot, where there is an information kiosk that explains the geology of the Sierra Nevada and the life of the Maidu who lived here before white settlers arrived. From the kiosk, bear left, following a boardwalk over a meadow that is green with corn lilies in the spring. At the bridge crossing over the Bear River, visitors eager to reach the waterfall quickly can head left, and those with more patience can head right and loop around to it. You might as well walk the whole loop—it's short, scenic, and educational.

The falls are only 12 feet high, but about 15 feet wide and completely surrounded by big-leaf maples and alders. The river drops in a solid block of water, and if you stay and watch for a few minutes, you're sure to see a water ouzel flitting in and out of the fall. A plaque at the overlook describes the life of this curious bird, the only American songbird that can swim below the surface of the water. They make their nests on rocky ledges behind waterfalls.

The wildflowers along this trail are best in June and July, but the waterfall is best even earlier. If you can, time your trip for just after the snow has melted in Bear Valley.

Directions

From Auburn, drive east on I-80 for 40 miles to the Highway 20 exit. Drive west on Highway 20 for 4.3 miles to Bowman Lake Road. Turn right and drive 0.6 mile to the Sierra Discovery Trail parking lot on the left side of the road, by Bear Valley Picnic Area.

Information and Contact

There is no fee. For more information, contact PG&E Recreation Areas at 916/386-5164, www.pge.com/recreation; or contact Tahoe National Forest, 530/265-4531, www.fs.fed.us/r5/tahoe.

11 HEATH FALLS AND PALISADE FALLS
Tahoe National Forest

Level: Strenuous

Best Season: May-July

Distance: 12.0-17.0 miles round-trip

Elevation Change: Total loss 1,700 feet

A hike to Heath Falls and Palisade Falls is like going on a vacation on your credit card. You can have all the fun you want, but when you return home, you gotta pay up.

That's because the trip to the Heath Falls Overlook is downhill nearly all the way, dropping 1,700 feet over the course of six miles, through scenery so stunning that you'll snap pictures, grin wide smiles at your hiking companions, and sing happy hiking songs as you go. The miles never seemed so easy. If you opt to visit Palisade Falls as well, it's even more

Heath Falls

© LEON TURNBULL/WATERFALLSWEST.COM

of a descent. But alas, eventually it's time for the return trip, a long and steady climb that lasts much longer than the trip down. If you plan to see both falls, be smart and plan to camp overnight in the vicinity of Palisade Falls (camping is forbidden near Heath Falls).

The Palisade Creek Trail begins at the dam between the two Cascade Lakes, the first of many lakes you'll pass on this trip. See that imposing chunk of rock straight ahead that juts out high above everything else around it? That's 7,704-foot Devil's Peak, and you'll head straight toward it, then lateral around its left (east) side. You'll be seeing a lot of it in the first two miles.

Walk across the dam and spillway, then pick up the trail through the lodgepole pine forest, heading to your right at a sign for the North Fork American River. (The left fork drops down to Long Lake, a worthwhile side trip.) You'll ascend slightly for the first mile, as you leave the trees and enter into polished granite country, all the while getting better and better views of Devil's Peak.

The first two miles of trail can be characterized in three words: lakes, granite, vistas. Not only do you pass the Cascade Lakes and shortly thereafter, Long Lake on your left, but half a dozen more lakes follow. They are small and unnamed, so you can name them anything you like. Granite surrounds you; this land is classic glacial moraine, where glaciers moved through and left mounds of rock in their wake. Watch for trail cairns to keep you on the right path. Few trees can grow in this territory, so the views are wide-reaching, not just of nearby Devil's Peak but also of far-off peaks to the north and east.

When you reach the southeast flank of Devil's Peak at 2.2 miles, you're in for a terrain change: suddenly you move into a thickly forested area, parallel a small creek, and then head into a sweet glen of aspens, ferns, vine maples, and corn lilies mixed in among the giant conifers. You may see some evidence of logging here; much of this land is private property that belongs to a lumber company. Luckily, they haven't cut much.

The downhill steepens and the trail begins some gentle switchbacks, dropping toward the American River Canyon. You're so deep in forest—mostly cedars, firs, and pines—that you cannot see the canyon unless you go off-trail and climb onto high rocks. Even then, you can't see all the way down to the river. You're still too far off.

At 5.2 miles, after a long downhill stint through the woods, you reach the Palisade Creek Bridge. Cross it, and in about 200 yards, there's a trail junction for the Heath Falls Overlook Trail heading east. Take care not to miss this fork; it's not usually signed. Now it's only 0.9 mile farther (still downhill) to the overlook of 50-foot Heath Falls on the North Fork American River. (It's not the greatest overlook; the view of the falls is somewhat obscured.) The fall is sheltered deep in the canyon, but you can still hear and see it thundering over rock cliffs and dropping into big pools. Having already come this far, most hikers are tempted to continue a bit farther, now off-trail and scrambling, to the river's edge at the base of the falls. But if you do this, be extremely careful not to step off Tahoe National Forest land and onto the private property that surrounds the falls. The property belongs to The Cedars at Soda Springs, and they don't like trespassers. Watch for No Trespassing signs and make sure you stay on Tahoe National Forest land.

Although the entire trail makes for excellent hiking any time it's snow-free, Heath Falls is most impressive in early summer, before the river level drops. It's best to make this trek as soon as the roads open to the trailhead, which is usually mid-June, but could be earlier or later.

From the Health Falls Overlook, you'll need to backtrack to join the main Palisades Creek Trail, then continue down the main path to see Palisades Falls. The extra distance is completely worth it; in fact, some waterfall-lovers have told me they conserve their energy by simply heading to Palisades Falls and skipping Heath Falls altogether. The North Fork American River is amazingly beautiful, and it's easy to linger on the bridge across it, admiring the view of magnificent Royal Gorge downstream. When you cross the bridge, continue downstream for about 200 yards to a fine view of Palisade Falls, a gorgeous and powerful 40-foot drop on the American. Like Heath Falls, Palisade Falls is best seen in early summer, as close to peak snowmelt time as possible.

Now it's time to pull up a rock, pull out your sandwich, and savor your lunch. After a visit here, there's nothing left to do but head uphill and pay that credit card bill. Unless of course you brought your camping gear; then you can put off that long climb until tomorrow.

Directions

From Auburn, drive east on I-80 for 55 miles to Soda Springs. Take the Soda Springs/Norden exit and follow Old Highway 40 east for 0.8 mile to Soda Springs Road. Turn south (right) and drive another 0.8 mile to Pahatsi Road. Turn right. Pahatsi Road turns to dirt in 0.2 mile, and its name changes to Kidd Lakes Road. At 1.5 miles, reach a fork and continue straight for 2.5 more miles, passing Kidd Lake on your left, and the Royal Gorge Devil's Lookout Warming Hut on your right. (Take the left fork after the warming hut; it's 0.5 mile farther.) The trailhead is on the north side of Cascade Lakes, signed as Palisade Creek Trail.

Information and Contact

There is no fee. Maps of Tahoe National Forest are available for a fee from the National Forest Store (406/329-3024, www.nationalforeststore.com), or can be downloaded for free from www.fs.fed.us/r5/maps/. For more information, contact Tahoe National Forest, Truckee Ranger District, 530/587-3558, www.fs.fed.us/r5/tahoe.

12 STEVENS CREEK FALLS
Bureau of Land Management (BLM) Folsom Resource Area

Level: Easy

Best Season: April-July

Distance: 3.0 miles round-trip

Elevation Change: Total loss 600 feet

The little gold-country town of Colfax is the secret land of waterfalls. The town doesn't look like much from I-80, but if you take any of Colfax's side roads or trails down into the American River canyon, you'll be on your way to a waterfall.

The Stevens Trail, which leads 4.5 miles one-way to the North Fork of the American River, passes by one of my favorite Colfax falls. To reach it, you need only hike 1.5 miles down the trail to the spot where it crosses Robbers Ravine Creek (not Stevens Creek, despite what everyone calls this waterfall). If you have the time and inclination, however, you should explore further and follow the trail all the way to the North Fork, where you'll find terrific wildflower displays and swimming holes. In 2002, this trail was designated on the National Register of Historic Places as a National Historic Trail, as it was originally part of a major livery trail that ran from Colfax to Iowa Hill. The latter city was a bustling metropolis during the Gold Rush. The bridge that crossed the North Fork to connect the two towns is long gone, but from 1870–1895, this was a heavily trafficked route. The trail is named for Truman A. Stevens, a miner who was responsible for the completion of the trail.

Stevens Creek Falls

Keep in mind that this well-graded trail goes down, down, down all the way to the river. If you're only going as far as the waterfall, you'll have a 600-foot gain on your return to the trailhead, spread out over 1.5 miles. If you hike all the way to the river, you'll have a 1,200-foot gain on the return, spread out over 4.5 miles. Be sure to bring plenty of water with you, and hike the trail as early in the year as possible, before it gets too hot.

The Stevens Trail requires a small leap of faith at the trailhead. When you get out of your car, you're inundated with highway noise from nearby I-80. The sound follows you for the first few minutes of trail, and it doesn't exactly make for a wilderness experience. But keep moving, because the path quickly drops below the highway, and the sound of rushing 18-wheelers is soon replaced by the twittering of birds and rustling of leaves.

Unquestionably, the best time to hike here is the spring, not only because that's when the waterfall is at its best, but also because that's when the wildflowers in the Sierra foothills are the most abundant. In April and May, you'll see dogwoods and redbuds busting out all over, and colorful clouds of baby blue eyes, shooting stars, and lupines at your feet.

The trail has a few junctions, which you should watch for. At 0.5 mile in, you leave the forest single-track and turn left on an open dirt road. A few minutes later, you come to an intersection of four dirt roads where you turn right. Finally, you reach another road intersection, but continue straight, then pick up the single-track on the left. The trail is well-signed the entire way, but the vegetation is so lush that it sometimes obscures the signs. In addition to all the vines and wildflowers, a dense forest of oaks, pines, and firs, as well as many buckeye trees growing along the creek, shade the trail to the waterfall.

The trail reaches a stream crossing at 1.4 miles; a small cascade spills just below the trail and a larger waterfall is just off the trail to the left, somewhat hidden in the foliage. A short spur trail will take you there. Because it's hidden from the trail by thick vines and branches, it's a good place for a quick dip. At the very least, take off your hiking boots and soak your feet. There's nothing quite like the cool, refreshing feeling of it.

Directions

From Sacramento, drive east on I-80 for 45 miles to Colfax. Take the Colfax/North Canyon Way exit and turn left at the stop sign. Drive east on the frontage road (North Canyon Way) for 0.7 mile, past the Colfax cemetery, to the trailhead parking area. On weekends, this parking lot can fill up, so if you can't fit your car into the lot, be sure to park legally alongside the road without blocking any driveways.

Information and Contact

There is no fee. For more information and a map/brochure, contact the Bureau of Land Management, Mother Lode Field Office, 916/941-3101, www.blm.gov/ca.

13 CODFISH CREEK FALLS
Auburn State Recreation Area

| **Level:** Easy | **Distance:** 3.0 miles round-trip |
| **Best Season:** April–September | **Elevation Change:** Total gain 50 feet |

It's unlikely that you'll see any codfish swimming in Codfish Creek, but you will have a chance at some private time by a pretty waterfall along the North Fork of the American River.

Nobody could tell me where this creek got its name, but everyone said that I had to see its waterfall in springtime. So off I went on a fair Saturday in May, following Ponderosa Way from the little town of Weimar down to the American River canyon. The final 2.5-mile stretch of this dirt road can be a white-knuckled ride or a mellow country drive, depending on what recent storms have done to the roadbed. Know in advance that there are very few pullouts along this very narrow thoroughfare, and that you will be driving quite slowly. A high-clearance vehicle is a very good idea, but plenty of passenger cars make the trip later in the season when the mud has dried. As long as you are mentally prepared for a bit of a driving adventure, you should be fine.

Park your vehicle along the road just before the river bridge and start hiking on the trail on the north side of the river. The route is surprisingly well-maintained, compared to many other river trails on this stretch of the American. You'll head

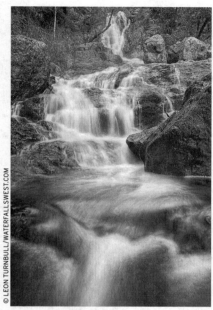

Codfish Creek Falls

west, paralleling the river for about a mile. You may spot occasional fortune-hunters looking for gold in the river and sun-lovers floating on their backs in the blue-green pools.

At 1.3 miles, the trail turns right and leads upstream along Codfish Creek, heading away from the river. I passed a hand-painted plaque naming the Codfish Creek Trail, with a dedication to a certain someone "and all others who love nature." It was put there by a group of wonderful people called PARC, which stands for Protect the American River Canyon, an Auburn-based conservation group. Before you start off on this trip, it's a good idea to download the "Codfish Creek Falls Discovery Trail" brochure from their website (www.parc-auburn.org). If you aren't familiar with the wildflowers and shrubs of this foothill country, this brochure will educate while hiking.

Although the trail along the river is very exposed, Codfish's canyon is shaded by big manzanitas and deciduous trees. After just a few minutes of walking under the forest canopy, you'll decipher the sound of falling water. The trail brings you to the smack-middle of the waterfall, which is a big cascade totaling about 80 feet.

The fall's lower reaches are gentle cascades, while the top is more vertical and dramatic. I climbed up the side of the fall and lay around on the rocks, which are a colorful black and gray with rust-colored highlights. A few clumps of Indian rhubarb grow with great enthusiasm by the water's edge.

Directions

From Sacramento, drive east on I-80 for 40 miles to Weimar. Take the Weimar/Cross Road exit, then turn south on Ponderosa Way. In three miles, Ponderosa Way turns to dirt. Continue for 2.5 additional miles (this dirt stretch can be very rough and rutted after winter rains; high-clearance may be required and the going is slow) until you reach a bridge over the American River, a total of 5.5 miles from Weimar/Cross Road. Don't cross the bridge, but park along the road near it. Begin hiking on the trail on the north side of the bridge, heading west (downstream).

Information and Contact

There is no fee. A map/brochure of Auburn State Recreation Area is available by free download at www.parks.ca.gov. For more information, contact Auburn State Recreation Area, 530/885-4527, www.parks.ca.gov. Or contact PARC (Protect American River Canyons), 530/885-8878, www.parc-auburn.org.

14 DEVIL'S FALLS   BEST 🌙
Auburn State Recreation Area

👫

Level: Easy   **Distance:** Negligible

Best Season: April–July   **Elevation Change:** 1,500 feet

It seems almost unfair that a waterfall this pretty is set right along the road. It's just too easy. Most of the year, it doesn't even take four-wheel drive to reach it. But visiting Devil's Falls by car can be the start of a day of adventure on the American River, with its emerald green pools, big fish, gold-panning prospects, and numerous camping and hiking possibilities.

Reach Devil's Falls by driving on Yankee Jim's Road, either from Colfax or from Foresthill. Whichever route you take, you must descend all the way to the bottom of the river canyon, a drop of about 1,200 feet. The road leads 3.8 miles from Colfax and 5.1 miles from Foresthill to the river, and although it's not paved, it's well-graded dirt the whole way. It traverses a narrow series of hair-

Devil's Falls

pin turns, the kind where you hope that nobody is coming in the opposite direction. The falls are located at one of those hairpins on the Foresthill side of the American River, just 0.5 mile south of the picturesque suspension bridge on Yankee Jim's Road.

When 75-foot Devil's Falls is running full, it divides into six or seven big chutes, then runs underneath Yankee Jim's Road and continues to drop till it joins Shirttail Creek, which empties into the American River. Considering the size of Devil's Falls, it's surprising that its creek is not a tributary to the American River, but only a tributary to a tributary.

Signs posted near the fall state "No parking 10 P.M. to 6 A.M." lest you should want to camp right here by the road. Auburn State Recreation Area has designated this area as Shirttail Picnic Area, for day-use only. On spring and summer weekends, the road from the old suspension bridge to the falls can be lined with parked cars, as this stretch of river is popular for both fishing and swimming. Local teenagers sometimes hang a long rope from the suspension bridge, then take turns swinging on it and jumping into the river. The scene looks like something right out of *Huckleberry Finn*.

Directions

From Sacramento, drive east on I-80 for 45 miles to Colfax. Take the Colfax/Grass Valley exit, turn right at the stop sign, then drive west on the frontage road (North Canyon Way) for 1.2 miles to Yankee Jim's Road. Turn left (south) on Yankee Jim's Road. The road turns to dirt; drive 3.7 miles to the bridge over the North Fork American River, then continue 0.5 mile farther to Devil's Falls on the right.

Information and Contact

There is no fee. A map/brochure of Auburn State Recreation Area is available by free download at www.parks.ca.gov. For more information, contact Auburn State Recreation Area, 530/885-4527, www.parks.ca.gov. Or contact PARC (Protect American River Canyons), 530/885-8878, www.parc-auburn.org.

15 INDIAN CREEK FALLS
Auburn State Recreation Area

Level: Moderate
Best Season: Late May–early July

Distance: 3.0 miles round-trip
Elevation Change: Total gain 50 feet

It took three trips till I finally got to see Indian Creek Falls. The hike starts off with a creek crossing, and you have to time it right to get across. In early May, it was too high. In early June, it was still too high. On the Fourth of July, I finally made it, but not by rock-hopping. I just took off my shoes and waded in.

You have to be lucky to time it right. Only a couple of weeks exist in the small

window of time when Shirttail Creek is
low enough to cross and Indian Creek
is high enough to have a good waterfall.
If you come too early, you can't access
the trail. If you come too late, there's no
reward at the end of the walk. In most
years, June or early July is just about
right.

From the parking pullouts at the south
side of the bridge, take the stairsteps
down from the road to the river canyon,
then walk to your right, upstream along
the river. You'll only go a few feet before you'll have to size up Shirttail Creek
and decide whether or not you can cross
without getting wet.

Once you're past Shirttail, the rest is
easy. Follow the miner's trail that runs
east along the south side of the river, a

Indian Creek Falls

© ANN MARIE BROWN

basically flat route that is in various states of repair and disrepair. Watch out for
some steep drop-offs. A few spur trails lead down to the river, giving you the option of cooling off on a hot day or staying on the high road if you want to head
straight for the falls.

Since there are no trail signs, count creek crossings to mark your distance traveled. You've already crossed Shirttail, and in 0.25 mile you'll cross a tiny, unnamed
stream—that makes two. The third and fourth streams are just over a mile out
and close together, and they have a decent flow in spring. The fifth creek at 1.5
miles is your ticket—Indian Creek. Even though the falls aren't visible from the
trail, it's easy to recognize the creek because just before it, the trail goes through
a large landslide of rounded rocks that flow right into the river. Pick your way
across the rocks and find the stream, which is sometimes marked by neatly placed
rock cairns on top of the haphazard rock piles.

Then start scrambling upstream, heading away from the river. The easiest and
quickest way to manage the scramble is to wear shoes that you can get wet. That
way, you can spend your time both in and out of the water, picking the most efficient route as you go. (A high trail travels above the landslide for those who don't
want to wade into the creek, but this seems needlessly treacherous. The stream
scrambling is safer and more fun, as long as the water is low enough.)

Fifteen minutes of this soggy but enjoyable travel brings you to Indian Creek

Falls, which are really two waterfalls, one right above the other. Their combined height is about 30 feet. The creek is very densely shaded, mostly by oaks, which contrasts with the exposed slopes along the river trail. Be sure to stick your head under the falls to cool off, or spend a few moments looking for gold flecks in the stream.

Directions

From Sacramento, drive east on I-80 for 45 miles to Colfax. Take the Colfax/Grass Valley exit, turn right at the stop sign, then drive west on the frontage road (North Canyon Way) for 1.2 miles to Yankee Jim's Road. Turn left (south) on Yankee Jim's Road. The road turns to dirt; drive 3.7 miles to the bridge over the North Fork American River, then cross it and park on the south side of the bridge.

Information and Contact

There is no fee. A map/brochure of Auburn State Recreation Area is available by free download at www.parks.ca.gov. For more information, contact Auburn State Recreation Area, 530/885-4527, www.parks.ca.gov. Or contact PARC (Protect American River Canyons), 530/885-8878, www.parc-auburn.org.

16 CHAMBERLAIN FALLS
Auburn State Recreation Area

Level: Strenuous

Best Season: March-May

Distance: 3.0 miles round-trip

Elevation Change: Total gain 200 feet

Trail? What trail? If it's a trail you're after, don't try the hike to Chamberlain Falls. Once upon a time, there was a trail, but a series of slides in the 1980s almost completely wiped it out. A route? Sure, there's a route. But it disappears in places, has plenty of death-defying drop-offs, and will leave you wondering why the heck you didn't just swim downstream to the falls instead.

The trip to Chamberlain Falls isn't for everybody. You have to be prepared for some fairly treacherous hiking along the steep North Fork American River Canyon, where a misplaced foot or a loose rock means a near-certain fall. Plus, only a small window of time exists when the waterfall runs and is accessible.

There's deception in the fact that the trip starts out so easy. From the day-use parking area at Mineral Bar Campground, a dirt trail leads steeply down to the river, then quite easily downstream for 0.5 mile. Auburn State Recreation Area keeps this part of the trail trimmed and maintained for people staying at the campground. You pass some old, rusted mining equipment as you hike through thick vines and foliage growing at the river's edge. Things look promising.

The trail leaves the river and heads uphill, along the steep oak- and bay-shaded canyon slopes. For another 0.3 mile, the trail gets progressively harder to follow but is still manageable. Views of the exquisite turquoise-green pools below spur you onward. The river water is unbelievably clear; the rocky canyon appears jewel-like. In the spring, the grassy slopes are sprinkled with wildflowers. River rafters and kayakers zip down the river. Life seems good.

But suddenly the route becomes dicey, if you can still find it. By the way, where is the route? It's nearly impossible to tell. Leaf litter makes the slopes treacherously slippery, and coupled with your near-perpendicular position to the river, it seems germane to start bargaining with some deity—any deity. Turning around looks just as dangerous as continuing onward, so take your pick.

Just creep along. Take your time and use extra caution. At nearly 1.5 miles from the trailhead, the route drops down to the river. Kiss the shoreline in gratitude, then scramble over the rocks for another 100 yards downstream to where Chamberlain Creek forms a 20-foot cascade over boulders as it drops into the American River. This is what is known as a "constriction" waterfall, where a big boulder chokes a stream canyon, and in high water forms a fall.

Chamberlain runs full until late May in most years, and by then, the creek has warmed up enough for swimming in its upper pools. The waterfall is most spectacular in March and April, however, and the same is true for the river canyon, when the wildflowers and the river boaters are out in full force.

Directions

From Sacramento, drive east on I-80 for 45 miles to Colfax. Take the Colfax/Grass Valley exit, turn right at the stop sign, and drive west on the frontage road (North Canyon Way) for 0.3 mile to Iowa Hill Road. Turn left (south) on Iowa Hill Road. In three miles, cross the bridge over the North Fork American River to Mineral Bar Campground. Park just beyond the bridge in the dirt parking lot on the right (day use only, across the road from the camp host). Begin walking southwest (downstream) along the river.

Information and Contact

There is no fee. A map/brochure of Auburn State Recreation Area is available by free download at www.parks.ca.gov. For more information, contact Auburn State Recreation Area, 530/885-4527, www.parks.ca.gov. Or contact PARC (Protect American River Canyons), 530/885-8878, www.parc-auburn.org.

17 BRIDAL VEIL FALLS
Eldorado National Forest

Level: Easy

Best Season: April-June

Distance: Negligible

Elevation Change: 3,500 feet

Bridal Veil Falls

Not to be confused with *the* Bridalveil Fall in Yosemite National Park, Highway 50's Bridal Veil Falls is spelled as two words, not one, and it bears little resemblance to the more famous cataract. The name's derivation is a mystery, but seeing the fall is not, because you drive right by it on Highway 50 heading from Placerville to South Lake Tahoe.

In the spring, Bridal Veil Falls is a winner, even as you fly by at 60 miles per hour. If you want to stop for a closer look, there are pullouts on both sides of the highway by the falls. Also, the waterfall is less than 0.5 mile west (and across the road) from Bridal Veil Picnic Area, which was once a campground but is now a day-use area that offers great swimming holes along the South Fork of the American River.

Bridal Veil Falls drops 80 feet over a big sheet of gray rock, and it's partially obscured by some tall maple trees growing in front. By late summer, you can drive right by without even noticing it, but in springtime, you can't miss its brilliant white stream.

The best way to view Bridal Veil is from across the road, rather than at the foot of the fall, because only from that distance can you see its full height. Your best bet: park at the picnic area, take a short walk west along the highway to the waterfall (don't bother crossing the highway), then walk back to the picnic area and claim your spot along the turquoise waters of the American River.

Directions

From Placerville, drive 19 miles east on Highway 50. Look for the waterfall on the right side of the road, 5.5 miles east of the town of Pollock Pines. There are parking pullouts on both sides of the road, or you can park at Bridal Veil Picnic Area on the north side of the road, east of the fall.

Information and Contact

A $3 day-use fee is charged per vehicle to park at Bridal Veil Picnic Area. To view the falls from the parking pullouts along the road, there is no fee. Maps of Eldorado National Forest are available for a fee from the National Forest Store (406/329-3024, www.nationalforeststore.com), or can be downloaded for free from www.fs.fed.us/r5/maps/. For more information, contact Eldorado National Forest, Pacific Ranger District, 530/644-2349, www.fs.fed.us/r5/eldorado.

18 BASSI FALLS
Eldorado National Forest

Level: Easy

Best Season: April-June

Distance: 1.0 mile round-trip

Elevation Change: Total gain 50 feet

The Sacramento Municipal Utility District, in conjunction with Eldorado National Forest, built an easy, lovely trail to Bassi Falls, near Union Valley Reservoir. People have been visiting Bassi Falls for decades, but there was never a formal trail until the summer of 2003. The well-built trail is a great bonus for campers and visitors to the Crystal Basin, who come to this spot in droves, carrying towels and wearing swimsuits for some watery Sierra summer fun.

To see it at peak flow, you must visit Bassi Falls in the late spring or early summer. Most years by mid-July there will still be some wading pools to splash around in at the base of 130-foot Bassi Falls, but not much in the way of a waterfall. The elevation here is less than 5,000 feet, so the snowmelt disappears early in the year.

Bassi Falls

© ANN MARIE BROWN

Of course, that means you can go visit Bassi Falls when other Tahoe-area waterfalls are still buried under the white stuff.

It's a mere 15-minute walk from the parking area to the base of the falls, first on the newly built trail through a forest of incense cedars and then along granite slabs marked with trail cairns. After the first few hundred yards, the sound of the falls will guide you, so there is no way to miss it. Big Hill Lookout, a fire tower near Ice House Reservoir, is an obvious landmark to the west.

The falls are popular with groups staying at nearby Big Silver Group Campground, so you are unlikely to have this place to yourself. But this isn't a party scene at the falls; it's more of a scout troop and family scene. Everybody's having a good time.

Directions

From Placerville, drive 21 miles east on Highway 50 and turn left (north) on Ice House Road. Drive 16.2 miles on Ice House Road, past the turnoff for Ice House Reservoir, to Big Silver Group Campground on the left. Don't turn into the campground; instead turn right across from it on a gravel road (Bassi Road). Drive 0.2 mile, then go left at the fork. Drive 1.5 miles to the signed trailhead.

Information and Contact

There is no fee. A map of Crystal Basin Recreation Area is available at the information station on Ice House Road (you'll pass it as you drive in). Maps of Eldorado National Forest are available for a fee from the National Forest Store (406/329-3024, www.nationalforeststore.com), or can be downloaded for free from www.fs.fed.us/r5/maps/. For more information, contact Eldorado National Forest, Pacific Ranger District, 530/644-2349, www.fs.fed.us/r5/eldorado.

19 HORSETAIL FALLS
Eldorado National Forest

Level: Easy   **Distance:** 2.0 miles round-trip

Best Season: April-September   **Elevation Change:** Total gain 200 feet

You'll know why they call it Horsetail Falls the minute you see it, while cruising west on Highway 50. Straight and narrow at the top and fanning out to a wide inverted V at the bottom, Horsetail Falls swishes hundreds of feet down Pyramid Creek's glacier-carved canyon. Its powerful stream is reinforced by four lakes: Toem, Ropi, Pitt, and Avalanche.

© ANDREW SAWADISAVI

Horsetail Falls

Don't be put off by the crammed parking lot at Twin Bridges, the trailhead for the falls. Many of the cars belong to backpackers who are far off in the Desolation Wilderness on multiday trips, and many more belong to people just milling around the trailhead, picnicking and admiring the falls from afar.

From the parking area at the highway bridge, pick up the trail at the large signboard. Hike through the dense cedar and pine forest, which smells like Grandma's cedar chest in the attic, only fresher and better. You leave most of your trail companions behind in the first 0.5 mile, as people drop off the route and choose their spots along Pyramid Creek. The trail continues into an exposed, rocky area—the glaciers paid a visit here—moving farther away from the creek and the cool shade of the forest.

About 0.5 mile in, you have a choice: Continue straight toward Horsetail Falls and the Desolation Wilderness boundary, or veer off and follow the 1.5-mile Pyramid Creek Loop Trail. The latter is a trail that was built in 1999 specifically with day users in mind. This well-marked trail offers terrific long-distance views of Horsetail Falls and is routed past a beautiful stretch of Pyramid Creek called the Cascades. If you haven't obtained a wilderness permit and just want to day hike to a waterfall vista and swimming holes, this is your ticket.

If you choose to continue toward the falls, in a short distance you may notice a bizarre phenomenon: arrows painted on the granite slabs pointing out the direction of the trail. Some ingrate vandalized this area in September 1995, spray-painting hundreds of green arrows on pristine granite. Apparently the culprit thought the trail was too difficult to follow and painted the arrows as some kind of a "service" to other hikers. (Go figure.) Eldorado National Forest rangers and various volunteer groups have made efforts to remove the graffiti, but it will take decades to get rid of it all.

Recreation managers in the Pacific Ranger District say that this trail has long been a source of controversy. Although the path up to the wilderness boundary is fairly well defined, beyond the boundary line it is an informal route, not a trail. Many visitors try to proceed to the base of Horsetail Falls, then get lost or hurt on the crude path. A slip near the waterfall or along the edges of fast-moving Pyramid Creek means near-certain death. Every year there are fatalities and injuries.

Despite the ruckus, Horsetail Falls is still a favorite hike around South Lake Tahoe. An estimated 15,000 people visit this trailhead and hike at least a portion of the trail each summer. Stay below the wilderness line and you're certain to stay out of trouble, although you'll have to be satisfied with long-distance views of Horsetail Falls. Aside from the beauty of Pyramid Creek and the falls, there is much more to see and enjoy. The up-close scenery includes ancient, twisted junipers and sturdy Jeffrey pines, and brightly colored lichens that coat the granite boulders.

When you reach the boundary sign, you may only continue farther if you have filled out a self-serve permit at the trailhead. If so, you can walk right to the base of the big fall, but remember, this is a route, not a trail. Be extremely careful near the edge of the creek. For most people, turning back at the boundary sign is no great compromise. The return trip offers views of Lover's Leap and surrounding peaks to the south, far across the highway. On your walk back, be sure to turn around every now and then for a parting look at Horsetail Falls.

Directions

From South Lake Tahoe, drive south on Highway 89 to Highway 50. Drive west on Highway 50 for about 15 miles to Twin Bridges, where there is a huge parking area on the north side of the highway just before the bridge. (It's 0.5 mile west of the turnoff for Camp Sacramento.) The trailhead is marked by a large signboard.

Information and Contact

A $5 parking fee is charged per vehicle. A wilderness permit is necessary if you are going to travel beyond the wilderness boundary. Maps of Eldorado National Forest are available for a fee from the National Forest Store (406/329-3024, www.nationalforeststore.com), or can be downloaded for free from www.fs.fed.us/r5/maps/. A more detailed map of the Desolation Wilderness or Lake Tahoe area is available from Tom Harrison Maps, 415/456-7940, www.tomharrisonmaps.com. For more information, contact Eldorado National Forest, 530/644-2349, www.fs.fed.us/r5/eldorado.

20 EAGLE FALLS
Lake Tahoe Basin Management Unit

Level: Easy   **Distance:** 0.5–2.0 miles round-trip

Best Season: April–July   **Elevation Change:** Total gain/loss 50–400 feet

There's the Eagle Falls you see from the short trail at Eagle Falls Picnic Area, and then there's the other Eagle Falls just downstream and across Highway 89. While you're in the neighborhood, you might as well go see both Eagle Falls. Let's face it, it's one of the rare things at Lake Tahoe that you can do without a bank loan.

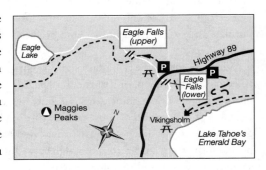

Start with the upstream Eagle Falls, the one that you reach via a 0.25-mile trail from the Eagle Falls Picnic Area. Unfortunately, they've made this into a "designer" trail by cutting the natural granite into flagstonelike stairsteps and building a wooden bridge with metal railings to escort you over the top of the falls. The route has been flattened by so many hikers' feet that even the sandy parts are packed smooth and hard.

It's a beautiful walk, nonetheless. It's also extremely popular, not just with people coming to see the falls, but also with those continuing into the Desolation Wilderness. For the most peaceful experience, visit as early in the morning as possible, like before 9 A.M.

The upstream Eagle Falls is only 50 feet tall, pouring directly underneath the hiker's bridge. In springtime, right after heavy snowmelt, the bridge can be an exciting place to stand. By fall, the flow of water is merely tame, and the overlook lacks its early-season drama.

If you decide to hike beyond Eagle Falls, you'll enter a vastly different land. The trail heads uphill and becomes very rocky, losing its "designer" quality almost immediately. You need a permit to enter the Desolation Wilderness, even for day hiking. Get one at the trailhead. The trail leads to Eagle Lake in one mile and to Velma Lakes in four, with spectacular views of exposed granite and dramatic, glaciated landscapes. Welcome to the Sierra high country. If you don't continue onward, the short walk back to the parking lot from Eagle Falls has its own drama—a terrific view of Lake Tahoe that was behind your back on the way in.

© ANDREW SAWADISAVI

Eagle Falls

Now that you've seen the upper Eagle Falls, head for the lower falls. From the Eagle Falls Picnic Area parking lot, carefully cross Highway 89 on foot (be very wary of drivers watching the lake instead of the road), then peer down over the top of the falls.

The lower fall is visible from the highway; it's a can't-miss-it traffic-stopper during spring snowmelt. During May and June, drivers constantly slam on their brakes, pull off the road, then risk their lives by dashing across the highway to get a closer look at the falls. Many people scramble down the side of Eagle Falls from the road, but this isn't recommended unless it's very late in the season, the water flow is low, and the surrounding granite is completely dry. There have been more than a few accidents here.

Instead, see the lower fall from the bottom up, by walking or driving 0.5 mile north on Highway 89 to the Emerald Bay Overlook parking lot on the lake side of the road. From there, hike down the steep, one-mile dirt road to Vikingsholm, an ornate replica of a Viking castle that once belonged to an heiress and is now a state park. From Memorial Day to Labor Day, you can pay a fee and tour the inside of the castle, or just walk right past it and go straight to the waterfall instead. The Eagle Falls Trail begins just beyond the Vikingsholm ticket office (signs direct you to the trailhead). A 0.25-mile walk takes you to the base of the falls. Although you can't see its entire length from here, in early summer this is a perfect spot to witness a vivid display of the churning power and force of snowmelt.

Directions

From South Lake Tahoe, drive northwest on Highway 89 for 8.5 miles to the Eagle Falls Picnic Area and Trailhead. Turn left into the parking area, or park in the pullout just beyond the picnic area on the west side of Highway 89. To hike to Vikingsholm and view only the lower fall, park in the Emerald Bay Overlook and parking area, 0.25 mile north of the Eagle Falls Picnic Area.

Information and Contact

A $5 parking fee is charged per vehicle at the Eagle Falls Picnic Area. Maps of the Lake Tahoe Basin are available for a fee from the National Forest Store (406/329-3024, www.nationalforeststore.com), or can be downloaded for free from www.fs.fed.us/r5/maps/. A more detailed map of the Lake Tahoe area is available from Tom Harrison Maps, 415/456-7940, www.tomharrisonmaps.com. For more information, contact Lake Tahoe Basin Management Unit, 530/543-2600, www.fs.usda.gov/ltbmu.

21 CASCADE FALLS
Lake Tahoe Basin Management Unit

Level: Easy   **Distance:** 2.0 miles round-trip

Best Season: April–July   **Elevation Change:** Total gain 100 feet

The hike to Cascade Falls is far and away the best easy hike at Lake Tahoe. It's short and level enough for almost anybody to make the trip, including children. It has enough spectacular scenery to keep even the biggest whiners-in-the-outdoors from complaining. And the trail leads you right to the edge of a stunning 200-foot cascade that drops into the southwest end of Cascade Lake. What more could you ask for?

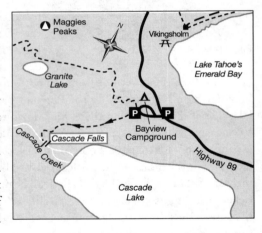

Cascade Falls has only one drawback—you have to see it early in the year. By August, the 100-yard-wide tower of water has become a thin, willowy stream, which greatly diminishes its dramatic effect. Plan your trip for sometime between the start of snowmelt and July, but no later.

From the trailhead parking lot at Bayview Campground, hike to your left on the well-signed trail. The route is a winner every step of the way. It meanders in and out of Jeffrey pine forest and open sunshine, alternately providing shade and views. After a mere five minutes of walking, you're rewarded with a tremendous vista of Cascade Lake, elevation 6,464 feet. The lake looks so large you may

© ANN MARIE BROWN

Cascade Falls

think it's part of Lake Tahoe, but with your bird's-eye view you can see that it's separated from Tahoe by a thin strip of forest and highway.

Moments later, the rumbling of the falls greets you as you break out of the forest and are given a clear view of the tumbling water. From here onward, the trail is out in the open on an exposed ledge trail with steep drop-offs. Watch your footing on the granite, and keep a firm handhold on small children. Watching your step is more difficult than you'd imagine, because the views of Cascade Lake and South Lake Tahoe will be vying for your attention.

The closer you get to the falls, the more the trail disintegrates, but numerous rock cairns show you the way. How far you go is up to you, but the best views of Cascade Falls are actually farther back on the trail. You lose sight of the falls in the last 0.25 mile of trail, and then if you walk right up to its edge, you can't see much of its 200-foot length. But upstream of the falls' lip are some lovely emerald green pools, as well as large shelves of granite where you can sit and picnic.

Cascade Falls was once known as White Cloud Falls. In the wind, it billows and scatters so much over its base of fractured granite that it creates a cloud of spray. Wildflowers enjoy all the water. Blue lupines and pink mountain prides present a superb springtime show as they cling to crevices in the rock.

Directions

From South Lake Tahoe, drive northwest on Highway 89 for 7.5 miles to the Bayview Campground and Trailhead. Turn left and drive to the far end of the campground to the trailhead parking area. If it's full, you can park across Highway 89 in the Inspiration Point parking lot.

Information and Contact

There is no fee. Maps of the Lake Tahoe Basin are available for a fee from the National Forest Store (406/329-3024, www.nationalforeststore.com), or can be downloaded for free from www.fs.fed.us/r5/maps/. A more detailed map of the

Lake Tahoe area is available from Tom Harrison Maps, 415/456-7940, www. tomharrisonmaps.com. For more information, contact Lake Tahoe Basin Management Unit, 530/543-2600, www.fs.usda.gov/ltbmu.

22 GLEN ALPINE FALLS AND MODJESKA FALLS
Lake Tahoe Basin Management Unit

Level: Easy

Best Season: May–August

Distance: 1.0 mile round-trip

Elevation Change: Total gain 50 feet

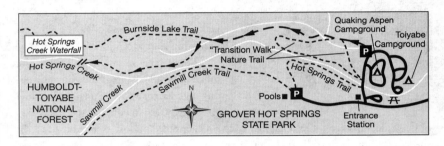

Glen Alpine Creek is abundant with waterfalls, affording hikers, bikers, and drivers the chance to "have it their way."

The biggest and most accessible fall on Glen Alpine Creek is on Road 1216, a left fork off Fallen Leaf Lake Road, on the way to the Desolation Wilderness Trailhead. In the spring, many people make the drive down impossibly narrow Fallen Leaf Lake Road to see the fall. Bike riders, too, enjoy the route. Because the road is so narrow, cars have no choice but to go slowly, which gives bikers a chance to ride in relative safety.

The falls are located right along the road, about 150 yards beyond the point where Fallen Leaf Lake Road forks and a sign points to the left for Lily Lake, Glen Alpine Falls, and the Desolation Wilderness Trailhead. The road deteriorates substantially at the fork, but you can park your car there and walk a few hundred yards to the falls, or drive a little farther and pull off right by the falls. There are several dirt pullouts, but they fill up on spring weekends. Just be sure that wherever you park, you aren't on private property or blocking someone's driveway.

Technically this is Lower Glen Alpine Falls, although some call it Big Falls; it's a 75-foot cascade that spills over jagged rocks that resemble stairsteps. It's

Glen Alpine Falls

an incredible sight in spring, when the water seems to be shooting out in every direction as it hits a multitude of ledges and outcrops. The best viewing is from the foundation of an old stone house, directly in front of the fall. Although this cabin is long gone, there are several others still standing nearby. They are on 99-year leases with the Forest Service, left over from the days when the government was trying to encourage recreational activity here. That means that a lucky few have weekend cabins surrounded by a waterfall, junipers, firs, and big pines, as well as Fallen Leaf Lake itself.

If you want to do a little hiking and see another waterfall on Glen Alpine Creek, drive past the first fall and continue 0.5 mile to the end of the road at the Desolation Wilderness Trailhead. Fill out a self-serve permit at the kiosk, then begin walking on the gated dirt road. Reach the waterfall in a mere 0.5 mile, hiking on a very rocky road past more leased cabins. The trail comes within 50 yards of the cascade, but you can scramble a little closer, making your way carefully through the scrub oaks that line the creek. This 35-foot cataract is Upper Glen Alpine Falls, although history buffs call it Modjeska Falls. It was named after Madame Helena Modjeska, a Polish actress of the late 19th century who performed at Glen Alpine Springs Resort, located another 0.5 mile up this trail. It's worth hiking the additional distance to the remains of this 19th- and early-20th-century resort, which includes a natural mineral spring and several buildings designed by famed architect Bernard Maybeck (who also designed San Francisco's Palace of Fine Arts).

From the site of the resort, you can continue hiking into Desolation Wilderness. The main trail leads to Grass Lake, 1.7 miles farther, or Susie Lake, 3.5 miles farther, with many more lakes beyond.

Directions

From South Lake Tahoe, drive northwest on Highway 89 for 2.9 miles to Fallen Leaf Lake Road. Turn left and drive 4.8 miles, first through a logged area and then through a stretch of lakeside homes on a very narrow road. Take the left fork onto Road 1216, signed for Lily Lake, Glen Alpine Falls, and the Desolation Wilderness Trailhead. You'll reach the trailhead in 0.7 mile. Begin hiking on the gated dirt road to the right of the trailhead sign.

Information and Contact

Hikers must fill out a self-serve permit at the wilderness trailhead. There is no fee. Maps of the Lake Tahoe Basin are available for a fee from the National Forest Store (406/329-3024, www.nationalforeststore.com), or can be downloaded for free from www.fs.fed.us/r5/maps/. A more detailed map of the Lake Tahoe area is available from Tom Harrison Maps, 415/456-7940, www.tomharrisonmaps.com. For more information, contact Lake Tahoe Basin Management Unit, 530/543-2600, www.fs.usda.gov/ltbmu.

23 HOT SPRINGS CREEK WATERFALL
Grover Hot Springs State Park

Level: Easy

Best Season: April–July

Distance: 3.0 miles round-trip

Elevation Change: Total gain 200 feet

Grover Hot Springs State Park in Markleeville is located only a half hour from the urban bustle of South Lake Tahoe, but it feels like a different world. Markleeville is a small town—a real small town. Although it's fairly well-known as a weekend meeting place for motorcyclists cruising the area's back roads, it's better known for its neighboring state park and mineral-water bathing pools. What is less known, however, is that a short trail from the state park campground leads to a spring and early summer waterfall, an easy walk of only 1.5 miles one-way.

Even if you're not camping, it's worth the day-use fee to take a walk to the waterfall, then laze around at the park's bathing pools for the rest of the day. If you

© ANN MARIE BROWN

Hot Springs Creek Waterfall

come during the week, especially before or after summer vacation from school, you can even get a little peace and quiet.

The trail begins on a dirt and gravel service road just beyond the campground, signed as Trail 1006. Hike to your left on the road, then take the left fork off the road and onto single-track. If you encounter any mountain bikers in your first few minutes of walking, have no fear; they'll be veering off shortly on their way to Charity Valley in Humboldt-Toiyabe National Forest. That fork comes up in just over 0.5 mile; you'll bear left for the waterfall.

Your route parallels Hot Springs Creek, although you aren't near enough to pay it much attention. You will notice the huge sugar pines all around you, which create a shower of needles in the wind, plus green meadows filled with sagebrush surrounded by hillsides bearing oddly shaped rock outcrops.

When the trail reaches a jumbled, boulder-filled area, there's no place to go but up and over. This is the first point where your trail is anything but flat. A good footpath leads over the boulders; find it and take it. Ignore any spur trails that go down to the creek and the wide trail you may spot on the opposite side; these will send you up the wrong fork of the canyon.

Pick up the trail again on the far side of the boulders; now the waterfall is only 5–10 minutes away. Keep the creek on your left, and hike up Hot Springs Canyon as it narrows to the waterfall. The fall is about 50 feet tall, dropping over a tower of rocks, with plenty of pools below it for swimming and admiring the small trout who live there. In spring, Hot Springs Creek's waterfall runs quite full, loud, and fast, calling lots of attention to itself, but by late summer, you have to look and listen carefully for it.

The official trail ends near the base of the waterfall, but various routes take you to the top, where there is a makeshift camp (this is now Humboldt-Toiyabe National Forest land, beyond the state park boundary, so camping is allowed). Hot Springs Creek is surrounded by pine, cedar, juniper, cottonwood, and willow trees, as well as elderberry bushes; it's a lush environment compared to the sandy pine forest at the start of the trail.

When you've finished your visit to the falls, you can hike back to the park and walk the pleasant interpretive trail that leads around the meadow, or just spend the rest of the day at the hot springs. A bonus at Grover is that, unlike many hot springs, these have very little sulphur, meaning you don't have to hold your nose from the smell. The park has two concrete pools, which are fed from six different springs and regulated to about 103°F. Natural hot springs and a waterfall in the same park? Wow, it just doesn't get any better than this.

Directions
From Meyers at the junction of Highway 50 and Highway 89, drive south on Highway 89 for 24 miles to Markleeville. At Markleeville, turn right (west) on Hot Springs Road and drive 3.5 miles to the state park entrance. Drive through the entrance kiosk, then take the left fork past the campground to the signed trailhead, a gated dirt road. (See map for Glen Alpine Falls and Modjeska Falls in this chapter.)

Information and Contact
An $8 day-use fee is charged per vehicle. A park map is available by free download at www.parks.ca.gov, or for $1 at the entrance kiosk. For more information, contact Grover Hot Springs State Park, 530/694-2248, www.parks.ca.gov.

24 WOLF CREEK FALLS
Carson-Iceberg Wilderness

Level: Moderate	Distance: 10.0 miles round-trip
Best Season: June–October	Elevation Change: Total gain 800 feet

It may take 10 miles of walking (round-trip) to see Wolf Creek Falls, but they are darn easy miles, with an almost negligible elevation gain. The 50-foot waterfall is worth the long miles, not only for a chance to sit alongside its sparkling whitewater plunge, but also to admire the rugged volcanic landscape that surrounds it.

Wolf Creek runs dependably even into early autumn, but the best time to see the waterfall is unquestionably soon after snowmelt, which means sometime in June or July. Then the fall will completely flood the steep, rugged volcanic chasm it cuts through. Later in the year, Wolf Creek Falls dwindles to a narrower, more streamlike cataract, although it's still worth a gander.

© ANN MARIE BROWN

Wolf Creek Falls

The first four miles of Wolf Creek Trail are practically level, with just a gentle, steady uphill grade. The route, an old jeep road, is almost completely shaded by Jeffrey pines and white firs. The only downer is that late in the summer, the trail is often dusty and carved up from horses' hooves. The soft volcanic soil can be as sandy as an ocean beach in places, making walking more difficult than you'd expect. Pine needles cover much of the path.

The trail parallels Wolf Creek the entire way, never very close to it but always within earshot. You'll cross a few feeder streams; one or two may require you to remove your shoes in the early season. At 4.3 miles from the trailhead, you reach your first junction, where Bull Canyon Trail forks to the right to Bull Lake. Stay left on Wolf Creek Trail. Finally the trail nears the creek. Right after this junction, you'll face a short, steep uphill that leads over and around a rock outcrop. At the top of the rise, you get your first expansive views of the day. The ridge on your right has two huge volcanic outcrops poking up into the sky. They stand like two castles on the hill, or giant sentries guarding this canyon.

Now you're clearly in volcanic country. Sagebrush is everywhere and the only trees left are a few hardy junipers. Scattered rock outcrops are covered with colorful lichens. The landscape looks barren but beautiful. From the high point, the trail starts to descend. You'll pass through a cattle fence and Wolf Creek Falls is only 50 yards farther, where Wolf Creek suddenly narrows and steepens and the stream drops over volcanic rock. Early in the summer, your ears will lead you to the falls. By autumn, you'll need to look carefully on your left for its sheltered chasm.

Wolf Creek Falls makes three drops. The middle one is the tallest, about 40 feet. Several smaller cascades frame it above and below. If you wish to leave the trail and scramble down to the edge of the creek, be careful—the volcanic rock is very crumbly and loose. Anywhere near the falls is a fine place to sit and enjoy the scenery.

Directions
From Meyers at the junction of Highway 50 and Highway 89, drive south on Highway 89 for 24 miles to Markleeville. Continue south on Highway 89 for four miles past Markleeville, then bear right (south) on Highway 4. Drive 2.5 miles on Highway 4, then turn south on Wolf Creek Road. Drive 4.9 miles to the trailhead. The road turns to dirt, but it is well-graded and suitable for most cars. The trail (a closed, gated road) begins on the right, about 100 yards before the campground at Wolf Creek Road's end.

Information and Contact
There is no fee. Maps of Humboldt-Toiyabe National Forest (Carson District) or the Carson-Iceberg Wilderness are available for a fee from the National Forest Store (406/329-3024, www.nationalforeststore.com) or from the office below. For more information, contact Humboldt-Toiyabe National Forest, Carson Ranger District, 775/882-2766, www.fs.fed.us/r4/htnf.

25 LLEWELLYN FALLS
Carson-Iceberg Wilderness

Level: Strenuous	**Distance:** 13.0 miles round-trip
Best Season: June–September	**Elevation Change:** Total gain 1,000 feet

Llewellyn Falls is not an extraordinary waterfall by Sierra standards. But it's a good waterfall, and conveniently located so it's in the exact middle of a 13-mile loop trip in the Carson-Iceberg Wilderness. That's reason enough to take this long day hike or easy backpacking trip through some beautiful scenery in the Northern Sierra. Although the mileage is long, the route has only moderate ups and downs, making the trip less strenuous than you'd expect. The only downer is that grazing is still permitted in this part of the wilderness, so you may have to put up with some bovine companions along the trail.

Start your trip at the Corral Valley Trailhead near the small town of Walker on U.S. 395 (a great place to stock up on supplies). The loop can be hiked in either direction. I've described it by taking the western (right) leg first, but since the elevation change is so minimal, it really doesn't matter. From the trailhead, head southwest along the Driveway Trail, ignoring the right fork to Antelope Valley Pack Station. You'll climb steadily through fir and pine forest, soon breaking out to a more exposed landscape with spectacular views of surrounding valleys. At less than one mile out, the climb is over and you

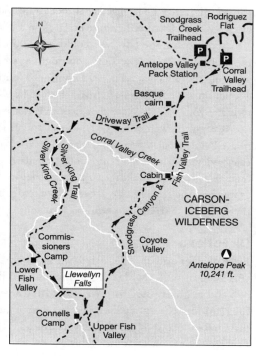

soon reach the start of the loop; I took the right fork, remaining on Driveway Trail. Immediately you pass the trail's historical highlight, an "ari mutillak," or rock pile that resembles a chimney, which was built by Basque sheepherders in the 1920s. At seven feet high, it looks something like a giant trail cairn. The rock piles served no purpose; building them simply helped to pass the time for the bored shepherds.

The trail proceeds on a generally downward trend all the way to Llewellyn Falls, passing by granite outcrops, green meadows, and forest. A ford of Silver King Creek at three miles out will require you to remove your boots; the water can be quite deep and fast, so exercise caution. On the far side, you join Silver King Trail heading south (bear left at the fork). Many campsites are found here along the stream. A second ford of trout-filled Silver King Creek closely follows the first. (Anglers, don't forget your tackle for this first leg of the trip.)

At just over six miles from the trailhead, you'll reach Commissioners Camp in Lower Fish Valley, a large camping area for packers. If you haven't seen any cows on your hike yet, this is where you'll find them. From the camp, continue another 0.5 mile to reach Llewellyn Falls. The 25-foot cascade is just off the trail by 100 yards (a sign may be in place to direct you; if not, use your ears). The waterfall curves around fractured granite bedrock in a boisterous, enthusiastic drop.

After enjoying the falls, you could return the way you came. But since this is the halfway point on the loop, you might as well continue on the other leg and see some more scenery. The trail continues south to another packer's camp and a junction with Snodgrass Canyon/Fish Valley Trail. Head northeast (left) here to make your return. Note that fishing is not permitted on this leg of the loop; upstream of Llewellyn Falls, the creeks are off-limits to protect a rare species of native Paiute trout. The second leg's landscape is more of the same lovely ilk as the first—views of close-up granite boulders, distant ridges and valleys, green meadows, and groves of quaking aspens near the streams. Take your time and soak in as much of the scenery as you can before returning to the start of the loop. From there, continue straight to head back to your car at Corral Valley in one mile.

Directions

From Walker on U.S. 395, drive two miles north on U.S. 395 to the Mill Canyon Road turnoff. (Mill Canyon Road is 7.5 miles south of the junction of U.S. 395 and Highway 89.) Turn west on Mill Canyon Road, then in 0.25 mile take the right fork. Continue six miles to a junction at Rodriguez Flat. Turn left and drive 0.5 mile to the Corral Valley Trailhead. (This last stretch is very rocky and may require a high-clearance vehicle.)

Information and Contact

There is no fee. Maps of Humboldt-Toiyabe National Forest (Carson District) or the Carson-Iceberg Wilderness are available for a fee from the National Forest Store (406/329-3024, www.nationalforeststore.com) or from the office below. For more information, contact Humboldt-Toiyabe National Forest, Carson Ranger District, 775/882-2766, www.fs.fed.us/r4/htnf.

26 SARDINE FALLS
Humboldt-Toiyabe National Forest

Level: Easy	**Distance:** 2.5 miles round-trip
Best Season: June–September	**Elevation Change:** Total gain 300 feet

You have to do some route-finding to reach Sardine Falls, but you can leave your compass at home. The falls are easily visible from the highway, and it's a one-mile

beeline walk through a high alpine meadow to reach them.

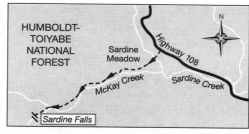

You might have to get your
feet wet, though. Any route you
take has to cross Sardine Creek,
and early in the year, it's easiest
just to take off your shoes and
wade right in.

Leave your car in one of the gravel pullouts along Sardine Meadow, 2.5 miles
east of Sonora Pass Summit on Highway 108. Because no real trail exists, it's easiest
to start walking on one of the overgrown jeep routes, most of which are marked
with the Forest Service's "No Motorized Vehicles" symbol. The shortest route is
an old jeep trail on the northwest side of the meadow that is clearly signed "Route
Closed" (to off-road vehicles, that is, not to hikers). If you look straight across the
meadow from that sign, you can see the largest cascade of Sardine Falls. From
there, it's obvious where to go—just head across the meadow and upstream.

Cross Sardine Creek, which parallels Highway 108, then start walking up the
right side of larger McKay Creek, making a more-or-less straight route for Sardine Falls. (The waterfall is actually on McKay Creek, not Sardine Creek. Go

figure.) A dirt path leads the way, lined
with yellow Sierra daisies, vibrant blue
lupines, monkeyflowers, purple wandering daisies, mariposa lilies, and mule's
ears. Dozens of small butterflies join in
the scene.

Climb uphill over a rise, then cross a
feeder stream coming in from the right.
At one mile, you first hear and then see
Sardine Falls. It drops boisterously over
a rocky cliff of about 75 feet, with a few
lodgepole pines framing the picture.
There are many good viewpoints and
picnic areas. Don't forget to pack along
the sardine sandwiches.

Directions

From Bridgeport, drive north on U.S.
395 for 17 miles to the junction of U.S.
395 and Highway 108. Turn west on

Sardine Falls

© LEON TURNBULL/WATERFALLSWEST.COM

Highway 108 and drive 12.5 miles. (You will be 2.5 miles east of Sonora Pass Summit.) Park along the road in the gravel pullouts, near the overgrown jeep roads on the northwest side of the meadow.

Information and Contact

There is no fee. Maps of Humboldt-Toiyabe National Forest (Bridgeport District) are available for a fee from the National Forest Store (406/329-3024, www.nationalforeststore.com) or from the Bridgeport Ranger Station on U.S. 395. For more information, contact Humboldt-Toiyabe National Forest, Bridgeport Ranger District, 760/932-7070, www.fs.fed.us/r4/htnf.

27 LEAVITT FALLS   BEST 🄲

Humboldt-Toiyabe National Forest

Level: Easy

Best Season: June–September

Distance: Negligible

Elevation Change: 7,000 feet

Highway 108, the Sonora Pass Road, has some of the most stunning drive-to scenery in the entire Sierra Nevada, and Leavitt Falls exemplifies it. You can't hike to the falls, because it's trapped in the back of a box canyon, but there's a great drive-to overlook that affords a stellar view.

To reach the Leavitt Falls Vista, drive 1.7 miles west of Leavitt Meadows Campground on Highway 108. The turnoff is well-signed and there is ample parking. A short walk leads you to a railed wooden overlook, which faces south; peering over its right side, you see across the canyon to Leavitt Falls. The fall cascades several hundred feet on Leavitt Creek, a tributary to the West

Leavitt Falls

Walker River. It plunges through a shadowy chasm, over and in between chiseled, rectangular boulders. Surrounded by majestic firs and junipers, Leavitt is a classic double waterfall with an upper drop, then a series of pools, followed by another, longer drop.

The Leavitt Falls Vista also provides a sweeping view of the West Walker Valley, hundreds of feet below, where the West Walker snakes its way through Leavitt Meadow and Leavitt Creek rushes to join it. Beyond the meadow are far-off views into the desert and mountains of Nevada to the east, and the snowy Sierra to the west.

The only possible downer at Leavitt Falls Vista is the wind, which can howl across Leavitt Meadow and nearly blow you off the overlook. The view can't be beaten, but if you want to stay a while to enjoy it, come dressed for a gale.

Directions

From Bridgeport, drive north on U.S. 395 for 17 miles to the junction of U.S. 395 and Highway 108. Turn west on Highway 108 and drive 8.7 miles to the signed falls vista on the left (south) side of the road. (You will be 6.3 miles east of Sonora Pass Summit and 1.7 miles west of Leavitt Meadows Campground.)

Information and Contact

There is no fee. Maps of Humboldt-Toiyabe National Forest (Bridgeport District) are available for a fee from the National Forest Store (406/329-3024, www.nationalforeststore.com) or from the Bridgeport Ranger Station on U.S. 395. For more information, contact Humboldt-Toiyabe National Forest, Bridgeport Ranger District, 760/932-7070, www.fs.fed.us/r4/htnf.

MORE WATERFALLS IN TAHOE
AND THE NORTHERN SIERRA

•**University Falls, Tahoe National Forest.** These easy-to-reach falls on Pilot Creek are popular with the locals in the Quintelle area (about 11 miles from George-town). The falls are a series of small cascades, each with a delightful swimming pool at its base—tons of fun for those who love water slides. For more informa-tion, phone the Nevada City Ranger District at 530/265-4531.

•**Scotchman Creek Falls, Tahoe National Forest.** These falls were listed in pre-vious editions of this book, but I have since omitted them because of concern by local landowners. Technically, this waterfall on a side canyon to the South Yuba River is on public land in Tahoe National Forest, but it's difficult to reach the fall without trespassing on private property. Unfortunately, trespassers were leaving tons of litter in their wake, and local landowners are sick and tired of it. For more information, phone the Nevada City Ranger District at 530/265-4531.

•**Crystal Basin Falls, Desolation Wilderness, Eldorado National Forest.** The popular Wrights Lake Campground off U.S. 50 near Tahoe is the start of several fantastic day hikes into the Desolation Wilderness. But plenty of campers never hike any farther than this one-mile jaunt to a waterfall and swimming hole just a short distance off the Twin Lakes Trail. For more information, contact the Pa-cific Ranger District at 530/644-2349.

•**Blue Canyon Falls, Emigrant Wilderness, Humboldt-Toiyabe National For-est.** Blue Canyon offers some of the most beautiful Sierra scenery on this side of Sonora Pass. Both Blue Canyon and Deadman Creek show off a series of falls that last most of the summer; some can be viewed from Highway 108 and others by following the unmaintained Blue Canyon Trail. For more information, contact the Bridgeport Ranger District at 760/932-7070.

•**Humbug Creek Falls, Malakoff Diggins State Historic Park.** An easy 1.5-mile hike along the Humbug Creek Trail will lead you to this 30-foot waterfall that can be quite impressive in the spring months. For more information, contact Malakoff Diggins State Historic Park at 530/265-2740.

SAN FRANCISCO BAY AREA

© ANN MARIE BROWN

BEST WATERFALLS

◖ **Long Backpacking Trips**
Alamere Falls, **page 192**

◖ **Bicycle**
Berry Creek Falls, **page 218**

◖ **State Parks**
Berry Creek Falls, **page 218**
Silver Falls and Golden Falls, **page 220**

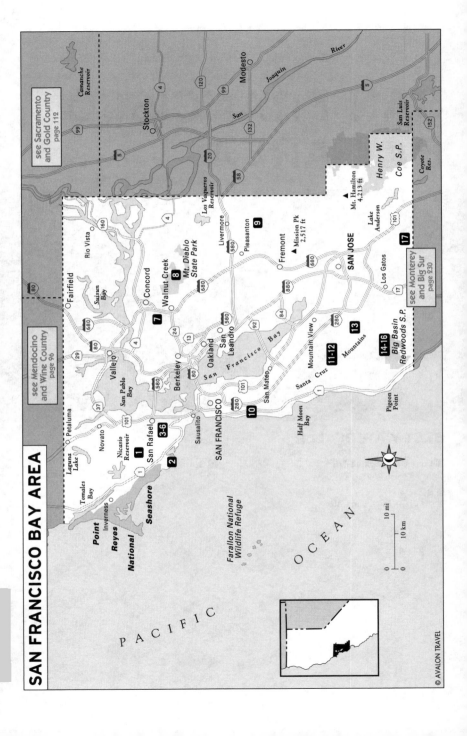

SAN FRANCISCO BAY AREA

see Mendocino and Wine Country page 96

see Sacramento and Gold Country page 112

see Monterey and Big Sur page 230

© AVALON TRAVEL

PACIFIC   OCEAN

Farallon National Wildlife Refuge

10 mi

10 km

TRAIL NAME	LEVEL	DISTANCE	ELEVATION	SEASON	FEATURES	PAGE
1 Stairstep Falls	Easy	2.5 mi rt	350 ft	Dec.-May	(icons)	190
2 Alamere Falls	Moderate	8.4-10.5 mi rt	500 ft	Dec.-May	(icons)	192
3 Carson Falls	Moderate	3.4 mi rt	500 ft	Dec.-May	(icons)	194
4 Cascade Falls	Easy/Moderate	1.6-4.8 mi rt	80 ft	Dec.-May	(icons)	197
5 Cataract Falls	Moderate	3.2 mi rt	600-800 ft	Dec.-May	(icons)	199
6 Dawn Falls	Easy	2.4 mi rt	240 ft	Dec.-May	(icons)	202
7 Abrigo Falls	Easy	2.6 mi rt	100 ft	Dec.-May	(icons)	204
8 Diablo Falls	Moderate	6.5 mi rt	900 ft	Dec.-May	(icons)	206
9 Murietta Falls	Strenuous	12.0 mi rt	3,500 ft	Jan.-Apr.	(icons)	208
10 Brooks Falls	Easy	1.6 mi rt	400 ft	Dec.-May	(icons)	211
11 Tip Toe Falls	Easy	2.0 mi rt	100 ft	Dec.-May	(icons)	213
12 Pomponio Falls	Easy	0.25 mile rt	Negligible	Dec.-May	(icons)	215
13 Castle Rock Falls	Easy	1.6 mi rt	200 ft	Dec.-May	(icons)	216
14 Berry Creek Falls	Moderate	12.0 mi rt	600 ft	Dec.-May	(icons)	218
15 Silver Falls and Golden Falls	Moderate	10.4 mi rt	1,600 ft	Dec.-May	(icons)	220
16 Sempervirens Falls	Easy	3.6 mi rt	200 ft	Dec.-May	(icons)	223
17 Uvas Canyon Falls	Easy	1.0-3.5 mi rt	700 ft	Dec.-May	(icons)	224

1 STAIRSTEP FALLS
Samuel P. Taylor State Park

Level: Easy

Best Season: December–May

Distance: 2.5 miles round-trip

Elevation Change: Total gain 350 feet

Samuel P. Taylor State Park gets somewhat overshadowed by its large and famous neighbor, Point Reyes National Seashore, but that's okay with the people who know and love the place. Even when the state park campground is filled with campers on summer weekends, you won't find too many people on Samuel P. Taylor's hiking trails. This means that Stairstep Falls has managed to

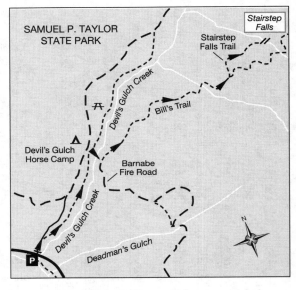

remain something of a secret in Marin County. Here you have a good chance of finding solitude at the base of a sparkling waterfall tucked into the back of a shady, fern-filled canyon.

The trailhead isn't at the main Samuel P. Taylor park entrance; rather it's a mile west on Sir Francis Drake Boulevard at Devil's Gulch Horse Camp. Park in the dirt pullout across the road from the camp, then walk up the paved camp road for about 150 yards until you see a trail leading off to the right along Devil's Gulch Creek, paralleling the road. Follow it and immediately you'll descend into a stream-fed canyon filled with Douglas firs, redwoods, oaks, bay laurels, and what must be a million ferns. In April, the ground near the stream is covered with forget-me-nots, buttercups, and milkmaids.

A few minutes of upstream walking brings you to a bridge over Devil's Gulch and an immense, hollowed-out redwood tree. It's the only redwood around, situated among many other kinds of hardwoods. Go ahead, climb inside its open trunk; a photo opportunity here is nearly impossible to resist. Then turn right and cross

© ANN MARIE BROWN

Stairstep Falls

the footbridge. Turn left on the far side of the bridge, following the sign marked "Bill's Trail to Barnabe Peak."

Climb gently above the creek, marveling at the walls of ferns and the long limbs of mossy oaks, gaining 350 feet over 0.75 mile. After crossing a bridge over a side creek, look for the Stairstep Falls Trail cutting off to the left of the main trail. It's usually signed, but sometimes not. Bear left and in 10 minutes of walking, you'll reach the trail's end near the base of Stairstep Falls.

True to its name, 40-foot-tall Stairstep Falls drops in three main cascades, with a rocky "staircase" at its base producing dozens of rivulets of water. Trail maintenance crews try to keep the area around the falls cleared of fallen trees and branches, allowing you to stand close to the cascading flow. It makes a lovely spot, perfect for quiet contemplation in the tranquil company of ferns, forest, and water.

If you want to take a longer hike, keep following Bill's Trail all the way to the summit of Barnabe Peak. A fire lookout tower on top offers a fabulous view of West Marin County and Point Reyes.

Directions

From San Francisco, cross the Golden Gate Bridge and drive north on U.S. 101 for 7.5 miles. Take the Sir Francis Drake Boulevard exit west toward San Anselmo, then drive about 15 miles (through the towns of Ross, Fairfax, and Lagunitas) to the signed entrance to Samuel P. Taylor State Park's campground. Don't turn here; continue on Sir Francis Drake for exactly one more mile. Park in the dirt pullout across the road from Devil's Gulch Horse Camp. Walk across the road and take the paved road to the campground, then cut off on the trail that parallels its right side.

Information and Contact

There is no fee if you park along Sir Francis Drake Boulevard in the roadside pullout across from Devil's Gulch Horse Camp. A park map is available at the entrance kiosk at the main campground, or by free download at www.parks. ca.gov. Wilderness Press (www.wildernesspress.com) publishes a more detailed map of the park and surrounding areas, Point Reyes, and West Marin Parklands. For more information, contact Samuel P. Taylor State Park, 415/488-9897, www. parks.ca.gov.

2 ALAMERE FALLS BEST (

Point Reyes National Seashore

Level: Moderate   **Distance:** 8.4-10.5 miles round-trip

Best Season: December-May   **Elevation Change:** Total gain 500 feet

Alamere Falls

Quick—which California waterfall leaps off high coastal bluffs and cascades gracefully down to the sand and surf below? Most people think of famous McWay Falls at Julia Pfeiffer Burns State Park in Big Sur, one of the most frequently visited and photographed waterfalls in the state. But don't forget the other coastal cataract that makes the same dramatic plunge from earth to sea, 150 miles up the coast in western Marin County. That would be Alamere Falls in Point Reyes National Seashore, which is less celebrated but no less dramatic than McWay Falls.

There may be no finer way to spend an April day than walking to Alamere Falls. If you time your trip for a clear day on the coast, when the lupine and Douglas iris are in full bloom and the waterfall is running hard, the trailside beauty will knock your socks off.

Start hiking on Coast Trail from the Palomarin Trailhead in Point Reyes, the southernmost trailhead in the national seashore. Despite its off-the-beaten-track location outside the town of Bolinas, the trailhead parking area is often full of cars. The occupants of those cars are usually hiking the entire 15-mile Coast

Trail, a spectacular backpacking trip. You'll follow the southern section of that route, where the Coast Trail is a wide dirt road beginning in stands of eucalyptus.

The first mile offers many excellent ocean views, then Coast Trail turns inland, climbing slightly to a junction with Lake Ranch Trail at two miles. Stay on the Coast Trail as it veers left, passing a couple of seasonal ponds that are usually covered with paddling water birds, then skirt the north edge of Bass Lake. Picnic and rest spots abound here; just follow the spur trail amid the Douglas firs. Bass Lake is a popular spot for swimming in the warm spring and summer months.

Reach another trail junction where Crystal Lake Trail heads right to Crystal Lake and tiny Mud Lake, but continue straight on the Coast Trail, now heading toward the ocean. Prepare yourself for a stunning view of Pelican Lake, which sits smack on a coastal bluff.

Here you must make a choice. If you are comfortable with off-trail scrambling on these rather unstable coastal bluffs, you can head downstream, then cross the stream where it is safe so that you wind up on the north side of Alamere Creek. At the edge of the bluffs and alongside the falls' lip, you'll find a well-worn route leading down to the beach. A rope is sometimes tied in place to help hikers over the most vertical spots. Still, be extremely wary of the loose sandstone and shale. Although park rangers try to discourage visitors from following this unofficial route to the base of Alamere Falls and the beach, on any spring weekend you'll find dozens of people doing so. If you are at all unsure of your abilities, or if you have children with you, it's a much better idea to stay on top of the falls.

At the beach, the full drama of Alamere Falls can be seen. Although the pristine coastline would be stunning even without the waterfall, it's made even more impressive by the sight of Alamere Creek dropping in a wide, effusive block over the cliff, then running across the sand and into the sea. The fall is 50 feet high, and although its width varies greatly according to how much water is flowing through the creek, it's always breathtaking.

Whereas day hikers will spend some time on this magical beach and then return to Palomarin Trailhead, backpackers can continue one mile northwest on Coast Trail, passing Ocean Lake and Wildcat Lake, to Wildcat Camp. Wildcat Beach is just a few steps away, and a network of trails leads north, east, and south from the camp. In fact, for backpackers the best approach to the base of Alamere Falls is to hike straight out to Wildcat Camp, drop your packs there, descend to Wildcat Beach, then hike south along the sand to see Alamere.

Directions

From San Francisco, cross the Golden Gate Bridge and drive north on U.S. 101 for 7.5 miles. Take the Sir Francis Drake Boulevard exit west toward San Anselmo and drive 20 miles to the town of Olema at Highway 1. Turn left (south) on Highway 1 and drive 8.9 miles to Bolinas Road, which is usually not signed (it's across from a white ranch house). Turn right and drive 2.1 miles to Mesa Road. Turn right and drive 5.8 miles to the Palomarin Trailhead.

Information and Contact

There is no fee. Backpackers spending the night at Wildcat Camp must have reservations and a backcountry camping permit. A park map is available at the Bear Valley Visitor Center on Bear Valley Road, or by free download at www.nps.gov/pore. A more detailed Point Reyes map is available from Tom Harrison Maps, 415/456-7940, www.tomharrisonmaps.com. For more information, contact Point Reyes National Seashore, 415/464-5100, www.nps.gov/pore.

3 CARSON FALLS
Marin Municipal Water District

Level: Moderate   **Distance:** 3.4 miles round-trip

Best Season: December-May   **Elevation Change:** Total gain/loss 500 feet

When flowing with vigor, Carson Falls appears like a miracle. Draining a large and steep canyon, Little Carson Creek drops 150 feet in four tiers, creating a series of rushing cascades that culminate in a 40-foot free-fall drop over rugged greenstone basalt. In the dry season, the fall is only a trickle, but its craggy cliff, which holds a series of basins and pools, remains a fascinating sight to behold.

Located in Marin Municipal Water District lands a few miles outside the town of Fairfax, Carson Falls is just far enough off the beaten path that it gets

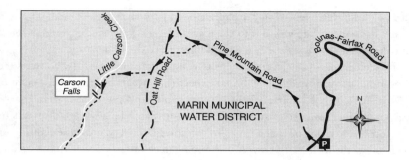

somewhat less traffic than other waterfalls in Marin County. However, since new trail signs and a reconstructed trail section were added in 2009, the waterfall is seeing a lot more visitors than it used to (and it's easier to find, too).

The trailhead is located along Bolinas-Fairfax Road at 1,078 feet in elevation. From the gravel parking area, cross Bolinas-Fairfax Road and pick up Pine Mountain Fire Road at the large Marin Municipal Water District signboard. Climb uphill for one mile, gaining slightly more than 300 feet in elevation. As you ascend, be sure to pause and look over your right shoulder to take in the sweeping view of Mount Diablo, San Pablo Bay, Marin County, the East Bay, and even the Richmond Bridge. The climb will get your heart pumping, but the views are more than fair compensation for your efforts.

Carson Falls

Keep your eyes and ears attuned for mountain bicyclists on this fire road. They sometimes come flying downhill at breakneck speed, most often after experiencing the agony and ecstasy of climbing nearby Pine Mountain.

After a mile of climbing, you reach a high point on the ridge and a junction. Look due north for a surprising view of Mount St. Helena in Napa, 45 miles distant, then turn left on Oat Hill Road, also a fire road. In only 0.25 mile, you'll see a sign for the Carson Falls turnoff on your right. Here you'll leave the fire roads behind and walk on the gorgeous new stretch of single-track that was built in 2007 and 2008, replacing the badly eroded path that once existed. The trail switchbacks gently downhill into the Carson Creek watershed through a forest of oaks and madrones. A bevy of sword ferns grace the understory.

This pleasant, shady stretch deposits you on a narrow, artfully constructed footbridge above Carson Falls. Don't expect that usual thunderous moment of "Wow! A waterfall!" Carson Falls is more subtle and mysterious than that—especially since you arrive at its crest, not at its base. This waterfall reveals its pleasures slowly, one pool at a time. To see it in its entirety, cross the footbridge, then follow the rocky path downhill, dropping in elevation along with the stream. Use caution heading down the steep footpath, especially when the rocks are wet from rain. Carson Falls' green-grey rock may look like serpentine, but it's actually greenstone basalt.

The pools of Carson Falls are home to threatened amphibians, including the foothill yellow-legged frog, which has been listed as a federal and state species of special concern. The frogs have disappeared from nearly 50 percent of their historic range in California and Oregon. Here in the Mount Tam watershed, only two populations exist, including this one at Carson Falls. To help protect these creatures, keep yourself and your canine companion out of the water, especially during the peak waterfall season of March–June, when the frog eggs and tadpoles are most vulnerable.

The trail continues downhill beyond Carson Falls' final drop, but for most people, the waterfall is the destination. Select any convenient rock near one of its pools, have a seat, and listen to the water music for a while. Even in summer, when Carson Falls is reduced to a mere trickle, a visit here feels restorative, like resting in a Zen garden with the sound of the wind and the tinkling of water as your only companions. But then, with the first multiday winter rain, Carson Falls roars. For visitors who are accustomed to the fall's placid summertime state, the effect is stunning.

Directions

From San Francisco, cross the Golden Gate Bridge and drive north on U.S. 101 for 7.5 miles. Take the Sir Francis Drake Boulevard exit west toward San Anselmo, then drive six miles to the town of Fairfax. Turn left by the "Fairfax" sign (on Pacheco Road), then turn right immediately on Broadway. In one block, turn left on Bolinas Road (also signed as Bolinas-Fairfax Road). Drive 3.8 miles on Bolinas Road, past the golf course, to the trailhead parking on the left side of the road. Park and walk across the road to the trailhead.

Information and Contact

There is no fee. Maps are available by free download from www.marinwater.org.

A more detailed map is available from Tom Harrison Maps, 415/456-7940, www.
tomharrisonmaps.com (ask for the *Pine Mountain* map). For more information,
contact Sky Oaks Ranger Station at 415/945-1181 or Marin Municipal Water
District, 415/945-1438, www.marinwater.org.

4 CASCADE FALLS
Marin County Open Space District

Level: Easy/Moderate

Distance: 1.6 miles round-trip (Lower Falls)
or 4.8 miles round-trip (Upper Falls)

Best Season: December–May

Elevation Change: Total gain 80 feet

Quiz question: Name three waterfalls located
on or nearby Mount Tamalpais, all within six
miles of each other, all with names that begin
with the letter C.

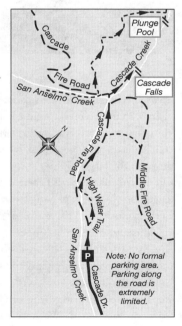

Answer: Cataract Falls on the back side of
Mount Tamalpais (see next listing in this chap-
ter), Carson Falls in Marin Municipal Water
District (see previous listing in this chapter),
and Cascade Falls in Marin County Open Space
District.

Too easy? Okay, now describe which is which.
Carson Falls? Isn't that the one with the trail
that starts at Alpine Dam and climbs the whole
way? Nope, that's Cataract. Cataract Falls? Isn't
that the one that falls in a long chain of pool-
and-drop stairsteps into rocky pools? No, that's
Carson. Cascade Falls? Isn't that the one that's
just outside the Fairfax suburbs? Well, you got
one right.

Of the three neighboring waterfalls, Cascade
Falls is by far the easiest to reach. While Cataract and Carson require some up-
and-down hiking, Cascade Falls is reachable by a nearly level two-mile round-
trip. It's a perfect waterfall to take small children to, or a great place to go for a
walk after work.

Because the trail begins at the end of a house-lined street, be careful where

Cascade Falls

you park your car so you're not blocking driveways or infringing on private property. Start walking on the gated fire road, then veer off it onto single-track. The trail stays close to San Anselmo Creek, which can look rather unpromising, even stagnant, at this end of the preserve. But don't be fooled. In periods of heavy rain, San Anselmo Creek can run like a river, as much as 30 feet wide and dark brown from sediment pouring off the hillsides. But this is a rare occurrence; usually the creek is tranquil.

Keep the creek on your left for the first 0.5 mile. Then cross a wooden footbridge and veer to the right. The trail leads you into a lovely oak and laurel forest, and as you travel, the anticipation builds. Quickly, the stream's flow picks up as you make your way upstream.

In 0.25 mile, you'll round a bend and hear the sound of falling water, then get your first look at Cascade Falls, tumbling 18 feet down a rough rock face. The trail leads up and over its lip, where you'll find many rock seats. Or you can drop down to the large boulder at the fall's base, a favored spot for waterfall-watching. On my first of many visits here, I was surprised to find two musicians sitting cross-legged on this rock, playing a duet on the violin and guitar. I stayed and listened to their music, and the music of the falls, for an hour or more.

Those who desire a longer hike and a greater chance at solitude can continue on for another 1.7 miles to see Upper Cascade Falls. Although a rough footpath travels along Cascade Creek to the upper falls, it is extremely steep in places and overgrown with poison oak. A better option is to retrace your steps to the footbridge you crossed on the way in, then turn right (west) on Cascade Fire Road. Walk 100 yards, then turn right on a single-track trail signed as "No bikes." (It's shortly beyond another single-track trail on the left.) This narrow path leads steadily up a wooded ridge, then drops down the other side to rejoin Cascade Creek. Where the trail forks, turn right and walk about 100 feet, then cross the creek. You'll come out at the brink of a beautiful two-tiered waterfall called the Plunge, the Ink Well, or just plain Upper Cascade Falls.

Directions

From San Francisco, cross the Golden Gate Bridge and drive north on U.S. 101 for 7.5 miles. Take the Sir Francis Drake Boulevard exit west toward San Anselmo, then drive six miles to the town of Fairfax. Turn left by the "Fairfax" sign (on Pacheco Road), then turn right immediately on Broadway. In one block, turn left on Bolinas Road. Follow Bolinas Road for 0.3 mile to a three-road intersection. Bear right on Cascade Drive (the middle road) and continue 1.5 miles. The road becomes very narrow and ends at Elliott Nature Preserve. Parking is extremely limited. Park alongside the road (be careful to avoid blocking driveways and obey the "No parking" signs in the last 100 feet before the trailhead). Begin hiking at the gate.

Information and Contact

There is no fee. Maps are available by free download at www.marinopenspace.org, or can be purchased from Tom Harrison Maps, 415/456-7940, www.tomharrisonmaps.com (ask for the *Pine Mountain* map). For more information, contact the Marin County Open Space District, 415/499-6387, www.marinopenspace.org.

5 CATARACT FALLS
Marin Municipal Water District

Level: Moderate

Best Season: December–May

Distance: 3.2 miles round-trip

Elevation Change: Total gain/loss 600–800 feet

Before you set out for Cataract Falls, you must do two things. First, check your calendar, because the falls only run in the wet half of the year. Second, decide whether you prefer to hike up and then down, or down and then up. Two separate trailheads access Cataract Falls, one from Alpine Lake leading uphill to the falls; the other from Mount Tamalpais leading downhill to the falls. The latter is a somewhat easier route, with less of a steep grade, as long as you don't travel the entire length of the trail.

Both routes are gorgeous, so take your pick. The trailhead at Alpine Lake requires a winding drive on Bolinas Road to reach, but it's more convenient if you're in northern Marin. The trailhead on Mount Tamalpais also requires a winding drive, but it's easier to reach if you're coming from San Francisco or southern Marin.

If you start hiking from the Alpine Lake Trailhead, you're treated to lake views

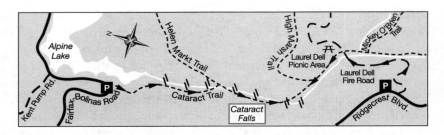

for the first 0.25 mile of trail, then dense redwood forest as you head steeply up-hill, often following rock stairsteps. You can hike as much or as little as you like, because Cataract Falls is a series of cascades that are spread out over 1.6 miles of the Cataract Trail. As soon as the trail leaves the lake and starts to climb, you start seeing waterfalls. Half a dozen of them cascade in the first 0.75 mile, from the edge of the lake to a signed turnoff for the Helen Markt Trail, just after a narrow footbridge where the trail crosses to the east side of Cataract Creek.

Most of the cascades are between 20 and 30 feet high, but their shapes and ap-pearances are all completely different. The common element they share, besides the life-giving flow of Cataract Creek, is that each one is completely surrounded by ferns. After a good rain, this hike is truly breathtaking, with the continual sound and sight of waterfalls providing nonstop excitement through every curve of the trail.

If you choose to hike from the trailhead on West Ridgecrest Boulevard, north-west of the big parking area at Rock Springs, you descend on a fire road to a clear-ing by Laurel Dell, 0.75 mile away. Cataract Creek often floods across this road in winter and spring, making your crossing a bit tricky. In summer, the route is dry, but of course, that means no waterfalls.

After rock-hopping across the creek, head to your left into Laurel Dell, a grassy flat. Walk through it, pick up the Cataract Trail at its far end, then begin a steep descent through redwoods and Douglas firs. Watch for an intersection with the High Marsh Trail on the right; continue straight and shortly you'll be at the up-permost cascade of Cataract Falls. The Cataract Trail curves in tightly, bringing you right by the stream, and you'll see the water tumbling over car-sized boulders as it rushes downhill. Pick a rock and watch the show.

From this upper waterfall, the magic continues as you head downhill, passing one cascade after another for another full mile of waterfall-watching. Just re-member that if you're hiking in this direction, your elevation loss will need to be regained on the return trip. The trail's slope gets steeper the farther you go; the last 0.75 mile before Bolinas Road are mostly rock stairsteps. At any point, you can cut your trip short and save yourself some of the climb back.

Directions

For the Bolinas Road Trailhead from San Francisco, cross the Golden Gate Bridge and drive north on U.S. 101 for 7.5 miles. Take the Sir Francis Drake Boulevard exit west toward San Anselmo, then drive six miles to the town of Fairfax. Turn left by the "Fairfax" sign (on Pacheco Road), then turn right immediately on Broadway. Drive one block and turn left on Bolinas Road. Drive 7.8 miles on Bolinas Road to the dam at Alpine Lake. Cross the dam and continue 100 yards farther to the hairpin turn in the road. Park in the pullouts along the turn; the trailhead is on the left.

Cataract Falls

For the West Ridgecrest Road Trailhead from San Francisco, cross the Golden Gate Bridge and drive north on U.S. 101 for four miles. Take the Mill Valley/Stinson Beach/Highway 1 exit and continue straight for one mile to a stoplight at Shoreline Highway (Highway 1). Turn left on Shoreline Highway and drive 2.5 miles, then turn right on Panoramic Highway. Drive 0.9 mile to a four-way intersection. Take the middle road (straight), continuing on Panoramic Highway for 4.3 more miles to Pantoll Road. Turn right on Pantoll Road and drive 1.4 miles to its intersection with Ridgecrest Boulevard. Turn left and drive 1.6 miles to a small parking area on the right. Park there and take the trail marked "Laurel Dell."

Information and Contact

There is no fee. Maps are available by free download from www.marinwater.org. A more detailed map is available from Tom Harrison Maps, 415/456-7940, www. tomharrisonmaps.com (ask for the *Mount Tamalpais* map). For more information, contact Sky Oaks Ranger Station at 415/945-1181 or Marin Municipal Water District, 415/945-1438, www.marinwater.org.

6 DAWN FALLS

Marin County Open Space District

Level: Easy

Best Season: December–May

Distance: 2.4 miles round-trip

Elevation Change: Total gain 240 feet

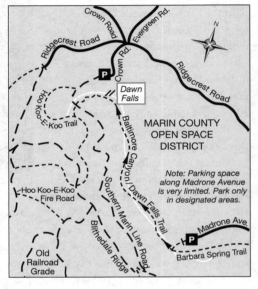

Dawn Falls is set in Baltimore Canyon, a deep green redwood- and fern-lined glen just outside of the tony neighborhood of Larkspur in Marin County. Only a short distance from Larkspur's collection of hip restaurants and shops du jour is this peaceful nature preserve, where the suburban world becomes a vague, distant memory.

From the end of Madrone Avenue, cross Larkspur Creek on a wooden footbridge and then turn right to head to the falls. Walking upstream, you head deeper into the canyon, a gorgeous basin filled with redwoods. Ignore the many spur trails and stay along the creek. The main trail winds its way through the dark and damp forest, which is best seen when the trees are dripping with moisture after a winter storm or dense fog. Don't hesitate to make this trip if it's raining or misting—that just makes the hike more beautiful.

The trail climbs slowly and gently. As it does, the forest changes to somewhat drier terrain, including oak and laurel trees. Dawn Falls is set among these mixed hardwoods, and because the trees are not as dense as the redwoods, you can easily spot the waterfall from the trail. The single-track leads to the top of the falls, which cascades 30 feet over a sheer rock ledge and is beautifully framed by a garden of ferns. The stream above the waterfall is almost as scenic as the fall itself, nourished by a little feeder creek coming in from the side.

Larkspur Creek often dries up by late summer, and the waterfall loses much of its appeal by late spring. For the best experience, visit Dawn Falls in winter or early spring. And because this canyon is so close to the Marin County suburbs, try to hike here early in the morning or during the week, when fewer people are likely to visit. This trail is especially popular with runners on weekends.

Your dog can accompany you on the stroll to Dawn Falls. Like nearby Cascade Falls in Fairfax, the land around Dawn Falls is managed by the Marin County Open Space District, so leashed dogs are permitted. On my trip, almost everyone on the trail had either a puppy or a child with them, and they seemed to be having an excellent time.

An even shorter route to Dawn Falls begins at the end of Crown Road in Kentfield. From the start of the gated fire road (Northridge Trailhead), it's only 0.25 mile to the Dawn Falls Trail cutoff on the left.

Dawn Falls

© ANN MARIE BROWN

Directions

From San Francisco, cross the Golden Gate Bridge and drive north on U.S. 101 for six miles. Take the Tamalpais Drive exit, then head west to Corte Madera Avenue. Turn right and drive 0.5 mile, then turn left on Madrone Avenue. Stay left at the fork and follow Madrone Avenue to its end, where it intersects with Valley Way. The trailhead is on the left side of the road. There is parking for about six cars. More parking is available farther along Madrone Avenue. Obey the "No parking" signs.

Information and Contact

There is no fee. Maps are available by free download at www.marinopenspace. org, or can be purchased from Tom Harrison Maps, 415/456-7940, www.tomharrisonmaps.com. For more information, contact the Marin County Open Space District, 415/499-6387, www.marinopenspace.org.

7 ABRIGO FALLS

Briones Regional Park

Level: Easy

Distance: 2.6 miles round-trip

Best Season: December–May

Elevation Change: Total gain 100 feet

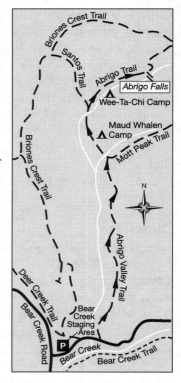

Waterfall-watchers who live in the East San Francisco Bay Area watch the skies carefully, keep their day packs packed, and make sure there's always gas in the car. That way, when conditions are just right, they can head out to see Abrigo Falls. Because water is not exactly plentiful in the East Bay, any waterfall is a big deal, even this thin-streamed cascade on Abrigo Creek in Briones Regional Park.

If you've ever hiked in Briones's vast acres of arid grasslands and oaks, especially in the hot summer months, you might wonder if Abrigo Falls really exists. But like many places in the San Francisco Bay Area, Briones comes to life with winter rain, and tiny Abrigo Creek starts to run, feeding larger Bear Creek. Although the waterfall is not large—it drops only 15 feet over a rock face—it's set in a cavelike canyon, creating an unusual, almost prehistoric-looking setting. With a little imagination, you might expect a brontosaurus to show up and start munching on the oak and bay leaves.

The big downer at Abrigo is that the waterfall is hard to see; the trail leads above and alongside the fall, not to its base. The creek and falls are set in a deep and narrow canyon, so it's hard to get a good perspective on the drop, even in the rare times when the waterfall is flowing hard.

The hike to Abrigo Falls is most pleasant in late winter and spring, preferably the day following a good rain. It's an easy route for families, with the creek meandering pleasantly alongside. Because the trail is really a ranch road, it can be heavily pocketed and eroded from cow traffic, making hiking boots necessary. In April and May, wildflowers bloom in the meadows.

Start hiking at the Abrigo Valley Trailhead, just past the kiosk at Briones's

Bear Creek entrance, walking an easy 1.3 miles up the dirt road. Mountain bikes, horses, and dogs are allowed on the route. Pass two group camping areas after the first mile, Maud Walen and Wee-ta-chi, and you'll find the waterfall shortly past the latter. The fall is located at the point where the road makes a short, steep climb, the first noticeable ascent along the route. (If the road makes a hairpin turn to the left and moves away from the creek, you've gone too far.) From the trail, you can see two small streams of water pouring over an exposed rock face, surrounded by ferns on the canyon walls.

Abrigo Falls

If you've come this far and want to keep walking, continue another 0.25 mile to where the Abrigo Valley Trail meets up with the Briones Crest Trail. Turn right and hike for 0.5 mile along Briones Crest for stellar views of Mount Diablo, Suisun Bay, San Pablo Bay, and Point Pinole. Then retrace your steps or loop back to Abrigo Valley on the Mott Peak Trail.

Directions

From I-580 in Oakland, take Highway 24 east. Go through the Caldecott Tunnel and continue another 1.5 miles. Take the Orinda exit, then turn left on Camino Pablo and drive north for two miles. Turn right on Bear Creek Road and drive 4.4 miles, then turn right into the Briones Regional Park/Bear Creek Staging Area entrance. Turn left just past the kiosk and park in the lower parking lot. Start hiking on the Abrigo Valley Trail.

Information and Contact

A $3 day-use fee is charged per vehicle. A free trail map is available at the entrance kiosk or by download at www.ebparks.org. For more information, contact East Bay Regional Park District, 888/327-2757, www.ebparks.org.

8 DIABLO FALLS
Mount Diablo State Park

Level: Moderate   **Distance:** 6.5 miles round-trip

Best Season: December–May   **Elevation Change:** Total gain 900 feet

Waterfalls? On Mount Diablo? It seems pretty unlikely, I know. But a trip to Clayton in the rainy season and a hike along the back side of the 3,849-foot mountain reveals half a dozen cascades, each about 30 feet tall. Scattered along the hillsides on two forks of Donner Creek, the falls drop in a canyon that is notoriously dry, steep, and hot as Hades most of the year. But pick the right day, soon after a good winter rain, and it's water, water everywhere. And it's cool and comfortable to boot.

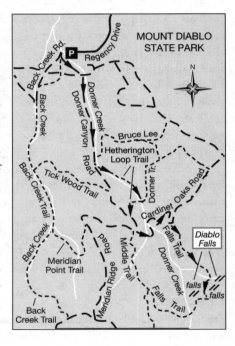

The closest trailhead to Diablo Falls, which is also known as Donner Creek Falls, is at the end of Regency Drive, a suburban neighborhood in Clayton. It's an unlikely start for an unlikely hike. Where the road ends, walk to your left along a gated dirt road, one of three possible trails, signed as "Donner Canyon Road to Cardinet Oaks Road." Right away, you hike along Donner Creek, so you can gauge how good the falls will be by how much water is flowing.

Keep walking upstream, and in 0.6 mile take the single-track route signed as "Trail to Donner Cabin Site." You'll stay along the creek and pass the remains of the Donner Cabin (a stone foundation and an old bathtub). Cross Donner Creek and reach a junction with Hetherington Loop Trail, which eventually leads back to Donner Canyon Road. Although you can stay on Donner Canyon Road for the whole distance, it's a steep and tedious climb. Hetherington Loop Trail, in contrast, is a longer, meandering route along Donner Creek, which adds only 0.5 mile and much enjoyment to your trip.

© ANN MARIE BROWN

Diablo Falls

Where Hetherington Loop Trail and Donner Canyon Road meet up again, continue to the left and uphill on the dirt road to Cardinet Junction, where Donner Canyon Road and Cardinet Oaks Road join. Bear left, then shortly thereafter cross the creek (if you're in luck, it will be widely flooding the road, an indicator of good waterfalls ahead). Then prepare to gain about 500 feet in elevation in five tight switchbacks on the dirt road. With these completed, you'll see the signed turnoff on the right for Falls Trail. You'll also gain some wide-reaching views of Clayton and far-off Suisun Bay.

Falls Trail is a pleasant, single-track path that laterals along the left side of the steep canyon. In moments, you spot waterfalls coming into view. The first, across the canyon on your right, is a 20-foot cascade. Then, moments later, you see another 20-footer straight ahead. Keep walking and you spot two more, including one perfect free fall about 30 feet high. The trail remains about 100 yards distant from the falls, so you won't get to admire them up close. But you do get the extraordinary experience of seeing as many as five waterfalls at once, in a very small area. (If you choose to scramble off-trail to get a closer look at any of the falls, be very careful. This canyon is remarkably steep.)

Note the occasional foothill pines along Falls Trail; their cones are extremely dense and can weigh up to four pounds. Among the eroding rock formations, you'll find scattered juniper trees bearing bright blue winter berries.

Falls Trail leads you right across the two forks of Donner Creek, the source of the falls, then loops back to Cardinet Junction. You can walk the entire loop if you wish, or just turn back and retrace your steps. An even longer loop (seven miles round-trip) is possible by taking Falls Trail to Middle Trail, Meridian Ridge Road, and Meridian Point Trail, then hiking into Back Canyon. The Back Creek Trail will return you to your starting point at the Regency Drive Trailhead.

Directions

From I-680 heading north in Walnut Creek, take the Ygnacio Valley Road exit.

Drive east on Ygnacio Valley Road for 7.5 miles to Clayton Road. Turn right on Clayton Road and drive 2.9 miles (it becomes Marsh Creek Road, but don't turn right at the sign for Marsh Creek Road) to Regency Drive. Turn right and drive 0.5 mile to the end of the road and the trailhead.

Or, from I-680 heading south in Walnut Creek, take the Treat Boulevard exit and go east. In one mile, turn right on Bancroft Road. In another mile, turn left on Ygnacio Valley Road and drive five miles to Clayton Road. Continue as above.

Information and Contact

There is no fee at the Regency Drive Trailhead. A park map is available by free download at www.parks.ca.gov. A more detailed map is available for $7.50 at www.mdia.org. For more information, contact Mount Diablo State Park, 925/837-2525 or 925/837-0904, www.mdia.org or www.parks.ca.gov.

9 MURIETTA FALLS
Ohlone Regional Wilderness

Level: Strenuous   **Distance:** 12.0 miles round-trip

Best Season: January–April   **Elevation Change:** Total gain/loss 3,500 feet

Everybody loves a waterfall, but do you love waterfalls enough to be willing to grunt out a 3,500-foot elevation change? Think it over. If your answer is yes, you're heading for a fine adventure in Ohlone Regional Wilderness, culminating in a visit to 100-foot Murietta Falls.

If your answer is "not sure," the first half-hour on this trail will be challenging enough to make up your mind, one way or the other.

Ohlone Regional Wilderness is one of the Bay Area's special places. No public roads lead through it or even near it. You have to hike to reach its boundary, starting either from Sunol Regional Wilderness to the west or Del Valle Regional

Murietta Falls

Park to the north. To be more specific, you have to hike uphill.

In the same vein, Murietta Falls is one of the Bay Area's most special waterfalls. That's partly because it's much taller than other area falls and partly because it's hard enough to reach that most people never make the trip. The difficulty doesn't just lie in the trail's many steep ups and downs, its sunny exposure, and its 12-mile-long round-trip distance. The real difficulty is that the waterfall has an extremely short season and must be seen immediately following a period of rain. More than a few hikers have made the long trip to Murietta and then been disappointed to find only a trickle of water. March is often the best month to see the fall flowing, but it depends on the current year's rain pattern. Depending on when the rains come, Murietta's top flow could happen anywhere from January to April. Keep your eyes on the skies.

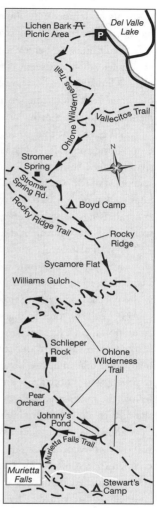

One thing to remember: this trail is absolutely not suitable for a warm or hot day. It offers very little shade and a ton of climbing.

A single element makes the trip easy. The trail is remarkably well-signed. Just pay attention at all junctions and keep following the red markers for Ohlone Wilderness Trail in the first five miles. Also, you must purchase a wilderness permit in order to hike on the Ohlone Wilderness Trail. With your permit, you get a free map, which comes in quite handy.

The trail starts by climbing and stays that way for 2.4 miles. (Don't forget to stop and sign in at the wilderness register one mile in.) The wide dirt road levels off in only a few brief stretches. Otherwise, it's up, up, up all the way to the top of Rocky Ridge, a 1,670-foot gain from the trailhead. Then all of a sudden, you start an incredibly steep descent—steep enough so that you'll wish you'd brought your trekking poles. You drop 530 feet in about 0.5 mile. The good news is that you're heading for water; you can hear its welcoming sound. The wide fire road narrows to single-track for the first time all day as you descend into the beautiful stream canyon of Williams Gulch. The sound of the cascading creek is so refreshing and inviting that you may suddenly remember why you are doing this hike after all. The half-mile stretch of path that cuts through the stream canyon is pure, refreshing pleasure.

You might as well enjoy it, because next you're going to climb out of the canyon in a 1,200-foot ascent. The single-track trail is surprisingly well-graded with some good switchbacks, however, so this climb isn't nearly as bad as some of the dirt road stretches. The path is fairly well-shaded. Prolific miner's lettuce and pink shooting stars grow alongside it.

You'll get a hint that you're nearing the falls when you start to notice rock outcrops along the trail. For the first four miles, you see mostly grasslands and massive oak trees, some with diameters that rival the size of giant redwoods. (The only exception to the oak savannah terrain is in riparian Williams Gulch.) But suddenly large rock outcrops start to pop up out of nowhere. One of these, on the left side of the trail, is signed as Schlieper Rock—named for Fred Schlieper, a silversmith who worked his trade in the mid-20th century. His ashes are scattered at the rock.

The trail also levels out substantially as you near the falls. At this 3,000-foot elevation, you'll gain some wonderful views to the north and west. (On my trip, I was amazed to see snow on the high ridges around us, and even a few lingering white patches right along the trail.)

At 0.7 mile beyond Schlieper Rock, you'll reach Johnny's Pond. Just beyond the small pond, turn right at the sign for Murietta Falls (signpost 35). Hike 0.25 mile farther, then turn left and start paying close attention to your surroundings. In just under 0.5 mile, you'll reach a hairpin turn in the road. If you've timed your trip well, you'll note a few streams of water crossing the road. Leave the trail and follow the main stream downhill to your right; it will deliver you to the brink of the falls in a few hundred feet.

A good use trail makes a steep descent to the base of the falls. Follow it carefully—you've come this far, you might as well get the full effect. The waterfall's cliff, an incredible rocky precipice with a 100-foot drop, is composed of greenstone basalt. At its base is a wide, round, shallow pool. Many good picnicking spots are found nearby. If you made it this far, you deserve to eat well. Pull out that turkey and avocado sandwich.

Birdwatchers, take note: the trailside oak savannah is home to many resident and migratory birds. I counted more western bluebirds on this walk than I had seen in my entire life previously. Bald eagles, too, are often seen commanding the skies above this trail.

Directions
From I-580 in Livermore, take the North Livermore Avenue exit and turn right (south). Drive south through the town of Livermore for 3.5 miles (North Livermore

Avenue becomes Tesla Road) and turn right on Mines Road. Drive 3.5 miles on Mines Road to its junction with Del Valle Road. Continue straight at the fork, now on Del Valle Road. Drive 3.2 miles to the entrance kiosk at Del Valle Regional Park. Purchase a wilderness permit at the entrance kiosk, then continue 0.75 mile to the dam and cross it. Turn right and drive 0.5 mile to the Lichen Bark Picnic Area. Take the signed Ohlone Trail.

Information and Contact

A $6 day-use fee is charged per vehicle. Hikers on the Ohlone Wilderness Trail must purchase a $2 wilderness permit, which includes a detailed trail map. (You may purchase a permit on the day of your hike at the park entrance station.) Maps are also available by download at www.ebparks.org. For more information, contact East Bay Regional Park District, 510/544-3246 or 888/327-2757, www.ebparks.org.

10 BROOKS FALLS
San Pedro Valley County Park

Level: Easy

Best Season: December–May

Distance: 1.6 miles round-trip

Elevation Change: Total gain 400 feet

If you live or work in San Francisco or on the San Mateo coast, Brooks Falls is the closest waterfall you can reach. It's a mere five-minute drive off Highway 1 in Pacifica, and less than 30 minutes from downtown San Francisco. You could leave your office job, drive to San Pedro Valley County Park, hike to the waterfall, and be back in your cubicle before anyone's suspicions get aroused. Just be careful not to leave your muddy shoes under your desk.

But keep in mind that if you prefer your waterfalls up close and personal, you're not going to feel satisfied at Brooks Falls. You'll have many chances along

Brooks Falls

© ANDREW SAWADISAVI

the trail to see and hear the waterfall, but you're always several hundred yards from the cascading stream. No matter how much it rains, Brooks Falls never appears as anything but a delicate silver strand pouring down a lush, foliage-congested canyon because you just can't get close enough to see more.

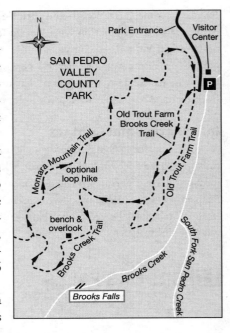

The hike around the Brooks Creek canyon is excellent, though, and it can be made into an easy 2.5-mile loop trip that provides numerous views of the waterfall and also of the wide blue Pacific Ocean. Or, if you're short on time, an out-and-back trip to a bench overlooking Brooks Falls requires only 1.6 miles of hiking.

Locate the trailhead for the Montara Mountain Trail alongside the restrooms in San Pedro Valley County Park. A few feet past the trailhead, the trail splits: Montara Mountain Trail heads right and Old Trout Farm Trail heads left. Go left and gently uphill through a dense eucalyptus grove. At trail junctions, small signs direct you "to Waterfall Viewing Area." Bear right at two forks, now following Brooks Creek Trail, and keep heading uphill. The path soon emerges from the trees to open views of the canyon amid coastal sage scrub, ceanothus, and monkeyflower.

Twenty minutes of well-graded climbing delivers your first glances of the waterfall, far off in the canyon on your left. Look for a narrow plume of water cascading down the mountainside, dropping in three tiers that total 175 feet. Brooks Falls' narrow, wispy length is reminiscent of the tropical waterfalls of Hawaii, especially since it's frequently viewed through the misty haze of coastal fog. The best viewing spot is at a conveniently placed bench right along the trail, where after a hard rain, you can hear as well as see the water crashing down the slopes, nearly a half mile away across the canyon.

By this point on the Brooks Creek Trail, you've climbed above the eucalyptus trees and are surrounded by manzanita and coastal brush. Your options are to turn around and head back, or continue on an excellent 2.5-mile loop. If you choose the latter, you get continual views of Brooks Falls as you continue upward, switchbacking to a trail junction and an overlook of the Pacific Ocean and

Pacifica State Beach. Here, turn right on Montara Mountain Trail, then start your descent back down the slope.

Directions

From San Francisco, take Highway 1 south for 10 miles to Pacifica. Turn east (left) on Linda Mar Boulevard, and follow it for two miles until it dead-ends at Oddstad Boulevard. Turn right and drive 50 yards to the park entrance on the left. Park in the upper parking lot (to the right of the visitor center as you drive in). Montara Mountain Trail is located next to the restrooms.

Information and Contact

A $5 day-use fee is charged per vehicle. Free maps are available at the visitors center or by free download at www.eparks.net. A detailed map of the area is available from Pease Press, 415/387-1437, www.peasepress.com (ask for the *Pacifica* map). For more information, contact San Pedro Valley County Park, 650/355-8289, www.eparks.net.

11 TIP TOE FALLS
Portola Redwoods State Park

Level: Easy	**Distance:** 2.0 miles round-trip
Best Season: December–May	**Elevation Change:** Total gain 100 feet

The name says it all. Tip Toe Falls is no loud watercourse thundering down over house-sized granite boulders. Rather, it's a petite little cataract, short and sweet, tiptoeing down a tiny cliff into a rounded rock pool. It's the smallest waterfall included in this book, but there's something special about it, a kind of je ne sais quoi that makes visitors draw in their breath and say, "Wow, look at that."

Tip Toe is one of the many jewels of Portola Redwoods State Park, a dark and shady redwood park that's tucked into the hillsides of the Santa Cruz Mountains. The park is like a smaller, less-visited version of nearby Big Basin Redwoods State Park, set in a canyon filled with big trees and ferns, although the majority of the redwoods here are second-growth. Biking, hiking, camping, and picnicking are all popular activities.

To hike to Tip Toe Falls, start your trip by the park office and visitor center. It's a good idea to ask a few questions inside because rangers remove many of the footbridges over Pescadero Creek in the winter, which may affect your trail

© ANDREW SAWADISAVI

Tip Toe Falls

options. Although Tip Toe Falls is on Fall Creek, you need to cross Pescadero Creek to reach it.

You have a couple of trailhead choices, all of which eventually put you on the Iverson Trail, a two-mile loop that leads to Tip Toe Falls' canyon. You can start from the Iverson Trail on the north side of the visitor center, the Sequoia Nature Trail on the south side of the visitor center, or you can walk or drive 0.2 mile past the visitor center to the group campgrounds and campfire center, where there's another trailhead for the Iverson Trail. If winter storms have ruled out all three routes, you can do what I did one rainy December day: walk 0.75 mile on the gated park service road, then turn right and pick up the Iverson Trail from there. It's not the prettiest way to go, but if you're determined to see the waterfall, it might just do the trick.

No matter how you do it, you'll eventually connect to the Iverson Trail on the far side of Pescadero Creek. It's easy streamside walking under dense redwoods and conifers, on a maze of well-signed and well-maintained trails. When Iverson Trail meets up with Fall Creek, a sign points to a spur trail leading upcanyon to Tip Toe Falls. A few steps on the spur trail take you to the narrow canyon's end, where two rock walls join and Tip Toe pours over a low notch. What's remarkable is the large and deep pool in front of the diminutive six-foot waterfall, and the strong breeze the stream creates when it's running hard. If you look carefully, you can see another cascade about 50 feet behind Tip Toe. The entire scene is bordered by cascade-loving ferns.

While you're in Portola State Park, take a walk on the short Old Tree Trail to see a fascinating 12-foot-wide fire-scarred redwood.

Directions

From I-280 in Palo Alto, take the Page Mill Road exit. Turn west and drive 8.9 miles to Highway 35 (Skyline Boulevard). Cross Highway 35 and continue on Alpine Road for 3.2 miles. Turn left on Portola State Park Road and drive 3.3 miles to park headquarters. (Note: do not take the Alpine Road exit off I-280; this section of Alpine Road dead-ends.)

Information and Contact

A $10 day-use fee is charged. A campground map that shows Iverson Trail and Tip Toe Falls is available by free download at www.parks.ca.gov. A more extensive park map is available at the visitors center for $2. For more information, contact Portola Redwoods State Park, 650/948-9098, www.parks.ca.gov or www.santa-cruzstateparks.org.

12 POMPONIO FALLS
Memorial County Park

Level: Easy

Best Season: December–May

Distance: 0.25 mile round-trip

Elevation Change: Negligible

Pomponio Falls is a 25-foot-tall cataract that drops just outside of Sequoia Flat Campground in Memorial County Park. It's easy to reach and worth a look. The waterfall cascades into wide, river-like Pescadero Creek, in a dense forest of ferns and redwoods.

To see it, you can follow the trail by campsite 12 in Sequoia Flat Camp, but that only takes you to a footbridge above the falls. To reach its base and get the best view, look for the gated road just to the left of the camp entrance. Hike down the road for about 100 yards to a concrete

Pomponio Falls

© ANN MARIE BROWN

apron where Pescadero Creek streams across the road. Don't cross the creek, just look to your right: there's Pomponio Falls. If Pescadero Creek isn't running too high, you can pick your way downstream on an old, broken concrete pathway. In about 30 yards, you're at the base of the waterfall. Five-finger, deer, maidenhair, and sword ferns grace its cliff. It drops onto the smooth rounded rocks along Pescadero's stream banks. To sum up: a nice waterfall, near a fine family campground, in a pretty county park.

Directions

From I-280 at Woodside, take Highway 84 west for 13 miles to La Honda. Turn left (southeast) on Pescadero Road and drive one mile, then bear right to stay on Pescadero Road. Continue 4.5 miles farther to the entrance to Memorial County Park on the left. Park at Sequoia Flat Campground or the amphitheater parking lot.

Information and Contact

A $5 day-use fee is charged per vehicle. A park map is available by free download at www.eparks.net. For more information, contact Memorial Park at 650/879-0238, www.eparks.net.

13 CASTLE ROCK FALLS
Castle Rock State Park

Level: Easy

Distance: 1.6 miles round-trip

Best Season: December–May

Elevation Change: Total loss 200 feet

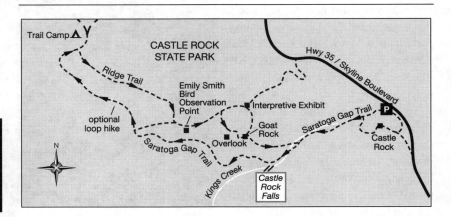

© ANN MARIE BROWN

Castle Rock Falls

It's hard to say which is better at Castle Rock State Park: the waterfall, the sandstone formations, or the views. It's a three-way tie for scenic beauty; the hikers who visit the park are the real winners.

To make the trip, set out on Saratoga Gap Trail from the far side of the parking lot, heading right. (The trail is signed as "To Campground.") The pleasure begins immediately as you hike downhill, walking along rocky, fern-lined Kings Creek through a mixed forest of Douglas fir, black oaks, and madrones. The stream begins as a trickle at the parking lot, then picks up flow and intensity as it heads downhill alongside the trail.

It's a mere 0.8 mile to Castle Rock Falls. After 15 minutes of trail time, you find yourself standing on a large wooden viewing deck, perched on top of the waterfall. Although the fall is tricky to see because you're at its brink, you'll be torn between searching for the best view of the 50-foot water drop and gazing outward at the miles of uninhabited Santa Cruz Mountains wildlands. It's hard to say whether the park built this deck for viewing the waterfall or the canyon vista. Both are incredible.

At Castle Rock Falls, Kings Creek leaps 50 feet off a vertical sandstone slab, then cascades onward, eventually joining the San Lorenzo River. Although you can't see the river from the overlook, you can gaze far off to its final destination in Monterey Bay and the Pacific Ocean.

From the observation platform, you can return to the parking lot or continue on a five-mile loop around the park, following Saratoga Gap Trail and then looping back on Ridge Trail. You'll pass by many beautiful sandstone displays, including the local rock climbers' favorite, Goat Rock. If you must turn back, be sure to take the short connector trail that leads 0.3 mile to Castle Rock, the park's namesake sandstone formation. It has many shallow caves that are fun to photograph or just climb around in.

Directions

From Saratoga, take Highway 9 west to its junction with Skyline Boulevard (Highway 35). Turn left (south) on Skyline and drive 2.5 miles to the Castle Rock State

Park parking area on the right. The trailhead is on the west side of the parking lot, opposite the entrance.

Or, from I-280 in Palo Alto, take Page Mill Road west for 8.9 miles to Skyline Boulevard. Turn left (south) on Skyline and drive 13 miles, past Highway 9, to the Castle Rock parking area on the right.

Information and Contact

An $8 day-use fee is charged per vehicle. A park map is available for $1 at the trailhead parking area, or by free download at www.parks.ca.gov. For more information, contact Castle Rock State Park, 15000 Skyline Boulevard, Los Gatos, CA 95033, 408/867-2952, www.parks.ca.gov.

14 BERRY CREEK FALLS   BEST 【
Big Basin Redwoods State Park

Level: Moderate   **Distance:** 12.0 miles round-trip (from Highway 1)

Best Season: December-May   **Elevation Change:** Total gain 600 feet

Berry Creek Falls is easily the most photographed waterfall in the San Francisco Bay Area. The first time you lay eyes on it, you may feel like you've seen it before. Its picture has graced calendars, greeting cards, and magazine covers, creating an eerie sense of déjà vu for many first-time visitors. But even being familiar with its image doesn't prepare you for the way the fall's beauty touches you. Berry Creek Falls can truly take your breath away.

You can reach the waterfall from two different trailheads, practically a world apart—one at the coast near Davenport, and the other at park headquarters in Big Basin Redwoods State Park near Felton. The route from the coast allows bicyclists to ride the first 5.2 miles of the trip along

Berry Creek Falls

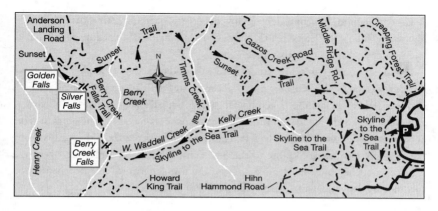

with hikers, but then everybody must walk the final 0.8 mile to the waterfall on foot. A bike rack is in place where bikers must dismount. Don't forget to bring your lock. The route from park headquarters is for hikers only, and is detailed in the Silver Falls and Golden Falls Cascade description, next in this chapter. It's a nine-mile round-trip to Berry Creek Falls, but most people hike a mile farther to Silver and Golden Falls as well.

Which route should you take? Both, if you get the chance. They are both first-class adventures in a beautiful, stream-fed redwood forest, leading to a destination that is as spectacular as any you'll find in the Bay Area. Why should you have to choose between them?

When you take the trip from Waddell Beach to Berry Creek Falls, a mountain bike can make the 12-mile trail length seem short and easy. Of course, you could always hike it, but most people use two wheels at this trailhead. Even beginning bike riders and children can ride the 5.2 miles on Skyline to the Sea Trail, a wide and smooth ranch road, usually covering the distance in about an hour. Along the way, your head is continually turned by beautiful scenery, including flowing Waddell Creek, fields of ferns, alders, Douglas firs, and, of course, big redwoods.

The ranch road ends at a stream crossing. If you're riding, lock up your bike at the bike rack and set out on foot, still on Skyline to the Sea Trail but now paralleling Berry Creek. A mere 15 minutes of walking on meandering single-track brings you to the fork where Skyline to the Sea heads east (right) to park headquarters, and you head left for Berry Creek Falls, now only moments away.

A large viewing platform with a bench is placed in front of the fall's large pool, so you can sit for a long, long time staring at the 70-foot cataract, which pours over a near-vertical drop. Berry Creek Falls creates a strong wind in peak flow, blowing and twisting the five-finger ferns growing at its edges. On sunny days, you can watch as light filters through the redwoods and makes beautiful patterns on the streams of water.

Berry Creek maintains a decent flow even in summer, making this one of the few waterfalls in the Bay Area that you can see outside of the rainy season. Still, late winter and spring are usually best.

If you have energy to spare, you can hike up and over Berry Creek Falls, following Berry Creek Falls Trail for one more mile and a 400-foot gain to Silver Falls and Golden Falls Cascade. Then it's an easy downhill hike back to the bike rack, and a coasting ride (or hike) homeward. Backpackers have the option of staying at Sunset Trail Camp near Silver Falls, or at one of three trailside camps along the first three miles of Skyline to the Sea Trail. If you're planning an overnight stay, contact the park for advance reservations and a permit. Not surprisingly, on summer weekends Skyline to the Sea Trail is a popular route.

Directions

From Half Moon Bay at the junction of Highway 92 and Highway 1, drive south on Highway 1 for 30 miles to the Rancho del Oso area of Big Basin Redwoods State Park (across from Waddell Beach and 7.5 miles north of Davenport). Park on the east side of the highway by the Rancho del Oso gate.

Information and Contact

If you hike or bike from the Rancho del Oso entrance at Highway 1, there is no fee. If you hike from Big Basin park headquarters, a $10 day-use fee is charged per vehicle. A park map is available for $2 at the Rancho del Oso visitor center and at park headquarters. A more detailed trail map is available for $8 at the park store or from www.mountainparks.org. For more information, contact Big Basin Redwoods State Park, 831/338-8860, www.bigbasin.org or www.parks.ca.gov.

15 SILVER FALLS AND GOLDEN FALLS   BEST C

Big Basin Redwoods State Park

🏃 🚲

Level: Moderate	**Distance:** 10.4 miles round-trip
Best Season: December–May	**Elevation Change:** Total gain/loss 1,600 feet

Even though Silver Falls and Golden Falls are less than a mile from Berry Creek Falls, they seem like a world apart. For starters, the two falls are vastly different in appearance from downstream Berry Creek Falls. Also, they are a little farther away from park trailheads, so they get fewer visitors. Furthermore, both of these falls are best visited not on a day hike, but on a spectacular overnight backpacking trip to Sunset Trail Camp.

Although you can get to Silver Falls and Golden Falls by taking the Skyline to the Sea Trail from the coast near Davenport (see Berry Creek Falls listing in this chapter), you'll be traveling on a dirt ranch road for much of the trip, and sharing the trail with horses and mountain bikers. The hikers-only route is on Skyline to the Sea Trail from Big Basin State Park Headquarters near Felton, where you can pick up a trail map and overnight permit if you're planning to backpack. Starting from park headquarters, you get a long and pleasant stroll on single-track through stands of old-growth redwoods, and a visit to all three waterfalls on Berry Creek—Berry Creek Falls, Silver Falls, and Golden Falls.

Silver Falls

© BILL RHOADES

The trail starts out good and stays that way, as it meanders among the big trees. After climbing 250 feet up a ridge in the first mile, the route drops down the other side to follow first Kelly Creek and then West Waddell Creek. The only things you need to watch out for are the huge yellow banana slugs that slowly cross the trail, and on rainy days, the cute little California newts that always seem to be right under your boots.

At 4.3 miles, just before the Skyline to the Sea Trail meets up with the Berry Creek Falls Trail, you get your first glimpse of Berry Creek Falls. It's enough to make you quicken your pace. Turn right on Berry Creek Falls Trail, and in moments, you'll be standing in front of the tremendous 70-foot cataract. Berry Creek Falls is truly awe-inspiring as it tumbles over a fern-lined cliff surrounded by big redwoods. Many people go this far and no farther.

But if you want more, you get more. Follow the trail up the left side of Berry Creek Falls, reaching some interesting overlooks above it, then climb for another 20 minutes until you're standing at the base of Silver Falls. The stream changes completely above Berry Creek Falls, becoming narrower, tamer, and more channeled. The streambed also changes, and nowhere is this more apparent than at Silver Falls. The 60-foot free fall spills over colorful sandstone and limestone rock, painted a bright tan, gold, and orange in contrast to Berry Creek Falls' dark cliff. There's no viewing platform holding you back from Silver Falls, so in summer, you can walk right up to its flow and stick your head in. Several redwoods have fallen around the fall's base, and they make good spots to sit down and take it all in.

Get accustomed to the orange glow of the rock underneath white water, because as you climb the wooden steps around the right side of Silver Falls, you'll see plenty more. The trail takes you to the top of the falls, where you walk on rocky sandstone steps. The park has put cables in place here, and in high water, it's wise to use them.

In moments, you're looking at the lower drop of Golden Falls, which is a long series of slippery orange sandstone, like a water slide for sea otters. There's one spot where the water funnels and plunges in a cascade, but most of Golden Falls is just a big orange Slip 'n Slide. The color of the rock is so striking, and the shape of the falls is so unusual, that you'll find it hard to believe you're still in Big Basin State Park, less than a mile from classic-looking, postcardlike Berry Creek Falls.

At Golden Falls, day hikers may want to consider retracing their steps for a 10.4-mile round-trip. The other option is to hike back on a loop, following Berry Creek Falls Trail for another 0.25 mile, then turning right on Sunset Trail and making a 12-mile round-trip. Backpackers need continue only another 0.25 mile to Sunset Trail Camp, where they can spend a peaceful night alongside Berry Creek, then visit the waterfalls again the following day. Now that's my idea of a good camping trip.

Directions

From the junction of Highways 35 and 9 at Saratoga Gap, drive six miles west on Highway 9 to Highway 236. Turn west on Highway 236 and drive 8.4 winding miles to Big Basin Redwoods State Park Headquarters. Park in the lot across from park headquarters, then begin hiking from the west side of the lot on a signed connector trail to the Skyline to the Sea Trail. For a trail map, see the listing for Berry Creek Falls in this chapter.

Information and Contact

A $10 day-use fee is charged per vehicle. A park map is available for $2 at the entrance station. A more detailed trail map is available for $8 at the park store or from www.mountainparks.org. For more information, contact Big Basin Redwoods State Park, 831/338-8860, www.bigbasin.org or www.parks.ca.gov.

16 SEMPERVIRENS FALLS

Big Basin Redwoods State Park

Level: Easy

Best Season: December–May

Distance: 3.6 miles round-trip

Elevation Change: Total gain 200 feet

Sempervirens Falls

Berry Creek Falls and its neighbors Silver Falls and Golden Falls Cascade are indisputably the prime destinations of hikers in Big Basin Redwoods State Park. Why? They are incredible, that's why. But not everybody has the time or energy required to make the trip to see Berry Creek's three waterfalls. If you're in that category, you can go find another, easier-to-reach cataract at Big Basin State Park, arriving at its side in less than two miles of nearly level hiking.

That would mean a trip to Sempervirens Falls, named for the many Sequoia sempervirens, or coast redwood trees, that surround its creek. The Sequoia Trail leads to the waterfall in 1.8 miles from park headquarters, and from there, you can just turn around and head back, or make a pleasant five-mile loop by returning on Shadowbrook Trail.

The route is well-marked all the way. You don't even have to remember that you're on the Sequoia Trail, because all the trail signs read "Sempervirens Falls" on your way in and "Park Headquarters" on your way out. Without trail directions to worry about, you can spend your time admiring the huge redwoods along the way, which reach more than 300 feet tall in Big Basin. Mixed in with the big guys are Douglas fir, tanoak, and laurel trees, as well as thousands of ferns lining the forest floor. Springtime brings wild ginger, trillium, and azalea blooms, especially near the feeder streams to Sempervirens Creek. Although portions of the Sequoia Trail are routed near a park road, it gets little traffic and shouldn't disturb your hike.

To see the waterfall, you must leave the Sequoia Trail and cross the park road,

0.5 mile after passing Wastahi Camp. Sempervirens Falls is a 25-foot drop that can be as wide as four feet at the top, with two miniature cascades flowing into it from above. The waterfall is perfectly framed by standing and fallen redwood trees on either side of its drop, and a large, clear pool at its base. From your position on the wooden viewing deck above the fall, you look straight down into its six-foot-deep pool.

A bonus is that if you're staying in Big Basin State Park at Sky Meadow Group Camp, Wastahi Camp, or Huckleberry Camp, you can access the waterfall directly from your tent on either Sequoia or Shadowbrook Trails, rather than hiking from park headquarters.

Directions

From the junction of Highways 35 and 9 at Saratoga Gap, drive six miles west on Highway 9 to Highway 236. Turn west on Highway 236 and drive 8.4 winding miles to Big Basin Redwoods State Park Headquarters. Park in the lot across from park headquarters, then begin hiking on the Sequoia Trail from the right side of the building.

Information and Contact

A $10 day-use fee is charged per vehicle. A campground map that includes Sempervirens Falls is available by free download at www.parks.ca.gov. A park map is available for $2 at the entrance station. A more detailed trail map is available for $8 at the park store or from www.mountainparks.org. For more information, contact Big Basin Redwoods State Park, 831/338-8860, www.bigbasin.org or www.parks.ca.gov.

17 UVAS CANYON FALLS
Uvas Canyon County Park

Level: Easy

Best Season: December–May

Distance: 1.0–3.5 miles round-trip

Elevation Change: Total gain 700 feet

Uvas Canyon County Park is a little slice of waterfall heaven on the east side of the Santa Cruz Mountains. Although the drive to reach it is a long route from the freeway through grasslands and oaks, it ends in a surprising redwood forest at the park entrance. Suddenly, you've entered another world.

Uvas is a small park, offering camping and picnicking facilities and a short

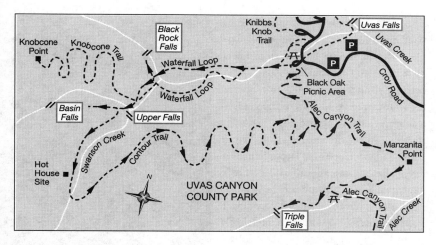

length of hiking trails in its 1,200 acres, but it's living proof that good things come in small packages. You can walk the one-mile Waterfall Loop Trail and see Black Rock Falls and several smaller cascades on Swanson Creek, or you can add on a 150-foot side trip to see Basin Falls and Upper Falls. If you're in the mood to stretch your legs, you can make a larger loop out to Alec Canyon, then take the uphill trail 0.5 mile to Triple Falls on Alec Creek.

Start your trip either at the Black Oak Group Picnic Area on the gated dirt road, or 100 yards farther down the park road, just before the turnoff to the campground. The latter access gives you an immediate audience with Granuja Falls, a tiny five-foot-tall cataract in a very photogenic setting, then leads across a bridge and up a set of stairsteps to join the picnic area trail/road. From Black Oak Picnic Area, head straight on the road to connect to the Waterfall Loop Trail through the canyon. Cross Swanson Creek on a footbridge, then bear right at the fork and head directly for Black Rock Falls, 0.25 mile away. You'll find the waterfall on your right, pouring 30 feet down a side canyon over—you guessed it—black rock.

Take a few pictures, then continue back in the canyon, heading for Basin Falls (20 feet tall, surrounded by moss-covered rocks and making a lovely S-curve as it carves its way downcanyon) and Upper Falls (15 feet tall with a fallen tree in front of it). Water pours down the canyon walls on all sides, creating a good deal of noise. The canyon is filled with oaks, laurels, and Douglas firs, all thriving in the wet environment around Swanson Creek.

At Upper Falls, it's decision time: either head back and take the other side of the Waterfall Loop Trail for a short and flat trip, or continue up Swanson Creek and follow the winding Contour Trail to Alec Canyon and Triple Falls. The latter adds 2.5 miles and a good hillclimb to your mileage. If you're heading for Triple, follow Contour Trail until it meets up with Alec Canyon Fire Road, then turn right and hike for 0.5 mile, passing Manzanita Point, where you get far-reaching views on clear days. Then turn right again on the spur trail to Triple Falls. True to its name, Triple Falls is a series of three cascades totaling 40 feet in height. You can climb off-trail and sit right alongside the cascading fall, and maybe munch on a sandwich and think about how great it is to be alive. Then make a short return trip by following the fire road back to Black Oak Picnic Area, a steep 0.75 mile descent.

Basin Falls at Uvas Canyon

If after all this you're still in a waterfall mood, walk down to the restrooms on the west side of the ranger station, near the family campground, and take the steep trail that leads down to Uvas Creek, where 20-foot Uvas Falls drops in the back of a canyon. The waterfall is formed by Swanson Creek near its junction with Uvas Creek.

So which waterfall at Uvas Park is the best? My favorites are Basin Falls and Triple Falls. Your favorite? Go see them all and decide.

Directions

From U.S. 101 in Morgan Hill, take the Bernal Road exit west. Turn left on Santa Teresa Boulevard. Travel south three miles and turn right onto Bailey Avenue. Follow Bailey Road 2.3 miles to McKean Road. Turn left on McKean Road and drive six miles (McKean Road becomes Uvas Road). Turn right on Croy Road and drive 4.5 miles to the park (continue past Sveadal, a private camp/resort). Park near park headquarters or in one of the picnic area parking lots, then walk down the park road to the trailhead. The trail begins at Black Oak Picnic Area, or you can access it 100 yards farther down the park road, just before the turnoff to the campground.

Information and Contact

A $6 day-use fee is charged per vehicle. A park map is available at the entrance station or by free download at www.parkhere.org. For more information, contact

Uvas Canyon County Park, 408/779-9232. Or contact Santa Clara County Parks and Recreation Department, 408/355-2200, www.parkhere.org.

MORE WATERFALLS IN THE SAN FRANCISCO BAY AREA

•**Green Valley Falls, Vallejo.** Two waterfalls—upper and lower Green Valley Falls—are located on private land in Fairfield that is owned by the city of Vallejo. Currently the only way to hike there is on a guided trip hosted by the Bay Area Ridge Trail Council (415/561-2595, www.ridgetrail.org). The hike to both falls is only two miles round-trip; the upper falls is much more spectacular than the lower.

•**Cascade Falls, Mill Valley.** Located in a small city park in downtown Mill Valley, this pretty 20-foot-high cataract can be seen via a 100-foot walk off Cascade Drive, near Cascade's junction with Throckmorton Avenue. For more information, phone 415/388-9700.

•**Big Carson Creek Falls, Marin Municipal Water District.** Seeing this waterfall requires a 14-mile round-trip on Pine Mountain Fire Road, best done on a mountain bike. For more information, phone Sky Oaks Ranger Station at 415/945-1181.

•**Golden Gate Park Falls, San Francisco.** More wedding photographs have been taken in front of these falls than probably anywhere else in San Francisco. So what if they are man-made? They flow even in summer. For more information, phone 415/831-2700.

MONTEREY AND BIG SUR

© ANN MARIE BROWN

BEST WATERFALLS

❰ Long Backpacking Trips
Pine Falls, **page 244**

❰ State Parks
McWay Falls, **page 240**
Limekiln Falls, **page 246**

❰ Wheelchair-Accessible
McWay Falls, **page 240**

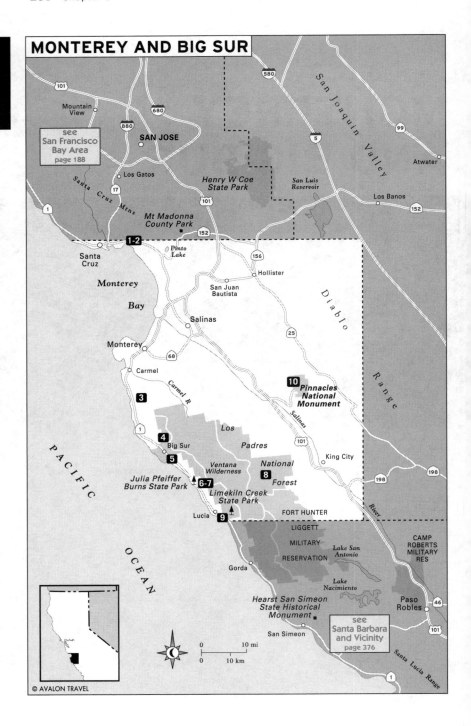

MONTEREY AND BIG SUR

see San Francisco Bay Area page 188

Mountain View

SAN JOSE

Los Gatos

Santa Cruz Mtns

Santa Cruz

Henry W Coe State Park

San Luis Reservoir

Los Banos

Atwater

San Joaquin Valley

Mt Madonna County Park

Pinto Lake

1-2

Monterey Bay

San Juan Bautista

Hollister

Salinas

Monterey

Carmel

3

Carmel R

Los Padres

4

Big Sur

5

Ventana Wilderness

National

Julia Pfeiffer Burns State Park

6-7

Limekiln Creek State Park

Lucia

9

Gorda

PACIFIC OCEAN

10 Pinnacles National Monument

Salinas

101

King City

Diablo Range

8 Forest

FORT HUNTER LIGGETT MILITARY RESERVATION

Lake San Antonio

Lake Nacimiento

CAMP ROBERTS MILITARY RES

Paso Robles

Hearst San Simeon State Historical Monument

San Simeon

see Santa Barbara and Vicinity page 376

Santa Lucia Range

0   10 mi
0   10 km

© AVALON TRAVEL

TRAIL NAME	LEVEL	DISTANCE	ELEVATION	SEASON	FEATURES	PAGE
1 Maple Falls	Moderate	9.0 mi rt	600 ft	Dec.-May	🥾 🏕 🚲	232
2 Aptos Creek Falls	Strenuous	7.0-12.0 mi rt	700 ft	Dec.-May	🥾 🏕 🚲	234
3 Garland Ranch Falls	Easy	1.6 mi rt	200 ft	Dec.-May	🥾 🧗	236
4 Andrew Molera Falls	Easy	0.5 mile rt	40 ft	Jan.-June	🥾	237
5 Pfeiffer Falls	Easy	0.8 mile rt	250 ft	Dec.-June	🥾 ◀	238
6 McWay Falls	Easy	0.5 mile rt	Negligible	Dec.-June	🥾 ♿	240
7 Canyon Falls	Easy	0.75 mile rt	200 ft	Dec.-June	🥾	242
8 Pine Falls	Moderate	10.6 mi rt	1,500 ft	Dec.-June	🥾 🏕 ◀	244
9 Limekiln Falls	Easy	1.0 mile rt	200 ft	Dec.-June	🥾 ◀	246
10 Bear Gulch and Condor Gulch	Easy	3.0 mi rt	500 ft	Dec.-Apr.	🥾	247

■ MAPLE FALLS
The Forest of Nisene Marks State Park

Level: Moderate

Best Season: December–May

Distance: 9.0 miles round-trip

Elevation Change: Total gain 600 feet

Maple Falls

Part of what makes visiting Maple Falls so enjoyable is that it's not so easy to get there. It's a four-mile hike from George's Picnic Area, the winter-season trailhead in The Forest of Nisene Marks State Park, followed by a half-mile stream scramble. By the time you complete the long walk through second- and third-growth redwoods, then squeeze your way upstream through a narrow canyon, you feel like you are due for a reward. Luckily, Maple Falls repays you for your effort.

In summer, you can hike from Porter Picnic Area, which cuts off two miles from your round-trip total. But Maple Falls is best seen in winter or spring, when you can only drive as far as the gated trailhead at George's Picnic Area. To shorten your trip, bring your mountain bikes and ride the first two miles on the dirt road to the Mill Pond Trail cutoff. Then lock up your bikes and start walking on single-track.

Whether hiking or biking, the trip starts on the Aptos Creek Fire Road by passing through the Mary Easton and Porter picnic areas and traveling under a thriving canopy of second-growth redwoods. A quarter mile past Porter Picnic Area, the Loma Prieta Grade Trail takes off on the left, and hikers can cut off Aptos Creek Road there or continue with bikers to the Mill Pond Trail cutoff, also on the left. Mill Pond Trail soon joins with the Loma Prieta Grade, where your route turns right and continues upcanyon.

As soon as you're on single-track, what was good becomes gorgeous. Looking at the lush, green forest around you, it's hard to imagine the park's not-so-distant history. In 1881, the Loma Prieta Lumber Company teamed up with Southern Pacific Railroad to log this tree-filled canyon. They built the Loma Prieta railroad grade you're walking on, and worked these tree-covered slopes with trains, oxen, skid roads, inclines, horses, and as many men as they could get. In 1922, when the loggers put their saws down, they had removed 140 million board feet of lumber. Not a single mature tree remained.

Today the forest has recovered, and it's prospering with young redwoods and Douglas firs. You hike among these second- and third-growth trees, first alongside Aptos Creek and later beside Bridge Creek. At a fork signed for Bridge Creek Historic Site, bear right for a shorter, more direct route to Maple Falls. (Loma Prieta Grade makes a loop, with the left fork following a longer, more meandering route to the historic site and the fall's canyon. Save it for the return trip, if you still have the energy.)

Bridge Creek Historic Site, the scene of a former logging camp, is reached at four miles from the trailhead. Here, get ready for a half-mile stream scramble up Bridge Creek to Maple Falls. It's the most fun part of the trip. The trail quickly disappears and the canyon walls narrow. When Bridge Creek is running strong, you must walk in the creekbed and cross the stream numerous times. If your shoes aren't waterproof, you may end up with wet feet.

Bridge Creek canyon is decorated with millions of ferns and mini-waterfalls dropping among the rocks and crevices. Keep going until you reach the back of the canyon, where the walls come together and 40-foot Maple Falls rushes over a rock wall, inviting admiration for its sparkling beauty and blocking any further progress upstream.

Directions

From Santa Cruz, drive south on Highway 1 for six miles to the Aptos exit. Bear left at the exit, then turn right on Soquel Drive and drive 0.5 mile. Turn left on

Aptos Creek Road. Stop at the entrance kiosk, then continue up the road and park at George's Picnic Area or Porter Picnic Area. (Porter Picnic Area is closer to the falls, cutting two miles off your round-trip, but it's closed in winter.)

Information and Contact

An $8 day-use fee is charged per vehicle. A park map is available at the entrance kiosk. For more information, contact The Forest of Nisene Marks State Park, c/o Sunset State Beach, 831/763-7062, www.parks.ca.gov.

2 APTOS CREEK FALLS
The Forest of Nisene Marks State Park

🚶 🚐 🚲

Level: Strenuous   **Distance:** 7.0-12.0 miles round-trip

Best Season: December-May   **Elevation Change:** Total gain 700 feet

If you've hiked to Maple Falls in The Forest of Nisene Marks State Park and you're looking for an even bigger adventure, Aptos Creek Falls is your ticket. Plan on a whole day for the 12-mile trip, and make sure you are properly dressed for some serious stream scrambling. Wear waterproof boots and bring dry clothes to change into. Then fill up your day pack with lunch and a water filter, and set out for a trip to a rarely visited waterfall.

© ANDREW SAWADISAVI

Aptos Creek Falls

As with the trip to Maple Falls, you can shorten your time and energy expended by riding your bike part of the way to Aptos Creek Falls (also called Five-Finger Falls and Monte Vista Falls). Starting from George's Picnic Area, you can bicycle 2.5 miles one-way along Aptos Creek Fire Road, then lock up and walk the Aptos Creek Trail for two miles until it ends, then scramble for the final 1.5 miles up Aptos Creek.

The trip starts out following the Aptos Creek Fire Road, passing Mary Easton and Porter picnic areas. The trail is wide, hard-packed, and smooth the whole way, with an almost imperceptible climb through the second-growth redwood canyon. Ride or hike on the road, passing several single-track cutoffs, for 2.5 miles. Look for a bike rack at a major hairpin turn in the road; a signboard commemorates this spot as the 1989 Loma Prieta earthquake epicenter (the sign is sometimes in place and sometimes not, so don't be misled if it's absent). This marks the junction where you will leave Aptos Creek Fire Road. Waterfall seekers must cross Aptos Creek and pick up the trail on the other side. This can require wading in the winter months, so be prepared to remove your shoes and socks.

Once on the far side of Aptos Creek, follow the single-track Aptos Creek Trail. You must cross the creek again, back to the north side, then in 0.5 mile you reach the exact center of the Loma Prieta quake, although there is nothing much to see. Another 1.5 miles of streamside travel brings you to an intersection with the Big Slide Trail, coming in from the left. The Aptos Creek Trail more or less peters out, but a decent use trail continues alongside the creek. Follow it, and sooner or later you'll have to cross the creek again because the north side becomes too steep to negotiate.

At times of high water, you may eventually have to give up the route along the bank and just slog along in the streambed. The canyon walls narrow, and after a slow 1.5 miles from where the Aptos Creek Trail ended, you'll reach the base of Aptos Creek Falls, tucked into the back of a fern-lined grotto on the right. The fall is not on Aptos Creek proper, but rather on a feeder stream that empties into Aptos Creek. The narrow 25-foot-high plume of water looks much different than nearby Maple Falls. In addition to the plentiful moss around it, you'll see many delicate five-finger ferns, the source of the cascade's common nickname, Five Finger Falls. Those ferns seem to be pointing the way to Nirvana.

Note that your experience at Aptos Creek Falls will be vastly different depending on when you visit. In the wet winter months, it can be a real challenge getting to the waterfall, with washed-out or submerged trails and high-water stream crossings. In the summer, getting to Aptos Creek Falls may be nothing more than a long walk. Not surprisingly, the waterfall's flow is also vastly different in the wet and dry months.

Directions

From Santa Cruz, drive south on Highway 1 for six miles to the Aptos exit. Bear left at the exit, then turn right on Soquel Drive and drive 0.5 mile. Turn left on Aptos Creek Road. Stop at the entrance kiosk, then continue up the road and park at George's Picnic Area or Porter Picnic Area. (Porter Picnic Area is closer to the falls, cutting two miles off your round-trip, but it's closed in winter.)

Information and Contact

An $8 day-use fee is charged per vehicle. A park map is available at the entrance kiosk. For more information, contact The Forest of Nisene Marks State Park, c/o Sunset State Beach, 831/763-7062, www.parks.ca.gov.

3 GARLAND RANCH FALLS
Garland Ranch Regional Park

🏃 🐎

Level: Easy

Best Season: December-May

Distance: 1.6 miles round-trip

Elevation Change: Total gain 200 feet

Garland Ranch Regional Park is the perfect place to take your kids to see a waterfall or to walk with a friend on a clear winter day in Carmel. The park has an excellent nature center that is dedicated to educating budding naturalists, and the riverside grasslands support a fine display of wildflowers. The park's waterfall is ephemeral, however, so you need to time your trip for just after a rain.

From the parking area alongside Carmel Valley Road, cross the Carmel River on either of two bridges and walk to the visitor center. After taking a look inside at some of the center's excellent brochures on the park's plants and animals, walk to the left on the Lupine Loop, a wide hiking and equestrian trail. In addition to the blooming lupine, you'll see monkeyflower and paintbrush growing in the flood plain along the river.

Garland Ranch Falls

In 0.5 mile, leave the Lupine Loop and continue straight on the Waterfall Trail. The trail climbs a bit as it enters an oak and laurel forest, an abrupt vegetation change from the grasslands in the river valley. The path changes to single-track, and horses aren't allowed on this short section of trail. In 10 minutes you'll reach Garland Ranch Falls. Watch for a footbridge just before the falls; if the stream underneath it is running full, you're in luck. Garland Ranch Falls pours (or cascades, or trickles, depending on when you visit) over a 70-foot-high sandstone cliff.

If you want a bit of a workout, you can continue uphill on the Waterfall Trail, climbing for another 0.75 mile to its end at a high meadow with views in all directions. You can return by taking the Mesa Trail to the Lupine Loop, then walk either side of the loop back to the nature center.

Directions

From Highway 1 at Carmel, turn left (east) on Carmel Valley Road. Drive 8.6 miles on Carmel Valley Road to the Garland Ranch parking area on the right side of the road. Walk across the river bridge to get to the visitor center and the trailhead for the Lupine Loop.

Information and Contact

There is no fee. A park map is available at the visitor center or by free download at www.mprpd.org. For more information, contact Garland Ranch Regional Park, 831/659-6065 or 831/372-3196, www.mprpd.org.

4 ANDREW MOLERA FALLS
Andrew Molera State Park

Level: Easy   **Distance:** 0.5 mile round-trip
Best Season: January–June   **Elevation Change:** Total gain 40 feet

Most people think of Andrew Molera State Park as a place to go camping and hiking on the spectacular Big Sur coast. Most of the park is located on the west side of Highway 1, perched on the beautiful Pacific shoreline. But on the east side of the highway lies the backcountry of Andrew Molera State Park and its hidden waterfall, a 35-foot-high gem that is seldom visited.

Getting to the waterfall requires a 10-minute walk on an easily navigated trail. It travels through a gorgeous

Andrew Molera Falls

© ANN MARIE BROWN

redwood forest, with a carpet of sorrel that looks so tidy and immaculate it seems like it has been manicured. The waterfall is a bit difficult to photograph, as it is tucked into the back of a box canyon and shaded by redwoods almost all day long. But it's a pretty spot that is a surprising contrast to the beaches and coastal bluffs that have made this park famous. Several tree trunks and branches have fallen over its lip, and the cascading water is forced to splash its way around the obstacles.

Directions
From Carmel, drive 20 miles south on Highway 1 to the entrance to Andrew Molera State Park on the right (four miles north of Big Sur). Don't turn here; instead continue one mile south on Highway 1 and park in the small dirt pullout on the east side of the road. (A gated dirt road leads from this pullout.)

Information and Contact
There is no fee at this trailhead. A park map is available at the entrance station to Andrew Molera or at Big Sur Station. For more information, contact Andrew Molera State Park, 831/667-2315, www.parks.ca.gov.

5 PFEIFFER FALLS
Pfeiffer Big Sur State Park

Level: Easy **Distance:** 0.8 mile round-trip
Best Season: December–June **Elevation Change:** Total gain 250 feet

The key factor to remember when you visit Pfeiffer Falls is that Pfeiffer Big Sur State Park is a busy place, especially on weekends. Unlike the other nearby state parks on the Big Sur Coast, Pfeiffer Big Sur has an abundance of amenities—a campground, lodge, restaurant, gift shop, and nature center—so it gets more visitors. It's critical to time your trip carefully so you can see Pfeiffer Falls without getting stuck in a long line of cars at the entrance kiosk.

Pfeiffer Falls

Your best bet is to visit during the week or on a rainy day, but you can always sneak in early in the morning, even on weekends. I visited one Saturday morning in June when the park campground and lodge were full to capacity, but most park visitors were still snug in their beds and sleeping bags. In the early dawn, I walked to Pfeiffer Falls in solitude. But on my return trip an hour or so later, I was joined by more than a dozen hikers.

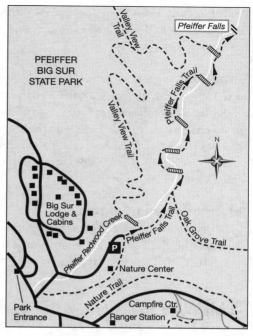

The Pfeiffer Falls Trail leads from the north side of the nature center. It's well signed and easy to follow. You'll pass trail junctions for Valley View and Oak Grove trails, but simply keep heading straight, following Pfeiffer Redwood Creek. The trail crosses the creek four times on wooden footbridges, making a decent little climb in its short distance. Stairsteps carry you up the steepest parts. The entire walk is shaded by giant redwoods, members of one of the oldest groves in Big Sur.

The trail ends at a viewing platform in front of Pfeiffer Falls, where Pfeiffer Redwood Creek drops 60 feet over a dark granite face. Most often, the fall flows in two skinny cascades, but after a big rain, the entire rock face can be covered with a wide sheet of white water. If you look carefully, you can spot another cascade high above the main drop, set back farther in the canyon. Very large ferns grow on the plateau between the two drops.

Pfeiffer Falls' pool is shallow and wide, largely due to a manufactured check dam that shores it up. Five-finger and maidenhair ferns grow on the granite around the waterfall, giving the damp grotto a tropical feeling. The fall can be difficult to photograph because its surroundings are so dark in contrast to the white cascade.

After visiting Pfeiffer Falls, you have many options for additional hiking, including walking the Valley View Trail from the junction near the waterfall's base. It leads uphill through chaparral and oaks to an expansive overlook of Point Sur and the Big Sur Valley, then returns to the trailhead by the nature center, where you began. Both Valley View Trail and the Pfeiffer Falls Trail suffered some minor fire damage from Big Sur and Carmel's massive 2008 wildfire, but the terrain has recovered nicely.

Directions

From Carmel, drive 26 miles south on Highway 1 to Pfeiffer Big Sur State Park, on the east side of the highway. (It's two miles south of Big Sur.) Drive through the entrance kiosk, turn left and pass the lodge, then turn right, following the signs to Pfeiffer Falls Trailhead and Nature Center. Park just beyond the nature center. The trail is on the left side of the parking lot, signed as "Oak Grove Trail, Valley View Trail, Pfeiffer Falls Trail."

Information and Contact

A $10 day-use fee is charged per vehicle. A park map is available at the entrance kiosk or at Big Sur Station. For more information, contact Pfeiffer Big Sur State Park, 831/667-2315, www.parks.ca.gov.

6 McWAY FALLS   BEST ◖
Julia Pfeiffer Burns State Park

Level: Easy

Best Season: December–June

Distance: 0.5 mile round-trip

Elevation Change: Negligible

Next to Yosemite Fall and Bridalveil Fall, McWay Falls is probably the waterfall that appears most often on family snapshots of California vacations. Although most people can't remember its name, no one can forget the image of the 80-foot waterfall leaping off a rugged ocean bluff and pouring gracefully into the Pacific.

Consider the setting. First, we're on the Big Sur coast, one of the most beautiful stretches

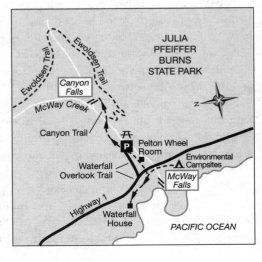

© ANN MARIE BROWN

McWay Falls

of sand, sea, and sky in the West. Here, McWay Creek intersects the beach, tumbling year-round through a pristine canyon of redwoods and over tall granite cliffs. Long, rolling ocean waves dissolve along the shoreline and crash against rock outcrops protruding from the sea. Seals and sea lions bask on the sands of McWay Cove, and California gray whales parade past on their annual winter and spring migrations.

The viewing point for the waterfall is on a short, level, paved trail, so it's suitable for wheelchairs. The trail leaves the parking area and parallels the park access road as it heads west, then enters a pedestrian tunnel (a glorified culvert) that travels underneath the highway. Once out of the tunnel and out on the open coastline, the path carves a few curves around McWay Cove's steep and craggy cliffs. Wooden railings keep you from venturing too near the edge.

It's a glorious moment when you first see the waterfall—streaming down the cliff and pouring to the sand like milk from a pitcher. Dropping into a perfect little pocket beach, McWay Falls is just like all those photographs you've seen, only better. Although its cliff is sheared off at an unforgiving right angle, McWay Falls leaps gracefully over the abrupt pitch.

A bench is situated along the trail for relaxing while you view the fall, but actually the best overlook is just 20 feet farther along the paved trail, where the angle of perspective is better. The path continues for another 50 yards, out of sight of the waterfall, to the ruins of the stone Waterfall House, which was the home of Lathrop and Helen Hooper Brown in the 1940s. In 1962, Helen Hooper Brown gave this land to the state of California for a park, with the stipulation that it be named after her friend Julia Pfeiffer Burns, a Big Sur pioneer and cattle ranch owner.

If the last time you visited McWay Falls was 30 years ago or more, you might notice that the waterfall isn't exactly as you remember. The cataract used to drop directly into the sea, but a major landslide in the winter of 1983 deposited so much earth and sand in McWay Cove that the waterfall now lands on the beach.

Unfortunately, there's no access to the cove's strip of sand, due to the constantly eroding coastal bluffs.

A little-known fact about McWay Falls is that a backpacking camp is located just south of it. Although you can't see the falls from the primitive camp, you do get a spectacular view of the Big Sur coast. Contact the park for reservations; the camp has only two sites and they are quite popular on weekends.

Directions

From Carmel, drive 37 miles south on Highway 1 to Julia Pfeiffer Burns State Park, on the east side of the highway. (It's 13 miles south of Big Sur.) Drive through the entrance kiosk, then park near the restrooms. The Waterfall Overlook Trail starts across the pavement from the restrooms, on a series of wooden stairs. Wheelchair users can ride over a bridge to bypass the stairs.

Information and Contact

A $10 day-use fee is charged per vehicle. A park map is available at the entrance kiosk or at Big Sur Station. For more information, contact Julia Pfeiffer Burns State Park, c/o Big Sur Station, 831/667-2315, www.parks.ca.gov.

7 CANYON FALLS
Julia Pfeiffer Burns State Park

| **Level:** Easy | **Distance:** 0.75 mile round-trip |
| **Best Season:** December–June | **Elevation Change:** Total gain 200 feet |

After you've visited the famous McWay Falls at Julia Pfeiffer Burns State Park (see listing in this chapter), don't be in a rush to drive down Highway 1 in search of your next waterfall. The state park harbors another cataract, far less renowned than McWay Falls on the coast. Your next trip need only be as far as the inland side of the parking lot, to the trailhead for the Canyon and Ewoldsen Trails.

If you've just walked the paved Waterfall Overlook Trail along the wide-open, wind-swept coast, it's a bit like culture shock to head into the dense, dark redwood forest along the Ewoldsen Trail. Your eyes have to adjust to the filtered light and the silent woods—a major contrast to the bright horizon and the crashing of the sea.

Immediately, you're taken by the beauty of fast-running McWay Creek, gurgling past tall redwoods and leafy, cloverlike sorrel. After passing through a picnic area, cross the creek and follow the Ewoldsen Trail for less than 0.25 mile until you reach the turnoff for Canyon Trail. Bear left, and a few more minutes of streamside rambling bring you to the back of the canyon, where a 30-foot waterfall drops in a hurried cascade. It carves two tiers, makes a smooth turn and drop, then forms another 10-foot cascade. You can sit at a bench at Canyon Trail's end, a few feet from the foot of the falls, and marvel at the incredible setting of ferns, huge trees, rocks, and cascading, musical white water.

Canyon Falls

© ANDREW SAWADISAVI

You'll have a chance of privacy at Canyon Falls because most park visitors are at the coast marveling at the other waterfall on McWay Creek, and most day hikers who make their way up the Ewoldsen Trail don't realize what lies at the end of the Canyon Trail fork. Ewoldsen is considered by many to be the finest day-hiking trail in Big Sur, and if you have the time, you should hike some or all of it. The trail makes a 4.3-mile semiloop, climbing 1,600 feet in the process. The payoff comes at the top of the climb, where there is a spectacular overlook of the Big Sur coast—now made more expansive thanks to Big Sur's 2008 wildfire, which took out many of the trees on this side of the park.

If you'd rather see waterfalls than coastal views, another small cataract lies just a few minutes' walk from Canyon Falls. Backtrack to the turnoff for Canyon Trail, and this time leave the main trail and scramble upstream along McWay Creek. You'll reach a 10-foot-high free fall in a few hundred feet. Climb above it (the right side of the stream is easiest) and you'll gain a view of a much larger free fall, about triple the size of this one.

Directions

From Carmel, drive 37 miles south on Highway 1 to Julia Pfeiffer Burns State Park, on the east side of the highway. (It's 13 miles south of Big Sur.) Drive through the entrance kiosk, then turn left, following the signs for the Canyon Trail and picnic area. Park in the parking lot by the restrooms. The trail starts from the inland side of the parking lot, signed as Canyon Trail/Picnic Area/Ewoldsen Trail.

Information and Contact

A $10 day-use fee is charged per vehicle. A park map is available at the entrance kiosk or at Big Sur Station. For more information, contact Julia Pfeiffer Burns State Park, c/o Big Sur Station, 831/667-2315, www.parks.ca.gov.

8 PINE FALLS   BEST €
Ventana Wilderness

Level: Moderate

Distance: 10.6 miles round-trip

Best Season: December–June

Elevation Change: Total loss 1,500 feet

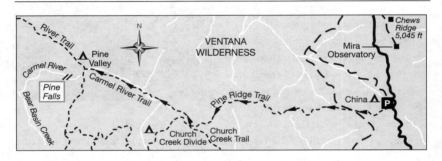

Lots of people want to explore the Ventana Wilderness, but they don't know where to start. Pine Falls on the Carmel River is the perfect place. You can make a long day trip to Pine Falls, or take it easy and go for a one-night backpacking trip, either out-and-back for 10.6 miles or on a loop of 13 miles. Either way, you're heading for a great journey into the rugged Ventana, one of the largest Forest Service wilderness areas in California.

Your route is on the Pine Ridge Trail, and although its western end from Highway 1 is one of the most well-used paths in the wilderness, up here things are a little more peaceful. That's especially true in winter or spring, which are the best seasons to see the waterfall. Keep in mind that the trailhead access roads can be impassable after heavy rain, however, so call to check on road conditions before setting out.

The Pine Ridge Trail leaves the parking area just south of the campground, at the signed trailhead on the west side of the road. It starts with a 0.5-mile climb through a tan oak forest, reaches a ridge, then follows an up-and-down course, lateraling along the grassy hillsides with wide-open views of the wilderness.

The trail begins to drop more steeply, till at 3.5 miles you reach a trail junction at Church Creek Divide. You have three choices: Pine Ridge Trail continues straight, eventually heading down to the redwoods at Big Sur; the Church Creek Trail heads left (south); and the Carmel River Trail heads right (north). Turn right on the Carmel River Trail, which descends gently as it meets the meager headwaters of the Carmel River. Your surroundings get more beautiful as you go: the stream picks up speed and flow, and the forest becomes more dense with firs and ponderosa pines in this two-mile stretch.

At 5.3 miles from the trailhead, you reach Pine Valley Camp, an established wilderness camp in lush Pine Valley, a spacious high meadow lined with ferns, ponderosa pines, and rocky sandstone formations. This large camp has many campfire rings, but it's often empty in wintertime, especially during the week. Water is dependable from a spring and the nearby Carmel River, which by this point on the trail is truly a river, no longer a stream.

To see Pine Falls, follow the well-worn route downstream for a little over 0.5 mile. The waterfall has an inviting pool below its drop, but getting to it is tricky, especially when the river is flowing hard. A route leads from the fall's brink, but is nearly vertical and often extremely muddy. Proceed slowly. If you can make it to the fall's base, this is the best spot for taking photographs.

From the waterfall and camp, you have the option of retracing your steps for a 10.6-mile round-trip or taking the trail from the upper end of the camp, which climbs steeply to the south and then southeast to meet up with the Pine Ridge Trail. From this junction, turn left on Pine Ridge Trail and hike back to Church Creek Divide, making an excellent 13-mile loop trip.

The Ventana Wilderness is rife with waterfalls, both named and unnamed. If the trip to Pine Falls whets your appetite, try a longer hike to the waterfalls on Pick Creek, Ventana Mesa Creek, or the Little Sur River. Contact the Monterey Ranger District for details.

Directions

From Greenfield on U.S. 101, take the G-16/Monterey County Road exit and drive west for 29 miles. Turn south on Tassajara Road and drive 1.3 miles to Cachagua Road. Turn left and drive nine miles to the trailhead, located just past the turnoff for China Campground. (The road turns to dirt; high-clearance vehicles are recommended. The county sometimes closes the road during bad weather; phone the Monterey Ranger District before traveling.)

Information and Contact

A national forest Adventure Pass is required. A free wilderness permit is required for overnight stays; they are available from the Monterey Ranger District Office (below). Maps of the Ventana Wilderness or Los Padres National Forest are available for a fee from the National Forest Store (406/329-3024, www.nationalforeststore.com), or can be downloaded for free from www.fs.fed.us/r5/maps/. For more information, contact Los Padres National Forest, Monterey Ranger District, 831/385-5434, www.fs.fed.us/r5/lospadres.

9 LIMEKILN FALLS   BEST ☾
Limekiln State Park

🏃 ⛰

Level: Easy   **Distance:** 1.0 mile round-trip

Best Season: December–June   **Elevation Change:** Total gain 200 feet

© ANN MARIE BROWN

Limekiln Falls

Don't tell everybody, but the waterfall at Limekiln State Park is more spectacular than Pfeiffer Falls at Pfeiffer Big Sur State Park. Limekiln's fall is so good, it even gives ocean-bound McWay Falls at Julia Pfeiffer Burns State Park a run for the money.

It used to be that getting to Limekiln Falls required some serious rock-hopping. You had to tango with the stream gods, tap dance over some slippery boulders, and take your chances on getting your feet wet. But in 2000, the park greatly improved the trail to the falls, installing good signs and sturdy bridges. Today this is a trip that almost anyone can make. Be sure to combine this walk with a short extension to see the park's namesake limekilns, which were used to manufacture limestone bricks and cement in the 1880s. The presence of the kilns gives you a clue as to what the waterfall is going to look like. Rather than dropping over a granite or basalt cliff, it fans out over a limestone face.

Start hiking from the end of the campground on the signed path through the redwoods. The route is similar to other coastal trails in Big Sur; it parallels a stream that's surrounded by big trees, ferns, rocks, and sorrel. Cross a bridge over Lime-kiln Creek immediately past the campground, then in another 0.25 mile, cross a second bridge. Just past this bridge is the right turnoff to the falls. Continuing straight leads you to the four limekilns, which look like giant smokestacks with mossy brick bottoms. Pay them a visit before or after seeing the falls.

Limekiln Falls pours down 100 feet over a nearly vertical sheet of limestone. On one May visit, its stream was so forceful that it fanned out to 25 feet wide at the bottom. The daylight is surprisingly bright by the waterfall, in contrast to the dark and shady forest you've been traveling in. The waterfall's rock cliff prevents any trees from growing nearby and blocking out the sun.

Limekiln is the northernmost limestone-based waterfall in California, although there are plenty more to the south: Rose Valley Falls in Ojai, Nojoqui Falls near San Luis Obispo, and several of the waterfalls in the Santa Monica Mountains.

Directions
From Carmel, drive 52 miles south on Highway 1 to Limekiln State Park, on the east side of the highway. (It's 2.5 miles south of Lucia, and 14.8 miles south of Julia Pfeiffer Burns State Park.) The trailhead is at the far side of the inland campground.

Information and Contact
An $8 day-use fee is charged per vehicle. A park map is available at the entrance kiosk, at Big Sur Station, or by free download at www.parks.ca.gov. For more information, contact Limekiln State Park, c/o Big Sur Station, 831/667-2315 or 831/667-2403, www.parks.ca.gov.

🔟 BEAR GULCH AND CONDOR GULCH
Pinnacles National Monument

Level: Easy

Distance: 3.0 miles round-trip

Best Season: December–April

Elevation Change: Total gain 500 feet

Pinnacles National Monument is not known as a watery place. Much of the year, it's darn hot and dry as a bone. But when the rains come in winter, a magical change occurs amid the spires, crags, and caves of the rocky park: the creeks in Bear and Condor Gulches start to run, creating short-lived but beautiful waterfalls.

Pinnacles is designed to be a hiker's park. No roads cross the park from east to west, although you can hike from one side to the other. It's a perfect setup for people who like their national parks to seem, well, natural. But it also means that if you don't have the time or energy to hike the four miles one-way across the park, you need to make sure you drive to the proper park entrance, east or west. To see the waterfalls in Bear and Condor Gulches, you want the east entrance to Pinnacles.

Bear Gulch Falls

Start hiking from the Bear Gulch Day Use Area, heading downstream along Bear Gulch. After passing a few park residences, cross the stream and walk parallel to the park access road. It's only 0.25 mile from the day-use parking lot to the waterfall. The path is nearly level until you reach the falls, then it steepens as you drop to its jumbled, boulder-choked base. Although the trail doesn't go right beside the 25-foot waterfall, it offers some good views of it and of the many cascades along the stream. The water snakes around big volcanic boulders, winds circuitously through the canyon bottom, and even pours through rock arches.

After getting a good look at Bear Gulch Falls, retrace your steps to the day-use parking lot, then pick up the trail across the road, signed as the Condor Gulch Trail. It's a good 30-minute climb to an overlook, which provides some aerobic exercise on a smooth trail with good switchbacks. In the wet season, you can hear the cascades as you climb because the stream parallels the trail, but you can't always see the water. The scent of wild sage and rosemary is enticingly aromatic, and your eyes will be drawn to the fascinating, colorful lichen growing on the equally colorful rocks. That is, until you start getting views of the high pinnacles and the cascades flowing down the hillside, which will surely divert your attention.

At the overlook, which is simply a metal railing on a ledge, you're standing on a huge, round boulder. In the rainy season, the headwaters of Condor Gulch's creek flow over the top. Its drop results in a narrow waterfall that pours a graceful 100 feet.

There are myriad hiking options at Pinnacles, especially in winter and spring when the weather is good and the wildflowers are in bloom. If this is your first visit to the park's east side, be sure to hike the Moses Spring Trail to Bear Gulch

Caves. Although these caves are closed in summer to protect nesting bats, at least some portion of the caves are open the rest of the year. Children and adults equally adore this trip. Just remember: bring a flashlight for the caves, preferably one for each person.

Directions

From the south: From King City on U.S. 101, take the First Street exit and head east. First Street turns into Highway G13/Bitterwater Road. Follow it for 15 miles to Highway 25, where you turn left (north). Follow Highway 25 for 14 miles to Highway 146. Turn left on Highway 146, and follow it for 4.8 miles to the park entrance and Bear Gulch nature center.

From the north: From Gilroy, drive south on U.S. 101 to the Highway 25/Hollister exit. Take Highway 25 south to Hollister, then continue 32 miles south on Highway 25 to Highway 146, where you turn right (west). From Highway 146, follow the directions above.

Information and Contact

There is a $5 entrance fee per vehicle at Pinnacles National Monument, good for seven days. Park maps are available for free at the entrance stations and visitor center, or by free download at www.nps.gov/pinn. For more information, contact Pinnacles National Monument, 831/389-4485, www.nps.gov/pinn.

MORE WATERFALLS IN MONTEREY AND BIG SUR

•**Pico Blanco Camp Waterfall, Ventana Wilderness.** This waterfall is on the Little Sur River and is accessible via the Pico Blanco Trail or Little Sur Trail. For more information, phone Los Padres National Forest, Monterey Ranger District, 831/385-5434.

•**Ventana Mesa Creek Waterfall, Ventana Wilderness.** The fall drops on Ventana Mesa Creek near the Carmel River. It's accessible via the Carmel River Trail out of Pine Valley Camp. For more information, phone Los Padres National Forest, Monterey Ranger District, 831/385-5434.

•**Pick Creek Falls, Ventana Wilderness.** Accessible via the South Fork Trail, Pick Creek Falls is found near South Fork Camp on the Big Sur River. For more information, phone Los Padres National Forest, Monterey Ranger District, 831/385-5434.

YOSEMITE AND MAMMOTH LAKES

© ANN MARIE BROWN

BEST WATERFALLS

❰ Easy Waterfall Walks
Rainbow, Lower, and Minaret Falls, **page 307**

❰ Swimming Holes
Rainbow Pool Falls, **page 256**

❰ Wheelchair-Accessible
Bridalveil Fall, **page 286**
Yosemite Falls, **page 289**

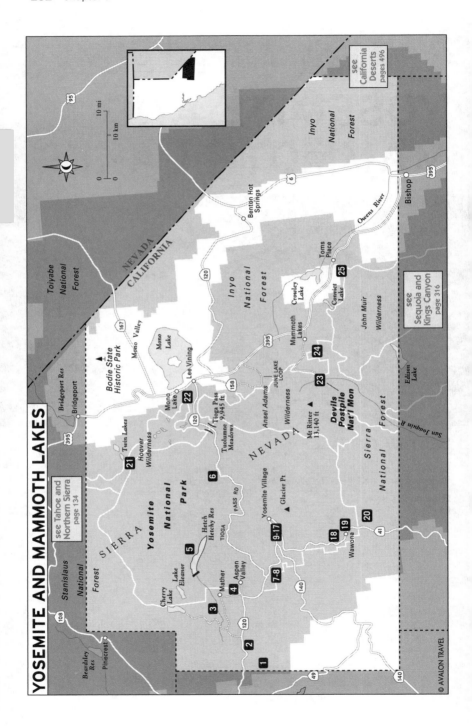

TRAIL NAME	LEVEL	DISTANCE	ELEVATION	SEASON	FEATURES	PAGE
1 Diana Falls	Easy	1.0 mile rt	50 ft	Apr.-Oct.	🥾🧗	255
2 Rainbow Pool Falls	Easy	0.25 mile rt	50 ft	Apr.-Oct.	🥾🧗	256
3 Preston Falls	Moderate	8.8 mi rt	500 ft	Mar.-May	🥾🧗	258
4 Carlon Falls	Easy	4.0 mi rt	350 ft	year-round	🥾	260
5 Tueeulala, Wapama, and Rancheria Falls	Easy/Moderate	4.8-13.0 mi rt	300-1,500 ft	Mar.-June	🥾	262
6 Foresta Falls	Easy	2.0 mi rt	500 ft	Mar.-July	🥾	265
7 Little Nellie Falls	Moderate	5.5 mi rt	600 ft	Apr.-Oct.	🥾	267
8 Cascades and Wildcat Falls	Easy	0.5 mile rt	Negligible	Mar.-June	🥾	269
9 Staircase Falls	Easy	Negligible	3,200 ft	Mar.-July	🥾	272
10 Ribbon Fall	Easy	0.5 mile	50 ft	Mar.-June	🥾♿	273
11 Silver Strand Falls	Moderate/Strenuous	7.6-13.0 mi rt	400-2,200 ft	Apr.-June	🥾	275
12 Sentinel Fall	Easy/Moderate	4.0 mi rt	500 ft	Mar.-June	🥾	277
13 Illilouette Fall	Moderate	4.0 mi rt-8.5 mi/one-way	1,200-3,200 ft	May-Oct.	🥾	279

TRAIL NAME	LEVEL	DISTANCE	ELEVATION	SEASON	FEATURES	PAGE
14 Vernal and Nevada Falls	Moderate/Strenuous	1.4–6.5 mi rt	400–2,000 ft	Mar.–July	[icons]	283
15 Bridalveil Fall	Easy	0.5 mile rt	50 ft	Apr.–July	[icons]	286
16 Yosemite Falls	Easy/Strenuous	1.0–7.4 mi rt	50–2,700 ft	Dec.–July	[icons]	289
17 Alder Creek Falls	Moderate	8.2 mi rt	1,000 ft	Apr.–July	[icons]	293
18 Chilnualna Falls	Strenuous	8.0 mi rt	2,400 ft	Mar.–July	[icons]	295
19 Fish Camp Falls	Easy	1.0 mile rt	250 ft	Apr.–Aug.	[icons]	298
20 Tuolumne, California, LeConte, and Waterwheel Falls	Moderate/Strenuous	9.0–16.0 mi rt	400–1,900 ft	June–Oct.	[icons]	299
21 Horse Creek Falls	Moderate	4.0 mi rt	950 ft	June–Sept.	[icons]	304
22 Lundy Canyon Falls	Moderate	4.5 mi rt	700 ft	June–Sept.	[icons]	305
23 Rainbow, Lower, and Minaret Falls	Easy/Moderate	2.0–8.0 mi rt	200–400 ft	June–Sept.	[icons]	307
24 Twin Falls	Easy	0.5 mile rt	Negligible	June–Sept.	[icons]	311
25 Horsetail Falls	Moderate	4.0 mi rt	600 ft	June–Sept.	[icons]	312

1 DIANA FALLS
Stanislaus National Forest

🏃 🏊 🏕

Level: Easy

Best Season: April-October

Distance: 1.0 mile round-trip

Elevation Change: Total loss 50 feet

You could think of it as a neighborhood backyard swimming hole, except there's no neighborhood anywhere nearby. Diana Falls is set in Stanislaus National Forest, not far from the towns of Groveland and Coulterville and within an hour's drive of Yosemite National Park. But it's not on the road to any of those places, so you won't come across it by accident. It's an out-of-the-way, known-to-locals-only 20-foot-tall waterfall on Bean Creek, near its confluence with the North Fork Merced River.

From the trailhead, follow the trail along the west side of the river, hiking along an old dirt road for 0.5 mile. Here, the Merced River is a tame, gentle stream—not like a river at all—with bright green bunches of large-leaved Indian rhubarb growing along its banks.

Diana Falls

The dirt road gets narrower as you walk, eventually becoming single-track. At a fork in the trail, bear right. You'll leave the river and hike along the Bean Creek canyon. In just a few minutes, or about 150 yards, you'll reach the brink of Diana Falls. Several spurs descend the slope to its base.

Although the small, picturesque waterfall looks tame enough, exercise extreme caution on the slick, slippery granite surrounding it. More than a few accidents have happened here. Still, Diana Falls and its canyon are lovely, its swimming holes are first-rate, and you could easily spend a fun-filled afternoon here.

Directions

From Groveland, drive east on Highway 120 for seven miles to Smith Station Road (also signed as County Road J132 to Coulterville). Drive 5.7 miles, then make a sharp left turn on Greeley Hills Road. Drive 4.2 miles to the trailhead, just before a one-lane bridge. The trailhead (a gated dirt road at a "Road Closed" sign) is on the right and a large parking pullout is on the left. Or, from Coulterville at the junction of Highways 132 and 49, go east on Coulterville Road (County Road J132) for 8.5 miles, then bear right on Greeley Hills Road for 4.2 miles.

Information and Contact

There is no fee. Maps of Stanislaus National Forest are available for a fee from the National Forest Store (406/329-3024, www.nationalforeststore.com), or can be downloaded for free from www.fs.fed.us/r5/maps/. For more information, contact Stanislaus National Forest, Groveland Ranger District, 209/962-7825, www.fs.fed.us/r5/stanislaus.

2 RAINBOW POOL FALLS   BEST ◖

Stanislaus National Forest

Level: Easy

Best Season: April-October

Distance: 0.25 mile round-trip

Elevation Change: Total loss 50 feet

Yosemite National Park is so spectacular that it overshadows the beautiful terrain just outside the park border. Visitors are often so busy trying to take in all of Yosemite that they miss the lesser-known special places located just minutes away.

Rainbow Pool Falls is such a place. It's a combination 20-foot waterfall and swimming hole, located on Highway 120 in Stanislaus National Forest, just 10 miles from the Big Oak Flat entrance to Yosemite. It's the perfect place to take your kids swimming for the afternoon when Yosemite Valley is too hot and crowded, or to go waterfall-watching and people-watching any time.

The entrance to Rainbow Pool can be

Rainbow Pool Falls

easy to miss as you cruise down Highway 120, so be sure to watch for its sign at the highway bridge over the South Fork of the Tuolumne River. From the parking lot, a paved path leads a few hundred feet down to the fall's giant-sized pool.

Rainbow Pool Falls is a river waterfall, so all year-round it is wide and powerful with a full, rushing flow. The pool of Rainbow Pool is a perfectly round rock basin, bigger than most backyard swimming pools, and edged by a small beach. This is where the timid onlookers set up their lawn chairs to watch the bold swimmers dive, jump, slide, and wade around the falls and in the pool.

Teenagers seem particularly drawn to the waterfall's rock cliffs, about 20 feet high, which they use as a jumping platform. Younger kids and more cautious adults prefer to slide down the granite chute next to the main body of the waterfall. Many people do this in their bathing suits, but the timid (or wise) wear denim to protect their backsides.

Besides the waterfall and the natural diving board and slide, another great bonus for swimmers is that the water warms up nicely in summer, thanks to the low elevation (about 3,000 feet). You don't have to jump in, scream like a banshee from the cold shock, and climb back out again as fast as possible. The pool is large enough that you can paddle around without fear of getting hit by other divers. It's good fun.

If you want privacy, try swimming in the smaller pools above the falls. A trail leads upstream along the west side of the river; just walk as far as you like until a particular basin strikes your fancy. (Look for the trail at the closed bridge just above the waterfall, at the far edge of the parking lot.)

In addition to all the watery theatrics, Rainbow Pool has an interesting history. A busy tourist inn known as Fall Inn and later the Cliff House was located here in the early 20th century. The resort had several cabins and was a popular spot for travelers heading to Yosemite. Some of the cabin foundations are still visible today. Before the advent of the automobile and the building of Highway 120, Rainbow Pool was the site of a toll bridge over the South Fork. The toll keeper built his cabin on a rock promontory that jutted out over the cataract at Rainbow Pool.

Not surprisingly, Rainbow Pool is a well-loved spot. During the summer of 2010, public access to the waterfall was closed for four months so the Forest Service could do some restoration work. During the closure, many waterfall lovers and swimmers were sorely disappointed, but lots of much-needed sprucing up took place: the paved road and parking areas were seal-coated, railings and walkways were upgraded, and best of all, the vault toilets were improved.

One caveat: be sure to time your visit between 8 A.M. and 6 P.M., because the Forest Service locks the gates after hours to prevent people from getting rowdy at the falls in the evening. Rainbow Pool Falls is meant for good clean fun, and rangers plan to keep it that way.

Directions

From Groveland, drive east on Highway 120 for 13 miles (toward Yosemite National Park). The Rainbow Pool turnoff is on the right, at the highway bridge over the South Fork of the Tuolumne River, just before the road to Cherry Lake/Sweetwater Camp on the left.

Information and Contact

There is no fee. Maps of Stanislaus National Forest are available for a fee from the National Forest Store (406/329-3024, www.nationalforeststore.com), or can be downloaded for free from www.fs.fed.us/r5/maps/. For more information, contact Stanislaus National Forest, Groveland Ranger District, 209/962-7825, www.fs.fed.us/r5/stanislaus.

3 PRESTON FALLS
Stanislaus National Forest

Level: Moderate

Best Season: March–May

Distance: 8.8 miles round-trip

Elevation Change: Total gain 500 feet

Preston Falls is a river waterfall on the Tuolumne River, so it's not particularly tall, but it is plenty wide and has the capacity to roar like a lion during spring snowmelt. The 15-foot-high falls drop just a half-mile downstream of the boundary line for Yosemite National Park, not far from Hetch Hetchy Reservoir in the stretch of the Tuolumne River canyon managed by Stanislaus National Forest.

The hike to the falls is as enjoyable as the falls itself, especially in spring. Although some day hikers choose to suffer through the nearly intolerable grade of the Poopenaut Valley Trail to access the swimming holes and fishing spots on the Tuolumne River's free-flowing stretch west of Hetch Hetchy Dam, the Preston Flat Trail is a much more pleasant approach to this fine stretch of river. The path travels 4.4 miles up the river's north side on a moderately undulating grade, passing under the occasional shade of oaks and pines. Spring wildflowers are abundant in the surrounding grasslands and bird-watching is often very rewarding. It's rare to share the trail with more than a few other hikers.

As you near the falls, you pass by an old stone chimney. A homesteader named Preston built a cabin here, although no one is quite sure why he chose this spot. The river narrows into an impressive granite gorge just a short distance before the actual waterfall. At the trail's end is a photogenic vista of Preston Falls, a cascade formed where the Tuolumne River drops 15 feet over a granite ledge into a wide, blue-green pool.

Waterfall lovers should hike this trail in the spring, when the raging river and falls provide the most exciting viewing. Those who wish to fish or swim should wait to visit until summer, when the river quiets down.

Preston Falls

© ANN MARIE BROWN

Directions

From Groveland, drive east on Highway 120 for 14 miles toward Yosemite. Turn left on Cherry Lake Road, signed for Cherry Lake and Sweetwater Camp. Follow Cherry Lake Road 8.5 miles to Early Intake and cross the bridge across the Tuolumne River. Turn right and drive 0.8 mile to the trailhead parking area at the end of the road, just beyond Kirkwood Powerhouse.

Information and Contact

There is no fee. Maps of Stanislaus National Forest are available for a fee from the National Forest Store (406/329-3024, www.nationalforeststore.com), or can be downloaded for free from www.fs.fed.us/r5/maps/. For more information, contact Stanislaus National Forest, Groveland Ranger District, 209/962-7825, www.fs.fed.us/r5/stanislaus.

4 CARLON FALLS

Stanislaus National Forest and Yosemite National Park

Level: Easy

Best Season: Year-round

Distance: 4.0 miles round-trip

Elevation Change: Total gain 350 feet

In the minds of most park visitors, the words "Yosemite" and "waterfalls" go together like peanut butter and jelly. Except in fall. That's when people show up in Yosemite Valley, look at all the dark, dried-up water stains on the granite walls, and have to squint real hard and visualize.

If you prefer your autumn waterfalls to be real and not imagined, autumn is a perfect time to make the trip to Carlon Falls, on the South Fork Tuolumne River in the northwest section of Yosemite. The trip begins on Stanislaus National Forest land, then enters the Yosemite Wilderness, so you can visit Carlon Falls without having to deal with the crowds and the day-use fees in Yosemite. The only downside is that as soon as the trail enters the national park boundary, your

Carlon Falls

dog must turn around and go home (dogs are allowed only on national forest land, not national park land).

The trip is an easy hike, suitable for every level of hiker. The key is to make sure you walk on the north side of the river and not on the south side, where the picnic area is located. The north side has an excellent trail with an easy grade, but the trailhead is unsigned except for a small "No Camping" marker, so it's easy to get confused. The south side has an unmaintained angler's route, which is fun to follow if you don't mind scrambling through branches, climbing over rocks, and doing the limbo under fallen trees.

Make it easy on yourself and hike on the river's north side, heading upstream. You'll pass a Yosemite Wilderness sign a few hundred feet in, and walk by some old concrete foundations. These provide a clue to this area's history: From 1916–1938, this was the site of the popular Carl Inn. The resort could lodge as many as 100 guests and had a swimming pool and several guest cabins.

The trail stays close to the river for the first mile, then moves away from it and climbs gently. You'll reach Carlon Falls in less than an hour of very enjoyable walking through a dense incense cedar and fir forest. Only one 100-yard stretch, in which the trail climbs steeply up and over a landslide, presents much of a challenge. The rest of the walk is a mellow stroll through a lovely forest.

The trail deposits you at the base of Carlon Falls, where the 35-foot cataract drops over a granite ledge with more flow than you might expect from the size of the river. In April and May, the water flows with such force that it launches horizontally off the fall's lip, rather than just dropping vertically. About 100 yards downstream of the main waterfall, a long, lacelike cascade pours over slick granite slabs, with water streaming over and around the rocky potholes. It's a gorgeous spot.

This area is open for hiking year-round, although you may need snowshoes in winter. In spring, the river and falls run with incredible velocity. In summer, the air temperature is warm for hiking, but the river offers plenty of swimming holes, including a deep, wide one at the waterfall's base. In autumn, the dogwoods and black oaks turn red and gold, respectively. And miraculously, even at this dry time of year, the waterfall still flows.

An incredible variety of plant speciation surrounds the river and waterfall. Adding to the dense conifer and hardwood forest is an abundance of ferns and reeds growing near the water. The Indian rhubarb that grows in large clumps around the falls is some of the largest you'll find anywhere. (Because of its massive leaves, some people call it "elephant ears.") Together with the ferns, it turns a dazzling yellow in October.

Directions

From Groveland, drive east on Highway 120 for 22.5 miles to the Evergreen Road turnoff signed for Hetch Hetchy Reservoir (one mile west of the Big Oak Flat entrance to Yosemite). Follow Evergreen Road north for one mile to the far side of the bridge, just past Carlon Day-Use Area. Park on the right at the closed-off road on the north side of the bridge. (There is room for about five cars.) Begin hiking on the closed road, heading upstream. The road turns to single-track in about 100 yards.

Information and Contact

There is no fee. Maps of Stanislaus National Forest are available for a fee from the National Forest Store (406/329-3024, www.nationalforeststore.com), or can be downloaded for free from www.fs.fed.us/r5/maps/. For more information, contact Stanislaus National Forest, Groveland Ranger District, 209/962-7825, www.fs.fed.us/r5/stanislaus.

5 TUEEULALA, WAPAMA, AND RANCHERIA FALLS
Yosemite National Park

Level: Easy/Moderate

Best Season: March–June

Distance: 4.8–13.0 miles round-trip

Elevation Change: Total gain 300–1,500 feet

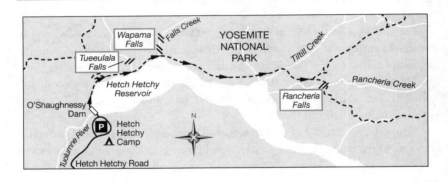

When people see pictures of what Hetch Hetchy Valley looked like before it was dammed and flooded in 1914 to provide water for San Francisco, they are struck by how much it resembles today's Yosemite Valley (minus the parking lots, pavement, and tour buses, of course). Photos show the stark, pristine granite of Kolana Rock and Hetch Hetchy Dome jutting upward from the valley floor, waterfalls dropping thousands of feet from hanging valleys like rivers falling from the sky, and lush, flower-filled meadows lining the edge of the meandering Tuolumne River.

You gotta wonder, what in the hell were those politicians thinking? Maybe it was something like: Hey, two Yosemites is one too many. Let's flood one, and keep the other for the tourists.

But here's the great irony: despite man's best efforts to destroy it, Hetch Hetchy remains beautiful. Of course, it's not the same as it was before it was flooded, and never can be again. But when you hike along the shoreline of Hetch Hetchy Reservoir and observe the higher sections of granite and waterfalls that still tower imposingly above the 400-foot-deep water line, you get the sense that

© ANN MARIE BROWN

Wapama Falls

Nature has ceased crying over Hetch Hetchy. Instead, she has done what she does best—heal, beautify, and make the most of what exists.

And waterfall-lovers still find plenty to treasure at Hetch Hetchy. For the best display, the key is to visit early in the year, no later than June 15. By July, Tueeulala Falls is usually dry and Wapama and Rancheria are less showy. Hetch Hetchy Reservoir is at a low elevation—3,800 feet—so it's imperative to hike here before the summer gets too hot. The elevation is the same as Yosemite Valley, but Hetch Hetchy is often about 10–15 degrees warmer. If you have to visit later in the summer, be sure to get an early-morning start and bring plenty of water or a water filter with you.

The low elevation means that Hetch Hetchy is one of the few places in Yosemite that is accessible for day hiking nearly year-round. The sun-baked north shore of the eight-mile-long reservoir can be warm even in the middle of winter, especially when you're climbing uphill on exposed granite. On rare occasions the park rangers have to close the trail during peak snowmelt in spring, because when Wapama Falls achieves flood level, high water and heavy spray make the trail impassable.

From the parking lot by O'Shaughnessy Dam, start your walk by crossing over the dam, then enter the long tunnel on the dam's far side and walk through its dimly lit 100-yard length. You'll exit into a leafy oak and bay forest and hear the water lapping along the deep reservoir's shore. After the first mile of trail, you'll reach a junction and head right, skirting the reservoir's edge for the entire length of your trip.

At this elevation, just about anything can grow. Springtime gives rise to a colorful wildflower display, including Indian paintbrush, mariposa lilies, purple brodiaea, and blue penstemon. These are a welcome addition to the omnipresent bear clover and plenty of poison oak.

Tueeulala is the first waterfall you reach at 1.5 miles out. It's tall, wispy, and becomes increasingly frail as the season wears on. If you arrive in July, it may have already disappeared, and you will wonder why they built all those trail bridges over a pile of dry rocks. The fall drops about 1,000 feet before it hits the lake's edge, so it must have been about 1,400 feet tall before the great flood.

The star waterfall of the trip is Wapama, which you reach at 2.4 miles. Wapama Falls on Falls Creek has such a wide, forceful flow that you can see it quite easily from O'Shaughnessy Dam and Hetch Hetchy Road even in midsummer. But the only place you can see the very top of the fall is from right below it, standing on one of its western bridges. In spring, you can't stand there for long without getting soaked. Bring your rain gear on cool spring days.

Many people simply hike to Wapama and back for an easy day hike that's just shy of five miles long. The trail is fairly level, and is pleasantly shaded by oaks, bays, and pines all the way up to Wapama Falls. Like at Tueeulala, you cross over Wapama's flow on a series of sturdy wood and steel bridges.

If you decide to stop for a rest or a picnic anywhere along the trail, keep in mind that the rules are strict at Hetch Hetchy: no swimming, no boating, no water contact, but fishing is okay. One ranger told us it was okay to wade into the creeks to cool off, but since the creeks empty into the reservoir, that logic seems rather strange.

For those continuing to Rancheria Falls, the trail now begins to climb and is less shaded than before, but it's still well-graded with lots of gentle switchbacks. It's all about the granite now. You walk on top of granite and you cast admiring glances at granite—Kolana Rock rises grandly from Hetch Hetchy's southern shore. From the bridges at Wapama Falls, four more miles and a 1,200-foot elevation gain take you to Rancheria Falls.

Because the trail rises, your wide-angle views of the reservoir improve. The water is so deep and so dramatically edged by granite, sand, and pines that some visitors say it reminds them of Lake Tahoe. Its depth creates a similar, rich sapphire color. In the afternoon, the sunlight does some dazzling twinkling on the reservoir's surface.

You reach Rancheria Creek at 5.7 miles out. Look for an unmarked fork 0.25 mile beyond your first peek at the creek, at a noticeable clearing along the right side of the trail. This spur trail leads to a section of stream 100 yards below 30-foot Rancheria Falls.

Here at creekside, under the shade of Jeffrey pines and black oaks, is a choice spot for waterfall-viewing, a picnic, and a rest. Keep on the lookout for bears—a small one tried to steal my lunch when I turned my back for 30 seconds to look at the falls. If you're backpacking, bear-proof food canisters are required in Hetch Hetchy, and for good reason. The bears at Hetch Hetchy are the boldest in all of Yosemite.

For another look at Rancheria Falls, continue on the main trail for 0.5 mile beyond the spur trail. At a trail junction, continue straight for Pleasant Valley. Less than 0.2 mile farther is a bridge above Rancheria Creek, where in high water you can glimpse the falls downstream.

Directions

From Groveland, drive east on Highway 120 for 22.5 miles to the Evergreen Road turnoff signed for Hetch Hetchy Reservoir (one mile west of the Big Oak Flat entrance to Yosemite). Follow Evergreen Road north to Camp Mather, then bear right and continue on Hetch Hetchy Road for a total of 16 miles to the dam and trailhead.

Information and Contact

There is a $20 entrance fee per vehicle at Yosemite National Park, which is good for seven days. Park maps are available for free at the entrance stations, or by download at www.nps.gov/yose. A more detailed map is available from Tom Harrison Maps, 415/456-7940, www.tomharrisonmaps.com. For more information, contact Yosemite National Park, 209/372-0200, www.nps.gov/yose.

6 FORESTA FALLS
Yosemite National Park

Level: Easy

Best Season: March–July

Distance: 2.0 miles round-trip

Elevation Change: Total loss 500 feet

If you're looking for an easy walk to a waterfall, and maybe a little solitude to go along with it, a drive to the small hamlet of Foresta can satisfy your desire.

Foresta is a group of private cabins tucked inside the border of Yosemite National Park. The little community is unknown to most park visitors because it's situated down in a valley below Big Oak Flat Road, hidden from sight to people driving by. Most of the cabins are owned by or rented to park employees.

Most people know the Big Oak Flat Road region as the fire-scarred stretch between Yosemite Valley and Tioga Road. In 1990, a lightning fire ignited here. Fueled by fierce winds, it created a firestorm that burned a total of 17,000 acres, including much of Foresta. The fire raged out of control for weeks.

But, as happens after a wildfire, Mother Nature got busy. Although many burned and blackened trees still stand, the undergrowth and young trees have come back in full force. Homeowners in Foresta have rebuilt their cabins and the area is quickly returning to its previous state.

Foresta Falls on Crane Creek sits on the perimeter of the burned area, a short distance from a cluster of cabins. When you hike around the falls, you'll notice the patchwork of burned and untouched vegetation. One tree is green and thriving; its neighbor is blackened. The effect is a little eerie, yet hauntingly beautiful.

To see the falls, you don't have to hike far. Park where the pavement ends on Foresta Road, then walk 0.4 mile down the dirt road and you're near the upper drop of the falls. The waterfall is a long series of cascades over granite, continuing for more than a mile. The most impressive stretch, a 40-foot-high cataract, is another 0.6 mile down the dirt road, where a bridge crosses the road. If the road is

Foresta Falls

open, technically you could drive to see this stretch of the cascade, but it's much more pleasant to walk it. In spring, when the waterfall is a glorious deluge, the road is often closed. That's the ideal time for a hike. A two-mile round-trip will provide you with plenty of cascading scenery, but if you can arrange a car shuttle, you can hike six miles one-way, following the closed road all the way downhill to El Portal. This is a great trip for those who love waterfalls and also spring wildflowers.

Even without the waterfalls, Crane Creek is a very attractive stream. Indian rhubarb grows in large clumps, poking out of the granite creekbed from the smallest of cracks. In the low water of late summer, mirrorlike pools lie below the cascades, only a couple of inches deep, with tiny granite islands poking up in the middle.

Directions

From Merced, drive 75 miles northeast on Highway 140 to Yosemite National Park. Follow the signs toward Yosemite Valley, entering through the Arch Rock entrance station. Continue 4.5 miles to the left turnoff for Tioga Road/Highway 120, looping back out of the valley on Big Oak Flat Road. In 3.4 miles, turn left on Foresta Road, which is 0.6 mile beyond the third tunnel on Big Oak Flat Road. Follow Foresta Road for 2.5 miles (stay left at the fork), to just beyond a group of cabins. Park where the pavement ends and start walking on the dirt road (the road is sometimes gated off at this point; if it's open, you can drive your car farther).

Information and Contact

There is a $20 entrance fee per vehicle at Yosemite National Park, which is good for seven days. Park maps are available for free at the entrance stations, or by download at www.nps.gov/yose. A more detailed map is available from Tom Harrison Maps, 415/456-7940, www.tomharrisonmaps.com. For more information, contact Yosemite National Park, 209/372-0200, www.nps.gov/yose.

7 LITTLE NELLIE FALLS
Stanislaus National Forest and Yosemite National Park

Level: Moderate

Distance: 5.5 miles round-trip

Best Season: April–October

Elevation Change: Total gain 600 feet

Little Nellie Falls on Little Crane Creek can be a drive-to waterfall or a hike-to waterfall. The driving option takes almost as long as the hiking option, so I highly recommend the latter. If you begin your trip in the small community of Foresta in Yosemite National Park, you can hike less than three miles one-way to the waterfall, out of the park boundary and into Stanislaus National Forest. The route is a rough, rarely used four-wheel-drive road. It's best taken on foot anyway, because it climbs above Foresta and Big Meadow to a rise just high enough for a view into the smack-dab-center of Yosemite Valley. There you are, 15 miles from Half Dome, and it looks close and imposing enough that you might think you could reach out and touch it.

Little Nellie Falls

Leave your car just outside of Foresta, near either Big Meadow or Foresta Falls (see Foresta Falls listing in this chapter), then hike along the four-wheel-drive road. Along the way, keep looking over your right shoulder for the incredible view of Yosemite Valley. It's a good climb to the top of the rise, heading northward with about a 500-foot gain, but the trail levels out as you veer west. You leave the fire-scarred area around Foresta and enter into thick conifer and hardwood forest on the border of Stanislaus National Forest.

About 0.5 mile from the fall, you pass through a metal gate that you must close behind you. Then the road drops down to where Little Crane Creek crosses it. Little Nellie Falls is just above the road in plain sight. It's a pretty drop of about 30 feet over a granite ledge, nestled in Indian rhubarb. There's a terrific campsite just across the road, next to Little Crane Creek, with a great view of the fall. You can spend the night here, if you like, with the sound of the water lulling you to sleep, but most people just hike in for the day, then make the easy trip back downhill to Big Meadow and Foresta. The road/trail beyond the falls leads six miles to the Merced Grove of Big Trees.

If you prefer to drive to the falls instead of hike, the best way to do so is to start near Yosemite's Big Oak Flat entrance station and access the falls via Stanislaus National Forest roads. Four-wheel-drive is highly recommended for this route: from Highway 120, turn south on the eastern end of Harden Flat Road, 1.5 miles west of the Big Oak Flat entrance. In less than 0.5 mile, bear left on Forest Service Road 2S30, which is also signed as Road 20 in places, and head for Five Corners. Follow 2S30 for 8.5 miles along Crocker Ridge until you reach Five Corners. Turn left on 1S12, a dirt road, heading for Trumbull Peak. Stay on 1S12 for 15 miles, following the road signs for Moss Canyon and then Little Nellie Falls.

Check out the incredible views into Yosemite Valley at approximately 13 miles on 1S12. At 15 miles, reach a hairpin left turn; take it and continue 0.3 mile to Little Nellie Falls. (If you miss the hairpin turn and continue straight, the road dead-ends.)

Whether you drive or hike to the falls, a map of Stanislaus National Forest is a necessity. A vast web of forest roads and spurs surrounds Little Nellie Falls.

Directions

From Merced, drive 75 miles northeast on Highway 140 to Yosemite National Park. Follow the signs toward Yosemite Valley, entering through the Arch Rock entrance station. Continue 4.5 miles to the left turnoff for Tioga Road/Highway 120, looping back out of the valley on Big Oak Flat Road. In 3.4 miles, turn left on Foresta Road, which is 0.6 mile beyond the third tunnel on Big Oak Flat Road. Follow Foresta Road for 1.8 miles to a fork, where you bear right and skirt along the edge of Big Meadow. Park off the road, being careful to stay off private property, and continue hiking up the dirt road, heading north and then west. (Most of the year, you can also drive this road, but high-clearance and four-wheel drive is necessary.)

Information and Contact

To access the falls from Foresta, you must pay a $20 per vehicle entrance fee at Yosemite National Park, good for seven days. The hike begins in Yosemite National Park but enters Stanislaus National Forest, so a Stanislaus National Forest map is recommended. Maps of Stanislaus National Forest are available for a fee from the National Forest Store (406/329-3024, www.nationalforeststore.com), or can be downloaded for free from www.fs.fed.us/r5/maps/. For more information, contact Stanislaus National Forest, Groveland Ranger District, 209/962-7825, www.fs.fed.us/r5/stanislaus.

8 CASCADES AND WILDCAT FALLS
Yosemite National Park

Level: Easy

Best Season: March–June

Distance: 0.5 mile round-trip

Elevation Change: Negligible

Of all the scenic places in California, only in Yosemite Valley can you have so many waterfall experiences so easily, and in such close proximity to one another.

Take Wildcat Falls and The Cascades, for example. To enter Yosemite National Park from the west, you make the narrow, winding drive along the Merced River on Highway 140. Then you pay your national park entrance fee and pick up a free map at the Arch Rock station. You drive less than three miles farther and—wham! Your head is turned by an incredibly tall and narrow spill of white water down the canyon wall on your left. Before you even have the chance to hit the brakes, your eyes are riveted to a wide, plunging cataract just 100 yards ahead. This time, you're prepared, and you make a quick turn into the parking lot to investigate.

© ANDREW SAWADISAVI

The Cascades

Welcome to Yosemite. Wildcat Falls and The Cascades in spring serve as the valley's welcoming committee on Highway 140—a sure sign that you're here, you've made the long trip, and now the fun is about to begin. Many first-time visitors to the park are so excited by the sight of these falls, especially The Cascades, that they think they are looking at Yosemite Falls. Almost every spring you hear someone at The Cascades' parking lot asking to have their picture taken in front of "Yosemite Falls." Well, these falls are certainly good, but they are just a warm-up.

The two waterfalls are only 100 yards apart, but they are vastly different in appearance and character. Wildcat Falls is by far the lesser known, mostly because it doesn't have a parking lot right in front of it. Some people drive by and don't even see it. The Cascades is impossible to miss, especially in springtime, but the waterfall is not signed in any way, so people rarely learn its name.

You can see both falls in the same visit, parking at either of the two lots near them and then walking a short route in between. You can park at Cascades Picnic Area on the south side of the road, which is actually closer to Wildcat Falls, or you can park at the parking lot by mile marker M1 on the north side of the road, which is where The Cascades falls.

The Cascades are easy to view. An overlook area by the M1 parking lot offers the best perspective, even though it's about 200 yards away from the base of the falls and off to the side. Many people get out of their cars, take a few pictures, and go sit somewhere close to the stream to inhale the sweet air of Yosemite. Huge boulders make climbing obstacles for kids and places for adults to claim as their picnic spot. Each rock has a slightly different view of the falls.

From here you can take a 10-minute walk to the west, paralleling the road on the north side, to see Wildcat Falls. Wildcat is more hidden by trees than The Cascades, so it's easier to see by foot than by car. From the M1 parking lot, you'll see a good use trail leading west that stays safely off the road. If you're parked in the Cascades Picnic Area lot, just cross the road and pick up the route on the other side, still heading west.

Wildcat is a tall, narrow free fall, and very different in shape from The Cascades. You can walk right to its base, but the view is better if you stand back about 50 feet, next to a large Jeffrey pine, where the cataract's great height is visible.

Surprisingly, both waterfalls continue to flow in autumn, when most waterfalls in Yosemite Valley are dry. They are not their lavish springtime selves, of course, but they run. Wildcat Falls is formed on little Wildcat Creek, which has a relatively small watershed but a lot of vegetation, whereas The Cascades is formed by two streams, Cascade Creek and Tamarack Creek. The two streams join several hundred feet above you, just below Big Oak Flat Road. Cascade Creek forms waterfalls all the way up and above Big Oak Flat Road, although none are equal in beauty to The Cascades.

To view Cascade Creek's higher falls on Big Oak Flat Road, take the left turnoff for Highway 120/Tioga Road 1.7 miles east of the M1 parking lot, then drive 1.9 miles, through two tunnels, to the parking pullouts on both sides of the bridge over Cascade Creek. You can walk on the bridge to look at the fall.

Many people stop to admire Cascade Creek's upper falls on Big Oak Flat Road without realizing that farther downstream, where Cascade Creek joins with its next-door neighbor, Tamarack Creek, the real falls begin. People often visit both sets of falls on Cascade Creek—those on Big Oak Flat Road and Highway 140—without realizing they are formed by the same creek.

For a look at the full 500-foot height of The Cascades, you must drive east on Big Oak Flat Road, coming from the Big Oak Flat park entrance or from Tioga Road into the valley. A half mile west of the bridge over Cascade Creek, a long pullout on the south side of the road offers an awesome view of the entire height of The Cascades, with Yosemite Valley as a backdrop.

Directions

From Merced, drive 75 miles northeast on Highway 140 to Yosemite National Park. Follow the signs toward Yosemite Valley, entering through the Arch Rock entrance station. Set your odometer at Arch Rock and drive 2.8 miles east, into the valley. Park at either The Cascades Picnic Area parking lot on the right side of the road, or the parking lot by the M1 road marker on the left side of the road. (The parking lot by the M1 road marker is 0.1 mile farther east.)

Information and Contact

There is a $20 entrance fee per vehicle at Yosemite National Park, which is good for seven days. Park maps are available for free at the entrance stations, or by download at www.nps.gov/yose. A more detailed map is available from Tom Harrison Maps, 415/456-7940, www.tomharrisonmaps.com. For more information, contact Yosemite National Park, 209/372-0200, www.nps.gov/yose.

9 STAIRCASE FALLS
Yosemite National Park

Level: Easy

Best Season: March–July

Distance: Negligible

Elevation Change: 3,200 feet

Staircase Falls delivers exactly what its name promises—a waterfall that drops in a perfect series of stairstepped right angles. Instead of seeing the "staircase" from the front, you see it from the side, and are treated to an unusual view of a tidy chain of linked L-shapes descending gracefully down the cliff behind Curry Village.

People who vacation in the village in springtime tend to think of Staircase Falls as their own private waterfall, but you can see it without staying at the hotel or camping in the tent cabins. The best vista is not in Curry Village at all, but in the large meadow just north of the village, called Stoneman Meadow on some maps.

Staircase is one of Yosemite Valley's ephemeral falls—the kind you have to act fast to see. By late July, it will have vanished. The fall is very narrow compared to many others in the valley, but it wins the Most Unusual Shape award, hands-down. Binoculars are a good idea, although you can see the outline of the falls without them.

From your viewpoint in the meadow, you also have a fine lookout on Half Dome, North Dome, Washington Column, and Glacier Point. If you time it just right, you may be able to spot Royal Arch Cascade on the opposite canyon wall, flowing downhill just to the left of the Royal Arches. (The Arches are easily distinguishable on the north canyon wall by their arch-like shape.)

Directions

From Merced, drive 75 miles northeast on Highway 140 to Yosemite National Park. Follow the signs toward Yosemite Valley, entering through the Arch Rock entrance station. Continue on El Portal Road, which becomes Southside Drive, for 11.6 miles to the Curry Village day-use parking area. Don't turn right into Curry Village; instead, continue straight to the pullouts on the north side of the big meadow. Park and look at the south canyon wall, behind Curry Village.

Information and Contact

There is a $20 entrance fee per vehicle at Yosemite National Park, which is good for seven days. Park maps are available for free at the entrance stations, or by download at www.nps.gov/yose. A more detailed map is available from Tom Harrison Maps, 415/456-7940, www.tomharrisonmaps.com. For more information, contact Yosemite National Park, 209/372-0200, www.nps.gov/yose.

10 RIBBON FALL
Yosemite National Park

Level: Easy

Best Season: March–June

Distance: 0.5 mile

Elevation Change: Total gain 50 feet

When all the waterfalls are flowing in Yosemite Valley, usually in that brief March–June period of snowmelt and spring rain, you may notice a curious pattern: At several places in the park, if you stand facing one waterfall, another waterfall can be found directly at your back.

Ribbon Fall

For instance, Yosemite Falls plunges off the canyon's north wall, while across from it, Sentinel Fall dives off the south wall. Staircase Falls stairsteps down the canyon's south wall, while across from it, Royal Arch Cascade tumbles down the north wall. Bridalveil Fall hurtles off the canyon's south wall, while across from it, Ribbon Fall leaps off the north wall. There's no logical or even geological explanation for this magical "pairing" of Valley waterfalls, and the phenomenon doesn't last long. Just enjoy the spectacle while you can, before most of these falls disappear for the summer.

One of the best spots to see the pairing effect is at the Bridalveil Fall overlook (a short walk from the Bridalveil parking area). If you stare up at Bridalveil, then do an about-face and turn your back to it, you're looking directly at 1,612-foot Ribbon Fall, a tall, delicate, silver thread of a waterfall. It seems impossibly long and narrow, just like its name. Many people see Ribbon from the Bridalveil overlook and mistake it for Yosemite Falls, probably because of its position on the north wall of the canyon, but Ribbon's yearly life span is far shorter than Yosemite's, and its flow is much weaker.

Although Ribbon Fall doesn't have the splashy, showy presence of other Valley falls, it holds the illustrious title of being the highest free-leaping waterfall in Yosemite. The operative phrase is free-leaping, because unlike most falls, Ribbon has no points where its stream contacts the granite wall behind it, forming a cascade. Instead, its fall remains unbroken. (Yosemite Falls, in contrast, free leaps 1,430 feet, then cascades 675 feet, then free-leaps another 320 feet.)

Ribbon Fall also has the distinction of having El Capitan for its neighbor. If you park your car in the parking pullouts on either side of Southside Drive near Cathedral Rocks (look for road marker V14, 0.5 mile east of the Highway 41/Bridalveil Fall turnoff), you get an incredible vista of El Capitan (7,042 feet) with Ribbon Fall on its left. And of course, if you simply turn around, you can see Ribbon's pair, Bridalveil Fall, dashing off the south canyon wall. Be sure to get a photo of Ribbon Fall arm-in-arm with El Capitan, because next to that huge piece of granite, Ribbon looks even more spectacular.

But remember, you have to make your trip early. By midsummer each year, Ribbon Fall disappears.

Directions

To see Ribbon Fall from the Bridalveil Fall Overlook, from Merced, drive 75 miles northeast on Highway 140 to Yosemite National Park. Follow the signs toward Yosemite Valley, entering through the Arch Rock entrance station. Continue on El Portal Road, which becomes Southside Drive, for 6.3 miles, then turn right at the fork for Highway 41/Wawona/Fresno. Turn left almost immediately into the Bridalveil Fall parking lot. The trail begins at the far end of the parking lot. (If you are driving into the park from the southern entrance near Wawona, watch for the Bridalveil Fall turnoff on your right as you drive into the valley on Highway 41.)

Another good viewing point for Ribbon Fall is near road marker V14 on Southside Drive, 6.6 miles east of the Arch Rock entrance (0.5 mile east of the Highway 41/Bridalveil Fall turnoff).

Information and Contact

There is a $20 entrance fee per vehicle at Yosemite National Park, which is good for seven days. Park maps are available for free at the entrance stations, or by download at www.nps.gov/yose. A more detailed map is available from Tom Harrison Maps, 415/456-7940, www.tomharrisonmaps.com. For more information, contact Yosemite National Park, 209/372-0200, www.nps.gov/yose.

11 SILVER STRAND FALLS
Yosemite National Park

Level: Moderate/Strenuous

Best Season: April-June

Distance: 7.6-13.0 miles round-trip

Elevation Change: Total loss/gain
400-2,200 feet

The funny thing about Yosemite waterfalls is that there are so many of them, you can get a little jaded. Even some cartographers have gotten blasé about Yosemite waterfalls—so much so that they don't bother drawing them in on maps, unless the falls happen to be world-famous, such as Yosemite Falls or Bridalveil. Many other excellent park waterfalls suffer from neglect because everybody is off visiting the celebrated ones.

Take Silver Strand Falls on the south canyon rim. Silver Strand would be worthy of its own park in any other part of California, but here in Yosemite, you can't even find it on the park map. It's a pity, because hiking to Silver Strand Falls is a stellar trip, complete with thick forest, a huge waterfall, and unparalleled scenic vistas.

Silver Strand Falls

© ANDREW SAWADISAVI

Silver Strand is perched between Inspiration Point and Stanford Point, closer to the latter, 0.25 mile off the Pohono Trail. There's a long way and a short way to get there, and most people choose to hike the short way, starting from the Wawona Tunnel Trailhead. Heading steadily uphill the whole way, the trail reaches stunning Inspiration Point at 1.3 miles, followed by Stanford Point at 3.8 miles. Stanford Point is accessible via a short spur trail to the left, which extends to the valley's rim, and from there, you can observe the waterfall's 1,170-foot drop, formed where Meadow Brook takes a dive off Yosemite's south canyon wall.

The Wawona Trailhead itself is a destination for many park visitors, because the views from here are as good as anywhere in the park, with the possible exception of Glacier Point. The parking lot has stellar vistas of Bridalveil Fall, Half Dome,

El Capitan, and the entire valley. Park on either side of the road just east of the Wawona Tunnel; then find the trailhead on the south side.

Three facts should be understood when planning your trip: First, the Pohono Trail does not go directly to Silver Strand Falls; in fact, no trail does. The only way to see it is to hike to Stanford Point, then look to the west. The fall is only 0.25 mile away, over your left shoulder as you face Yosemite Valley. The view from the point is remarkable, taking in Silver Strand Falls, Bridalveil Fall, Ribbon Fall, and the valley floor 3,000 feet below you.

Second, the waterfall's duration is short—it flows only in spring. By July, Meadow Brook (Silver Strand's stream) dries up completely. And finally, there are no bridges on this part of the Pohono Trail. Hiking from the Wawona Tunnel, you must cross Meadow Brook to reach Stanford Point, and this can be a challenge. When Silver Strand is at its strongest flow, conditions will be either very wet or very snowy along the Pohono Trail, especially at the stream crossing. When I hiked it, snow still covered the ground and a snow bridge carried me across. You must check with rangers about springtime trail conditions before you head out.

It's a grunt of a climb to get to Stanford Point from the Wawona Tunnel Trailhead, with a gain of 2,200 feet. This explains why some people opt for the longer but more level route, which starts at the McGurk Meadow Trailhead on Glacier Point Road. From there, you head out on the McGurk Meadow Trail for 2.2 miles, then turn left on the Pohono Trail. Hike four miles, then take the right cutoff for Stanford Point. In addition to an easy grade, this longer route has some incredible scenic offerings, including pristine McGurk Meadow (1.2 miles in) and three vista points: Dewey (5.2 miles in), Crocker (5.8 miles in), and Stanford (6.5 miles in). Perched at 7,300 feet in elevation, these three points have unique perspectives on just about everything in the valley.

Directions

For the Wawona Tunnel Trailhead: From Merced, drive 75 miles northeast on Highway 140 to Yosemite National Park. Follow the signs toward Yosemite Valley, entering through the Arch Rock entrance station. Continue on El Portal Road, which becomes Southside Drive, for 6.3 miles, then turn right at the fork for Highway 41/Wawona/Fresno. Continue 1.5 miles to the parking lots on either side of the road just before you enter the Wawona Tunnel. The trailhead is at the parking lot on the left (south) side of the road.

For the McGurk Meadow Trailhead: Follow the directions as above, but continue through the Wawona Tunnel and beyond for another eight miles to Glacier Point Road. Turn left on Glacier Point Road, and drive 7.5 miles to the McGurk Meadow Trailhead on the left. Park in the pullout about 75 yards farther up the road.

Information and Contact

There is a $20 entrance fee per vehicle at Yosemite National Park, which is good for seven days. Park maps are available for free at the entrance stations, or by download at www.nps.gov/yose. A more detailed map is available from Tom Harrison Maps, 415/456-7940, www.tomharrisonmaps.com. For more information, contact Yosemite National Park, 209/372-0200, www.nps.gov/yose.

12 SENTINEL FALL
Yosemite National Park

Level: Easy/Moderate

Best Season: March–June

Distance: 4.0 miles round-trip

Elevation Change: Total gain 500 feet

© KENT SUMMERS

Sentinel Fall

In the list of the 10 Highest Free-Falling Waterfalls in the World, waterfalls in Yosemite Valley claim two spots—number five and number eight. Yosemite Falls on the north valley wall is rated as a free fall of 2,425 feet, and Sentinel Fall on the south valley wall is rated as a free fall of 2,000 feet. (These two are only beaten by Angel Falls in Venezuela at 3,212 feet, Tugela Falls in South Africa at 3,110 feet, and a few hard-to-spell Norwegian waterfalls in the 2,500-foot range.)

Well, just about anybody who has ever been to the Sierra Nevada has seen Yosemite Falls. But in an unofficial poll I took one spring day in Yosemite Valley, few people had even heard of Sentinel Fall, even though they were all standing within easy view of it.

You can see it by car or you can see it by foot. I first found it while driving on Northside Drive, heading west out of the valley. When I pulled into a small parking area between the Three Brothers and El Capitan and walked a few yards down to the Merced River's edge, I spotted an incredibly long, thin waterfall leaping and sliding down the right side of Sentinel Rock, far across the canyon.

Of course, if you are going to view Sentinel Fall from this far away, you'll need to bring your binoculars. Or do what I did, which was to loop back around the valley to get a better look from Southside Drive, near the Four Mile Trail Trailhead. Pullouts are located on both sides of the road, and if you aren't too distracted by the views to the north of Yosemite Falls, you'll be able to spot Sentinel Fall to the south. To make it easy, first locate Sentinel Rock, then look for the fall pouring down to the right. Sentinel Fall is set back slightly from Sentinel Rock, and it has three main free-leaping sections connected by brief cascades.

So if Sentinel Fall is the eighth-largest waterfall in the world, why doesn't it get more attention? Sentinel Fall, like dozens of other waterfalls in Yosemite, is an ephemeral waterfall, which means it doesn't run year-round. In fact, if you don't get to Yosemite in springtime, you have to wait until your next trip for another chance to see Sentinel Fall. Although Yosemite Falls is also an ephemeral fall, its creek is full enough and drains a large enough watershed so that it runs a few months longer than Sentinel, and with a more spectacular show.

If you prefer to see Sentinel Fall close-up, drive to Glacier Point Road and lace up your hiking boots. In addition to having the chance to see the fall from its brink, you also get to take a classic Yosemite high-country hike that is short enough and easy enough for families to enjoy. The trip is a great four-mile loop from the Sentinel Dome and Taft Point Trailhead, and if you add an extra mile to it, you can visit Taft Point, with its spectacular rock fissures and view of the valley floor 3,000 feet below.

It's best to start the loop by heading left, toward Taft Point. After 0.5 mile, take the right fork to go directly to Sentinel Fall (the trail is signed for Sentinel Dome and Glacier Point), or take the left fork for a 0.5-mile side-trip to Taft Point, then return to the junction. If you head directly to Sentinel Fall, you'll walk through dense Jeffrey pine forest for a mile and then meet up with Sentinel Creek. There's no bridge, so if the creek is flooding, cross it with great care.

Take the spur trail on the far side of the creek that runs for 50 yards to the canyon rim, where you can peer over the edge (very carefully) at Sentinel's big drop. In springtime, the sight of the powerful plunge can make your toes curl. Check out the interesting view of the back side of Sentinel Rock, which is just ahead of you.

From Sentinel Creek, the trail climbs for a mile, reaching some spectacular overlooks of Yosemite Valley and Yosemite Falls, then reaches a junction where you head right for Sentinel Dome, 0.5 mile away. Climb some more to reach its base, where you can decide whether or not to take another side-trip off your loop—ascending to the top of the dome for spectacular views to the north and east. If you have any energy left, go for it. It only takes about 10 minutes to reach the top, and it makes you feel like a real mountaineer.

At the base of the dome, pick up the paved trail that curves around to its south side, then head back to the dirt single-track path for the final leg of your loop. It's just one mile back to the trailhead.

Directions

From Merced, drive 75 miles northeast on Highway 140 to Yosemite National Park. Follow the signs toward Yosemite Valley, entering through the Arch Rock entrance station. Continue on El Portal Road, which becomes Southside Drive, for 6.3 miles, then turn right at the fork for Highway 41/Wawona/Fresno. Continue 9.2 miles, then turn left on Glacier Point Road and drive 13.2 miles to the Taft Point/Sentinel Dome Trailhead parking lot, on the left side of the road.

Information and Contact

There is a $20 entrance fee per vehicle at Yosemite National Park, which is good for seven days. Park maps are available for free at the entrance stations, or by download at www.nps.gov/yose. A more detailed map is available from Tom Harrison Maps, 415/456-7940, www.tomharrisonmaps.com. For more information, contact Yosemite National Park, 209/372-0200, www.nps.gov/yose.

13 ILLILOUETTE FALL
Yosemite National Park

Level: Moderate	**Distance:** 4.0 miles round-trip or 8.5 miles one-way (via shuttle)
Best Season: May–October	**Elevation Change:** Total loss 1,200–3,200 feet

There are two good ways to make the trip to Illilouette Fall: you can take an easy and unbelievably scenic out-and-back hike from Glacier Point, or a longer one-way journey from Glacier Point all the way to the valley floor, passing Illilouette, Vernal, and Nevada Falls on your way.

Both trips offer mind-boggling scenery—the kind that gets imprinted on your brain so that you can't forget it—on the well-named Panorama Trail from Glacier Point. The trail offers bird's-eye views of Vernal and Nevada Falls, Half Dome, and plenty more of the valley's stunning geological features.

Both trips are moderate day hikes. But the out-and-back to Illilouette from Glacier Point takes only about two hours as you cover four miles, downhill on the way to the falls and uphill on the way back. The one-way hike from Glacier Point to the valley floor is 8.5 miles, downhill almost all the way, but with some knee-jarring descent as you stairstep alongside Vernal and Nevada Falls. It takes about five hours. In addition, you need to leave your car parked in Yosemite Valley and ride the shuttle bus to Glacier Point to begin your hike. (There is a fee for the shuttle bus to Glacier Point. Phone the Yosemite Lodge Tour Desk at 209/372-1240 for rates, pickup times, and locations.) Adding in the transportation arrangements, the 8.5-mile hike usually expands into a full day.

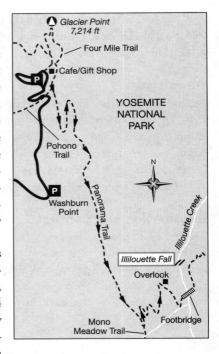

Which trip you take to Illilouette is really a decision based on time and logistics more than anything else. Either way, you start at Glacier Point, elevation 7,214 feet, the trailhead with what is probably the grandest view in the West, encompassing Half Dome, Basket Dome, North Dome, Liberty Cap, and Vernal and Nevada Falls. When you leave your car and begin hiking on the Panorama Trail, you get the same vista as from Glacier Point, but more of it. Your view changes with every footstep; a different angle on the scene is offered with each passing moment. A trail sign tells you that Illilouette Fall is two miles away, but you quickly forget about the destination as the journey provides eyefuls upon eyefuls of grandeur.

The Panorama Trail slowly switchbacks downhill, curving through a fire-scarred area. Shrub-type growth proliferates, typical after a fire, including ceanothus, bear clover, and young dogwoods. Deer adore the newly grown foliage found on the slopes. A few does or a big buck are common companions along the trail.

After a series of downhill switchbacks, Panorama Trail junctions with a trail leading to Mono Meadow, but you continue left for Illilouette. In a few minutes, you'll reach an overlook directly across from the fall, and you may be surprised to see that you've approached it from a sideways angle, rather than from behind or in front. That's because Illilouette doesn't pour from the back of a canyon, rather it rushes over its side wall, where the creek drops 370 feet over a granite lip. The canyon is pencil-thin with vertical rock walls, so the only vantage point is from the side. It's a spectacular sight.

Illilouette Fall

Illilouette must be one of the greatest place names in all of Yosemite. It sounds French, but it's not; it's actually a bastardized English translation of a Yosemite Indian word, which was originally something like "Tooloolaweack." To the Native Americans, the word was the name for the place where they gathered to hunt for deer.

After you've rested a while and enjoyed the view, follow the trail as it descends and then crosses a bridge over Illilouette Creek, just above the falls. Posted signs warn people not to swim here because the bridge is only about 50 yards above the drop. Don't try it in a barrel, either.

Those opting for the shorter hike should turn around at the Illilouette bridge, preparing themselves for the 1,200-foot climb back to Glacier Point. Hikers continuing all the way to the valley floor will find that the trail now switchbacks uphill for the first time, leading to the high southeast canyon wall. From there, you can see all the way across Yosemite Valley to Upper Yosemite Fall, and after a few more minutes of walking, you can see all the way to Lower Yosemite Fall as well. Your perspective on the falls is an unusual one: from most vantage points, Upper and Lower Yosemite Falls appear to be right on top of each other, but from here, you can clearly see how far apart they are. The middle cascades, which separate them, are long and nearly horizontal.

Keep walking; more waterfalls await. In a little more than an hour from the Illilouette Fall bridge, you reach a cutoff trail for 594-foot Nevada Fall, now only 0.2 mile away.

The trail takes you to a bridge just above the big drop, where the Merced River gathers steam to form the fall's tremendous flow. You can cross the bridge to an overlook area on the fall's north side, although you can't see very much when you're at its brink. If you lean over the piped railing (hold on tightly), you can look deep into the swirling mist at the bottom of the fall, which appears like a giant block of dry ice, clouded and mysterious.

From here, you have two choices for your descent: you can take the John Muir

Trail (on the south side of the falls) or the Mist Trail (on the north). The Mist Trail is more dramatic, but both trails offer great views. If your knees or ankles are bothering you from the five-plus miles of downhill hiking you've already done, give yourself a break and take the John Muir Trail, which is less steep. You can always cut over to the Mist Trail at Clark Point, just before Vernal Fall, so you get a taste of both routes.

The John Muir Trail offers a tremendous full-length view of Nevada Fall as its route leads along a rocky cliff edge. Keep looking back at the fall as you walk away from it. (If you take the Mist Trail, you'll be so busy watching your step as you descend on the slippery, rocky staircase—and watching out for other hikers ascending—that you probably won't be admiring the scenery much.) Watch for the cutoff on your right for the Mist Trail, which will take you to 317-foot Vernal Fall. Even if you choose to take the John Muir Trail all the way down to the valley, at least take the cutoff trail 0.5 mile back and forth to the top of Vernal Fall. (The John Muir Trail does not go to Vernal.)

Vernal Fall, like Nevada, has a railed overlook area at the fall's lip, but again this on-top perspective is not your best view. From the top of Vernal Fall, you can return to the John Muir Trail (adding an extra mile to your trip, but with less of a steep downhill grade) or take the Mist Trail's stunning staircase descent. If you want to see the best views of Vernal Fall, continue downcanyon on the Mist Trail. This is the time to don your rain gear, especially in spring, when the waterfall's spray can be a downpour.

The most famous vista of Vernal Fall is farther downstream at the Vernal Fall footbridge, only 0.7 mile from Happy Isles. After taking a few pictures here, it's an easy stroll back to the trail's end. Be sure to check out the last-minute bonus view of Illilouette Fall in the final half mile of trail beyond the Vernal Fall footbridge. This time you see it from the bottom looking up. When you reach Happy Isles, you simply ride the free Yosemite Valley shuttle bus to your car parked in the valley.

For more information about the Mist Trail, John Muir Trail, and Vernal and Nevada Falls, see the listing for Vernal and Nevada Falls in this chapter.

Directions

From Merced, drive 75 miles northeast on Highway 140 to Yosemite National Park. Follow the signs toward Yosemite Valley, entering through the Arch Rock entrance station. Continue on El Portal Road, which becomes Southside Drive, for 6.3 miles, then turn right at the fork for Highway 41/Wawona/Fresno. Continue 9.2 miles, then turn left on Glacier Point Road, and drive 16 miles to Glacier Point at the end of the road. Park in any of the parking lots, then walk to the point. The trailhead is on the right side of Glacier Point. (If you are taking the one-way hike from Glacier Point to Yosemite Valley, leave your car in any day-use parking area in the Valley, then ride the free shuttle bus to Yosemite Lodge at the Falls, where the bus departs for Glacier Point.)

Information and Contact

There is a $20 entrance fee per vehicle at Yosemite National Park, which is good for seven days. Park maps are available for free at the entrance stations, or by download at www.nps.gov/yose. A more detailed map is available from Tom Harrison Maps, 415/456-7940, www.tomharrisonmaps.com. For more information, contact Yosemite National Park, 209/372-0200, www.nps.gov/yose.

14 VERNAL AND NEVADA FALLS
Yosemite National Park

Level: Moderate/Strenuous

Distance: 1.4-6.5 miles round-trip

Best Season: March-July

Elevation Change: Total gain 400-2,000 feet

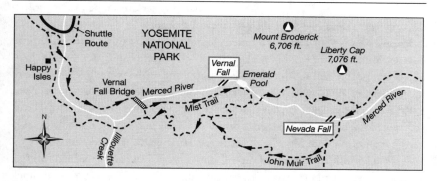

Vernal and Nevada Falls are best described with a long line of superlatives punctuated by commas: awesome, majestic, breathtaking, magnificent, and so on. Or maybe they are best described not with words at all, but by the millions of photographs, famous and not so famous, that have been taken of them over the years.

All the same disclaimers apply with Vernal and Nevada Falls as with other celebrated sights in Yosemite Valley: 1) Come ready for hordes of people. 2) Bring rain gear if you don't like getting wet. 3) Start as early in the morning as possible to avoid the crowds. 4) Prepare to be awed.

First, a little geology lesson. Whereas Yosemite Fall and Bridalveil Fall are

© ANN MARIE BROWN

Vernal Fall

classic examples of waterfalls that drop over a "hanging valley"—an upper canyon perched high above a valley after glaciers eroded away the lower portion—Vernal and Nevada Falls merely drop over soft or fractured rock masses that glacial ice has eroded into huge "stairsteps." These rocky "stairs" on the eastern end of Yosemite Valley are called the Giant Stairway, with Vernal Fall being the lower step and Nevada Fall the upper step.

Some aficionados would argue that a hanging valley waterfall is more dramatic than a stairstep waterfall. Hanging valley falls have a sensational jumping-off-the-edge-of-the-world appearance. They are usually described as leaping off their cliffs in some heroic fashion. But a stairstep waterfall can be just as theatrical, and Vernal and Nevada Falls are cascading proof.

Happy Isles is your trailhead, unless you opt for a one-way shuttle hike from Glacier Point to Vernal and Nevada Falls (see Illilouette Fall listing in this chapter). Some people will recall Happy Isles as the site of the incredible rockslide of the summer of 1996, when a huge chunk of Glacier Point broke off and dropped 3,000 feet to the valley floor, devastating the area and killing one bystander. Today, you must look hard to see evidence of the slide, since the granite rubble quickly becomes a normal-looking part of the ever-changing glacial landscape.

Walk 0.75 mile on the paved, uphill-but-easy trail to the Vernal Fall bridge. There you get your best view of the beautiful 317-foot fall, a voluminous block of water that forms where the Merced River drops over vertically jointed rock. At peak flow, the fall can be as much as 80 feet wide.

Many people shoot off a bunch of pictures and turn around here, but if you don't mind some stair-climbing, you should continue to the fall's lip, 0.5 mile farther up the trail. This famous route is called the Mist Trail, and it's as good as all the guidebooks say. Just make sure your knees are in good shape before you attempt it; the trail climbs up a steep granite staircase, which curves tightly around the waterfall's right side. Sections of the trail are completely covered by the fall's billowing mist and spray. Raincoats are often a necessity in spring, especially if the day is not particularly warm.

(One note: If you are traveling the Mist Trail with kids, keep a hand-hold on them. The wet, rocky stairs, combined with the hundreds of people coming at you from ahead and behind, can be hazardous.)

If you can look up from the sight of your feet clinging to the granite stairs, you'll notice a tremendous amount of moss and deep green foliage growing alongside the fall. This lush vegetation thrives even on granite because of Vernal Fall's nonstop misting action. When you reach the top of the fall and the overlook, you'll find that you're in barren, exposed granite country again. It's stark, dramatic, and awe-inspiring.

Nevada Fall

© ANN MARIE BROWN

From the top of Vernal Fall, you have a choice: turn back or continue onward another two miles to the top of Nevada Fall. If you opt to head uphill, you can take one of two routes: the Mist Trail or the John Muir Trail. The latter is far less steep but slightly less dramatic. My choice would be to continue upward on the Mist Trail, then take the John Muir Trail back downhill, so you can sample both trails. (Besides, steep uphills are good for your heart; steep downhills are bad for your knees.)

Tighten your boot laces and climb, climb, climb up the Mist Trail, finally ascending the left flank of Nevada Fall. The ascent is hard work, but your heart will pound more from the stunning waterfall view than from the cardiovascular workout. Continually fed by upstream snowfields and glaciers, Nevada Fall occurs where the Merced River funnels through a narrow, rocky chute. Named for the Spanish word for snow-covered, Nevada drops 594 feet like a liquid avalanche—a seemingly endless cataract of white, churning water. Whereas Vernal Fall is a square, block-type waterfall, Nevada has a more unusual shape, something like a horsetail or an inverted V. Ansel Adams took what is probably the most famous photograph of Nevada Fall in 1947, on a day when a rainbow was draped gracefully across its white plunge.

You'll notice that from the fall's summit and overlook area, you have less of a vista than you had on your climb up. Looking down at the fall, it is difficult to see its full grandeur. Not to worry; you get more views on the way back downhill.

Take the John Muir Trail back for variety and a lesser grade. Watch for tremendous vistas of Nevada Fall framed by Liberty Cap and Half Dome as you lateral away from the fall along a rocky cliff edge. (Keep looking over your shoulder, or stop and turn around.) At a clearing alongside the trail, you get a picture-perfect view of both Nevada and Vernal Falls simultaneously. It's a great spot for picture-taking or just admiring the scene.

If all the steep downhill hiking is giving your joints and muscles a hard time, you can walk the entire route back to the valley floor on the John Muir Trail, although it adds an extra mile to your trip. If you'd prefer to see Vernal Fall again and hike at least a portion of the Mist Trail again, you can transfer over at Clark Point, just above Vernal Fall.

Directions

From Merced, drive 75 miles northeast on Highway 140 to Yosemite National Park. Follow the signs toward Yosemite Valley, entering through the Arch Rock entrance station. Continue on El Portal Road, which becomes Southside Drive, for 11.6 miles to the day-use parking lot at Curry Village. Then ride the free Yosemite Valley shuttle bus to Happy Isles, stop #16. In winter, when the shuttle does not run, you must hike from the day-use parking lot in Curry Village, adding an additional two miles to your round-trip.

Information and Contact

There is a $20 entrance fee per vehicle at Yosemite National Park, which is good for seven days. Park maps are available for free at the entrance stations, or by download at www.nps.gov/yose. A more detailed map is available from Tom Harrison Maps, 415/456-7940, www.tomharrisonmaps.com. For more information, contact Yosemite National Park, 209/372-0200, www.nps.gov/yose.

15 BRIDALVEIL FALL   BEST (
Yosemite National Park

| **Level:** Easy | **Distance:** 0.5 mile round-trip |
| **Best Season:** April-July | **Elevation Change:** Total gain 50 feet |

There's a story about a guy who visits Yosemite National Park for the first time and says to a park ranger, "I only have one day to spend in Yosemite. What should I do with my time?" And the park ranger says, "If I only had one day to spend in Yosemite, I'd just sit down and have myself a good cry."

© ANN MARIE BROWN

Bridalveil Fall

Well, if you've only got one day in Yosemite, stop your cryin' and make a beeline for Bridalveil Fall, which drops 620 feet over the south wall of Yosemite's valley in a spectacular display of spray and mist. In spring, the water can flow with such force that seasoned waterfall-goers know to wear rain gear when visiting the fall's overlook. Otherwise, you just get wet.

Probably the best thing about Bridalveil, besides its incredible beauty, is its reliability. Whereas other falls in Yosemite Valley can dry up completely by late summer, Bridalveil Fall has a dependable flow year-round. That's because Bridalveil Creek drains a large area, including a lush upper valley with plenty of vegetation and deep, rich soil, which acts as a sponge, releasing water slowly and steadily. Many other Yosemite falls are situated at the base of stark granite terrain, where snow melts all at once off the rocks. When the snow is done melting, the waterfall display ends. Not so with Bridalveil, which in most months is a continually replenished, swaying plume of white water pounding over the canyon's rock wall.

It's less than a 0.25-mile walk to the fall's overlook on a paved trail that is suitable for wheelchairs and baby strollers, and even leashed dogs are permitted—a rarity in Yosemite. Follow the trail from the parking lot, then take the right cutoff that is signed "Vista Point." The path also continues straight to Southside Drive for folks who choose to walk to the falls from other points in the valley.

The name "Bridalveil" is fairly recent, given by the editor of the Mariposa newspaper in the 1850s. The fall was called "Pohono" by the Yosemite Indians, and some translations suggest that Pohono meant "evil wind" or "puffing wind." When the fall's flow is heaviest, you can feel the wind it creates long before you see the water. The trees within a quarter mile of Bridalveil suffer from wind-pruning, the result of constant exposure to the downdrafts and spray of the fall. They look as if they've been tended by a mad gardener who pruned only one side of each tree. The sound of the waterfall in spring and early summer is often as loud and staccato as gunshots, with the water dropping in great sheets and then billowing out in layers of mist.

As with the other famous sights of Yosemite Valley, a good trick is to visit Bridalveil Fall between 6 and 7 A.M., when nobody is around but the morning light is perfect. From the Bridalveil Fall overlook, you also get a great view of Ribbon Fall on the opposite canyon wall—just do an about-face, turning your back to Bridalveil. Check your calendar first, though, because Ribbon Fall usually disappears by July, while Bridalveil keeps right on flowing.

Like its taller neighbors Upper and Lower Yosemite Falls, Bridalveil Fall can often be seen swaying or scattering in strong wind. When the breeze really kicks up, Bridalveil Fall can even blow sideways. This effect is best seen from a slight distance, such as from the Bridalveil Fall parking lot. On a windy day, you can photograph dozens of pictures of the fall in just a few minutes, each revealing a different shape and character of the plunging water. From the fall's vista point, you're too close to see Bridalveil's full length, but from the western side of the parking lot, the entire waterfall is framed perfectly for photos.

Another good viewpoint is along Northside Drive as you drive west out of the valley, at a parking pullout near Bridalveil Meadow, just before you reach the turnoff for Highway 41. But my absolute favorite long-distance view is from the Wawona Tunnel parking lot on Highway 41. From here, all of Yosemite Valley is in view, including El Capitan, Half Dome, Sentinel Rock, and Cathedral Rocks, with sweet Bridalveil Fall flowing into the edge of the frame. It gives you the feeling that perhaps you are entering the Garden of Eden.

Your perspective from the tunnel is such that without prior knowledge, you cannot guess at the enormity of Yosemite's canyon walls and the gigantic proportions of all that is within them. When John Muir first saw Bridalveil Fall from a spot near here, he guessed it was a 50-foot waterfall, and he said he would like to camp at its base to see the pretty ferns that might grow there.

When Mr. Muir finally made the trip to Bridalveil, he found that his 50-foot cascade was actually a 620-foot white-water plunge of amazing force and power. As he learned about the vegetation above the fall and how it feeds and moderates the flow of water, Muir pushed for legislation that would expand the park's boundaries to protect Bridalveil's entire watershed, not just the fall alone. Eventually, this was accomplished, and visitors to Bridalveil Fall have Muir and others to thank for the fact that Bridalveil Creek remains undammed, pristine, and awesome in its perpetual flow.

Directions

From Merced, drive 75 miles northeast on Highway 140 to Yosemite National Park. Follow the signs toward Yosemite Valley, entering through the Arch Rock entrance station. Continue on El Portal Road, which becomes Southside Drive, for 6.3 miles, then turn right at the fork for Highway 41/Wawona/Fresno. Turn left almost immediately into the Bridalveil Fall parking lot. The trail begins at the far end of the parking lot. (If you are driving into the park from the southern entrance near Wawona, watch for the Bridalveil Fall turnoff on your right as you drive into the valley on Highway 41.)

Information and Contact

There is a $20 entrance fee per vehicle at Yosemite National Park, which is good for seven days. Park maps are available for free at the entrance stations, or by download at www.nps.gov/yose. A more detailed map is available from Tom Harrison Maps, 415/456-7940, www.tomharrisonmaps.com. For more information, contact Yosemite National Park, 209/372-0200, www.nps.gov/yose.

16 YOSEMITE FALLS   BEST (

Yosemite National Park

Level: Easy or Strenuous   **Distance:** 1.0-7.4 miles mile round-trip
Best Season: December-July   **Elevation Change:** Total gain 50-2,700 feet

At a combined height of 2,425 feet—almost a half mile—Yosemite Falls is ranked as the fifth—highest free-falling waterfall in the world and the highest in North America. It is also probably the most visited and most famous waterfall in the world. Upper Yosemite Fall alone is a whopping 1,430 feet of plunging water. It leaps off the canyon rim, reaches a less vertical chunk of rock and cascades for 675 feet, then hits a ledge and forms Lower Yosemite Fall, which plunges for another 320 feet. In the words of John Muir: "Yosemite Fall comes to us as an endless revelation."

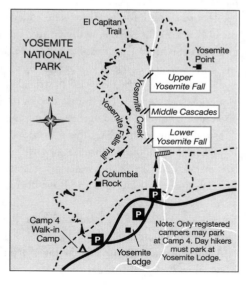

There are several good ways to view Yosemite Falls, but an important distinction should be made: hiking to the base of Lower Yosemite Fall is basically a walk in the park, suitable even for tourists in high heels. Hiking to Upper Yosemite Fall is a different story, requiring a 7.4-mile tromp with 2,700 feet of elevation gain.

The Lower Yosemite Fall trail is one of the most popular attractions in Yosemite Valley, and as such, the route is perpetually crawling with people. Still, it is an absolute must for visitors to Yosemite Valley—even seasoned visitors who have seen the falls many times before. When Lower Yosemite Fall is roaring with snowmelt in the spring and early summer, they never disappoint even the most seasoned hiker.

The Lower Yosemite Fall Trail received a major facelift in 2004. The old

Upper Yosemite Fall

parking lot was removed, the trail was extended to make a pleasant loop, and modern restrooms and facilities were added. The only problem is that now that the old parking lot is gone, many visitors can't figure out where to leave their car and start the hike. Your best bet is to ride the shuttle bus from other points in the Valley, which deposits you at the "new" Yosemite Fall Trailhead, an attractive log structure right alongside Northside Drive. It is possible to park your car alongside the road near the shuttle stop or in the Yosemite Lodge parking lot, but good luck finding a space in the summer months.

However you get to the trailhead, once you get started, the trail is simple enough to follow. With about 10 minutes of walking, you are standing at the footbridge below the falls. To view the waterfall at is most magnificent stage, plan your trip for sometime between April and June, during peak snowmelt. When the falls are at full flood, you will need to wear your rain gear if you wish to stand within a few hundred yards of the waterfall's base. Spray and mist will still fall so heavily that it feels like rain.

Another great time to view the lower fall is on full moon nights in April and May, when lucky visitors get the chance to see pale-colored "moonbows" dancing in the waterfall's spray. It's the most romantic sight in Yosemite Valley. And speaking of romantic, check out Yosemite Falls in winter, when a giant ice cone forms at the base of the upper fall. Composed of frozen spray and fallen chunks of ice, the ice cone can sometimes grow to a height of 300 feet.

Inevitably, many who visit the lower fall and feel the thrill of its tumultuous presence get a hankering to get close to the upper fall, too. But if you haven't done it before, keep in mind that hiking to the upper fall is a strenuous endeavor. It should not be done without good hiking boots and a serious supply of water and snacks. Although some hikers start their trek from the Lower Yosemite Falls trail, where a side trail takes off to the west and travels alongside Northside Drive to the Upper Yosemite Falls trailhead in Camp 4, it's much more efficient to ride the free Valley shuttle bus straight to Camp 4 and save yourself that extra mile or so of hiking. The 7.4-mile round-trip is strenuous enough without adding extra mileage. By the standards of the average fit hiker, it's a grunt of a trip, climbing 2,700 feet with more than 100 switchbacks. An early start is a very good idea; you want to avoid climbing this south-facing slope in the heat of the day. The trail is a workout, but if you're reasonably fit, you shouldn't miss it.

From its start, the route begins to climb immediately, twisting and turning through countless switchbacks under a canopy of oaks. At 1.2 miles and 1,000 feet up, you reach Columbia Rock (5,031 feet), an extraordinary viewpoint that looks out over the valley floor and east toward Half Dome. Many people tire of the climb and are satisfied with the view here, but it's wise to continue at least another 100 yards, where an unsigned right spur trail leads 30 feet downhill to an awe-inspiring view of Upper Yosemite Fall. Many, many hikers miss this turnoff completely. Continuing on the main trail, all hikers are rewarded with tremendous views of the falls at 1.4 miles, after a brief downhill stretch. From several points along the trail, you get a front-seat perspective on the towering plume of water. You're eye to eye with the waterfall, close enough to feel its tremendous energy.

More ascent lies ahead, as the trail switchbacks above the trees and into a rocky area that is the recipient of frequent slides. In 1980, a rockfall covered about a mile of the trail here. The moral is: don't stand still for long. But keep drinking water. This section of trail is completely exposed and can be very warm, especially because your legs are pushing through a steady climb. Luckily, the view keeps getting more and more expansive, distracting you from the hard work.

At 3.4 miles, you've completed your ascent, and the trail levels out and heads east, reaching a trail junction. Head right toward Yosemite Point, then follow the short right spur trail signed as "Overlook," which leads downhill on a treacherous set of granite stairsteps to near the edge of roaring Yosemite Creek. You are literally on top of Upper Yosemite Fall. Check out the fascinating vista of the plummeting upper fall and showering Middle Cascades from this incredible vantage point, and the stunning view of the valley, but stay safely behind the metal railing.

Still haven't had enough? Go back to the main trail and continue another 0.75 mile, crossing a bridge above the falls, to Yosemite Point (6,936 feet). There you get an even better view of the south rim of the canyon, as well as Half Dome and North Dome, and a look at the top of Lost Arrow Spire, a single shaft of granite jutting into the sky.

For waterfall-lovers who are less fond of heights and the climb they require, a great feature of Upper Yosemite Fall is that it is so clearly visible from various points in the valley. The best "no sweating" way to view Upper Yosemite Fall is on a bike on the bike path. From the saddle of a bike, you can see various views of the falls on the looping section of the paved path that runs west of Yosemite Village. If you're on foot, that's a lot of pavement-walking, but on a bike, it's perfect. Plus, there are bike racks positioned near the foot trail to the base of Lower Yosemite Fall, so you can lock up your bike and walk the short path to the falls.

Even people who don't want to get out of their cars can get a dozen good chances to view the falls. The best roadside falls vista is along Southside Drive as you head east into the valley. Smart park planners built pullouts along the road because they understood that so many drivers would have no choice but to stop and rubberneck. It's practically a requirement to take a photo from your car window or through your sunroof along this stretch. The pullouts provide a perfectly framed shot of Upper Yosemite Fall with a verdant meadow in the foreground. Check out the view from near road marker V19. If you drive to the farthest end of the parking pullout (near the Yosemite Chapel), you get a vista of Upper Yosemite Fall that also includes a glimpse of Lower Yosemite Fall.

If there is any downer to Yosemite Falls, it's that it doesn't flow year-round. Plenty of first-time visitors show up in August or September, or any time during serious drought years, and wonder why the park rangers turned off the waterfall. Yosemite Falls drains a watershed that is composed of smooth, bare granite and little vegetation. Runoff from snowmelt and rainfall is rapid—the all-or-nothing effect of water on a hard, impenetrable surface. Once the rain and snow have drained, the waterfall show is over for the year. For the fullest flow of water, visit between March and the Fourth of July.

Directions

From Merced, drive 75 miles northeast on Highway 140 to Yosemite National Park. Follow the signs toward Yosemite Valley, entering through the Arch Rock entrance station. Continue on El Portal Road, which becomes Southside Drive, for 10.5 miles. Just beyond the Yosemite Chapel, bear left at the fork and head toward the village and visitor center. Park in any of the signed day-use parking areas and ride the free Yosemite Valley shuttle bus to either the Lower Yosemite

Fall Trailhead, shuttle stop number 6 (if you want to hike to Lower Yosemite Fall) or Camp 4, shuttle stop number 7 (if you want to hike to Upper Yosemite Fall). If you plan to hike to both the upper and lower fall, you can walk the 0.5-mile trail between the two trailheads or take the shuttle bus from one stop to the next. (Note: there is limited parking alongside Northside Drive near the Lower Yosemite Fall trailhead, but unless you arrive very early in the morning, these spots are usually full. Parking in the Yosemite Lodge at the Falls parking lot, or at Camp 4, is reserved for overnight guests/campers only.)

Information and Contact

There is a $20 entrance fee per vehicle at Yosemite National Park, which is good for seven days. Park maps are available for free at the entrance stations, or by download at www.nps.gov/yose. A more detailed map is available from Tom Harrison Maps, 415/456-7940, www.tomharrisonmaps.com. For more information, contact Yosemite National Park, 209/372-0200, www.nps.gov/yose.

17 ALDER CREEK FALLS
Yosemite National Park

Level: Moderate

Best Season: April-July

Distance: 8.2 miles round-trip

Elevation Change: Total gain 1,000 feet

Yosemite National Park is home to some of the world's most famous waterfalls. But after you've tromped around and made your obligatory visit to Bridalveil, Vernal, Nevada, and Yosemite Falls, you may want to seek out a waterfall that few people know about and even fewer visit.

Alder Creek Falls is your ticket. It's a waterfall you can call your own for a while, but you have to work a little to earn it. For starters, you have to find the unmarked trailhead along Wawona Road—no small feat. (Follow the directions exactly.) Then you have to hike

© KENT SUMMERS

Alder Creek Falls

straight uphill into the Yosemite Wilderness, with nary a switchback, for just shy of a mile. After that, things start to get easier.

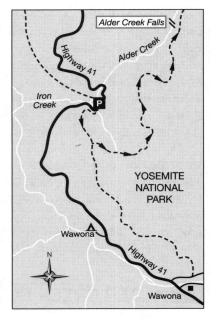

The first stretch of this trail leads uphill through a fire-scarred forest, the result of a controlled burn set by the Park Service in 2008 (not a wildfire). Catch your breath after your one-mile ascent, then make a left turn at the signed trail junction, which indicates that Alder Creek is 3.2 miles away (the trail on the right goes to Wawona in 2.9 miles). Your route continues to climb through dense ponderosa pines and incense cedars, although the grade is now a bit tamer.

After a total of three miles of climbing through the forest—just trees, trees, and more trees—the trail suddenly levels out and goes completely flat. You're now walking on an old railroad grade, and if you look carefully, you'll occasionally see wooden railroad ties still embedded in the dirt. It was on this section of trail that I surprised a big black bear lumbering along in front of me, making his morning rounds. He turned around and looked at me with a shocked expression on his face, then darted off into the woods.

You may be as surprised as he was when suddenly you hear pounding water through the silence of the trees. In a few moments, your view opens up to Alder Creek and its 250-foot fall, pouring grandly over a granite lip. The railroad grade laterals alongside it, heading upstream, taking you near the brink of the falls. The best view of the entire drop is right along the trail, about 100 yards before the falls. (Stay on the trail; there is no way to get any closer by scrambling off-trail because the waterfall's canyon is too steep.)

Beyond the fall, the trail continues along Alder Creek, paralleling it for 3.5 miles all the way to Deer Camp and Empire Meadow. If you're backpacking, Deer Camp is the best place to spend the night. I walked just 0.25 mile beyond the falls, where there is a tiny feeder stream that inspires some great wildflowers, including mariposa lilies, iris, blue lupine, and purple vetch, and an interesting rock formation with trees growing on top. Any number of places make good stopping points along the creek, where you can drop your packs and pull out your lunch.

Directions

The easiest way to find this unmarked trailhead is to travel north from Wawona. Follow the directions for Chilnualna Falls (see listing in this chapter), but from the turnoff for Chilnualna Falls Road, drive north on Highway 41 for 4.2 miles. (You can also set your odometer at Wawona Campground; the trailhead is 3.4 miles north of the camp.) The trailhead is at a hairpin turn on the east side of Highway 41. (There is another trailhead for the Alder Creek Trail on the west side of the road, about one mile north, but don't take this trail.) There is no marker except for a Yosemite Wilderness sign, which you can't see from the road. A dirt pullout on the west side of the road is large enough for about eight cars.

Information and Contact

There is a $20 entrance fee per vehicle at Yosemite National Park, which is good for seven days. Park maps are available for free at the entrance stations, or by download at www.nps.gov/yose. A more detailed map is available from Tom Harrison Maps, 415/456-7940, www.tomharrisonmaps.com. For more information, contact Yosemite National Park, 209/372-0200, www.nps.gov/yose.

18 CHILNUALNA FALLS
Yosemite National Park

Level: Strenuous **Distance:** 8.0 miles round-trip
Best Season: March-July **Elevation Change:** Total gain 2,400 feet

Most people don't expect too much from the southern section of Yosemite National Park. Sure, everyone visits the Mariposa Grove to see the big sequoias, but other than that, the area doesn't take up too much of the average visitor's itinerary. But while everyone else is in the valley or at Glacier Point or Tuolumne Meadows, you can sneak off to the southern part of the park, take a rigorous hike, and be rewarded with a terrific waterfall: Chilnualna Falls near Wawona, one of my favorite falls in Yosemite.

Remember, however, that you'll begin hiking at low elevation—4,200 feet—and you'll gain 2,400 feet over four miles to reach the falls. It's a steady, nonstop climb through only partial shade. If you don't like to hike up, don't sign up. If you relish a good climb, bring plenty of water for your two-hour aerobics session, plus the long downhill return.

You don't have to walk four miles to see falls. From the Chilnualna Falls parking

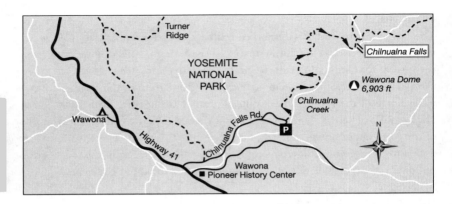

lot, hike about 10 minutes uphill and already you're at a tremendous cascade on Chilnualna Creek, where the stream rushes furiously over room-sized boulders. It looks like someone took Stonehenge apart, piled up all the rocks, then started a downpour over them. Plenty of large, flat rocks abound where you can sit and watch the spectacle. It's beautiful and very loud in spring and early summer.

When you're ready to continue, say farewell to the creek, because you won't see it again for a few miles. Heading up the trail, you'll reach a Yosemite Wilderness sign and begin to switchback your way up, up, and up through manzanita, mountain misery, and bear clover. In spring, the aroma of all this flowering brush is intoxicating—it's easy to see why bears and deer munch it down.

After nearly an hour of climbing (about two miles), you come to a large granite overlook with a terrific view of the tree-filled canyon below and Wawona Dome (6,897 feet) across from you. Stop here to stretch your hamstrings, eat a snack, and make comments like, "Geez, these falls better be good."

They are, and you're halfway there. The nearby roar of Chilnualna Creek assures you that you're doing the right thing. A half mile past your rocky perch, start looking for glimpses of Chilnualna Falls on the far back wall of the canyon, way up high. What you can see is only a small section of the fall, and as you switchback uphill, your view of it will change to include more and more length. It provides an incentive to spur you on.

At three miles, you reach a small stream crossing the trail, which makes a lovely miniature stairstepped waterfall just above the trail. Since you've gained so much elevation, the forest is now dense with shady pines and incense cedars. Finally, you come to what seems like the canyon rim and start to lateral toward the fall. From here it looks like a giant free-falling plume of water. Your trail turns to granite, and it is pleasingly flat after so much uphill.

Now for the bad news: you never get to see that big free-falling plume close up

© ANN MARIE BROWN

Chilnualna Falls

because the trail brings you on top of it, not in front of it. But the good news is that the free fall is just the lower part of Chilnualna Falls, a series of cascades totaling hundreds of feet, and you can climb some more to get to the upper tiers.

Walk on granite, over rocky stairsteps, on a ledge at the edge of the world, until you reach a cascade above the long free fall. Pause to admire it, then keep climbing. In another 0.5 mile, you'll reach a trail sign where the trail leads off to Turner Meadows, Grouse Lake, and Chilnualna Lakes. On your right is another huge Chilnualna cascade, my favorite of the trip—a series of six rounded granite pools connected by a continually descending flow of water. Leave the trail and walk 100 yards to your right to reach the waterfall's edge. Here, on the bare outcrop of granite surrounding the waterfall, is the perfect place to open up your pack and have lunch.

Directions

From Merced, drive 75 miles northeast on Highway 140 to Yosemite National Park. Follow the signs toward Yosemite Valley, entering through the Arch Rock entrance station. Continue on El Portal Road, which becomes Southside Drive, for 6.3 miles, then turn right at the fork for Highway 41/Wawona/Fresno. Drive south on Highway 41 for 25 miles to Wawona, then turn left on Chilnualna Falls Road. Drive 1.7 miles east and park in the lot on the right side of the road. Walk back to Chilnualna Falls Road and pick up the single-track trail across the pavement.

Alternatively, from the Wawona/southern entrance to Yosemite National Park on Highway 41, drive north on Highway 41 for 7.5 miles to Wawona. Turn right on Chilnualna Falls Road and follow the directions as above.

Information and Contact

There is a $20 entrance fee per vehicle at Yosemite National Park, which is good for seven days. Park maps are available for free at the entrance stations, or by download at www.nps.gov/yose. A more detailed map is available from Tom Harrison Maps, 415/456-7940, www.tomharrisonmaps.com. For more information, contact Yosemite National Park, 209/372-0200, www.nps.gov/yose.

19 FISH CAMP FALLS
Sierra National Forest

Level: Easy

Best Season: April-August

Distance: 1.0 mile round-trip

Elevation Change: Total gain 250 feet

Fish Camp Falls is not one waterfall but three, and if they weren't five miles from Yosemite, they'd be good enough to be the centerpiece of their own state park. Unlike most of Yosemite's waterfalls, Fish Camp Falls have a dependable supply of water long into late summer. Their swimming holes are clear, cool, and inviting.

© ANN MARIE BROWN

Fish Camp Falls

The three falls are all about 25 feet in height. They free-fall gracefully off smooth granite ledges along a 300-yard-long section of Big Creek. The trail to reach them begins at a locked gate off Big Sandy Road. You simply hike to the right, passing a private cabin, and stay on the trail until you reach Big Creek. You'll see the first waterfall in about 10 minutes from your car. Head upstream a few hundred yards to see the next two; the last one is the largest and most photogenic.

In addition to your bathing suit and sunscreen, it wouldn't be a bad idea to bring a fishing rod along on this trip. Big Creek is filled with hungry rainbow trout.

Directions
From Oakhurst, drive north on Highway 41 for 15 miles to the right turnoff for Big Sandy Road (0.5 mile south of Fish Camp). Turn right and drive 2.5 miles to

a dirt pullout on the left, near a small building located alongside a flume. Park there and walk across the road to the gate.

Information and Contact

There is no fee. Maps of Sierra National Forest are available for a fee from the National Forest Store (406/329-3024, www.nationalforeststore.com), or can be downloaded for free from www.fs.fed.us/r5/maps/. For more information, contact Sierra National Forest, Bass Lake Ranger District, 559/877-2218, www.fs.fed.us/r5/sierra.

20 TUOLUMNE, CALIFORNIA, LECONTE, AND WATERWHEEL FALLS
Yosemite National Park

Level: Moderate/Strenuous   **Distance:** 9.0-16.0 miles round-trip

Best Season: June-October   **Elevation Change:** Total loss 400-1,900 feet

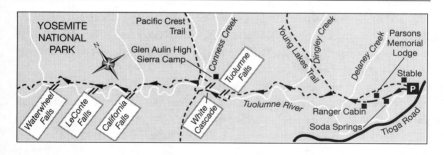

This hike is the Epic Waterfall Trip. If you hike the entire route, you'll see so many waterfalls and so much water that you'll have enough memories to get you through a 10-year drought.

Before you start, it's important to know what you're in for. There's a great deal of discrepancy between various maps and park trail signs as to the actual mileage of this route, but the blisters on my big toes say that the round-trip from the Lembert Dome parking lot all the way to Waterwheel Falls is a whopping 16 miles. You can do the trail as a long day hike if you're in good condition, or you can get a camping permit and have a great two- or three-day backpacking trip. Or you can snag a reservation for one or two nights at the Glen Aulin High Sierra Camp. You'll enjoy great meals and a warm bed, spending the night about 50 yards from

Glen Aulin Falls. The High Sierra Camp is only 1.5–3.5 miles from the other falls (go to www.yosemitepark.com for High Sierra Camp reservations; cancellations are often available at the last minute). Most camp guests spend at least some part of their visit parked in a lawn chair by the huge pool of Glen Aulin Falls. Lucky them.

Finally, you could choose to hike only a portion of the route, making a short day trip to Tuolumne Falls (9.0 miles round-trip and nearly flat). California and Le-Conte Falls are midway in between Tuolumne and Waterwheel, and these also make good day-hike destinations.

In choosing your route, keep in mind one fact: although there is a mere 400-

Tuolumne Falls

© ANN MARIE BROWN

foot elevation difference between the trailhead and Tuolumne Falls, followed by only a 1,500-foot elevation difference between Tuolumne Falls and Waterwheel Falls, it's downhill on the way out and uphill on the way back. As a day hike, 16 miles can get pretty long when you're going uphill on the return. You need plenty of food, water, and energy for the trip home.

If you choose to make the Epic Waterfall Trip an overnight excursion, you'll need to get a wilderness permit, then hike in about five miles to one of the back-packer's sites along the river, which are spaced 0.5–2.5 miles beyond Glen Aulin High Sierra Camp and Tuolumne Falls. (If you have a reservation at the High Sierra Camp, you don't need a permit; your reservation is your permit.) Most people spend the night, then wait till the next day to hike three more miles down to Waterwheel Falls. After enjoying the day there, they return to camp, get a good night's sleep, and hike five miles homeward on the third day. It's a perfect entry-level backpacking trip, the kind of vacation that turns people into lifelong outdoors enthusiasts.

If you must make the trip as a day hike, follow a few tips: first, be in good hiking shape, accustomed to walking at least 10 miles a day. Start early in the morning, say by 7 or 8 A.M. Hike the full one-way distance out to Waterwheel Falls with only short breaks, covering the eight miles in about four hours. (The best place for a snack and a stretching break is at the bridge below Tuolumne Falls.) Have lunch and relax at Waterwheel. Then, since you have some uphill

© ANN MARIE BROWN

Waterwheel Falls

climbing on the way back and you're already somewhat fatigued, take the route home slowly and in sections. Stop and swim in the placid sections of the river. Stop and eat in all the shady spots. Climb a granite staircase and stop to drink some water. Take a nap along the river somewhere. You can do the whole trip, all 16 miles, between 8 A.M. and 6 P.M., hiking for a total of about eight hours and fooling around for the other two.

The Waterwheel trip is only doable as a day hike because the trail has a relatively small elevation gain. Hiking to Half Dome is about the same trail distance, but far more exhausting because of the elevation gain and loss. The key to your trip: drink a ton of water—you're at a very high elevation from the trailhead onward. Bring your canteen and be sure to filter water out of the river; it can be a heavy load if you try to carry enough bottled water for the entire trip.

Start your trip at the trailhead parking area for Dog Lake, Lembert Dome, and Soda Springs. Begin hiking on the gated dirt road that is signed "Soda Springs 0.5 mile," walking until you near Parson's Lodge and see the trail sign for the Glen Aulin Trail. The sign says it's 4.7 miles to Glen Aulin High Sierra Camp (located at the base of Tuolumne Falls) and 5.2 miles to Glen Aulin backpackers' camp (where you'll spend the night if you have a wilderness permit).

The first couple miles of trail are quite flat, only faintly downhill, but the downhill increases as you near Glen Aulin and waterfall country. The scenery is spectacular all the way; after leaving the forest in the first mile, the trail gets closer to the Tuolumne River and moves from trees to granite. The result is wide-open views of Cathedral and Unicorn Peaks and Fairview Dome to the south. The trail meanders through a mix of meadows, granite, and woodland, where deer and other wildlife abound. On my trip, I saw what has to be the cutest of all High Sierra mammals—baby marmots—playing hide-and-seek with me from behind rocks, while Mom marmot watched a bit more cautiously from a distance.

When the trail reaches its first footbridge over the Tuolumne River, a sign states that Glen Aulin is now only 1.7 miles away. In fifteen minutes of walking, you reach the top section of Tuolumne Falls, a stunning 100-foot drop, but that's merely a preview of good things to come. Now you begin a steep downhill to the base of the falls and another bridge, which takes you across the river again to Glen Aulin High Sierra Camp. (If you want to stay here or at any High Sierra Camp, you must make reservations a year in advance through the High Sierra Camp lottery system. However, if you just want a terrific hot meal, you can show up any time and see if they have room for you.)

When you cross the river bridge to the Glen Aulin side, be sure to descend to the small, pebbly beach at the river's edge, where there's a great spot for viewing and taking pictures of the lower drop of Tuolumne Falls. From the bridge itself, your view is slightly obstructed by trees, but from this beach, you have a clear shot. Some people call this waterfall Glen Aulin Falls or White Cascade, but most consider it to be a section of Tuolumne Falls.

The second bridge to your right heads to the High Sierra Camp, but continue straight; then take the left fork, which continues downstream along the river. As you climb up on granite, turn around for a parting look at some of the upper cascades of Tuolumne Falls.

Day hikers looking for a nine-mile round-trip should call it a day here, have a picnic near the river, and then head back up the granite alongside Tuolumne Falls. A turnaround here will make your trip 4–5 hours long, and although the homeward route climbs, the worst of it is in the first half mile—getting up and around Tuolumne Falls. After that, the grade is fairly tame.

Those continuing on will find that the path drops down to a level section in a beautiful meadow, where backpackers make their camps near the river. If you're spending the night, pick out your spot. Here the lupine grows waist high, the river is placid, and ferns and aspens make their home. You may never want to leave, but if you want to see more falls, you'll have to move on. Waterwheel, the final fall on this stretch, is only three miles away, and cascading California and LeConte Falls can be enjoyed along the way.

Another section of granite leads you to another flat, flower-filled meadow, a place where the river is so quiet that it's hard to believe it could produce any more falls.

But then a roaring sound comes from up ahead, and you pass by boisterous California Falls, just off the trail by a few hundred feet. A side trail on your left leads to a huge block-shaped waterfall with some great swimming holes near its base.

Note that while the stretch of river between Glen Aulin High Sierra Camp and California Falls is extremely flat, the stretch downstream from California Falls is almost nonstop cascades and falls, separated only by brief quiet pools. Because of the continual series of cascades and the fact that the river is sometimes obscured by the forest, it can be tricky for first-time visitors to identify California and LeConte Falls' exact locations—where one ends and the other begins. If you're not certain, just take all the short spur trails that fork from the main trail, each of which brings you to either a stunning vista of the falls or a perfect swimming/fishing hole. You can't miss.

Officially, LeConte Falls shows up about 0.5 mile after California Falls, following a large, placid, green pool. At the edge of the pool it seems that the world drops off and disappears, but you're just at the top of LeConte Falls' main cascade.

The trail, which was a fairly even grade up to California Falls, now drops steeply downhill on rock for just shy of eternity. As you descend, watch for a trail sign for Pate Valley and Tuolumne Meadows, and near it, another spur trail on your left. This one takes you to your final destination, Waterwheel Falls, often billed as Yosemite's most unusual waterfall. Shortly, you'll discern why; the side trail brings you to the center of the giant Waterwheel cascade, where you are directly across from some of the lower "waterwheels." These are sections of churning water that dip into deep holes in the granite, then shoot out with such velocity that they seem to double back on themselves, appearing to circle around like waterwheels. As soon as you see them, you understand the fall's moniker. Six different waterwheels spin in the middle section, and a few more circle up above. Find a spot on the granite alongside them, pull out your camera, and linger a while.

Directions

From Merced, drive 75 miles northeast on Highway 140 to Yosemite National Park. Follow the signs toward Yosemite Valley, entering through the Arch Rock entrance station. Continue 4.5 miles to the left turnoff for Tioga Road/Highway 120, looping back out of the valley. In another 9.5 miles, turn right on Highway 120 and drive 40 miles to the parking lot for Dog Lake/Lembert Dome/Soda Springs on the left. Park as far to the west of Lembert Dome as possible, and start hiking at the gated dirt road that is signed "Soda Springs 0.5 mile."

Information and Contact

There is a $20 entrance fee per vehicle at Yosemite National Park, which is good for seven days. Park maps are available for free at the entrance stations, or by download at www.nps.gov/yose. A more detailed map is available from Tom Harrison Maps, 415/456-7940, www.tomharrisonmaps.com. For more information, contact Yosemite National Park, 209/372-0200, www.nps.gov/yose.

21 HORSE CREEK FALLS
Inyo National Forest and Hoover Wilderness

🥾 🐴 ⛰️

Level: Moderate   **Distance:** 4.0 miles round-trip

Best Season: June–September   **Elevation Change:** Total gain 950 feet

The Horse Creek Trail is one of the busiest trails in the Hoover Wilderness, but the worst of the crowds are found in the first half mile. On my first trip, I hiked in only to the lowest cascade along Horse Creek, a mere 0.5-mile from Twin Lakes and huge Mono Village campground, and passed several dozen people along the way, mostly families with children. Feeling discouraged, I left the area and found someplace quieter to hike. But on my next trip, I hiked two miles on the Horse Creek Trail, passing several cascades along the way, and saw almost no one after the initial stretch.

The hardest part of the trip is finding the trailhead. The friendly attendant at the campground entrance kiosk usually gives out directions, but if no one is available, here's what you do: walk past the entrance kiosk, and take the left fork through Mono Village Campground. Look for a dirt road on your left; follow it and cross a footbridge. Hike to your right on the far side of the bridge, passing some tent campers on the hillside. Cross the creek again, and reach a wilderness information sign. From the sign, take the trail to your right, switchbacking uphill.

The trail stays roughly parallel to Horse Creek, as it winds back and forth and uphill into the Hoover Wilderness. The views are great from the get-go, both of Twin Lakes below you and the spectacular Sawtooth Ridge all around you. After 10 minutes of walking past the wilderness sign, you're right alongside the first rushing cascade on Horse Creek, and the white water continues above and below you for as far as you can see.

Keep hiking uphill through more switchbacks. These can be extremely hot and dry in summer, so bring plenty of water with you. In about an hour of nearly relentless climbing, you'll reach the best falls on Horse Creek, often referred to as Horsetail Falls. The stream drops over a low hanging valley. The trail continues beyond the waterfall to a startlingly beautiful meadow. It's wise to come prepared with a picnic.

Directions

From U.S. 395 at Bridgeport, drive west on Twin Lakes Road for 13.2 miles. Park near the far end of the lake, just before the Mono Village Campground entrance kiosk, then walk into the campground.

Information and Contact

There is no fee. Maps of Humboldt-Toiyabe National Forest (Bridgeport District) are available for a fee from the National Forest Store (406/329-3024, www.nationalforeststore.com) or from the Bridgeport Ranger Station on U.S. 395. A more detailed map of the Hoover Wilderness is available from Tom Harrison Maps, 415/456-7940, www.tomharrisonmaps.com. For more information, contact Humboldt-Toiyabe National Forest, Bridgeport Ranger District, 760/932-7070, www.fs.fed.us/r4/htnf.

22 LUNDY CANYON FALLS
Inyo National Forest and Hoover Wilderness

Level: Moderate

Distance: 4.5 miles round-trip

Best Season: June–September

Elevation Change: Total gain 700 feet

If you're a wildflower-lover, Lundy Canyon will float your boat. If it's autumn colors you seek, Lundy Canyon will be the pearl in your oyster. If you're a waterfall aficionado, Lundy Canyon is your cat's meow.

There just aren't enough clichés to describe how good Lundy Canyon is. The camping is good. The fishing is good. The backpacking is good. The day hiking is good. What's not good? The season's not good. It's too short; you can never get enough time here. Lundy Canyon usually isn't snow-free until late June, and it can snow again by October. Plan on July as the best month to see the waterfalls.

Lundy Canyon Falls

It takes 5.4 miles of hiking in Lundy Canyon to reach the spectacular 20 Lakes Basin, but you don't have to go that far to see waterfalls. I hiked just over two miles into the canyon, until just before the trail starts to climb in earnest, and I saw more waterfalls than I could keep track of.

The Lundy Canyon Trail leads into the Hoover Wilderness, a remote and rugged land of granite, mountains, lakes, and glaciers. The trail follows Mill Creek, which has two main falls on it in the first two miles of trail. In addition, many smaller streams cascade for hundreds of feet down the surrounding canyon walls, feeding into Mill Creek. Within half an hour of hiking, you are surrounded by falls. As you walk deeper into the canyon, every couple of minutes you have to stop and count how many you can see.

From the trailhead, the path briefly meanders through an aspen grove and then climbs abruptly and steeply on loose shale, but in 15 minutes, you're rewarded with your first view of a waterfall on Mill Creek. It's a doozy. In the next 15 minutes, you'll pass two more falls on your right. And so it goes. The trail ascends for the first 0.75 mile, then goes completely level in a forested grove along the stream, where I came upon some Boy Scouts on a camping trip. The route passes a dilapidated trapper's cabin, then opens out to a large clearing where the vista is wide, expansive, and humbling. You can look around and see half a dozen cascades dropping along the back and side walls of the canyon.

At two miles out, the trail starts to climb again, slowly working its way off the canyon floor, and shortly you reach my favorite fall on Mill Creek. It has three main cascades, the first being a long stairstepped drop, which you hike right alongside. The smell of wild spearmint is almost intoxicating near the falls. I was compelled to stop here to spread out a picnic and admire the scenery.

What scenery? You already know about the waterfalls; let's talk wildflowers. They are so good in Lundy Canyon that rangers from nearby Yosemite bring visitors here on guided tours. (And Yosemite is no slacker in the wildflower department.) You can identify at least 30 different species, including wandering daisies, Indian paintbrush, mariposa lilies, purple vetch, mule's ears, columbines, Sierra daisies, and tiger lilies. And if you're so unlucky as to miss the June–August wildflower season, you can always visit in September or October and watch the quaking aspens do their golden autumnal dance.

It will be difficult, but when you bring yourself to leave Lundy Canyon, you'll have an easy downhill walk back to the trailhead. Along the way, you'll witness the wonders of the canyon all over again, plus a bright spot of blue in the distance that is Lundy Lake.

If you find Lundy Canyon so captivating that you want to see more, consider a hike up the South Fork of Mill Creek. To access the South Fork, you'll need to start hiking at Lundy Resort or farther back at the dam on the east end of Lundy Lake. A seven-mile round-trip from the dam will take you to spectacular Lake Canyon and its historic gold mine. There's plenty of beauty and history to be seen.

Directions

From Lee Vining, drive 6.8 miles north on U.S. 395 to the Lundy Lake Road turnoff on the left. Drive west on Lundy Lake Road for five miles, past Lundy Lake Resort, to the signed trailhead parking area. (Beyond the resort, the road turns to dirt. It is two miles from the resort to the trailhead.)

Information and Contact

There is no fee. Maps of Inyo National Forest are available for a fee from the National Forest Store (406/329-3024, www.nationalforeststore.com), or can be downloaded for free from www.fs.fed.us/r5/maps/. A more detailed map of the Hoover Wilderness is available from Tom Harrison Maps, 415/456-7940, www.tomharrisonmaps.com. For more information, contact Inyo National Forest, Mono Basin Scenic Area Visitor Center, 760/647-3044, www.fs.fed.us/r5/inyo.

23 RAINBOW, LOWER, AND MINARET FALLS   BEST C
Devils Postpile National Monument

Level: Easy/Moderate   **Distance:** 2.0–8.0 miles round-trip

Best Season: June–September **Elevation Change:** Total loss 200–400 feet

Rainbow Falls is one of the prized geologic possessions of Devils Postpile National Monument. The Devils Postpile, of course, is the other. Add in Minaret Falls and Lower Falls, which can be seen with the others in an easy-to-moderate hiking trip, and we're talking about a treasure chest trail filled with natural wonders. That's three stunning waterfalls, and one intriguing volcanic formation, within four miles of each other. You can see them all in one eight-mile hike, or you can visit just one or two in a shorter trip.

Let's start with the whole enchilada. If you decide to see it all, you can expect a long, scenic hike through wildflower-filled meadows and lodgepole pine forest. You'll have many lingering looks at the fly-fishing paradise of the Middle Fork of the San Joaquin River, plus up-close views of three waterfalls.

Begin your trip at the Devils Postpile parking lot, near the ranger station. Hike south past the ranger station, following the sign for Devils Postpile in 0.4 mile. Immediately you are wowed by a pristine meadow filled with purple shooting stars. Hang on to your hat; this is just the beginning. Pass by the Postpile, a formation of towering "posts" composed of columnar basalt remaining from a lava flow nearly 100,000 years ago. Be sure to take either of the trails along the sides of the Postpile, which climb to its crest. From there, you'll see that the top of the formation looks like a somewhat off-kilter parquet floor.

Continue hiking south past the Postpile. Watch as the thriving pine forest transitions to a mostly regenerated fire-scarred area, the result of a 1992 wildfire. The forest has recovered nicely from the burn. Keep heading gently downhill until you reach the first overlook of Rainbow Falls, which plummets 101 feet over a volcanic

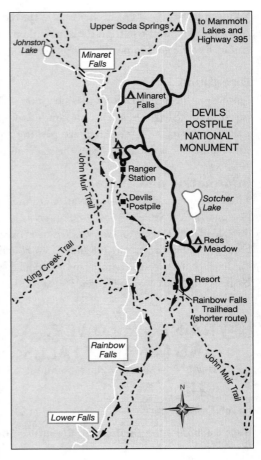

cliff. If you arrive at midday, when direct light rays are passing through water droplets, you'll see the rays refracted and separated into their component colors. That means the fall's namesake rainbows are dancing through the mist.

Although Rainbow Falls drops over volcanic rock, it's a different volcanic rock than the basalt of Devils Postpile. It's rhyodacite, and it has two extremely hard horizontal rock layers at the top of its cliff, much like Niagara Falls. That keeps the San Joaquin River from eroding the waterfall and eventually beveling it off. Rainbow Falls has been here for a long time, and it's going to stick around.

If you're taking pictures, the best spot is at a second overlook, just 30 yards farther downstream, where you can walk down a set of stairs to the fall's base. Ferns and moss grow on the rock at the cliff bottom; they benefit from the waterfall's constant mist.

Rainbow Falls

When you're ready, head downstream for 0.25 mile to often-snubbed Lower Falls. Always in the shadow of big brother Rainbow Falls, Lower Falls gets much less recognition. Rainbow Falls has its picture taken by hundreds of tourists each day in the summer. Lower Falls doesn't even get an imaginative name. But it is beautiful in its own right, with a nearly vertical drop of about 40 feet. Because its cliff is not as wide as Rainbow Falls', Lower Falls' flow is channeled, creating greater volume as the river drops through a narrow chute. Almost no foliage grows near its cliff, except for a few fire-scarred trees standing on top. At the waterfall's base is a wide pool filled with small- to medium-size trout.

After visiting Lower Falls, retrace your steps, heading back uphill past Rainbow Falls and the Devils Postpile again. The climb is steady and sustained enough to get your heart working. After passing the Devils Postpile, watch for the trail fork on your left where a scenic footbridge crosses the San Joaquin River. This is your route to the third waterfall in the park, Minaret Falls, less than a mile away. Turn right on the bridge's far side, hike 0.5 mile upstream, then bear right on the Pacific Crest Trail. The trail brings you near the base of the falls, and with a short cross-country scramble over rocks and fallen trees, you choose your own viewing spot.

Whereas Rainbow Falls and Lower Falls are classic river falls—imposingly wide but not immense in height—Minaret Falls drops on Minaret Creek, cascading 300 feet in length and 100 feet wide at peak flow. The fall is composed of a dozen or more side-by-side streams, running down the hillside. Even in July, the fall is so loud that conversation is nearly impossible. Shout a few words to your hiking partner, take some photographs, then retrace your steps back to the bridge, turning left to return to the Devils Postpile ranger station and parking lot.

Now that's a fine eight-mile day. But if you're not up for the whole trip, try one of these shorter hikes instead: from the Devils Postpile ranger station, hike out-and-back to Rainbow and Lower Falls, passing by the Devils Postpile formation, for a 5.5-mile round-trip. Or hike out-and-back to Minaret Falls for a three-mile round-trip.

If you want to see Rainbow and/or Lower Falls via an even shorter walk, you can start from the trailhead at Reds Meadow (see *Directions* below) for a two-mile round-trip, plus an extra 0.5-mile round-trip to Lower Falls.

Directions

From U.S. 395 in Lee Vining, drive 25 miles south to the Mammoth Lakes/ Highway 203 cutoff. Take Highway 203 west for four miles, through the town of Mammoth Lakes, then turn right at Minaret Road (still on Highway 203) and drive five miles to the Devils Postpile entrance kiosk, near Minaret Overlook. Unless you are camping in Devils Postpile, you will board a shuttle bus here and ride into the monument. Disembark from the bus at either the Devils

Lower Falls

Postpile parking area (for the longer hike) or the Rainbow Falls Trailhead near Reds Meadow (for the shortest hike). At the Devils Postpile parking area, the trail begins from the left (south) side of the parking area, just past the ranger station.

Information and Contact

Between 7 A.M. and 7:30 P.M. daily, you must purchase an access pass at the Mammoth Mountain Adventure Center on Highway 203 at Mammoth Ski Area and ride the park shuttle bus into the monument. Access passes cost $7 per adult over age 16; $4 per child ages 3–16. If you are camping in the monument, you may drive your own car, but you still must purchase an access pass for your vehicle. Park maps are available for free at the ranger station in Devils Postpile, or by download at www.nps.gov/depo. A more detailed map is available from Tom Harrison Maps, 415/456-7940, www.tomharrisonmaps.com. For more information, contact Devils Postpile National Monument, 760/934-2289, www.nps.gov/depo. Or contact Inyo National Forest, Mammoth Ranger District, 760/924-5500, www.fs.fed.us/r5/inyo.

24 TWIN FALLS
Inyo National Forest

Level: Easy

Distance: 0.5 mile round-trip

Best Season: June–September

Elevation Change: Negligible

Twin Falls can be seen plainly enough from the bridge between the two campgrounds at Twin Lakes in Mammoth. Plenty of folks stand on that bridge, cast a line into the water, and admire the view of the two lakes, the falls, and the surrounding granite crags. Some of them even hope to catch a fish or two while they are standing there. But if the waterfall interests you more than the fishing, take a little walk and inspect it more closely.

From the bridge, head into the west loop of the campground to the gravel road between sites 36 and 37. Walk down it until you see a trail marked "Private road, public trail." The private road to the right leads to some cabins, so follow the single-track trail to the left. The route

Twin Falls

is only a few hundred yards long, tunneling through a very lush glen. Be careful not to trample any of the columbine blossoms and corn lilies growing at your feet.

In minutes, you're at the base of 250-foot Twin Falls, where the stream pours down the mountainside and drops into Upper Twin Lake. Late in the summer, you can cross the stream at the waterfall's base by rock-hopping. You get a perfect view of the falls on one side of you and the lakes and bridge on the other.

For a different angle on Twin Falls, you can drive two miles farther on Lake Mary Road, past the turnoffs for Twin Lakes and Lake Mary, to the Twin Falls Picnic Area across from Lake Mamie. The picnic area is perched at the top of Twin Falls, where Lake Mamie's outlet stream cascades down the hillside. There's a fine view of Twin Lakes from here, although the waterfall view is better from below.

Directions
From U.S. 395 in Lee Vining, drive 25 miles south to the Mammoth Lakes/

Highway 203 cutoff. Take Highway 203 west for four miles, through the town of Mammoth Lakes, to the intersection of Highway 203/Minaret Road and Lake Mary Road. Continue straight on Lake Mary Road for 2.2 miles, then bear right on Twin Lakes Road and follow it for 0.5 mile to the Twin Lakes store. Park and walk across the bridge toward the west loop of Twin Lakes Campground (you can see the falls from the bridge).

Information and Contact

There is no fee. Maps of Inyo National Forest are available for a fee from the National Forest Store (406/329-3024, www.nationalforeststore.com), or can be downloaded for free from www.fs.fed.us/r5/maps/. A more detailed map of the Mammoth Lakes area is available from Tom Harrison Maps, 415/456-7940, www.tomharrisonmaps.com. For more information, contact Inyo National Forest, Mammoth Ranger District, 760/924-5500, www.fs.fed.us/r5/inyo.

25 HORSETAIL FALLS
Inyo National Forest

Level: Moderate   **Distance:** 4.0 miles round-trip

Best Season: June–September   **Elevation Change:** Total gain 600 feet

Several waterfalls in California go by the name Horsetail Falls. But the Horsetail Falls in McGee Creek Canyon, just off the McGee Creek Trail, really lives up to its moniker. The instant you see it, you know what it is, because its shape is a perfect inverted V, with a wide drop at the bottom that appears to swish back and forth in the wind. The only question is: Where's the rest of the horse?

But the waterfall is perhaps only a sidelight on this trip. The mountain vista surrounding McGee Creek Canyon is so large and looming, it actually dwarfs the falls. There's Mount Baldwin on the right and Mount Crocker on the left, but what really dominates the canyon is Red and White Mountain straight ahead at 12,816 feet, as colorful as its name implies. One of the most incredible sights I have ever seen in the Eastern Sierra is McGee Creek Canyon at sunset, backed by towering Red and White Mountain. Talk about the "range of light."

The view from the trailhead itself is awe-inspiring—the path leads back into a narrow pass, surrounded on both sides by huge peaks jutting straight upward. Reaching Horsetail Falls requires a two-mile walk up this pass, heading into the John Muir Wilderness, climbing the whole way on a slow grade. The trail is a

© ANN MARIE BROWN

Horsetail Falls

typical Eastern Sierra wilderness trail—rocky and sandy. It's a where-desert-meets-mountains hike, but it's not all sagebrush country. Thick groves of aspens, birches, and cottonwoods create incredible autumn colors. In summer, bright orange paintbrush, white lupine, and huge yellow mule's ears paint the hillsides. The trail gets more lush, and more beautiful, the farther you travel.

The McGee Creek Trail does not go right to Horsetail Falls; instead, it passes by the waterfall on its way to Steelhead Lake and the McGee Lakes. You can take a rough spur trail that brings you closer. At two miles out from the trailhead, cross the waterfall's creek (it flows right across the trail), then continue walking for two or three more minutes until you spy a crude route on the right. Follow it for a few hundred yards off the main trail and you come to a rock outcrop with a view of the fall and its dramatic mountain backdrop. You can see only about 50 feet of Horsetail's length, because the rest of it is obscured in dense foliage.

Ideally, you want to see Horsetail Falls early in the day—morning is best—while it is lit from the front by the sun. If you don't see it until later, the fall will be completely shaded. Of course, in the late afternoon, you can witness the miracle of the range of light in the colorful peaks. It's as if Mother Nature shines her spotlight on one mountain after another as the sun drops below the horizon. They light up one at a time, on cue, like each member of a jazz band taking turns playing lead. It's a sight you'll never forget.

Directions

From U.S. 395 in Lee Vining, drive approximately 33 miles south to the McGee Creek Road turnoff on the right. (It's eight miles south of the Mammoth Lakes turnoff and 30 miles north of Bishop.) Drive three miles southwest on McGee Creek Road to the trailhead (past the pack station).

Information and Contact

There is no fee. Maps of Inyo National Forest are available for a fee from the

National Forest Store (406/329-3024, www.nationalforeststore.com), or can be downloaded for free from www.fs.fed.us/r5/maps/. A more detailed map of the Mammoth Lakes area is available from Tom Harrison Maps, 415/456-7940, www.tomharrisonmaps.com. For more information, contact Inyo National Forest, White Mountain Ranger District, 760/873-2500, www.fs.fed.us/r5/inyo.

SEQUOIA AND KINGS CANYON

© ANN MARIE BROWN

BEST WATERFALLS

SEQUOIA AND KINGS CANYON

see Yosemite and
Mammoth Lakes
page 252

140
Fish Camp
Sierra
John Muir
Wilderness
395
6
49
1
National
Bishop
Inyo
National
Forest
2 **3**
Lakeshore
Forest
6
41
4
Big Pine
Millerton
Lake
168
5
Kings
Prather
Canyon
7
Pine Flat
Lake
National
Independence
Giant Sequoia
Nat'l Mon **9**
Park
395
Fresno
8
Cedar
Grove
John Muir
180
Wilsonia
180
10
11
Wilderness
12
Lone Pine
99
198
Selma
13
Sequoia
National Park ▲ Mt Whitney
14,494ft
Orosi
14-15
41
17-20
Lake
Kaweah
Golden Trout
Wilderness
Hanford
198
Visalia
Three Rivers
16
Lemoore
63
Olancha
21-22
Tulare
23-24
Lindsay
Giant Sequoia
National
Monument
25
Sequoia
National
Stratford
99
Forest
Corcoran
43
65
26
27
Dome Land
Wilderness
28
5
Delano
Kern R.
33
Isabella
Lake
Onyx
Blackwells
Corner
46
Wasco
Lake
Isabella
178
99
58
Bakersfield
McKittrick
0   10 mi
0   10 km
see
California
Deserts
page 496
5
58
Mojave
14
14

© AVALON TRAVEL

TRAIL NAME	LEVEL	DISTANCE	ELEVATION	SEASON	FEATURES	PAGE
1 Corlieu and Red Rock Falls	Easy	4.0 mi rt	200 ft	May-Oct.		319
2 Angel and Devil's Slide Falls	Moderate	4.8 mi rt	400 ft	May-Sept.		321
3 Whiskey Falls	Easy	Negligible	5,800 ft	May-Sept.		324
4 Rancheria Falls	Easy	2.0 mi rt	350 ft	May-July		325
5 Upper and Lower Dinkey Creek Falls	Easy	0.6 mile rt	Negligible	May-Sept.		327
6 Bear Creek Falls	Moderate	11.6 mi rt	1,000 ft	June-Sept.		329
7 First and Second Falls	Moderate	3.0 mi rt	300 ft	May-Sept.		331
8 Ella and Viola Falls	Moderate	4.5 mi rt	1,000 ft	Apr.-Aug.		333
9 Grizzly Falls	Easy	Negligible	4,400 ft	May-Sept.		336
10 Roaring River Falls	Easy	0.4 mile rt	Negligible	May-July		337
11 Mist Falls	Moderate	8.0 mi rt	650 ft	May-July		339
12 Tokopah Falls	Easy	3.6 mi rt	500 ft	Apr.-July		341
13 Marble Falls	Moderate	7.0 mi rt	1,500 ft	Feb.-June		343
14 Panther Creek Falls	Moderate	6.0 mi rt	600 ft	Feb.-June		345

TRAIL NAME	LEVEL	DISTANCE	ELEVATION	SEASON	FEATURES	PAGE
15 Middle Fork Kaweah River Falls	Easy	0.5 mile rt	50 ft	Feb.–June	[icons]	347
16 South Fork Kaweah River Falls	Moderate	3.4 mi rt	800 ft	Feb.–Sept.	[icons]	348
17 East Fork Kaweah River Falls	Easy	2.0 mi rt	600 ft	May–Aug.	[icons]	351
18 Three-Falls-Below-The-Gate	Moderate	4.0 mi rt	100 ft	June–Oct.	[icons]	352
19 Tufa, Crystal, and Franklin Falls	Moderate	4.0 mi rt	450 ft	June–Sept.	[icons]	354
20 Black Wolf Falls	Easy	0.5 mile rt	50 ft	May–Aug.	[icons]	357
21 Hidden Falls	Easy	0.25 mile rt	30 ft	May–Sept.	[icons]	358
22 Galena Creek Falls	Easy	1.5 mi rt	100 ft	May–Sept.	[icons]	361
23 Wishon Fork Tule River Falls	Moderate	6.0 mi rt	800 ft	May–Sept.	[icons]	362
24 Middle Fork Tule River Falls	Easy	0.5 mile rt	100 ft	May–Sept.	[icons]	364
25 Peppermint Creek Falls	Moderate	0.5 mile rt	150 ft	May–Aug.	[icons]	365
26 Nobe Young Falls	Moderate	1.0 mile rt	100 ft	May–Aug.	[icons]	367
27 South Creek Falls	Easy	Negligible	3,800 ft	May–Sept.	[icons]	369
28 Salmon Creek Falls	Moderate	9.0 mi rt	600 ft	May–July	[icons]	370

1 CORLIEU AND RED ROCK FALLS
Sierra National Forest

Level: Easy

Best Season: May–October

Distance: 4.0 miles round-trip

Elevation Change: Total gain 200 feet

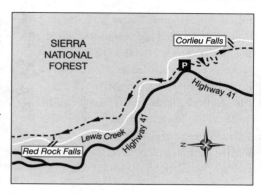

You wouldn't expect a hiking trail with a trailhead right along a busy highway to be this pleasurable. But the Lewis Creek National Recreation Trail, which is accessible from Highway 41 just south of Yosemite and north of Oakhurst, is pure pleasure. In addition to two good waterfalls, Corlieu and Red Rock, the trail offers trout fishing in Lewis Creek, myriad wildflowers, and an interesting historical perspective.

Apparently, it's also one of the best trails around for holding hands with your hiking partner, because I passed three different couples, ranging from teenagers to senior citizens, all of them hand-in-hand and smiling. It's just that kind of place.

Although the Lewis Creek Trail has three access points, at both ends and in the middle, most people start from the middle, because that trailhead is easiest to locate. From this access point, Corlieu Falls is a mere 10 minutes away. Just follow the trail from the parking pullout, then take the signed right fork and continue to the top of the falls.

You can look down at Corlieu Falls from an overlook on the main trail, or follow a use trail that continues to Corlieu's base. It requires some short but steep scrambling to get there. The waterfall is reported to be Madera County's tallest waterfall with a total height of 80 feet, descending in several stairsteps. It has several fallen logs clustered at its base, and a forest of elephant ears growing on tall stalks around its stream. Many rocks and wayward branches have collected below Corlieu, providing a seating gallery for viewing the falls.

The fall is named for Clifford Corlieu, who built a cabin overlooking the falls and lived here from 1910–1929. He was a rancher and logger who came from the Fresno area and later in life became a nature lover and a poet; a book of his verse was published in 1962. In the 1930s, a rustic cabin resort was built near

Corlieu Falls to take advantage of the picturesque waterfall and also a nearby warm spring. A few remnants of the old homestead and resort can still be seen near the falls.

When you're ready for the next waterfall, scramble back to the main trail and follow it upstream. You're walking on the path of an old logging route, where the Madera Sugar Pine Company built a section of a 54-mile-long flume to carry milled boards from the town of Sugar Pine to the railroad in the San Joaquin Valley. The flume operated from 1900–1931. Evidence of the old flume—in the form of boards, nails, and metal scraps—can be spotted along the trail if you look carefully.

Red Rock Falls

To hike upstream to Red Rock Falls, cross Lewis Creek on a sturdy footbridge that carries you to its eastern banks then head left. Colorful wildflowers pepper the banks of Lewis Creek. May apples, big-leaf maples, bear clover, blackberries, and huge ferns proliferate along the stream, all happily growing under a filtered canopy of oaks, ponderosa pines, and incense cedars. If you've been traveling around the stark higher elevations of Yosemite, it's a pleasant change to be in this lush mixed forest.

In the last half mile before Red Rock Falls, the trail departs from its mostly level meandering and begins to climb a bit above the creek. Here your surroundings become drier and more exposed, and at 1.8 miles from Corlieu Falls you see a left spur, which descends steeply to the creek. Take it to the base of Red Rock Falls, which is a wide river-type waterfall, about 20 feet high. Unlike Corlieu Falls, Red Rock has almost no foliage or delicate nooks and crannies. Instead, the water pitches over a rock ledge in one bold sheet, creating a loud downpour. The red-hued rock that the fall is named for can be seen only when the water level drops. Several fallen logs have gathered in front of the falls; they are casualties that washed downstream in a season of harsh storms.

There's not much of a viewing area for Red Rock Falls; you have to sit on the ground alongside it, at an angle to the falls and about 50 feet distant. Although this is a fine spot for picture taking, it's not much of an up-close-and-personal waterfall experience. Of the two falls, Corlieu seems much more intimate.

From Red Rock Falls, you can simply head back 1.5 miles to the trailhead and your car, or you can continue one mile to the trail's north terminus at Sugar Pine. If you wish to hike the entire length of the Lewis Creek Trail rather than just visit the waterfalls, start hiking at Cedar Valley Road (the trail's south terminus) and walk four miles one-way to Sugar Pine. And don't forget to bring along a hiking friend, preferably someone you like to hold hands with.

Directions
From Oakhurst, drive north on Highway 41 for eight miles to the signed trailhead for the Lewis Creek Trail on the east (right) side of the highway. (The trailhead is four miles south of Westfall Picnic Area.)

Information and Contact
There is no fee. Maps of Sierra National Forest are available for a fee from the National Forest Store (406/329-3024, www.nationalforeststore.com), or can be downloaded for free from www.fs.fed.us/r5/maps/. For more information, contact Sierra National Forest, Bass Lake Ranger District, 559/877-2218, www.fs.fed.us/r5/sierra.

2 ANGEL AND DEVIL'S SLIDE FALLS
Sierra National Forest

Level: Moderate
Distance: 4.8 miles round-trip
Best Season: May–September
Elevation Change: Total gain 400 feet

When you hear of waterfalls named Angel and Devil's Slide, you have to wonder what they are going to look like. The answer is that they look a lot like you'd expect. Angel Falls looks like an angel's wings, fanning out in thousands of delicate rivulets over light gray granite. Devil's Slide looks like the place where a laughing devil would play—a series of water chutes, holes, and dips, running for a 200-yard length along Willow Creek.

To hike to Angel and Devil's Slide falls, follow Willow Creek Trail from the north end of Bass Lake. The trail makes for a beautiful walk along its whole route; the only difficulty is figuring out how to access it. Officially, Willow Creek Trail (also called the McLeod Flat Trail) starts at Road 274 on the east side of the highway bridge over Willow Creek. But there's limited parking on the west side of the bridge, and the lot is often full. If you can't park there, you must park on North Shore Road between the Bass Lake Dam and Falls Beach Picnic Area. Then walk along the lake for a short distance to the east side of the Willow Creek bridge, and follow an access trail up along the North Fork of Willow Creek. When you reach Road 274, walk 50 feet to your left and access the dirt driveway on the northeast side of the highway bridge, then walk 50 yards on the driveway and take the left cutoff onto single-track. There, finally, you'll find the trail sign and the official start of the Willow Creek Trail.

Even so, things are still a bit confusing because you'll see three different routes—one up high, one right along the creek, and another somewhere in the middle. Take the highest trail above the creek; the lower trails are short spur routes for anglers and swimmers who aren't going all the way to the falls.

The route has many gentle ups and downs, but no steep pitches, as long as you stay off the side trails, which descend to the creek. Spring and early-summer wildflowers are resplendent: orange columbines, white western azaleas, deep purple lupines, wild strawberries, mariposa lilies, and even the unusual harlequin lupine that has both purple and yellow flowers on the same plant. All of these are tucked in amid myriad ferns and a canopy of black and white oaks and mixed conifers. Because of its huge variety of flora, the Willow Creek Trail is an excellent tree- and wildflower-identification trail.

Hike above the rushing flow of Willow Creek as it carves its way through and around its granite streambed. You reach Angel Falls at 0.7 mile from the trailhead, and true to its name, it looks like the gossamer wings of an angel. You can hike to its base on one of several side trails, or follow the main trail to the top of the falls.

Although many other small cascades tumble above and below it, Angel Falls is distinct. Willow Creek's stream runs like latticework over the granite, dropping into granite pockets and then pouring back out. It forms an intricate and beautiful cascade. A small dam controls the water above Angel Falls. Water pipes run by its side. Although these signs of mechanization slightly mar the beauty of Angel Falls, it's only slightly.

© ANN MARIE BROWN

Devil's Slide Falls

Because Angel Falls is so close to the parking area, this can be a major party spot for teenagers in late spring and summer, as soon as the water warms up. Avoid a weekend visit here if at all possible; weekdays before school is out are the best times to visit. Still, if you get stuck with the crowds, just keep hiking. You'll leave almost everyone behind as you walk upstream from Angel Falls, heading for Devil's Slide. In the stretch between the two falls, the creek is so placid that it's difficult to believe you will find any more waterfalls. But at 2.4 miles from your car, you'll reach the left spur off the main trail that leads to Devil's Slide. The spur trail ends at a chain-link fence, built to keep people off the slippery granite near the cascade. It's wise to stay behind it. Many injuries and deaths have occurred along Willow Creek due to the slick granite and fast-moving water.

Devil's Slide is not impressively tall, but rather impressively long. It's the perfect water slide for a river otter or a beaver, or perhaps the Devil himself. The water runs cold, fast, and loud.

On your return trip, watch for views of bright blue Bass Lake as you descend on the trail. And since you've just been visiting the Devil's playground, you might want to stop and pay homage to saintly Angel Falls once more before returning to the trailhead.

Directions

From Oakhurst, drive north on Highway 41 for four miles, then turn right on Road 222. Drive four miles and bear left on Road 274. Drive one mile to the trailhead parking area on the left side of the road, on the west side of the highway bridge over Willow Creek. Or bear right on the Bass Lake cutoff (Road 222), then bear left on North Shore Road and drive one mile to Falls Beach Picnic Area. Park there or farther west in the dirt pullouts along the road, closer to the dam. A use trail begins across the road from the dam; follow it up and across Road 274 to the official start of the Willow Creek Trail.

Information and Contact

There is no fee. Maps of Sierra National Forest are available for a fee from the National Forest Store (406/329-3024, www.nationalforeststore.com), or can be downloaded for free from www.fs.fed.us/r5/maps/. For more information, contact Sierra National Forest, Bass Lake Ranger District, 559/877-2218, www.fs.fed.us/r5/sierra.

3 WHISKEY FALLS   BEST C
Sierra National Forest

Level: Easy

Distance: Negligible

Best Season: May–September

Elevation Change: 5,800 feet

Usually the waterfalls you can drive to don't interest me as much as the ones you must hike to. Drive-to falls are often too well-known and crowded; hike-to falls are usually more secluded and remote. But Whiskey Falls in Sierra National Forest is the exception. Even though the waterfall drops right along the Whiskey Falls Campground access road, it somehow manages to stay a secret. Maybe the long, unpaved access road keeps it isolated, or perhaps the other campgrounds and attractions around Bass Lake draw the crowds away. Whatever it is, it's a good thing.

You can combine your visit to Whiskey Falls with a camping trip at the adjacent Forest Service camp, where your stay will cost you nothing. Then you can get up in the morning and head off on

Whiskey Falls

© ANN MARIE BROWN

various hiking and fishing adventures in the area. At the end of each day, you return to Whiskey Falls, always running wide and clear, and go to sleep at night with the sound of a waterfall accompanying your dreams.

Whiskey Falls can be found just beyond the campground entrance sign at a bridge over Whiskey Creek. The 40-foot waterfall drops just upstream over two stairstepped granite slabs, which are framed by big western azaleas blooming bright white along the creek. The fall's width is almost double its height, and its stream provides excellent flow year-round. Large sheets of granite at the waterfall's base furnish a place to sun yourself and admire the shimmering, lacy cascade. Big conifers nearby offer a shady respite.

Whiskey Falls is two side-by-side cataracts, one wide main drop and one alongside it that's a beautiful, narrow stairstep, with large clumps of elephant ears growing between the two. The waterfall's secret is that the larger cascade has a shallow cave behind it, lined with greenery, mosses, and ferns of all variety. My hiking partner insisted on going underneath the spray of water to crawl into the cave. Then, just to prove he'd done it, he took a picture of me on the other side of the running water. It's one of the most unusual photographs I've ever seen, something like Kodachrome crossed with Impressionism.

Directions

From Oakhurst, drive north on Highway 41 for four miles, then turn right on Road 222. Drive four miles and bear left on Road 274, following it approximately 10 miles into North Fork. At the four-way stop sign where roads 274 and 225 intersect, turn left on Road 225. Drive one mile, then turn left onto Cascadel Road (Road 233). Drive two miles, then bear left on Road 8S09. Follow Road 8S09 for about seven miles, then turn right and drive 1.2 miles to Whiskey Falls Camp. The falls drop right along the road.

Information and Contact

There is no fee. Maps of Sierra National Forest are available for a fee from the National Forest Store (406/329-3024, www.nationalforeststore.com), or can be downloaded for free from www.fs.fed.us/r5/maps/. For more information, contact Sierra National Forest, Bass Lake Ranger District, 559/877-2218, www.fs.fed.us/r5/sierra.

4 RANCHERIA FALLS
Sierra National Forest

Level: Easy   **Distance:** 2.0 miles round-trip
Best Season: May–July   **Elevation Change:** Total gain 350 feet

The Rancheria Falls National Recreation Trail is so well-groomed, it's hikeable in tennis shoes—even little four-inch-long Reeboks made for three-year-old feet.

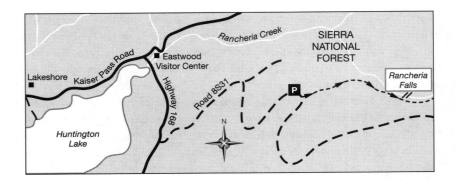

I know because I found one on the trail, and then a few moments later, I came upon its owner, walking along with one shoe on and one shoe off. She seemed nonplussed by the missing Reebok, but feigned gratitude for its return.

Why worry about footwear when you're hiking to Rancheria Falls? There's so much else to concern yourself with. It's a gorgeous one-mile trail, smooth and wide, that takes a gentle uphill grade to the waterfall. You'll share it with blue butterflies and noisy cicadas flitting by. The route leads through a mix of sunshine and shady fir forest. At your feet are low-growing gooseberry, chinquapin, and colorful wildflowers, mostly hardy lupine and paintbrush.

Rancheria Falls

You don't see or hear water until you're almost on top of the falls. It's a big surprise when you suddenly get your first glimpse of white water through the trees. This initial view can take your breath away, particularly in the early summer when the fall is at full flood. Rancheria Falls plummets 150 feet over a 50-foot-wide rock ledge, then continues in a long, boisterous cascade that greatly increases its magnitude. As Rancheria Creek's flow hits assorted smaller ledges below its lip, the water pushes off and sprays outward like fireworks exploding. It's the kind of sight you want to watch for a long, long time.

From the end of the trail, you can climb over rocks and pick your viewing spot, either closer to or farther from the voluminous spray. Even if there is a crowd here, as there often is because of the fall's proximity to popular Huntington Lake, you can usually find a private spot downstream. Make sure you check out the vista downcanyon; it's almost as compelling as the waterfall view.

Directions

From Fresno, drive northeast on Highway 168 through Clovis for 70 miles, past Shaver Lake. A half mile before reaching Huntington Lake, take the right turnoff signed for Rancheria Falls (Road 8S31). Follow the dirt road for 1.3 miles to the signed trailhead at a sharp curve in the road. Park off the road.

Information and Contact

There is no fee. Maps of Sierra National Forest are available for a fee from the National Forest Store (406/329-3024, www.nationalforeststore.com), or can be downloaded for free from www.fs.fed.us/r5/maps/. For more information, contact Sierra National Forest, High Sierra Ranger District, 559/855-5355, www.fs.fed.us/r5/sierra.

5 UPPER AND LOWER DINKEY CREEK FALLS

Dinkey Lakes Wilderness

Level: Easy

Best Season: May–September

Distance: 0.6 mile round-trip

Elevation Change: Negligible

Don't plan on coming to Dinkey Creek just to see the waterfall. Once you get out of your car and start walking into the Dinkey Lakes Wilderness, there's almost no chance you'll be willing to turn around at the falls, which are only 0.3 mile from the trailhead. The place is just too good to pass up.

Before you jump in your car and head out, though, make sure you pack along the bug spray. On my July visit, I pulled up in the parking lot, opened the doors of my air-conditioned car, and was immediately attacked by about eight million mosquitoes. In the middle of the day, no less. I dove back in the car and slathered my skin with repellent, then braved the onslaught. The odds were much better this time.

Another odd fact about the trailhead is that it's located right next to a popular off-road-vehicle area. While I was swatting mosquitoes, three guys on all-terrain motorcycles roared up to me and asked, "Hey, how far is it to the first Dinkey

Lake?" I told them it was just over a mile, but they weren't allowed to ride their machines in the wilderness area. They were shocked. "A mile?! That's way too far to walk." Then they roared off in the other direction. To each his own.

Immediately beyond the parking area, the trail crosses Dinkey Creek, which can make things a bit tricky, depending on the stream level. You'll be instantly wowed by the colorful striated rock formations in the creekbed and along the edges of the trail. After hopping across the creek, walk for only about two minutes down the trail, until you see a huge 100-yard-wide rock slab on your left. It looks like a gray lava field. Leave the trail and cross over to it, then walk across it and you'll find the upper falls on the far side. Total walking time from the parking area? About seven minutes. (Which might be fortunate, if the famous Dinkey Creek mosquitoes are out in force.)

Dinkey Creek Falls

Upper Dinkey Creek Falls is only about 25 feet high, dropping through a notch in the fractured granite, then fanning out in a wide horsetail shape and hitting a single wide stairstep below. Except for this one clifflike section at the waterfall, the stream around it is otherwise level. The water is very clear, showing off the colorful rock beneath it. Tiny pink and white mountain wildflowers grow out of cracks in the granite alongside the fall, and if you wear enough bug spray you can actually stand still for a minute and enjoy the scene.

You won't want to stop here. The trail continues along Dinkey Creek to a right turnoff for Mystery Lake at 1.3 miles. The lake is only 0.25 mile farther from this junction. Or continuing straight along Dinkey Creek brings you to First Dinkey Lake, as it is prosaically named, in three miles. You're sure to have company at these and the more distant lakes. A popular backpacking trail links several of them. The loop trip is flat and short enough for hikers of any level, and the scenery is world-class, replete with verdant meadows, colorful wildflowers, stark granite walls, and deep blue lakes.

If you're here to see waterfalls, there's one more fall you should check out: just downstream from where you parked your car is a much larger fall on Dinkey

Creek, which is more impressive than the 25-footer you just visited. Lower Dinkey Creek Falls is nearly 100 feet high, and can be accessed by crossing the creek at the parking lot and following the dirt road on the far side downstream. This will bring you right to the brink of the falls.

Directions

From Fresno, drive northeast on Highway 168 through Clovis for 50 miles to the town of Shaver Lake. Turn right on Dinkey Creek Road and drive nine miles. Turn left on Rock Creek Road (9S09) and drive six miles, then turn right on 9S10 and drive 4.7 miles. Turn right at the sign for Dinkey Lakes on Road 9S62 and drive 2.2 miles to the trailhead. These last two miles are very rough road. (Stay left at the fork to bypass the four-wheel-drive area and go straight to the trailhead.)

You can also reach the trailhead from the northern end of Road 9S09, at Tamarack Winter Sports Area, nine miles north of Shaver Lake. Drive 6.4 miles on 9S09, then bear left on 9S10 and drive 4.7 miles. Follow the rest of the directions as above.

Information and Contact

There is no fee. Maps of the Dinkey Lakes Wilderness or Sierra National Forest are available for a fee from the National Forest Store (406/329-3024, www.nationalforeststore.com), or can be downloaded for free from www.fs.fed.us/r5/maps/. For more information, contact Sierra National Forest, High Sierra Ranger District, 559/855-5355, www.fs.fed.us/r5/sierra.

6 BEAR CREEK FALLS
John Muir Wilderness

🏃 🚐 🏊 🐴

Level: Moderate

Best Season: June–September

Distance: 11.6 miles round-trip

Elevation Change: Total gain 1,000 feet

The drive to the trailhead is a big part of this adventure to Bear Creek Falls. Four-wheel drive or very high clearance is necessary for the final two miles of the trip, but even the paved stretch on narrow, winding Kaiser Pass Road is exciting.

Bear Creek Falls is located in the John Muir Wilderness just outside of Mono Hot Springs in Sierra National Forest. The nearest major development is at Huntington and Shaver Lakes, 20 miles to the west. After you leave these recreation areas and set out over Kaiser Pass, all you'll find are a few spartan resorts and campgrounds and the incredible granite landscape of the Central Sierra. The scenery is priceless—a nonstop parade of granite slabs and domelike structures. This is the type of landscape that defines the word "Sierra" in the minds of so many nature lovers.

Be sure to stop in at the rustic resort at Mono Hot Springs to fill up your day pack or backpack with supplies, then head for the wilderness boundary and a gorgeous hike along Bear Creek. Bear Creek Trail leads past Bear Creek Reservoir and then follows alongside the creek's rushing cascades. If you've ever hiked along the Tuolumne River in Yosemite, you'll find this experience to be similar—the stream is always in close proximity, but its many cascades are partially hidden from the trail. The greenish colored water, clear pools, and nearly nonstop sound of waterfalls will force you to detour from the main path to get a closer look. If you are thinking about swimming, be forewarned—the water in Bear Creek is icy cold. Stick in one big toe before you make a bigger commitment. Anglers, take note: there are many good-sized trout in this stream.

The stream stays on your right side for the entire trip. Along its banks are groves of quaking aspens, which turn a brilliant gold in October. The trail has a constant but gentle elevation gain, and although much of the route is exposed, occasional welcome shade is provided by Jeffrey pines and firs.

At 5.8 miles out, you'll spot 25-foot Bear Creek Falls from the trail. It is formed where two cascading branches of Bear Creek pour into an enormously wide, shallow pool. Stay on the trail for a few more yards as it leads up and around the pool. Take off your shoes and socks and ford the creek where you can. On the far side, you'll gain access to a lovely beach, which is composed of tiny, rounded pebbles. Pull out your lunch and your camera. You won't be leaving soon.

Directions

From Fresno, drive northeast on Highway 168 through Clovis for 70 miles to Huntington Lake. Turn right on Kaiser Pass Road and drive 17 miles (narrow and winding) to a fork. Bear left for Mono Hot Springs and Edison Lake. Drive 2.5 miles to the Bear Creek turnoff on the right (it's one mile past the Mono Hot Springs turnoff and before the Mono Creek Campground turnoff). Turn right and drive 2.3 miles on rough dirt road (four-wheel drive is required) to Bear Creek Reservoir parking area and trailhead. Park on the granite slabs, then follow the trail that leads downhill toward the reservoir.

Information and Contact

There is no fee. Maps of the John Muir Wilderness or Sierra National Forest are available for a fee from the National Forest Store (406/329-3024, www.

nationalforeststore.com), or can be downloaded for free from www.fs.fed.us/r5/
maps/. For more information, contact Sierra National Forest, High Sierra Ranger
District, 559/855-5355, www.fs.fed.us/r5/sierra.

7 FIRST AND SECOND FALLS
Inyo National Forest

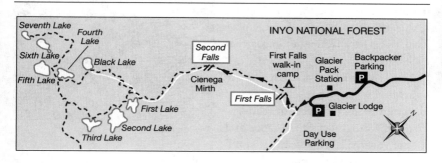

Level: Moderate

Best Season: May–September

Distance: 3.0 miles round-trip

Elevation Change: Total gain 300 feet

Looking for a perfect beginner-level backpacking trip where you can camp on
top of a waterfall? How about an easy day hike near the border of the John Muir
Wilderness, visiting two waterfalls on the way? Then sign up for the trip to First
and Second Falls, just 10 miles off U.S. 395 in Big Pine.

The trip begins at the trailhead near Glacier Lodge. You start off easy with a
stroll down a paved and dirt road by some privately owned cabins, paralleling
Big Pine Creek. In moments, you cross a bridge over First Falls, which is a long
200-foot cascade that pours down the mountainside. Because its edges are completely overgrown with willows and cottonwoods, you can't see much of it, but it
creates a terrific noise even late in the summer.

After the bridge, take the right fork and begin a steep uphill climb, switchbacking up and over First Falls. It takes a dozen or more tight curves in the trail to get
above it, and your body will feel the 7,800-foot elevation if you aren't acclimated.
You get great views straight into Big Pine Canyon, though, and the sound of the
creek will spur you on.

You won't be heading into the great expanse in front of you, which is Big
Pine Canyon's South Fork. Instead you're stealing away to a hidden canyon off
to your right, the North Fork Canyon of Big Pine Creek, which you can't see

until you get on top of First Falls. Cross a bridge to your right, then take a hard left onto a dirt road, staying along the creek. Note that if you turn right instead, you'll reach First Falls Walk-in Camp in 100 yards, with its six campsites, fire rings, and picnic tables. This is a perfect backpacking destination for families, only a mile's hike from the backpackers' parking lot. The camp sits along the stream just above First Falls, nestled in the pines. (A single-track trail option at this junction, signed only as "Upper Trail," is for backpackers heading farther back into the canyon.)

Second Falls

Now that you've made all those switchbacks, you can relax a while and just cruise along the level dirt road, enjoying the proximity of the creek and the canyon vistas. At 1.2 miles, you'll get your first view of Second Falls, which looks more impressive from a distance than it does close up. Like First Falls, Second Falls is a 200-foot cascade, but it delivers much more visual impact than First Falls does. The fall is surrounded by interesting rocks and has a few sparse Jeffrey pines growing on top.

The dirt road you're hiking on eventually narrows to single-track, then switchbacks to the right to join the upper trail in the canyon. But an unmaintained route continues to the left, bringing you closer to the waterfall if you choose to follow it. The view is best about a quarter mile back from the falls (look for a large rock near a lone pine tree). From there, the scenery is superb: in addition to Second Falls and the surrounding mountains, the profusion of plant life in the canyon can be surveyed. In one glance, you can see mountain mahogany, lodgepole pines, creekside aspens, sagebrush, and even some scrubby cactus growing near the waterfall's edge.

Backpackers and day hikers wishing to hike farther can continue beyond the falls to Cienega Mirth at 3.0 miles. The mirth is a lush, meadowy area that is overflowing with lupine, larkspur, and leopard lilies in July. Fed by a natural spring, the area can be quite swampy until late summer. The wetness produces spectacular wildflowers but also, alas, prolific mosquitoes. Near the creek at Cienega Mirth is a beautiful stone cabin that was built by movie star Lon Chaney. Today it's a backcountry ranger residence. Beyond the mirth are First Lake (4.5 miles out), Second Lake (4.8 miles out), and Third Lake (5.5 miles out). By Second Lake, you've climbed to more than 10,000 feet, and the lakes take on the blue-green hue of glacially fed waters. A popular summer trip is to hike all the way to the edge of the Palisade Glacier, the southernmost glacier in the Sierra, but the trek is not for casual hikers. It's a long, hard pull of nine miles one-way, with a 5,000-foot elevation gain.

Directions

From Bishop, drive 15 miles south on U.S. 395 to Big Pine. Turn right (west) on Crocker Street, which becomes Glacier Lodge Road, and drive 10.5 miles to Glacier Lodge and the Big Pine Canyon Trailhead at the end of the road. Day hikers may park in the day-use area near the lodge, but backpackers must park 0.5 mile east on Glacier Lodge Road in the backpackers' parking lot.

Information and Contact

There is no fee. Maps of Inyo National Forest are available for a fee from the National Forest Store (406/329-3024, www.nationalforeststore.com), or can be downloaded for free from www.fs.fed.us/r5/maps/. For more information, contact Inyo National Forest, White Mountain Ranger District, 760/873-2500, www.fs.fed.us/r5/inyo.

8 ELLA AND VIOLA FALLS

Kings Canyon National Park

🚶 🔼

Level: Moderate	**Distance:** 4.5 miles round-trip
Best Season: April-August	**Elevation Change:** Total loss 1,000 feet

Ella Falls was the destination of my first hiking trip ever in Kings Canyon National Park. What an introduction. I've been a Kings Canyon believer since. Ella Falls was also the place where I got educated about exploring off-trail on the slick granite around southern Sierra waterfalls. While looking for a good spot to take a photograph, my hiking boots suddenly lost all traction, and I slid on my backside about 10 feet into a freezing pool. Luckily, I landed in a basin, so I didn't tumble farther downstream. I hiked back feeling very humble, and carrying my pants, which were soaking wet. I learned my lesson.

The trail to Ella Falls starts at Sunset Campground, right across the road from

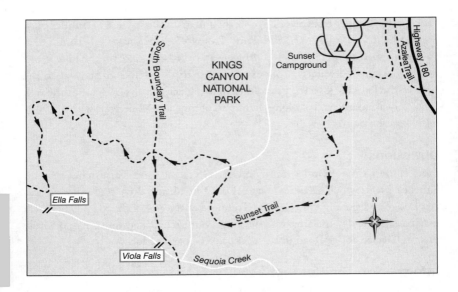

Grant Grove Village. The trip is downhill all the way, with a 1,000-foot elevation loss that you must gain back on the return. It's a well-built trail with an even grade and sturdy wooden bridges to carry you across streams. The trail descends through big pines and firs and winds through stands of ceanothus and flowering western azalea. Although the forest is partially burned in places around the trail, incredible foliage and ferns surround all the side streams.

At 1.5 miles from the trailhead, reach a junction where the South Boundary Trail crosses Sunset Trail. Turning left will take you on a 0.25-mile side trip to what the park rather liberally calls Viola Falls. Although the area around it is lovely—it's set in a rock garden of sculptured granite pools—Viola Falls is a bit of a disappointment. The diminutive fall is only about five feet high, and lacking drama. The best thing about the side trip is not Viola Falls at all, but a huge sequoia tree that grows just upstream. Chunks of granite are permanently fused in its above-ground roots. The big old tree grew right around the rocks, imprisoning them in its grasp.

More cascades drop downstream from Viola Falls and the South Boundary Trail, but they can't be accessed because of the slick, polished granite of the streambed and the steep canyon walls. Take the side trip to Viola if you choose, or continue straight on Sunset Trail to Ella Falls.

Like Viola, Ella Falls drops on Sequoia Creek. It's a 50-foot-long narrow cascade that shimmers bright white against a background of gray granite and dense green foliage. The rock-sculpted streambed has been continually rounded and eroded by the coursing stream. Alders and willows are clustered tightly along the water's edge. Look for tall cow parsnips and colorful leopard lilies growing along the banks.

If you'd like to continue hiking before making the uphill return trip to Sunset Campground, you can follow Sunset Trail for another 0.25 mile to a YMCA camp on Sequoia Lake. Although Sequoia is a privately owned lake and not part of the park, you're allowed to walk along the lake's edge as long as you stay out of the camp area.

© ANN MARIE BROWN

Ella Falls

Directions

From Fresno, drive east on Highway 180 for 55 miles to the Big Stump Entrance Station at Kings Canyon National Park. Continue 1.5 miles and turn left for Grant Grove. Drive 1.5 miles to Grant Grove Village and park in the large parking lot near the visitor center. Cross the road and walk on the paved trail toward Sunset Campground's amphitheater. Continue heading left through the campground to site #179, where the trail begins.

Information and Contact

There is a $10 entrance fee per vehicle at Sequoia and Kings Canyon National Parks, which is good for seven days. Park maps are available for free at the entrance stations, or by download at www.nps.gov/seki. A more detailed map is available from Tom Harrison Maps, 415/456-7940, www.tomharrisonmaps.com. For more information, contact Sequoia and Kings Canyon National Parks, 559/565-3341, www.nps.gov/seki.

🄝 GRIZZLY FALLS

Giant Sequoia National Monument

BEST ☾

Level: Easy

Distance: Negligible

Best Season: May–September

Elevation Change: 4,400 feet

Most people don't notice the difference, but Grizzly Falls is not in Kings Canyon or Sequoia National Parks, it's in Giant Sequoia National Monument. The national park/national monument boundary line is drawn in such a way that the Kings Canyon Highway enters the national park near Grant Grove, then leaves it, then re-enters it again near Cedar Grove after passing through 27 miles of Giant Sequoia National Monument. Grizzly Falls is in the final few miles of the monument before the winding highway re-enters the national park.

Grizzly Falls

But government jurisdictions matter little when you're looking at a waterfall as breathtaking as 80-foot Grizzly Falls, which pours just 50 yards from the road. A small parking lot and picnic area near the waterfall's base make Grizzly an easy destination. A stop here breaks up the long and winding drive into the heart of Kings Canyon.

The water from Grizzly Falls starts at Grizzly Lakes, deep in the Monarch Wilderness below the Monarch Divide, and drains all the way down to the Kings River along the Kings Canyon Highway. The falls are on the edge of the Monarch Wilderness, a roadless land of steep and rugged terrain. Hikers can make their way into the wilderness by way of the Deer Cove Trailhead two miles east of the falls, but relentless ups and downs and limited water keep all but the hardiest of hikers away.

Grizzly is a waterfall for people who have little interest in hiking, or a lot of interest in waterfalls, since the fall is only 50 yards from where you park your car. The waterfall is loud and powerful, dropping 80 feet over a 35-foot-wide granite ledge. The first time you see it, you may have a sense of déjà vu, because photos of this fall frequently appear on park brochures and local travel magazines.

If you're making the drive all the way out here to see Grizzly Falls, you might want to take a look at another natural wonder just five miles away. Boyden Cave, a limestone cavern gilded with crystalline stalactites and stalagmites, can be seen via guided tours that are offered daily from May through October.

Directions

From Fresno, drive east on Highway 180 for 55 miles to the Big Stump Entrance Station at Kings Canyon National Park. Continue 1.5 miles and turn left for Grant Grove and Cedar Grove. Continue 27 miles on Highway 180 to Grizzly Falls on the left, 5.5 miles past Boyden Cave.

Information and Contact

Although the waterfall is in Giant Sequoia National Monument, the only way to reach it is by entering Kings Canyon National Park on Highway 180. There is a $10 entrance fee per vehicle at Sequoia and Kings Canyon National Parks, which is good for seven days. Park maps are available for free at the entrance stations, or by download at www.nps.gov/seki. A more detailed map is available from Tom Harrison Maps, 415/456-7940, www.tomharrisonmaps.com. For more information, contact Giant Sequoia National Monument, Hume Lake Ranger District, 559/338-2251, www.r5.fs.fed.us/sequoia.

10 ROARING RIVER FALLS   BEST ◖

Kings Canyon National Park

Level: Easy	**Distance:** 0.4 mile round-trip
Best Season: May-July	**Elevation Change:** Negligible

You might think that Roaring River Falls is the cute and clever name for a Kings Canyon waterfall that makes lots of noise, but no; Roaring River Falls is a waterfall that falls on the Roaring River. So the next question is: Does the Roaring River actually roar? The answer is yes, but not as much as the South Fork Kings River, into which the waterfall drops. It just goes to show that in the waterfall business, you can't take everything literally.

A great feature of Roaring River Falls is that it's the only waterfall in Kings

© ANN MARIE BROWN

Roaring River Falls

Canyon and Sequoia National Parks that is accessible via wheelchair. The trail is paved, wide, and only 0.4 mile round-trip. If able hikers want a longer trip, they can continue upstream on the River Trail to Zumwalt Meadow in 1.6 miles or Road's End in 2.7 miles.

Getting to the falls is a breeze. After leaving your car in the Roaring River Falls parking lot, just follow the trail through the forest and you arrive in about five minutes. At the overlook area, you have a perfect view of the falls, nicely framed by a big Jeffrey pine on the right and two red firs on the left. The river funnels down through a narrow rock gorge, forming two water chutes. One is 40 feet tall; the one behind it is about half that size. Your overlook is directly across from the waterfall, on the north side of the dark gray rocky bowl into which the water pounds.

Roaring River Falls' pool is so large—probably 50 feet wide—and the cliffs surrounding it are so tall and sheer that the falls are somewhat dwarfed. Keep in mind, however, that you are seeing only their final drop. The cascades extend for hundreds of feet upstream, but they are hidden from view and inaccessible. Park officials estimate that from the overlook, you see only one-third of Roaring River Fall's total drop.

Directions

From Fresno, drive east on Highway 180 for 55 miles to the Big Stump Entrance Station at Kings Canyon National Park. Continue 1.5 miles and turn left for Grant Grove and Cedar Grove. Continue 35 miles on Highway 180 to the sign for Roaring River Falls and the River Trail, three miles past the Cedar Grove campground and ranger station. The trailhead and parking area are on the right side of the road.

Information and Contact

There is a $10 entrance fee per vehicle at Sequoia and Kings Canyon National Parks, which is good for seven days. Park maps are available for free at the entrance stations, or by download at www.nps.gov/seki. A more detailed map is available from Tom Harrison Maps, 415/456-7940, www.tomharrisonmaps.com. For more information, contact Sequoia and Kings Canyon National Parks, 559/565-3341, www.nps.gov/seki.

11 MIST FALLS
Kings Canyon National Park

Level: Moderate

Best Season: May–July

Distance: 8.0 miles round-trip

Elevation Change: Total gain 650 feet

The Mist Falls Trail is easily the busiest hiking trail in the Cedar Grove area of Kings Canyon National Park. Although it's an eight-mile round-trip to Mist Falls, they are easy miles, with a well-marked trail and only 650 feet of elevation gain. The route is equally shared by day hikers heading to the falls and backpackers heading to Paradise Valley and beyond, so if you want to have any solitude on your walk, you must start early in the morning. It's also much cooler if you get an early start.

The trail begins level and stays that way for the first two miles. The scenery is spectacular from the start; you find yourself

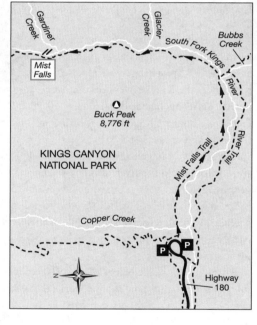

craning your neck a lot, always looking up at the imposing canyon walls on both sides of the trail. In the spring, a tall, narrow waterfall on Avalanche Creek pours down the right canyon wall. The surrounding oak, pine, and cedar forest is sparse at first, then becomes increasingly dense. Giant boulders are scattered around the trail, having dropped from the cliffs sometime during the last 100,000 years. The roar of the South Fork Kings River is a pleasant accompaniment.

After a lovely, shaded stretch where the forest closes in and ferns grow squeezed in between big boulders, you reach a junction at 2.0 miles. Bear left and climb gradually, rising above the river. As you leave the forest and enter a granite landscape, the long-distance views become increasingly spectacular. At 3.0 miles, turn around and check out the vista of the Kings River canyon behind you, framed by big mountains on both sides. The epitome of classic Sierra drama is the silhouette of The Sphinx, a distinctive granite pinnacle, side-by-side with 10,007-foot Avalanche Peak.

At exactly 4.0 miles out, after a few switchbacks on exposed granite and some heavy breathing, you reach the spot where the Kings River fans out over a wide granite ledge and plummets 40

Mist Falls

feet into a boulder-lined pool, forming well-named Mist Falls. Famous for exuding mist and spray, Mist Falls is perhaps more impressive for its noise level. In springtime, you have to shout at your hiking partner to be heard. A short right spur drops you to the river, about 150 feet downstream of the waterfall, to a large granite slab that gets exposed at low water. This river waterfall actually looks prettier when it is not at full flood. During heavy snowmelt, the details of the cascade are completely obscured by rushing water and spray. The first time I saw Mist Falls, in a wet June, it looked like a big white blob. A month later, it showed off its finer points.

Angling is popular below Mist Falls, especially in late spring and early summer. One angler told me that he works this stretch of river every June, commonly catching 50 fish a day between Mist Falls and the trailhead.

If the crowds get too heavy for you on the Mist Falls Trail, there's a less-used alternate route for the homeward trip: when you return to the trail junction at 2.0 miles, turn left and cross Bailey Bridge. Walk 0.3 mile, passing by the Bubbs Creek Trail junction, then turn right, heading back on the River Trail on the south side of the Kings River. In addition to leaving most of the crowds behind, this trail has great views. You'll need to walk slightly downstream of the trailhead to reach a bridge where you can cross the river and head back to your car.

Directions

From Fresno, drive east on Highway 180 for 55 miles to the Big Stump Entrance Station at Kings Canyon National Park. Continue 1.5 miles and turn left for Grant Grove and Cedar Grove. Continue 38 miles on Highway 180 to Road's End, six miles past the Cedar Grove campground and ranger station. The trailhead is at the east end of the parking lot, near the wilderness ranger station.

Information and Contact

There is a $10 entrance fee per vehicle at Sequoia and Kings Canyon National Parks, which is good for seven days. Park maps are available for free at the entrance stations, or by download at www.nps.gov/seki. A more detailed map is available from Tom Harrison Maps, 415/456-7940, www.tomharrisonmaps.com. For more information, contact Sequoia and Kings Canyon National Parks, 559/565-3341, www.nps.gov/seki.

12 TOKOPAH FALLS

Sequoia National Park

Level: Easy

Best Season: April-July

Distance: 3.6 miles round-trip

Elevation Change: Total gain 500 feet

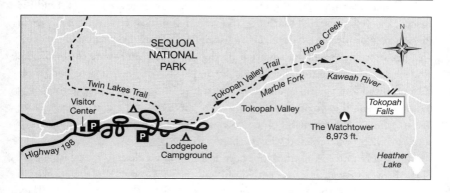

Tokopah Falls is hands-down the best waterfall in Sequoia and Kings Canyon National Parks. To get the most out of your hike to the falls, head to Lodgepole Campground and the Tokopah Falls Trailhead in late spring or early summer, when the waterfall is a showering spectacle.

Sure, the trail can be crowded. Why wouldn't it be? The walk to the falls is only

1.8 miles of level trail through gorgeous High Sierra scenery, culminating at the base of 1,200-foot-high Tokopah Falls. But if you follow the cardinal rule for popular outdoor destinations and start hiking early in the morning, the crowds will still be sleeping in their tents. You can be out to the falls and back before most people have finished brushing their teeth.

the bottom cascade of Tokopah Falls

© ANN MARIE BROWN

The trail offers almost as many rewards as its destination. In a little more than a mile and a half, you get incredible views of the Watchtower, a 1,600-foot-tall glacially carved cliff on the south side of Tokopah Valley. Your perspective on the Watchtower changes with every few steps you take. Then there's Tokopah Valley itself, with Tokopah Falls pouring down the smooth back wall of its U shape. Tokopah Valley is similar in geological type and appearance to Yosemite Valley, formed partially by the river flowing in its center but mostly by slow-moving glaciers.

The Tokopah Falls Trail also provides a near guarantee of seeing some wildlife, specifically yellow-bellied marmots, the largest and most charming member of the squirrel family. In a completely nonscientific survey, I determined that this area has more marmots per square mile than probably anywhere in the Sierra. The marmots' great abundance here is due in part to the proximity of Lodgepole Campground and the furry creatures' great love of food. (Don't give them any handouts.) You'll have dozens of chances to photograph the cute little guys, or just to admire their beautiful blond coats as they sun themselves on boulders or stand on their back legs and whistle their warning calls.

The trail is a mix of conifers and granite and follows close to the Marble Fork of the Kaweah River. It leads gently uphill all the way to the falls, then downhill all the way back. If the route seems rather rocky at the start, don't fret; its surface changes. Sometimes the trail winds along a soft forest floor of conifer needles, other times it travels over bridges that cross tiny feeder creeks, and still other times it traverses meadows overflowing with ferns, orange columbines, yellow violets, and purple nightshades. The trail passes through so many different habitats, you can find 40 different kinds of wildflowers along its brief length.

The final 0.25 mile crosses a rockslide area and gives you wide-open views of Tokopah Falls' impressive 1,200-foot height. The trail has been dynamited into the granite; in one section, you must duck your head as you walk under a ledge. The path ends just before the edge of the waterfall, which drops over fractured granite. Choose a rock to sit on and marvel at the cacophony of cascading water, but don't get too close. Tokopah flows fast, and can be dangerous in springtime.

If you're visiting Sequoia National Park in winter, try strapping on a pair of snowshoes and trekking out to Tokopah Falls. If you've seen it previously in warm weather, you won't believe the sight of this cascading waterfall frozen in ice.

Directions

From Fresno, drive east on Highway 180 for 55 miles to the Big Stump Entrance Station at Kings Canyon National Park. Continue 1.5 miles and turn right on the Generals Highway, heading for Sequoia National Park. Drive approximately 25 miles on the Generals Highway to the Lodgepole Campground turnoff, then drive 0.75 mile to the Log Bridge Area of Lodgepole Camp. Park in the large lot just before the bridge over the Marble Fork Kaweah River, and walk 150 yards to the trailhead, which is just after you cross the bridge.

Information and Contact

There is a $10 entrance fee per vehicle at Sequoia and Kings Canyon National Parks, which is good for seven days. Park maps are available for free at the entrance stations, or by download at www.nps.gov/seki. A more detailed map is available from Tom Harrison Maps, 415/456-7940, www.tomharrisonmaps.com. For more information, contact Sequoia and Kings Canyon National Parks, 559/565-3341, www.nps.gov/seki.

13 MARBLE FALLS
Sequoia National Park

Level: Moderate

Best Season: February-June

Distance: 7.0 miles round-trip

Elevation Change: Total gain 1,500 feet

Marble Falls is a series of wide cascades that swoop and scatter over white granite on the Marble Fork of the Kaweah River in Sequoia National Park. But the beauty of the falls is only one of its great features; the other is that its trail is open year-round for hiking, even when other trails in Sequoia and Kings Canyon parks are closed down with heavy snow.

The Marble Fork Trail begins on a dirt road at the upper end of Potwisha Campground. After crossing a flume filled with flowing water in springtime, watch for a sign that marks the official start of the trail, which climbs a steep bank to the right.

You're in chaparral country here at 2,100 feet in elevation. It's hard to believe that this dry habitat is in the same park as all those giant sequoia trees and snowy peaks, but it's true. As the trail leads through hillsides covered with canyon oak, chamise, poison oak, and yerba santa, you may find yourself wondering if you're in San Diego rather than the Sierra.

Marble Falls

© ANN MARIE BROWN

After the initial climb, the trail occasionally levels and curves into gullies where you'll find blessed shade and foliage that is more lively than the continual chaparral and oaks. Buckeye trees bloom in springtime in these marginally wet areas. Although you can hear the roar of the river continually as you hike, you are a few hundred feet above it. The ascent remains gradual but steady.

Amateur geologists will enjoy the many outcroppings of colorful marble, which increase in number underfoot and alongside the trail as you approach Marble Falls. At 3.5 miles, the trail descends to the river's edge near the falls. Take the short spur trail on your left (before the main trail ends) for a better view. Marble Falls drops in a series of cascades; the tallest is about 40 feet. Many of the cascades are upstream from the trail, in a rocky gorge and out of sight. Trying to reach them is dangerous and not recommended. (Beware fast water and slick granite.) Instead, choose a spot on the riverbank near the trail's end to watch the action.

Remember, what's good about this trail in winter—that it's located at low elevation and snow-free—can be a curse in summer. With a 1,500-foot climb and little shade along the route, you don't want to be hiking here at midday in August. If you want to see Marble Falls in summertime, head out early in the morning, reach the falls by 9 A.M., and make the downhill return trip before the sun reaches high noon.

Directions

From Visalia, drive east on Highway 198 for 44 miles to the turnoff on the left for Potwisha Campground, 3.8 miles east of the Ash Mountain entrance station to Sequoia National Park. The trail begins next to site #16 in Potwisha Campground; park in the day-use parking area in the camp.

Information and Contact

There is a $10 entrance fee per vehicle at Sequoia and Kings Canyon National Parks, which is good for seven days. Park maps are available for free at the entrance stations, or by download at www.nps.gov/seki. A more detailed map is available from Tom Harrison Maps, 415/456-7940, www.tomharrisonmaps.com. For more information, contact Sequoia and Kings Canyon National Parks, 559/565-3341, www.nps.gov/seki.

14 PANTHER CREEK FALLS
Sequoia National Park

Level: Moderate   **Distance:** 6.0 miles round-trip

Best Season: February–June   **Elevation Change:** Total gain 600 feet

You want to be alone? You don't want to see anybody else on the trail? Okay, just sign up for this trip any time between June and September. I hiked the Middle Fork Trail to Panther Creek Falls on Labor Day Weekend, when every campground in the national park was jammed and every trail was a veritable parade of hikers, and mine was the only car at the trailhead. Of course, the price for solitude is the summer heat, but if you start early enough in the morning, you can beat it.

Don't let the name mislead you. The Middle Fork Trail does indeed parallel the Middle Fork of the Kaweah River, but this is no streamside ramble. You are high, high above the river for the entire length of your trip, traversing steep canyon slopes. The trail is mostly flat to Panther Creek, but there is almost no shade and very little water available. Because the route is so high and open, it often catches breezes blowing through the canyon, making the exposed slopes more comfortable for hiking.

After leaving the trailhead, you immediately cross over Moro Creek, a cascading stream that is practically a waterfall in its own right. Enjoy the shade around its banks, then say goodbye and put on your sun hat. Hike through chamise, manzanita, yucca, and scrub oak—nothing tall enough to obscure the incredible views in all directions. The first two miles of trail provide sweeping vistas of the Upper Middle Fork canyon area, Moro Rock, the Great Western Divide, and Castle Rocks. With all the peaks and ridges in your scope, there's enough stunning geology to keep anyone enthused, even on a hot day.

At three miles, the Middle Fork Trail brings you right on top of the waterfall on Panther Creek, which drops into the Middle Fork Kaweah River. Now's the time to warn anyone in sight to be darn careful if they look over the edge. The view of the Middle Fork Kaweah River below is awesome, with its many green pools and small falls, and the sight of Panther Creek's 150-foot free-fall drop is stunning, but the granite you're standing on is extremely slippery. You have to peer very carefully over the edge to see any of Panther Creek Falls' drop or the scenic and largely untouched river below, and it's hard to do this without endangering yourself. Use extreme caution.

The safer upstream areas of Panther Creek warrant exploration. If you want to swim and see another small fall, head upstream and off-trail for a few hundred feet, where there are several cascades and cold, clear pools for cooling off.

If you'd prefer to hike this trail in the winter, when the air is cool and the foothills are moist and green, you'll have to earn it. The road to Buckeye Flat Campground is closed during winter months, so you must park at Hospital Rock and walk an extra 1.8 miles one-way to the trailhead. If this sounds like a lot of work, take along a backpack and make it an overnight trip. A few campsites are situated along the trail shortly following Panther Creek Falls. One of the many charms of the foothill areas of Sequoia National Park is that the weather is warm enough for backpacking even in January.

Directions

From Visalia, drive east on Highway 198 for 47 miles to the turnoff on the right for Buckeye Flat Campground, across from Hospital Rock. Turn right and drive 0.5 mile to a left fork shortly before the campground. Bear left on the dirt road and drive 1.3 miles to the trailhead and parking area. (In the winter, both the Buckeye Flat Camp road and the trailhead road are closed to vehicles, but you can begin your hike at Hospital Rock, adding an extra 3.6 miles to your round-trip.)

Information and Contact

There is a $10 entrance fee per vehicle at Sequoia and Kings Canyon National Parks, which is good for seven days. Park maps are available for free at the entrance stations, or by download at www.nps.gov/seki. A more detailed map is available from Tom Harrison Maps, 415/456-7940, www.tomharrisonmaps.com. For more information, contact Sequoia and Kings Canyon National Parks, 559/565-3341, www.nps.gov/seki.

15 MIDDLE FORK KAWEAH RIVER FALLS

Sequoia National Park

🚶 🏊 ⛰

Level: Easy   **Distance:** 0.5 mile round-trip

Best Season: February–June   **Elevation Change:** Total gain 50 feet

---

When it's summertime in the foothills region of Sequoia National Park, most people don't feel like hiking in the hot and dry afternoons. Swimming, on the other hand, is a better draw. How about swimming at the foot of a Kaweah River waterfall? Sounds great. Just don't forget the sunscreen.

Campers at Buckeye Flat Camp have the best access to the Paradise Creek Trail and its spur to Middle Fork Kaweah River Falls. All they have to do is saunter over to site #28, where the trail begins. Day hikers, on the other hand, must park alongside the road outside the camp or 0.5 mile back at Hospital Rock, then walk into the campground and pick up the trail.

From the Paradise Creek Trailhead, you hike only a few hundred feet under

Middle Fork Kaweah River Falls

the shade of blue oaks, buckeyes, and ponderosa pines before reaching a 40-foot-long bridge over the Middle Fork Kaweah River. There's a huge swimming hole on its downstream side that looks nearly Olympic-size. Teenagers sometimes dive off the bridge into the river here.

After crossing the bridge, leave the main trail and make a hard left turn, following the use trail upstream along the river. It's only 100 yards farther to the falls, which are surrounded by jagged, colorful rocks. Even in late summer, your ears will lead you right to it, because although the fall is only about 20 feet tall, it's 35 feet wide and creates a tremendous volume of water.

Kids often climb up on the rocks here, walk to the crest of the waterfall, then slide down its chute. Shorts made of heavy cloth, such as denim, are the required attire for this pursuit. A bathing suit won't protect your backside from the sharp edges on the rocks. Then again, if you prefer a tamer form of swimming, head farther upstream to more pools, or walk back to the river bridge and its big basin downstream.

Directions

From Visalia, drive east on Highway 198 for 47 miles to the turnoff on the right for Buckeye Flat Campground, across from Hospital Rock. Turn right and drive 0.6 mile to the campground. Park in any of the dirt pullouts outside of the camp entrance; no day-use parking is allowed in the campground. (You can also park at Hospital Rock and walk to Buckeye Flat Campground.) The trailhead is near campsite #28.

Information and Contact

There is a $10 entrance fee per vehicle at Sequoia and Kings Canyon National Parks, which is good for seven days. Park maps are available for free at the entrance stations, or by download at www.nps.gov/seki. A more detailed map is available from Tom Harrison Maps, 415/456-7940, www.tomharrisonmaps.com. For more information, contact Sequoia and Kings Canyon National Parks, 559/565-3341, www.nps.gov/seki.

16 SOUTH FORK KAWEAH RIVER FALLS   BEST 🄲
Sequoia National Park

Level: Moderate	**Distance:** 3.4 miles round-trip
Best Season: February–September	**Elevation Change:** Total gain 800 feet

It was Labor Day Weekend in the foothills section of Sequoia National Park and I braced myself for the worst. I expected swarms of people, no room at the campgrounds, and boiling daytime heat. What could be worse than a national park on a holiday weekend? Combine it with low elevation and a hot day.

Well, I drove out to South Fork Campground and the Ladybug Trailhead, and discovered I was wrong on all counts. The camp still had open campsites—the only available sites in the whole park. Not a single soul was hiking on the Ladybug Trail. And since I started my trip early in the morning, I actually got chilled from swimming in the waterfall pool, and was happy to hike uphill in the sunny foothills.

© ANN MARIE BROWN

South Fork Kaweah River Falls

In short, I started out dreading and wound up loving my trip to the South Fork Kaweah River Falls, better known as Ladybug Falls. Why Ladybug? Because of its location below Ladybug Camp, where the little brick-red beetles predominate. Thousands of ladybugs come here by the stream to nest in the winter, but you can find at least a few hundred at any time of the year. I didn't see any until I sat down next to the creek; then I noticed they were all around me, on every rock and blade of grass. There are so many, it's hard not to step on them.

The Ladybug Trail starts from the far end of the South Fork Campground, where a sign says that Ladybug Camp is 1.7 miles, Cedar Creek is 3.2 miles, Whiskey Log Camp is 4.0 miles, and the trail dead-ends at 5.1 miles. A few hundred feet from the camp, the route crosses the South Fork Kaweah on the Clough Cave Footbridge.

The hike to Ladybug Falls leads through dry foothill country, but with a surprising amount of shade from canyon oaks and bay trees. The route is only slightly uphill, so the 1.7 miles can be easily covered in about 45 minutes. You travel parallel to the river for the entire trip, with occasional views of tree-covered ridges to the south, and increasingly wider views of the entire canyon as you climb. In spring, look for Putnam Creek across the canyon; it has an excellent but short-lived white-water cascade.

No signs alert you to when you've reached Ladybug Camp and Falls at 1.7 miles; you'll simply notice a few primitive campsites between the trail and the river, in a level clearing beneath shady incense cedars. If you reach a point where the trail switchbacks to the left and a sign points to Whiskey Log Camp, you've walked right by Ladybug Camp. The falls are hidden from view, downstream.

To reach them, walk the few feet from the camp down to the river and you'll come upon a 10-foot water slide and a narrow, deep swimming hole. Keep walking to your right on a well-used, short but steep route. In the last few yards, you may have to use your hands to help you descend. The waterfall is tucked into a rocky corner in the river gorge, so the only way to see it is to position yourself at its base. Once there, you'll see that it's a perfect 25-foot free fall, shooting over rocks and ferns.

In the morning, it can be quite shady and cool in this grotto, and the river water is not warm by any stretch of the imagination, so you might want to head back up to the camp to sunnier pools for swimming. But before you do, pause a while to admire the beauty of this sheltered spot.

If you decide to camp at Ladybug, remember to bring a filter for pumping water out of the river, and if you are thinking about catching fish for dinner, forget it. The rules are catch-and-release only from downstream of the Clough Cave Foot-bridge to an elevation of 7,600 feet. But for catch-and-release angling, or for just a picnic, head upstream of Ladybug Camp, beyond where the trail switchbacks away from the river. There's a marvelous stretch of stream with pristine pools, rounded boulders, and ferns growing in huge clumps, making little rock-and-waterfall gardens. The conifers growing along the river here provide a welcome contrast to the foothills and grasslands along the trail.

There's one more positive and one more negative to the hike to Ladybug Falls. The positive: you don't have to pay a park entrance fee to visit the South Fork section of Sequoia National Park, and although there is a fee for camping at South Fork Campground, there is no fee for camping at Ladybug Camp. The negative: there's poison oak all over the place. The trail and the camp are usually cleared of it, but use caution if you venture off-trail.

Directions

From Visalia, drive east on Highway 198 for 35 miles to one mile west of Three Rivers. Turn right on South Fork Drive and drive 12.8 miles to South Fork Campground. (At nine miles, the road turns to dirt.) Day-use parking is available just inside the campground entrance. Walk to the far side of the campground to the Ladybug Trailhead.

Information and Contact

There is a $10 entrance fee per vehicle at Sequoia and Kings Canyon National Parks, which is good for seven days. Park maps are available for free at the entrance stations, or by download at www.nps.gov/seki. A more detailed map is available from Tom Harrison Maps, 415/456-7940, www.tomharrisonmaps.com. For more information, contact Sequoia and Kings Canyon National Parks, 559/565-3341, www.nps.gov/seki.

17 EAST FORK KAWEAH RIVER FALLS

Sequoia National Park

Level: Easy

Distance: 2.0 miles round-trip

Best Season: May–August

Elevation Change: Total loss 600 feet

It's a gentle descent to East Fork Kaweah River Falls, a picturesque cascade that arches gracefully over big boulders. This short trip on the Hockett Trail is one of the few hikes in the Mineral King area of Sequoia National Park that is suitable for families, or anyone who doesn't want a long and arduous hike. And it's downright gorgeous every step of the way.

The trail begins between sites 16 and 17 at Atwell Mill Camp, and you take the fork that is signed for Hockett Meadow. Pass by many huge sequoia stumps, 12–15 feet wide, left from the days when people thought it was a good idea to cut down the mammoth trees. In a small meadow, you'll find remains of an 1880s sawmill, where the sequoias were transformed into fence posts and shingles.

© ANN MARIE BROWN

East Fork Kaweah River Falls

Be prepared for olfactory bliss, because the scent of mountain misery is ubiquitous on the downhill route to the river. (This shrub is also called bear clover because bears love to munch on it.) Listen for the tap-tap-tap of woodpeckers as you walk, and look for the large pileated variety with their bright red heads. I spotted two.

Hike through a variety of big conifers, including pines, cedars, firs, and young sequoias, many with velvety mosses growing on their bark. At 0.5 mile, you'll start to hear the rumble of the East Fork Kaweah River. Cross a small stream, and in just a few minutes you come to a picture-perfect footbridge over the river. A 20-foot waterfall descends into an aquamarine pool just upstream of the bridge. Many more luxurious pools and cataracts can be seen both up- and downstream, bounded by the bright red berries of currant bushes and lavish fern banks. In springtime, it seems that everywhere you look, cascading white water drops over car-size boulders. Perfecting the scene are a few giant sequoias that grow along the riverbanks; apparently these were just far enough from the mill to escape its giant saw.

Most people set up a picnic right here by the bridge, or just take a few photographs and head back uphill. If you choose to continue, you'll find that the trail climbs uphill through a burned area on its way to the East Fork Grove of Sequoias and Deer Creek, one mile farther. Both make good destinations.

Directions

From Visalia, drive east on Highway 198 for 38 miles to Mineral King Road, 2.5 miles east of Three Rivers. (If you reach the Ash Mountain entrance station, you've gone too far.) Turn right on Mineral King Road and drive 20 miles to the Hockett Trail parking area on the right, 0.3 mile past Atwell Mill Camp. Park there and walk into the campground. Take the left fork to sites 16 and 17, where the Hockett Trail begins.

Information and Contact

There is a $10 entrance fee per vehicle at Sequoia and Kings Canyon National Parks, which is good for seven days. Park maps are available for free at the entrance stations, or by download at www.nps.gov/seki. A more detailed map is available from Tom Harrison Maps, 415/456-7940, www.tomharrisonmaps.com. For more information, contact Sequoia and Kings Canyon National Parks, 559/565-3341, www.nps.gov/seki.

18 THREE-FALLS-BELOW-THE-GATE
Sequoia National Park

Level: Moderate	Distance: 4.0 miles round-trip
Best Season: June–October	Elevation Change: Total loss 100 feet

Three-Falls-Below-The-Gate: Now that's an unusual name for a waterfall. That's what the prominent falls on the East Fork Kaweah River are called, according to Louise Jackson's *Beulah: A Biography of the Mineral King Valley of California*. The "gate" in the waterfall's moniker marks the beginning of the Mineral King Valley proper. In the 1870s, homesteaders placed a wooden gate across a narrow opening between granite rocks on either side of the wagon road, in what is now the vicinity of Cold Springs Campground. Its purpose was to keep cattle and pigs from roaming out of the valley, but it soon became a reference point for explaining where significant features were located. Hence, Three-Falls-Below-The-Gate.

In 1879, when that original wagon road into the valley was being constructed, the Native Americans on the work crew refused to go above these falls. They believed that evil lurked in Mineral King Valley and wanted none of it. Pick up a copy of Jackson's book at Mineral King's Silver City Resort to find out more about the fascinating history of this area; it makes great campfire reading.

The waterfall has been tempting Mineral King visitors for as long as people have been coming here. It's easily spotted from the slow-going Mineral King Road, about two miles from the road's end at Mineral King Valley. A spectacular river fall with a year-round water supply, it drops a total of about 200 feet in three tiers. But how to gain access to the falls? It certainly isn't possible from this one-lane stretch of road. First, there's no place to pull over and park. Second, the river canyon is so steep that an off-trail descent to the waterfalls' narrow, rocky gorge would require a nearly impossible climb back up.

There is only one possibility, and that's to start at the cluster of privately owned cabins in Mineral King Valley. A dirt road leads westward from these cabins, then disintegrates into a narrow trail. With a good topo map, you can make your way to the top of Three-Falls-Below-The-Gate in about two miles of cross-country travel. You'll see bits and pieces of an informal use trail guiding the way, although it's not particularly easy to follow. A map is a must. When you reach the brink of Three-Falls-Below-The-Gate, you may be tempted to work your way to the bottom. Stay far away from the fall's slick granite if you do; instead, keep to the side of the falls where you have the luxury of dirt under your feet. And remember that however far you go down, you're going to have to come back up. There are rewards for those bold enough to make their way to the falls: the stretch of water below the rushing rapids is a mecca for intrepid anglers.

Directions

From Visalia, drive east on Highway 198 for 38 miles to Mineral King Road, 2.5 miles east of Three Rivers. (If you reach the Ash Mountain entrance station, you've gone too far.) Turn right on Mineral King Road and drive 22 miles (1.3 miles past Silver City Resort), to a 0.25-mile stretch of road from which you can view the falls, deep in the canyon on your right. The road is only one lane wide in this stretch, so use caution.

Information and Contact

There is a $10 entrance fee per vehicle at Sequoia and Kings Canyon National Parks, which is good for seven days. Park maps are available for free at the entrance stations, or by download at www.nps.gov/seki. A more detailed map is available from Tom Harrison Maps, 415/456-7940, www.tomharrisonmaps.com. For more information, contact Sequoia and Kings Canyon National Parks, 559/565-3341, www.nps.gov/seki.

19 TUFA, CRYSTAL, AND FRANKLIN FALLS
Sequoia National Park

Level: Moderate   **Distance:** 4.0 miles round-trip

Best Season: June–September   **Elevation Change:** Total gain 450 feet

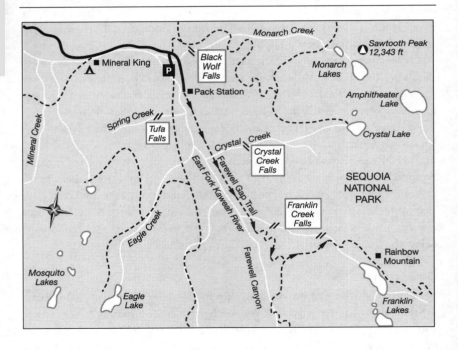

You can say "farewell" when you begin hiking from the Farewell Gap Trailhead, but it doesn't have to be for long. Sure, you can hike for more than 20 miles from the trailhead and be gone for days, or you can just head out for two miles, visit three waterfalls, and return.

The Farewell Gap Trail begins at the end of the road in Mineral King Valley in Sequoia National Park, one of the most beautiful places in California.

© ROGER HOOPER

Crystal Creek Falls

The glacial valley, a peaceful paradise of meadows, streams, and 19th-century cabins, is surrounded by 12,000-foot granite and shale peaks that are colored rust, red, white, and black. The headwaters of the East Fork Kaweah River flow through the valley, encouraging aspen groves and wildflowers along its banks. Farewell Gap Trail traces its path.

Ah, paradise. You know you're in it as soon as you park your car at the end of Mineral King Road, in the Eagle/Mosquito Trailhead parking lot. Don't start walking on the trail that leads south from the lot; walk back up the road you drove in on, cross a bridge over the river, then turn right and walk past the Mineral King Pack Station. All the horses will turn to look at you. If they could talk, they would ask the inevitable question: Do you have any extra apples?

The path officially begins at the trail sign by the pack station, where you continue straight, heading south into a beautiful glacial canyon. You see your first fall almost immediately—it's Tufa Falls on Spring Creek, dashing off the far canyon wall just across from the pack station. The trail you didn't take from the Eagle/Mosquito parking lot leads across the fall's stream on a wooden footbridge, but you get no view from that trail. From close up, the stream is almost completely hidden in foliage. But from your vantage point on the Farewell Gap Trail, you can see and especially hear all of Tufa's remarkable 500-foot cascade as it flows down from Spring Creek's spring. The spring's porous layer of calcified minerals gives Tufa Falls its name.

Continue walking on the Farewell Gap Trail, which stays level as it wanders up the canyon. At one mile from the trailhead, Crystal Creek Falls surprises you on your left. The falls are hidden around a corner, invisible from the trail until you're practically at their base. A short walk on a spur trail brings you alongside the waterfall, which drops about 50 feet. (The spur can be found just after crossing the stream on the main trail; it leads up the right side of the fall.) Crystal Creek flows downhill from Crystal Lake and the Cobalt Lakes, both at more than 10,000 feet in elevation.

An unmarked right fork just beyond Crystal Creek Falls leads farther up the canyon bottom to Aspen Flat, a lovely grove of aspens, and Soda Springs, a bubbling natural spring alongside the river that has colored the nearby earth bright orange. Many people take this fork up the river, visit the little spring and the aspens, maybe fish in the river or have a picnic, and then head back to the trailhead for a level 2.5-mile round-trip. But if you want to see another waterfall, the best one yet on the Farewell Gap Trail, stay on the main trail and begin to climb, gaining 350 feet on your way to Franklin Creek Falls, a little less than a mile away.

Your view up Farewell Canyon, which has been stellar all along, keeps getting better as you climb. Your perspective changes as you leave the canyon floor and begin to meet this steep, rocky terrain on its own terms. Colorful Rainbow Mountain at 12,000 feet reveals its rings of pigmented rock on your left, and massive Vandever Mountain looms straight ahead. In a few heart-pumping minutes, you arrive at Franklin Creek at the base of a 15-foot cascade. An impressive series of falls continues hundreds of feet up and down the slope.

Directions

From Visalia, drive east on Highway 198 for 38 miles to Mineral King Road, 2.5 miles east of Three Rivers. (If you reach the Ash Mountain entrance station, you've gone too far.) Turn right on Mineral King Road and drive 25 miles to the end of the road and the Eagle/Mosquito Trailhead. (Take the right fork at the end of the road to reach the parking area.)

Information and Contact

There is a $10 entrance fee per vehicle at Sequoia and Kings Canyon National Parks, which is good for seven days. Park maps are available for free at the entrance stations, or by download at www.nps.gov/seki. A more detailed map is available from Tom Harrison Maps, 415/456-7940, www.tomharrisonmaps.com. For more information, contact Sequoia and Kings Canyon National Parks, 559/565-3341, www.nps.gov/seki.

20 BLACK WOLF FALLS
Sequoia National Park

Level: Easy

Best Season: May–August

Distance: 0.5 mile round-trip

Elevation Change: Total gain 50 feet

Black Wolf Falls

© ROGER HOOPER

Black Wolf Falls in Mineral King is a waterfall of many names: it's alternately called Black Wolf Falls, Black Wall Falls, or Monarch Falls. The latter moniker is easy to explain, because the waterfall drops on Monarch Creek in the Mineral King Valley. The first two names are related: Black Wolf is apparently a bastardization of Black Wall, the original name of the falls. It was named by miners in the 1870s who weren't as interested in waterfalls as they were in minerals. Black Wall was the name of the copper mine at the base of the falls, clearly designated as such because of the dark-colored, sheer cliff over which the fall drops.

You can drive right by Black Wolf Falls. It's set just 500 feet from the edge of Mineral King Road, shortly before the road ends in the valley. If you want to see it from close up, park at the Sawtooth Trailhead, then walk farther up the Mineral King Road toward the Mineral King pack station. Continue past where Monarch Creek flows under the road, about 150 yards before the left fork for the pack station. Look for the "No Parking Any Time" sign. Across the road from the sign is a wide, usually dry wash. The best, most well-worn route to the falls is on its left (north) side.

Follow the rough footpath, and shortly it crosses the wash to its south side, taking you up and over the scrubby, sagebrush-covered hillside to the right of the falls. From there, you can scramble down to the water's edge. If you do, you'll see what looks like a small cave near the base of the falls, but as you move closer you'll see that it's an abandoned mining tunnel, a leftover from the Black Wall Mine. Do not enter the tunnel, as its walls are unstable.

Black Wolf Falls drops 50 feet over a dark cliff, with a flow that's quite full and lively even as late as July. Big clumps of yellow flowers grow in between the streams of water when the level drops in late summer. During my visit, one of the hundreds of black-tail deer that abound in Mineral King was trying to get near the falls to mow down those tasty yellow blooms.

If you time it right, you can take a free ranger-led tour to Black Wolf Falls. These occur periodically over the summer, usually on Saturdays, and a call to the Mineral King ranger station can get you the current schedule. Your short walk to the waterfall is combined with an interesting talk on Mineral King's mining history.

Directions

From Visalia, drive east on Highway 198 for 38 miles to Mineral King Road, 2.5 miles east of Three Rivers. (If you reach the Ash Mountain entrance station, you've gone too far.) Turn right on Mineral King Road and drive 24.5 miles to the Sawtooth Parking Area, 0.5 mile before the end of the road. The waterfall is visible from the road.

Information and Contact

There is a $10 entrance fee per vehicle at Sequoia and Kings Canyon National Parks, which is good for seven days. Park maps are available for free at the entrance stations, or by download at www.nps.gov/seki. (See Tufa, Crystal, and Franklin Falls listing in this chapter for trail map.) A more detailed map is available from Tom Harrison Maps, 415/456-7940, www.tomharrisonmaps.com. For more information, contact Sequoia and Kings Canyon National Parks, 559/565-3341, www.nps.gov.seki.

21 HIDDEN FALLS   BEST **C**
Mountain Home Demonstration State Forest

Level: Easy   **Distance:** 0.25 mile round-trip

Best Season: May–September   **Elevation Change:** Total loss 30 feet

It's one heck of a drive to get to Hidden Falls. Maybe that's why they call it Hidden. Or maybe it's because the waterfall is so carefully tucked into a dark and narrow corner of a gorge, you could camp right on top of it and not even know it's there.

Hidden Falls is in Mountain Home Demonstration State Forest, a state-managed preserve that is home to several of the largest and oldest giant sequoia trees in the world—some reaching 240 feet tall and 27 feet in diameter. Many of the sequoias are more than 2,000 years old.

This special place is not easy to get to. The state forest is a long, slow, winding 22-mile-drive from Springville. Plan on more than an hour for this stretch, and make sure you follow the directions exactly, because if you just follow the road signs you might be inclined to take Balch Park Road all the way to Hidden Falls, and that makes for an even longer trip (on one of the most narrow, winding roads in the Southern Sierra).

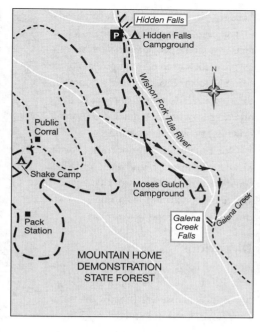

Once you get to Mountain Home, the fun begins. The giant sequoias are an unexpected sight—cool, dark green, and welcoming if you've driven in from the hot Central Valley. In addition to the mammoth trees, which number in the thousands, many young sequoias are also getting their start here.

Pick up a free map at park headquarters, then drive on paved and dirt roads to the Hidden Falls Recreation Area, where there's a campground and some hiking trails. Hidden Falls is a walk-in camp, which means you must park your car in the lot and then walk a few hundred feet to your campsite. Day hikers park in a separate lot above the campground, just before where the road crosses the Wishon Fork Tule River. The falls drop on the river, right by the camp, but you can only glimpse the top of them from the campground area. To get a better view and to access the fall's pools for swimming, walk through the camp to site 6, where an easy route leads down to the water. From there, you can walk upstream to the falls, which drop in a chiseled gorge just below site 2. (A rough route leads directly down to the falls from site 2, but it's much steeper.)

The waterfall's total height is about 50 feet, falling in a series of pools and drops. The best way to get a look at the whole picture is to climb on top of a giant sequoia trunk that sits in the streambed. From there, you can see three lovely tiers of falling water nestled between giant sequoias. The tallest drop is 20 feet high, with a wide and shallow pool at its base. Some people swim here, but others prefer the stretch of river upstream of the camp (across the road), where an unmaintained trail leads a short distance to more and deeper swimming holes. The water is downright cold, but refreshing.

One note of great importance: bears are very hungry at this park and they have gotten used to humans. Even if you're only visiting for an hour or two, don't leave any food in your car.

Hidden Falls

Directions

From Porterville, drive east on Highway 190 for 18 miles to Springville. At Springville, turn left (north) on Balch Park Road/Road 239 and drive 3.5 miles, then turn right on Bear Creek Road/ Road 220. Drive 14 miles to Mountain Home State Forest Headquarters, pick up a free map, then continue 0.75 mile on Bear Creek Road and turn right. Drive two miles and turn right again, then drive 1.5 miles and turn left. Hidden Falls Campground is 0.25 mile farther. (Obtaining a park map is highly recommended. See the Galena Creek Falls listing in this chapter for a trail map.)

Information and Contact

There is no fee. A free map/brochure of Mountain Home Demonstration State Forest is available at park headquarters or by free download at www.fire.ca.gov. For more information, contact Mountain Home Demonstration State Forest, 559/539-2321 (summer) or 559/539-2855 (winter), www.fire.ca.gov.

22 GALENA CREEK FALLS
Mountain Home Demonstration State Forest

🏃 🏊 🐴 ⛺

Level: Easy

Best Season: May–September

Distance: 1.5 miles round-trip

Elevation Change: Total loss 100 feet

Galena Creek Falls in late summer

If you've driven all the way to Mountain Home Demonstration State Forest to see Hidden Falls (see listing in this chapter), you should take a little hike to see Galena Creek Falls, too. The trail begins from the state forest's other campground, Moses Gulch, just a few miles from Hidden Falls Campground and its waterfall. The nicest thing about Galena Creek Falls is that you have to hike a bit to reach it, and once you're there you may have your own private swimming hole.

You'll pass the River Trail on the drive into campsites 6–10 in Moses Gulch. Park in the pullouts at the beginning of the campground loop near the restrooms (not in any of the campsite spaces), then walk back down the road for about 50 yards to where the trail crosses the road. River Trail leads to the North Fork of the Middle Fork of the Tule River, less complicatedly known as the Wishon Fork of the Tule River.

The hike is only 0.75 mile from Moses Gulch Campground, heading downstream and downhill through a lovely mixed forest with many big sequoias. After 0.25 mile, you reach the river. Cross it, pick up the trail on the other side, and continue hiking, now on more level ground. In another 0.5 mile, you'll spot an old wooden sign stating "Galena Creek." Look for a spur trail to your right near this sign; there are several. Follow any of the spurs and, in a few yards, you'll be right on top of Galena Creek Falls.

The creek cascades 20 feet into a narrow slot in the Wishon Fork of the Tule River. Use caution climbing down to the base of the falls; the granite is typically slick. You can swim in the skinny, tublike pool below the falls, or just hang out on the granite alongside the falls. Galena Creek runs dependably even in autumn, but it is best seen in June or July.

Directions
From Porterville, drive east on Highway 190 for 18 miles to Springville. At Springville, turn left (north) on Balch Park Road/Road 239 and drive 3.5 miles, then turn right on Bear Creek Road/Road 220. Drive 14 miles to Mountain Home State Forest Headquarters, pick up a free map, then continue 0.75 mile on Bear Creek Road and turn right. Drive two miles and turn right, then drive 1.5 miles and turn right. Drive one mile to Moses Gulch Campground. Take the fork for sites 6–10.

Information and Contact
There is no fee. A free map/brochure of Mountain Home Demonstration State Forest is available at park headquarters or by free download at www.fire.ca.gov. For more information, contact Mountain Home Demonstration State Forest, 559/539-2321 (summer) or 559/539-2855 (winter), www.fire.ca.gov.

23 WISHON FORK TULE RIVER FALLS
Giant Sequoia National Monument

Level: Moderate

Best Season: May–September

Distance: 6.0 miles round-trip

Elevation Change: Total gain 800 feet

You can see plenty of falls and cascades on the Wishon Fork of the Tule River just by driving around, but if you want a good walk and some solitude at a waterfall, the Doyle Trail to Wishon Fork Falls is your ticket.

If you're staying at Wishon Camp, you can start the hike right from your campsite, but if you're a day visitor, you should drive to the gated trailhead that is signed for the Doyle Trail in 0.25 mile. Start hiking on the paved, gated road; then at the bridge, bear left (just before the "No Trespassing" sign at Doyle Springs, a

© ANN MARIE BROWN

Wishon Fork Tule River Falls

small community of cabins). The route is clearly signed as "Trail to Upstream Fishing."

The Doyle Trail is a great alternative to the heat of the Springville and Porterville valleys. It's in the transition zone between foothills and conifers, with plenty of shade from tall manzanitas, hardwoods (oaks, madrones, and dogwoods), and some pines. Squirrels and lizards are your main trail companions, making plenty of noise as they scurry among the dry leaves and clumps of bear clover on the ground. The path ascends gently but steadily, lateraling along the slopes above the Wishon Fork. Ignore any side trails leading down to the river. Always stay on the main route, heading uphill.

After 2.5 miles, you'll finally stop climbing and descend to the same level as the river, where you'll find some primitive campsites along the banks and good swimming holes, in case you can't wait for the waterfall. Soon you climb again, and in another 0.5 mile, you reach a clearing along the trail. The trees suddenly open up, and you see huge chunks of jagged, greenish rock lining the river. If you leave the trail and cross the rocks on your right, you'll find yourself on top of Wishon Fork Falls, which is composed of two tiered cascades hidden in a narrow, angular gorge. The lower fall is the tallest, about 25 feet high. An incredible range of color is visible in the river rock, primarily in shades of red and gray. Multicolored lichens add to the display.

Have a seat on the rocks, and chew on a few sandwiches. If you want to swim, you'll find long, deep pools among the rectangular rocks here, but it's easier to scramble into the river downstream and then wade your way up to the waterfall's pools.

Directions

From Porterville, drive east on Highway 190 for 18 miles to Springville. From Springville, continue east on Highway 190 for 7.5 miles to Wishon Drive (Road 208), a left fork. Turn left and drive four miles on Wishon Drive, then take the left fork, which is signed for day-use parking (above the campground). Drive 0.25 mile and park off the road, near the gate.

Information and Contact

There is no fee. Maps of Giant Sequoia National Monument and Sequoia National Forest are available for a fee from the National Forest Store (406/329-3024, www.nationalforeststore.com), or can be downloaded for free from www.fs.fed. us/r5/maps/. For more information, contact Giant Sequoia National Monument/ Sequoia National Forest, Western Divide Ranger District, 559/539-2607, www. r5.fs.fed.us/sequoia.

24 MIDDLE FORK TULE RIVER FALLS   BEST ◖
Giant Sequoia National Monument

Level: Easy

Best Season: May–September

Distance: 0.5 mile round-trip

Elevation Change: Total loss 100 feet

The Middle Fork Tule River has more waterfalls and swimming holes than you can shake a stick at. Its granite bed is as slick and smooth as any you'll find in the Sierra—a shining example of water-sculpted rock. In addition, the river is a spectacular aquamarine color, with deep pools so inviting that it's tempting to jump into every single one you find.

One of the best and easiest-to-access stretches of the Tule features a 50-foot-high waterfall with a good trail leading down to it. Unfortunately, this region suffered a major forest fire in 2000. Its manzanita-covered slopes went up in smoke, so the scenery surrounding the trail leaves a lot to be desired. But the falls are still a winner, and in a couple of years, the foliage will return. It won't take long before it is difficult to discern that a fire ever occurred here.

Middle Fork Tule River Falls

© ANN MARIE BROWN

To see the falls, begin hiking at the Forest Service signboard from the roadside pullout 1.7 miles above the powerhouse. A semisteep footpath leads 0.25 mile down to the river. At a fork in the trail, go right. You'll pass alongside the lip of a spectacular free-falling waterfall, where the Tule River drops in an even, rectangular block over smooth granite. Even in autumn, the fall runs about 15 feet wide and 50 feet high.

If you continue all the way down to the canyon bottom (another 25 yards), you'll wind up at the pool below the falls. Swimming here is as sweet as it gets, with a terrific view of the big fall. When I visited, teenagers were jumping off the waterfall's 50-foot-high brink. Watching them leap from this height nearly gave me a heart attack. I wouldn't try this if you paid me a million bucks, but it was exciting to watch them.

Directions

From Porterville, drive east on Highway 190 for 18 miles to Springville. From Springville, continue east on Highway 190 for 7.5 miles to the powerhouse and highway bridge near the turnoff for Camp Wishon and Wishon Drive (Road 208). Reset your odometer and continue on Highway 190 for 1.7 miles. Park in the roadside pullout on your right. A use trail leads down to the river from the Forest Service sign.

Information and Contact

There is no fee. Maps of Giant Sequoia National Monument and Sequoia National Forest are available for a fee from the National Forest Store (406/329-3024, www.nationalforeststore.com), or can be downloaded for free from www.fs.fed.us/r5/maps/. For more information, contact Giant Sequoia National Monument/Sequoia National Forest, Western Divide Ranger District, 559/539-2607, www.r5.fs.fed.us/sequoia.

25 PEPPERMINT CREEK FALLS
Giant Sequoia National Monument

Level: Moderate

Distance: 0.5 mile round-trip

Best Season: May–August

Elevation Change: Total loss 150 feet

In a word, it's awesome. Peppermint Creek Falls is a classic 150-foot granite waterfall, with wide slabs and ledges, a steady flow of water all summer, and big Jeffrey pines growing along its sides. It's the only waterfall in this book that drops over the edge of a rounded granite dome.

To reach it, take the scenic drive on Road 22S82, the road that parallels the Western Divide Highway in Giant Sequoia National Monument. Try to stay on the pavement and between the lines as you view all the stunning geology of the area. You get views of Sentinel Peak, Elephant Knob, and the Needles, all of which look remarkably like their names.

© ANN MARIE BROWN

Peppermint Creek Falls

Park your car in Camping Area 6, the informal dispersed camping area shortly past Lower Peppermint Camp. Usually, a few families or groups are camped along the creek. Just beyond the campers is where Peppermint Creek plummets over smooth, rounded granite. In several places, sheets of the granite dome's exterior have peeled off and broken into chunks, creating a pile of rubble at the base of the fall, which the creek cascades over.

Peppermint Creek Falls has a wide pool at its base, just deep enough for wading. The falls are impressive even in late summer, although by then the stream flows more delicately over the granite, rather than pouring down in a thick sheet over the rounded crest.

The route to the base of the fall is a steep drop and not for the faint of heart, mostly because of the brief, breathtaking climb back up. Start by scrambling over the rocks at the top of the cliff, then take any of several use trails down the side of the falls. As much as possible, try to stay off the waterfall's granite and on the dirt paths because the rock is much more slippery than it looks.

Directions

From Kernville on the north end of Lake Isabella, drive north on Sierra Way/Mountain 99 for 27 miles to 0.5 mile north of Johnsondale R-Ranch. Turn right on Road 22S82 and drive 11.3 miles to Road 22S82F, signed for Camping Area 6. (It's on the right, 0.25 mile past Lower Peppermint Camp on the left.) Turn right on 22S82F, then drive 0.3 mile to a large clearing near a cliff edge.

Information and Contact

There is no fee. Maps of Giant Sequoia National Monument and Sequoia National

Forest are available for a fee from the National Forest Store (406/329-3024, www. nationalforeststore.com), or can be downloaded for free from www.fs.fed.us/r5/ maps/. For more information, contact Giant Sequoia National Monument/Sequoia National Forest, Kern River Ranger District, 760/376-3781, www.r5.fs. fed.us/sequoia.

26 NOBE YOUNG FALLS
Giant Sequoia National Monument

Level: Moderate

Best Season: May–August

Distance: 1.0 mile round-trip

Elevation Change: Total loss 100 feet

© ANN MARIE BROWN

Nobe Young Falls

Nobe Young is the secret waterfall of Giant Sequoia National Monument. It has no signs or markers to identify it, not even a trailhead. The first time you visit, you practically need someone to hold your hand and show you the way. You'll need route-finding skills and also some scrambling ability because there's no formal trail to the falls. Even so, the route takes only about 15 minutes from where you leave your car.

Follow the driving directions below to the letter, and once you've parked in the dirt pullout, look for sign markers for 22S11 and 304 015. (They are not visible from the road, only from the pullout.) This is the secret code that tells you you're in the right place.

Next, start hiking on the dirt road off to your left. When it forks, follow it to the right. (The fork is signed as "304 186," and the left branch is very overgrown.) You're on a real trail at this point, and the going is easy. Pass a makeshift camp and campfire ring, with a short spur trail leading from it to Nobe Young Creek. You'll hear the creek along this stretch, but now start to listen for the change in its sound, going from a steady gurgle to more of a pouring or spraying sound. Keep your eyes peeled for spur routes leading off the main trail to your left. The best route comes up after you walk for about three minutes past the campfire ring, or about five minutes past the fork in the trail.

It's a steep route down to the falls, so be cautious. Anglers and waterfall-lovers have made a good path to Nobe Young Fall's base, but it has some sheer drops. The falls spill and splash for 125 feet over three granite ledges, creating a watery playground. Between the top and middle ledges is a tall, wide cave behind the falling water, where some people like to climb in and look out from behind the waterfall. If you choose to do so, be careful scrambling your way up to it.

Exploring around below the falls, you'll find many little trout in the stream, plus thimbleberries (red berries that look like raspberries) and currants. Big wood-wardia ferns and dogwoods grow along the creek, thriving in the abundant shade of surrounding oaks and cedars.

Many big, smooth boulders are situated directly in front of the falls, just a few feet from the spray, perfect for picnicking. Choose your spot, and know that you are in on the big waterfall secret of Giant Sequoia National Monument. Shhh...

Directions

From Kernville on the north end of Lake Isabella, drive north on Sierra Way/Mountain 99 for 27 miles to 0.5 mile north of Johnsondale R-Ranch. Turn left on Road 50, then in 5.5 miles, turn right on Road 107, the Western Divide Highway. Drive eight miles to the fall's parking pullout on the east (right) side of the road, which is unsigned. Look for a dirt pullout exactly one mile north of the turnoff for Camp Whitsett and Lower Peppermint Camp, and 0.25 mile south of the Crawford Road turnoff.

If you are coming from Porterville, drive east on Highway 190 for 54 miles to the falls turnoff, 6.7 miles south of Ponderosa Lodge.

Information and Contact

There is no fee. Maps of Giant Sequoia National Monument and Sequoia National Forest are available for a fee from the National Forest Store (406/329-3024, www.nationalforeststore.com), or can be downloaded for free from www.fs.fed.us/r5/maps/. For more information, contact Giant Sequoia National Monument/Sequoia National Forest, Kern River Ranger District, 760/376-3781, www.r5.fs.fed.us/sequoia.

27 SOUTH CREEK FALLS   BEST 🅒
Sequoia National Forest

Level: Easy

Best Season: May–September

Distance: Negligible

Elevation Change: 3,800 feet

If you want to see a waterfall in Sequoia National Forest without a long drive and long hike, cruise up Mountain 99 from Kernville and Lake Isabella and pay a visit to South Creek Falls.

South Creek Falls

© ANN MARIE BROWN

At 120 feet tall, South Creek Falls is a spectacular plume of vertical white water. It bears an uncanny resemblance to Cedar Creek Falls in San Diego, hundreds of miles away, except that South Creek Falls drops right along the road. From the side of the pavement, the fall plunges into the bottom of a steep-walled canyon, surrounded by foothill pines, sagebrush, and rocks—hallmarks of the hot, dry, rugged land of the Kern River Canyon.

If you drive to South Creek Falls from the north, you'll notice a small sign that says "Caution: Waterfall 300 Yards Ahead," and then you'll see a chain-link fence, but you can't see the fall itself unless you look back over your right shoulder as you drive. A better approach is from Kernville to the south. The waterfall seems to come suddenly and magically into view shortly after you cross the huge Johnsondale Bridge over the Kern River. You can park in one of the pullouts near the fence above the fall, then walk south on the road for about 100 yards to get the best view or take a few pictures.

Don't get any ideas about hiking down to the big pool at the base of South Creek Falls. The slope is extreme, almost vertical. A sign states "South Creek Falls: Stay alive; stay behind the railing. Extremely dangerous area." For once, obeying authority is a wise idea.

Directions
From Kernville on the north end of Lake Isabella, drive north on Sierra Way/

Mountain 99 for 17 miles to Fairview (a small settlement). Continue north from Fairview for 5.5 miles to South Creek Falls. (The falls drops right alongside the highway, exactly 0.5 mile north of the Johnsondale Bridge, the highway bridge over the Kern River.) There is a small parking pullout at the chain-link fence just above the falls.

Information and Contact

There is no fee. Maps of Sequoia National Forest are available for a fee from the National Forest Store (406/329-3024, www.nationalforeststore.com), or can be downloaded for free from www.fs.fed.us/r5/maps/. For more information, contact Sequoia National Forest, Kern River Ranger District, 760/376-3781, www.r5.fs.fed.us/sequoia.

28 SALMON CREEK FALLS
Sequoia National Forest

Level: Moderate

Best Season: May–July

Distance: 9.0 miles round-trip

Elevation Change: Total loss 600 feet

Salmon Creek Falls

Don't be fooled by the clearly marked sign on Mountain 99 north of Kernville that says "Salmon Creek Falls." Just 2.1 miles north of Goldledge Camp, the sign appears on the left. A parking pullout and trail show up on the right. The next thing you know, you're slamming on the brakes and envisioning a great hike to a waterfall. Better envision something else, at least from this spot. What looks like a trail from here to Salmon Creek Falls is hopelessly overgrown with encroaching brush. In less than a mile, the path becomes nearly impassable. The only evidence of a trail is that darn misleading sign, and in the wet season, a long-distance view of the falls. While attempting this brush-laden path, my hair got hopelessly tangled in scratchy chaparral, and in frustration I almost pulled out my pocketknife and cut off my ponytail.

But the good news is that you can get to Salmon Creek Falls, as long as you're willing to take a long drive to the Salmon Creek Trailhead at Horse Meadow Campground. It's a nine-mile round-trip hike, and unfortunately, the trail ends at the top of the falls, where your view is less than optimal. Still, it's a stellar walk through lodgepole pines and white firs, with a chance for fishing, skinny-dipping, and getting close to the lip of a 70-foot-high waterfall. The hike is an ideal day trip or an easy, one-night backpacking jaunt in early summer.

Although the drive to the Salmon Creek Trailhead at Horse Meadow is nearly 20 miles on dirt roads, they are incredibly smooth and well-graded, easily passable in a passenger car. The only hazard is logging trucks, which you must be on the lookout for. When you see one, get out of its way. Along the drive, check out the small waterfalls on Alder Creek, 0.75 mile down Road 22S12.

Hiking to Salmon Creek Falls from Horse Meadow is a vastly different experience than the hot, dusty, brush-laden, cross-country route off Mountain 99. Once you've made the drive to Horse Meadow, you've gained 4,000 feet in elevation, and you're in granite and conifer country. There's plenty of cool mountain air and pretty scenery.

The trailhead is well-signed, and the path begins in big trees and then skirts the edge of Horse Meadow, where cattle sometimes graze. When you first meet up with Salmon Creek, it's just a tiny little stream meandering through the meadow, but it quickly gathers a stronger flow and picks up speed as it hits steeper, rockier terrain.

At the edge of the meadow, you have two choices: you can continue along the north side of Salmon Creek on a well-worn use trail, or you can turn left and cross the creek, hiking on the official Salmon Creek Trail on the stream's south side. The two trails meet up again about two miles downstream, where the official trail crosses back to the north side of Salmon Creek. My suggestion is to take the use trail on the way in to the falls, when your energy level is highest, then return on the main trail. The creekside use trail is more scenic, but it requires careful footing over granite slabs.

Occasionally, you may lose sight of the use trail in the huge football field–sized sheets of granite lining the creek, but since you're always paralleling the water, the route is simple. Just keep heading downstream and downhill. The shade of tall pines alternates with a few sunny stretches. While you're out in the sun, you may want to dip into some of the many smooth granite swimming holes. Be forewarned—the water is cold. Trout like it, though; you'll find them in almost every deep pool.

At two miles out, the two trails meet. Continue to amble on the smooth downhill path toward the falls. Look for plentiful wildflowers in shady areas tucked among the increasingly drier, sunnier slopes. The trail ends with a bit of a climb to a rocky ridgeline, where you can see the stream ahead of you disappear off what seems like the edge of the earth. Clamber downhill carefully, over more slick granite slabs, to reach the pools above the falls.

If you brought lunch with you, be sure to eat it here, so your pack is lighter for the uphill return trip. If you want to camp, you'll see a few campfire rings in this area, and more at various points along the creekside route.

If you're determined to gain access to Salmon Creek Falls from Mountain 99, there is a way to do so, and it's a much shorter hike than the jaunt described above. The locals aren't inclined to talk about it, but they know the route well, because the pool at the base of Salmon Creek Falls is filled with hungry golden trout. See if you can pry (or charm) it out of one of the local anglers. I was only able to do so after being sworn to secrecy!

Directions

For the Salmon Creek Trailhead: From Kernville on the north end of Lake Isabella, drive north on Sierra Way/Mountain 99 for 22 miles to the right turnoff for Sherman Pass Road (22S05) to Big Meadow and Horse Meadow (before the highway bridge over the Kern River). Turn right and drive 6.1 miles on Sherman Pass Road, then turn right on Road 22S12, the road to Horse Meadow Campground. Drive 6.3 miles on Road 22S12 (it turns to dirt at 5.8 miles but is still manageable for passenger cars) until you reach a fork; stay straight. At 8.0 miles, bear left. At 9.3 miles, turn right at the Horse Meadow Campground sign (Road 23S10). You'll reach the camp at 10.7 miles, but turn right just before the camp to reach the trailhead.

Information and Contact

There is no fee. Maps of Sequoia National Forest are available for a fee from the National Forest Store (406/329-3024, www.nationalforeststore.com), or can be downloaded for free from www.fs.fed.us/r5/maps/. For more information, contact Sequoia National Forest, Kern River Ranger District, 760/376-3781, www.r5.fs.fed.us/sequoia.

MORE WATERFALLS IN SEQUOIA AND KINGS CANYON

•**Cascade Creek Falls, Sequoia National Park.** If you go to visit Crystal Cave in Sequoia National Park (tour tickets required in advance), you'll walk right past Cascade Creek Falls on the way to your cave tour. This 25-foot cataract is popular with picnickers. For more information, phone Sequoia National Park, 559/565-3134.

•**Silver Spray Falls and Blue Canyon Falls, Tehipite Valley, Kings Canyon National Park.** Two spectacular waterfalls are set in a spectacular valley, best accessed from the Rancheria Trailhead near Wishon Reservoir. Plan on a 35-mile round-trip. For more information, phone Sierra National Forest, High Sierra Ranger District, 559/855-5360.

•**Ninemile Creek Falls, Golden Trout Wilderness.** Accessible via a backpacking trip on Ninemile Creek and Hells Hole Trails near the Kern River and Jordan Hot Springs. For more information, phone Sequoia National Forest, Kern River Ranger District, 760/376-3781.

•**Tenmile Creek Falls, Giant Sequoia National Monument.** These falls can be seen near Kings Canyon Lodge on Highway 180 as you drive into the heart of Kings Canyon National Park. To hike to the lower reaches of the 200-foot cascade, follow the Yucca Point Trail from Highway 180. Just before reaching the river, a spur trail cuts off to the left to access the falls. For more information, phone Giant Sequoia National Monument, Hume Lake Ranger District, 559/338-2251.

•**Chagoopa Falls and Hamilton Creek Falls, Sequoia National Park.** These falls are accessible via a backpacking trip on the High Sierra Trail out of Bearpaw Meadows. For more information, phone Sequoia National Park, 559/565-3134.

SANTA BARBARA AND VICINITY

© ANN MARIE BROWN

BEST WATERFALLS

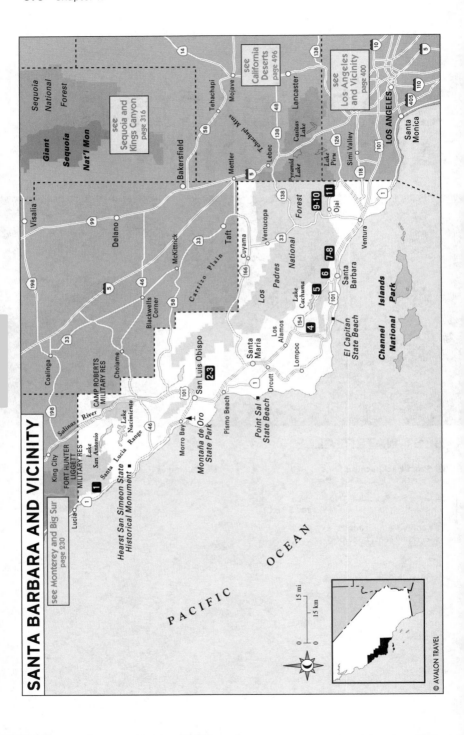

TRAIL NAME	LEVEL	DISTANCE	ELEVATION	SEASON	FEATURES	PAGE
1 Salmon Creek Falls	Moderate	0.8 mile rt	50 ft	Dec.-June		378
2 Big Falls	Moderate	3.0 mi rt	350 ft	Dec.-June		379
3 Little Falls	Easy	1.0 mile rt	50 ft	Dec.-June		381
4 Nojoqui Falls	Easy	0.6 mile rt	50 ft	Dec.-May		383
5 Wellhouse Falls	Strenuous	3.5 mi rt	800 ft	Dec.-May		384
6 Seven Falls and Mission Falls	Moderate	2.8 mi rt	350 ft	Dec.-May		386
7 West Fork Cold Springs Falls	Strenuous	2.0 mi rt	700 ft	Dec.-May		389
8 San Ysidro Falls	Moderate	3.6 mi rt	1,200 ft	Dec.-June		391
9 Rose Valley Falls	Easy	0.6 mile rt	50 ft	Dec.-May		393
10 Potrero John Falls	Moderate	5.4 mi rt	700 ft	Jan.-May		394
11 Santa Paula Canyon Falls	Moderate	6.0 mi rt	800 ft	Dec.-May		396

1 SALMON CREEK FALLS
Los Padres National Forest

🏃 🐕

Level: Moderate   **Distance:** 0.8 mile round-trip

Best Season: December–June   **Elevation Change:** Total loss 50 feet

What's the best waterfall on the Big Sur Coast? It's impossible to choose. How about a three-way tie for McWay Falls, Limekiln Falls, and Salmon Creek Falls? They are about as different from each other as any waterfalls could be, but all of them have the capacity to make you rejoice in your existence on this planet. That good? Yes, they are that good.

Salmon Creek Falls is the only one of the three that's located on national forest land, and it is visible from the highway. Sort of. Driving north on Highway 1 from San Simeon, you go right past Salmon Creek Falls without seeing it because it's over your right shoulder and set back in the canyon. But heading south on Highway 1 from Gorda, you can't miss the sudden splash of white along the hillside. More than a few travelers have

Salmon Creek Falls

slammed on the brakes and pulled off the highway to get a better look.

From the large pullouts along the road, it's a short walk to reach Salmon Creek Falls, following the Salmon Creek Trail partway. The trick is to know where to exit the trail and scramble up the creek, because the trail leads high above the fall without going to its base.

Start from the south end of the guardrail at the signed trailhead. Immediately, you'll see several cutoffs on the left; don't take the first one, which is right by an old wooden gate. If you do, you'll have an unnecessarily long and difficult upstream scramble, especially when the water is high. Instead, walk up the Salmon Creek Trail for about five minutes, and when you hear the falls loud and clear, take one of the spur trails on the left and head down to the stream. You can climb over the huge boulders at the fall's base to get up high and obtain a good vantage point.

Salmon Creek is a "wow" waterfall, the kind that when you stare at it, not much else comes to mind but the word "wow," so you say it over and over. The fall drops about 120 feet in a huge crash of water, with three big chutes plummeting down to join at the bottom. A gigantic boulder is balanced at the top, separating the streams.

I visited the waterfall in May and was soundly impressed, but when I told a Forest Service ranger about it the next day, he sniffed, "Well, it doesn't have as much water as it did a few weeks ago." Wow.

Directions

From Big Sur, drive 33 miles south on Highway 1 to Gorda, then continue 7.6 miles south of Gorda to the trailhead for the Salmon Creek Trail on the east side of the highway, at a hairpin turn. (The trailhead is 70 miles south of Carmel on Highway 1.) Park in the large parking pullout along the road. You can see the waterfall from the pullout. Salmon Creek Trail leads from the south end of the guardrail.

Information and Contact

A national forest Adventure Pass is required. Maps of Los Padres National Forest are available for a fee from the National Forest Store (406/329-3024, www.nationalforeststore.com), or can be downloaded for free from www.fs.fed.us/r5/maps/. For more information, contact Los Padres National Forest, Monterey Ranger District, 831/385-5434, www.fs.fed.us/r5/lospadres.

2 BIG FALLS   BEST (

Santa Lucia Wilderness

🏃 🏊 🐕

Level: Moderate	**Distance:** 3.0 miles round-trip
Best Season: December–June	**Elevation Change:** Total gain 350 feet

Big Falls is a remarkable waterfall, but the thing that people remember most about it is the drive. That's because the trailhead is 17 miles from the freeway on a narrow road, the last several miles of which are prone to frequent rockslides. But in all honesty, that's the easy part. Where the pavement ends, you must drive another 3.5 miles on a dirt road that gets crossed by Lopez Creek dozens of times, and I don't mean via bridges or culverts. The stream crosses the road, and your vehicle must cross the stream. Here and there, the stream simply becomes the road, and you just keep driving.

On my first trip here, on a fine June day, I drove my low-clearance, two-wheel drive Toyota, but I was foiled at the second stream crossing, which was more than a foot deep. I knew there were at least a dozen more crossings to negotiate, so my chances weren't good. I turned back, and two weeks later, I returned with a high-clearance truck, which made it through easily. Another Big Falls Canyon hiker told me that during the wettest weather, the only way into the canyon is on horseback.

"Medium Falls" in Big Falls Canyon

Once you get to the trailhead, the rest is easy. The trail is well-built and sees plenty of use. It winds through a dense, wooded canyon, crossing and recrossing Big Falls Creek. Many people just hike in 0.5 mile to the first waterfall in the canyon, which they assume is Big Falls. It's actually only a preview of things to come; the real Big Falls is another mile farther down the trail. This waterfall, which I call "Medium Falls," is a 30-foot drop over a limestone cliff that is almost completely covered with foliage. The fall's pool is filled with small trout. A much deeper rock pool lies above the fall's lip, with a 20-foot cascade known as "The Slide" flowing into it. Only the very brave or very foolish slide down the cascading chute, and even they wear something thick on their backsides.

The trail continues above this fall to Big Falls, located off a short left spur. The one-mile walk covers a few easy switchbacks uphill, heading up a chaparral-lined ridge. Watch for an interesting outcrop of quartz alongside the trail. The canyon has lovely wildflowers in spring and early summer, including plentiful orange monkeyflower, but also a good crop of poison oak. When you arrive at Big Falls, the facts are clear: Medium Falls and The Slide are just right for people who like water play, but Big Falls is for true waterfall aficionados. An easy 80 feet tall, Big Falls has less flow than its downstream brethren because it doesn't benefit from the lower feeder streams. But just after a big rain, Big Falls roars. Time your trip for soon after a storm and see it at its best.

Directions

From San Luis Obispo, drive 15 miles south on U.S. 101 to Arroyo Grande and the Highway 227/Lopez Lake exit. Head east on Highway 227, then Lopez Drive, following the signs toward Lopez Lake for 10.3 miles. Turn right on Hi Mountain Road (before Lopez Lake's entrance station). Drive 0.8 mile, then turn left on Upper Lopez Canyon Road. Drive 6.3 miles, passing a Boy Scout Camp, then turn right. In 100 yards, the pavement ends and you pass a Christian camp. Continue 3.5 miles on the dirt road, crossing the stream dozens of times, to the trailhead for Big Falls. (It's not always marked, so set your odometer and look for a small waterfall on the left side of the road. The trail is directly across the road on the right.) Four-wheel drive or high-clearance may be necessary if the road is wet.

Information and Contact

A national forest Adventure Pass is required. Maps of Los Padres National Forest are available for a fee from the National Forest Store (406/329-3024, www.nationalforeststore.com), or can be downloaded for free from www.fs.fed.us/r5/maps/. For more information, contact Los Padres National Forest, Santa Lucia Ranger District, 805/925-9538, www.fs.fed.us/r5/lospadres.

❸ LITTLE FALLS
Santa Lucia Wilderness

Level: Easy

Best Season: December–June

Distance: 1.0 mile round-trip

Elevation Change: Total gain 50 feet

Little Falls Canyon is the next-door neighbor of Big Falls Canyon in the Santa Lucia Wilderness. Getting to the trailhead requires the same rugged drive as the trip to Big Falls, but less of it, because it's only 1.6 miles from the pavement. That means that even if your car can't manage the stream-crossed dirt access road, you can walk in and visit the falls anyway, adding 3.2 miles to your one-mile hike (provided you don't mind wading through the stream). Not only that, but later in the summer as the water level drops, Little Falls becomes a more impressive waterfall than Big Falls.

Little Falls is an easy walk from the trailhead, following the creek on a well-used trail into the Santa Lucia Wilderness. The trail stays close to the cool, shady stream of Little Falls Creek, which is teeming with small trout. The streambanks are lined with oaks, sycamores, bays, and maples. In spring, wildflowers are abundant, and maidenhair and giant woodwardia ferns edge the rocky pools.

After 15 minutes of hiking, you'll reach an unsigned junction where a spur trail leads off to the left, and the main trail heads up and away from the creek. Keep to the left and scramble upstream for a few hundred feet until you reach 50-foot-high Little Falls. You'll need good hiking boots to keep your feet dry, but the scramble is easily accomplished in about five minutes.

The waterfall occurs where Little Falls Creek plummets downward between giant sheets of limestone, which look like freshly poured concrete that has somehow been frozen in midpour. A maple tree grows about halfway up the fall, and others hang over its lip. The fall's pool is about three feet deep, perfect for wading amid the reeds and ferns.

Little Falls

If you scramble back to the main trail, you can continue up and above Little Falls, where you'll find deeper, water-carved pools, perfect for cooling off. If the sculpted basins don't invite you to continue, the wildflowers might—they are prolific along the next mile of trail as you climb out of the canyon.

Directions

Follow the same directions as in the listing for Big Falls (see listing in this chapter), but drive only 1.6 miles on the dirt road. There's parking alongside the road, and the trail leads from the right side. Four-wheel drive or high-clearance may be necessary if the road is wet.

Information and Contact

A national forest Adventure Pass is required. Maps of Los Padres National Forest are available for a fee from the National Forest Store (406/329-3024, www.nationalforeststore.com), or can be downloaded for free from www.fs.fed.us/r5/maps/. For more information, contact Los Padres National Forest, Santa Lucia Ranger District, 805/925-9538, www.fs.fed.us/r5/lospadres.

4 NOJOQUI FALLS
Nojoqui Falls County Park

Level: Easy	**Distance:** 0.6 mile round-trip
Best Season: December-May	**Elevation Change:** Total gain 50 feet

Let's start with the right pronunciation. The park and its namesake waterfall are "na-HO-wee," not "no-jo-kee." If you don't say it properly, the locals will mock you without mercy. Get it right and you're ready to visit the park, which is easily accessed off U.S. 101 heading south from San Luis Obispo or north from Santa Barbara. It's only a couple miles off the highway.

The hike to the park's waterfall is short and sweet, requiring a mere 15-minute commitment on a smooth, wide trail through a canopy of 200-year-old California laurels and oaks. Small footbridges carry you over the wet stretches, so you can leave your hiking boots at home. Even Fido is allowed to make the trip, as long as he is on a leash and can appreciate a good waterfall.

Nojoqui Falls

© ANN MARIE BROWN

Nojoqui Falls is an unusual-looking waterfall—intriguing to look at no matter what its flow level. It drops more than 100 feet over a mossy sandstone cliff that is covered with delicate Venus maidenhair ferns. This is one of the few places in Santa Barbara County where maidenhairs thrive. They require acidic, calcium-rich soil and plenty of moisture, which are rarities in this arid coastal climate.

A sign at the waterfall explains that Nojoqui Falls is formed where the shale of the lower canyon meets the sandstone of the upper canyon. Rather than being continually eroded by its stream flow like most waterfalls, Nojoqui Falls is continually built up. Calcium deposits from the sandstone of the upper canyon trickle over the face of the waterfall, adding layer upon layer to its cliff.

A stairstepped rock perch awaits by the fall's pool, where you can sit in the shade of sycamores and have a picnic lunch, or just gaze in admiration at the falls' moss- and fern-covered drop. It's such a perfect spot—it's probably no surprise to learn that many marriage proposals have taken place here.

Directions

From Santa Barbara, drive 40 miles north on U.S. 101 to the signed turnoff for Nojoqui Park, north of Gaviota State Beach. Drive one mile on the Old Coast Highway, then turn east on Alisal Road. Drive 0.8 mile, then turn right into the park entrance. Drive 0.25 mile on the park access road to the parking lot and trailhead. The trail starts from the far end of the parking lot loop.

From Buellton, drive four miles south on U.S. 101, then turn left at the sign for Nojoqui Park and continue as above.

Information and Contact

There is no fee. For more information, contact Nojoqui Falls County Park at 805/688-4217. Or contact Santa Barbara County Parks, 805/934-6123, www.sbparks.com.

⑤ WELLHOUSE FALLS
Los Padres National Forest

Level: Strenuous

Distance: 3.5 miles round-trip

Best Season: December–May

Elevation Change: Total loss 800 feet

Knapp's Castle is one of the historical oddities that give Santa Barbara its character; the stone ruins of George Knapp's mansion intrigue visitors in much the same manner as Hearst Castle. It also has the capacity to awe; the site's 180-degree views of the Santa Ynez River Canyon and Lake Cachuma are downright inspiring. The site also gives waterfall collectors a cataract with a good story: a downhill walk leads to Wellhouse Falls, a natural waterfall that was once an integral part of Knapp's luxurious estate.

George Knapp was the former chairman of the board of Union Carbide, and in 1916 he built a five-bedroom sandstone mansion, complete with a pipe organ, on this mountain site. In addition to the main house, Knapp built servants' quarters, a groundskeeper's house, and a road that led down to Lewis Canyon below his home, where a cascading waterfall flowed in winter and spring. Not content with the natural seasonal changes of the waterfall, Knapp installed a pumphouse and system of locks in Lewis Creek, so he could store up water and make the waterfall run at his leisure or for the entertainment of guests. Going completely over the top, he installed an observation deck for the falls, a bathhouse, spotlights for nighttime viewing, and a speaker system so organ music could be piped down from the main house. It may seem obsessive, but the guy liked his waterfall.

Knapp's mansion burned in a canyon fire in 1940. Wellhouse Falls still flows after winter rains, but it no longer does so at Knapp's (or anyone's) beck and call.

The ruins of Knapp's Castle are located near the top of the Snyder Trail, a well-maintained Forest Service route that runs from Santa Ynez Canyon six miles uphill to East Camino Cielo. Although the property around Knapp's Castle is private, you can hike Snyder Trail 1.4 miles downhill, and take a short cutoff to see the falls. At present, you can also take another short cutoff and visit the castle ruins, although this is completely at the landowner's discretion. The dirt road to reach the castle ruins is public, but the ruins are privately owned.

Start hiking at the gated dirt road on East Camino Cielo that is signed "Private Property Ahead." Where the road reaches another gate, bear left and head downhill on the unsigned Snyder Trail. (The main road continues to the castle ruins, which you should visit on your return trip.)

Snyder Trail quickly turns to well-graded single-track as it drops below the Knapp's Castle site. Follow it for 1.4 miles from the road, about 35 minutes of downhill walking, enjoying tremendous views of the Santa Ynez River Canyon over the entire distance. A terrific display of wildflowers, including purple nightshade and pink wild roses, is found in the grasses in springtime.

As you descend, keep watching for some gray metal electrical towers and power lines. (There are power lines at the start of the trail as well, but you'll move away from these and reach a second, more prominent set.) A quarter mile beyond where the power lines cross the trail, look for a side trail on the right, the unsigned route to Lewis Canyon and Wellhouse Falls. (At this fork, the Snyder Trail is marked with a rusted "Trail" sign.)

Now things get a bit dicey. The route gets progressively more eroded, and the chaparral closes in, but if you're willing to scramble for a third of a mile, you'll come out to several points where you can view Wellhouse Falls. Just keep your fingers crossed that it's running full of water, because Lewis Canyon drains quickly. Time your trip for immediately after a good rain, preferably the following day. Otherwise, you'll find yourself wishing that Lewis Creek still had Knapp's pumphouse and locks on it so you could flip the switch and make the waterfall pour.

Directions

From U.S. 101 in Santa Barbara, take the Highway 154/State Street exit and drive north for 10.5 miles. Turn right on East Camino Cielo and drive 2.9 miles to the parking pullout on the right, across from a locked gate and dirt road on the left. The gate is signed "Private Property Ahead."

Information and Contact

A national forest Adventure Pass is required. Maps of Los Padres National Forest are available for a fee from the National Forest Store (406/329-3024, www.nationalforeststore.com), or can be downloaded for free from www.fs.fed.us/r5/maps/. For more information, contact Los Padres National Forest, Santa Barbara Ranger District, 805/967-3481, www.fs.fed.us/r5/lospadres.

6 SEVEN FALLS AND MISSION FALLS BEST ℂ
Los Padres National Forest

Level: Moderate   **Distance:** 2.8 miles round-trip

Best Season: December-May   **Elevation Change:** Total gain 350 feet

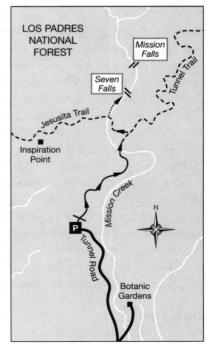

Seven Falls is a perfect springtime day trip in Santa Barbara. It has a little bit of everything: waterfalls, swimming holes, vistas, wildflowers, and a good trail. The only problem is that the route to Seven Falls, one of the most popular paths in Santa Barbara, is also one of the most poorly signed. You have to know where you're going before you set out.

From the parking area at the end of Tunnel Road, there are three possible roads to follow; you want the middle one, which is the continuation of Tunnel Road. Walk past a water tank and around a gate, continuing uphill on pavement for 0.75 mile. On any given day, you may pass any or all of the following characters on this road: families coming to splash around in the lower pools of Mission Creek, serious power-walkers on training hikes on

Seven Falls

the fire roads, an old guy who leads a three-horse pack train up and down the canyon, and college kids going to explore the falls. It's a busy trail, but the ocean views are awesome.

At a bridge over Mission Creek, look for 25-foot-high Fern Falls, which drops below the footbridge in winter and early spring only. It has a lovely pool below it. From the bridge, look up at the rocky peaks ahead and admire the sandstone jutting upward. Yes, Virginia, this is waterfall country. Sometimes you'll spot hang gliders soaring above the cliffs.

Cross the bridge and continue walking uphill on the deteriorating paved road. Where the pavement ends, a dirt road leads straight ahead and also to the right. Go straight, hiking among red wild fuchsias and peach-colored monkeyflowers. In about 100 yards, a sign appears on your left: Jesusita Trail to Inspiration Point and San Roque Road are to the left; Tunnel Trail is the single-track to your right. Walk 100 yards to the left, then bear left on Jesusita Trail, cutting downhill to parallel Mission Creek. You reach small cascades and rocky pools in short order, and families with small children usually stop here and choose a pool to play in.

To see Seven Falls, cross the creek, but on the far side, don't continue on Jesusita Trail, which leads up the slope to Inspiration Point. Instead, follow the well-worn use trail 0.25 mile upstream, on the left (west) side of Mission Creek. It takes only 15 minutes of scrambling on fairly good trail to reach the sandstone-carved cascades of Seven Falls. The trail paralleling the creek is well-defined, but which spur you take to descend to the falls is up to you—there are several of them, all steep. The first cutoff leads you to a rocky overlook near the main set of falls; the rest take you to various swimming holes and other cascades. Use extreme caution as you negotiate your way around the slick streambed. Plenty of accidents happen at Seven Falls.

The Seven Falls designation is a little nebulous; it's more like "Nearly Seven Falls" because there are five falls right in a row and then a couple more sprinkled up- and downstream. None of them are huge, but they are all beautiful. Their pools are as much as eight feet deep, perfect for swimming when there's enough water in Mission Creek. (If you do swim, don't step on the salamanders.) Fervent believers of truth in advertising would say that after about May 15th, this place should be called Seven Pools, not Seven Falls, because the water flow dwindles as soon as the rains stop. Nonetheless, the crowds keep coming. Seven Falls is a popular place throughout the spring.

Farther upstream of Seven Falls is Mission Falls, accessible by another 0.5 mile of scrambling. Considering how difficult (and sometimes dangerous) it is to get past Seven Falls to access Mission Falls, it is amazing how many people do so on spring weekends. First, you have to scramble and/or climb your way to the top of Seven Falls. From here, you simply follow the streambed, often walking directly in the water, although you can sometimes make use of a rough path that edges along Mission Creek's left side. Mission Falls has four main drops, all in the 15–20-foot range and with deep swimming holes. The first of these can be reached about 0.2 mile upstream of Seven Falls. Figure on a total round-trip of about four miles if you want to see all of Mission Falls' and Seven Falls' cascades. But if you're smart, you'll go slowly, and don't try anything that looks like it is beyond your abilities.

Directions

From U.S. 101 in Santa Barbara, take the Mission Street exit and follow it east for just over a mile, crossing State Street. When Mission Street ends, turn left on Laguna Street and drive past the Santa Barbara Mission, turning right on Los Olivos directly in front of the Mission. As you pass the Mission, bear left on Mission Canyon Road for 0.8 mile. Turn right on Foothill Boulevard. In 100 yards, turn left onto the continuation of Mission Canyon Road. Then bear left on Tunnel Road, and follow it for 1.1 miles until it ends. Park alongside the road, on the right.

Information and Contact

A national forest Adventure Pass is required. Maps of Los Padres National Forest are available for a fee from the National Forest Store (406/329-3024, www.nationalforeststore.com), or can be downloaded for free from www.fs.fed.us/r5/maps/. For more information, contact Los Padres National Forest, Santa Barbara Ranger District, 805/967-3481, www.fs.fed.us/r5/lospadres.

7 WEST FORK COLD SPRINGS FALLS
Los Padres National Forest

Level: Strenuous

Distance: 2.0 miles round-trip

Best Season: December–May

Elevation Change: Total gain 700 feet

West Fork Cold Springs Falls is a locals-only waterfall, a "secret" gem that Santa Barbara hikers would like to keep to themselves. Of course, it isn't that much of a secret, since most everybody in town knows about it. Also called Tangerine Falls due to the peach-colored tint of its sandstone face, this waterfall can only be reached by hiking off-trail. In the winter and spring when the falls are flowing at their best, you'll have to scramble a bit, get a little muddy, and rub elbows with a fair amount of poison oak to get a close-up look. The payoff is incredible, though, with West Fork Cold Springs being the most beautiful waterfall in the Santa Barbara area.

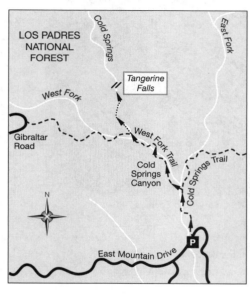

The trail starts in a suburban neighborhood, then leads away from the road into Cold Springs Canyon. In 0.25 mile, the East and West Forks of Cold Springs Creek converge at a small cascade. A wooden bench is in place nearby. Here, you must cross the creek at a sometimes-signed trail junction, now heading up the less-maintained West Fork Trail on the West Fork of Cold Springs Creek. At your feet, you'll find millions of ferns, thriving in the leafy shade of the canyon.

As the trail starts its ascent above the canyon, watch for the point where the view suddenly opens up, about 0.75 mile from the junction. Look ahead and slightly to the right and you'll catch a glimpse of Tangerine Falls, aka West Fork Cold Springs Falls. Hike 100 yards farther to where the main trail turns away from the creek, curving to the left. Keep your eyes peeled on this stretch for a narrow spur trail that leads right, continuing along the creek.

Take the spur and follow some obvious water pipes up the creek canyon. In

© ANN MARIE BROWN

West Fork Cold Springs Falls

the early season, before many folks have taken this trail, you'll have to do a little bushwhacking as you follow the use trail along the stream bank. Be prepared to climb over a lot of rocks, and be wary of erosion, slides, and ubiquitous poison oak. In about 20 minutes of scrambling, you'll reach a series of small sandstone falls about 15 feet tall, each with a lovely pool at its base. Admire them, then keep heading farther back in the canyon.

Finally, you'll reach the base of West Fork Cold Springs Falls, a sandstone monolith more than 100 feet tall. The reason for its nickname Tangerine is readily apparent in the peach- and green-colored moss and lichen on the fall's white cliff. The waterfall has a giant pool, from which the stream cascades down the hillside in a series of pools and drops. As if all this isn't enough to thrill your senses, you can stand at the waterfall's base, turn your back to it, and look to the south for an exquisite view of the coastline beyond Montecito.

Directions

From Santa Barbara, drive south on U.S. 101 for four miles and exit on Hot Springs Road. Turn left on Hot Springs Road and drive 2.5 miles to Mountain Drive. Turn left and drive 1.2 miles to the Cold Springs Trailhead. Park off the road, near where the creek runs across the road.

Information and Contact

A national forest Adventure Pass is required. Maps of Los Padres National Forest are available for a fee from the National Forest Store (406/329-3024, www.nationalforeststore.com), or can be downloaded for free from www.fs.fed.us/r5/maps/. For more information, contact Los Padres National Forest, Santa Barbara Ranger District, 805/967-3481, www.fs.fed.us/r5/lospadres.

8 SAN YSIDRO FALLS
Los Padres National Forest

Level: Moderate

Distance: 3.6 miles round-trip

Best Season: December-June

Elevation Change: Total gain 1,200 feet

If you like running water, San Ysidro Canyon is your chance at seeing some, even long after the last rain. Other streams in the Santa Barbara area are often nearly dry by May, but San Ysidro keeps on flowing year-round, creating two lovely waterfalls and many small cascades that are accessible by an easy walk.

Not only that, but the falls in San Ysidro Canyon win an award: they are the only waterfalls in Santa Barbara that you can actually walk to on a well-maintained trail! No bushwhacking or rock scrambling required. But there's a price to be paid—a healthy climb of 1,200 feet over 1.8 miles—so get ready to give your heart and lungs a workout.

Start hiking on the signed San Ysidro Trail by the stables at San Ysidro Ranch,

© ANN MARIE BROWN

lower San Ysidro Falls

a popular playground of the rich and famous. You'll pass blooming lantana, bougainvillea, and geraniums along this trail stretch, not exactly wildflowers but certainly flowers that have gone wild. In the first mile, your route goes from single-track to pavement to wide fire road and then finally back to single-track, following San Ysidro Creek the whole way and passing a continual series of rushing cascades. Sandstone outcrops rise above the stream; rock climbers are often seen practicing their craft on them. The canyon is almost completely shaded by oaks and bays, making it cool even in summer.

At 1.5 miles from the trailhead, just before the trail climbs a steep slope on a series of rocky stairs lined with a guide rail, take the left cutoff, which leads to the stream and a small five-foot-tall waterfall and sculpted sandstone pool. (They are easily visible from the trail.) If you don't mind a little scrambling, you can take the side trail upstream of this cascade for about 100 feet to a much larger and prettier waterfall about 25 feet high. Two cascades come together over sandstone boulders, with a plethora of ferns and mosses growing in between. The fall has a great swimming hole, and is just hidden enough so that many people miss it.

After this little side trip, continue up the trail on the rock stairway, which the trail-builders have scored deeply so the surface isn't too slippery. (Still, watch your footing and use the handrail on your downhill return.) You move away from the creek, heading for another fork of it.

At 1.75 miles, a stream, which sometimes rushes wildly and sometimes seeps slowly, crosses the trail. A few hundred feet beyond it, just before the trail curves right and moves away from the creek, take the left cutoff for 30 yards to see a sandstone waterfall set in the back of a canyon. It's 60 feet tall and completely different from the canyon's other cascades. The waterfall exhibits an incredible array of colors, much like nearby West Fork Cold Springs Falls. Lichen, mosses, and ferns appear yellow, green, peach, and gold against the cascade's gray sandstone cliff. The stream flow can be thin or wide, depending on recent rains, but the cliff and its fern-filled grotto are stunning any time.

Directions
From U.S. 101 in Montecito, take the San Ysidro Road exit and head east for one mile to East Valley Road/Highway 192. Turn right on East Valley Road/Highway 192 and drive a mile, then turn left on Park Lane. Drive 0.5 mile on Park Lane, then bear left on East Mountain Drive. Follow East Mountain Drive to its end in 0.25 mile. Park alongside the road; the trail is on the right.

Information and Contact
A national forest Adventure Pass is required. Maps of Los Padres National Forest are available for a fee from the National Forest Store (406/329-3024, www.nationalforeststore.com), or can be downloaded for free from www.fs.fed.us/r5/maps/. For more information, contact Los Padres National Forest, Santa Barbara Ranger District, 805/967-3481, www.fs.fed.us/r5/lospadres.

9 ROSE VALLEY FALLS

Los Padres National Forest

BEST C

Level: Easy

Distance: 0.6 mile round-trip

Best Season: December–May

Elevation Change: Total gain 50 feet

Rose Valley Falls is the kind of place where you take your kids when they want to have an adventure, but they're not quite old enough for adventures. The trip to the falls is like a Shirley Temple cocktail—colorful and exciting, but without potential hazards.

Start your hike at the signed trail by campsite 4 in Rose Valley Campground. Head into the woods, cross Rose Creek, then cross it a few more times. From a clearing in the canyon, you get a glimpse of the waterfall far off in the distance— a tall, narrow stream pouring through a notch. If that sight doesn't motivate your five-year-old to keep walking, nothing will.

Rose Valley Falls

Bordered on both sides by oaks and fragrant bays, the path is smooth and nearly level, and it parallels the stream all the way. Several side trails head down to small cascades and pools on Rose Creek— good swimming spots on a warm day. You'll continue to get peek-a-boo glances at the falls as you head upcanyon.

In a mere 15 minutes, you're standing at the base of Rose Valley Falls, which looks nothing like what you saw coming up the canyon. That's because this is only the very bottom of the huge 200-foot fall, which drops in two tiers. The lowest tier is an immense 100-foot slab of sandstone and limestone, bearing the strange molten-rock appearance that is characteristic of this type of fall. It appears as if the cliff melted down the hillside in sheets of sand-colored lava. Its entire surface is encased in moss. Water cascades over the limestone and mossy surface in thin, separate streams. Many large boulders are sprawled at the waterfall's base, where you can sit and marvel at this unusual geologic feature.

The upper tier, which you spotted from a distance, is accessible only by following a spur trail that begins about 75 feet before the base of the lower tier. The trail curves its way up above the lower falls. Where the path forks, stay left and you'll find yourself at the base of another waterfall located on a side canyon to Rose Creek. From here, follow the narrow trail to your left down to Rose Creek for another 75 yards and you'll be at the upper tier, which will take your breath away. Upper Rose Valley Falls is as tall as the lower tier, but has a much more graceful, showering flow of water. This Yosemite-quality waterfall will leave you shaking your head. Can this really be Ojai?

Directions

From Ojai, drive north on Highway 33 for 16 miles to Rose Valley Road and the sign for Rose Valley Recreation Area. Turn right, drive three miles, then turn right again at the sign for Rose Valley Camp. Drive 0.6 mile to the campground. The trail starts by site 4.

Information and Contact

A national forest Adventure Pass is required. Maps of Los Padres National Forest are available for a fee from the National Forest Store (406/329-3024, www.nationalforeststore.com), or can be downloaded for free from www.fs.fed.us/r5/maps/. For more information, contact Los Padres National Forest, Ojai Ranger District, 805/646-4348, www.fs.fed.us/r5/lospadres.

🔟 POTRERO JOHN FALLS   BEST 🅲
Los Padres National Forest and Sespe Wilderness
🚶 🚐 🐕 ⛺

Level: Moderate   **Distance:** 5.4 miles round-trip

Best Season: January-May   **Elevation Change:** 700 feet

Depending on when you visit, you may not do a lot of hiking on the way to Potrero John Falls. If the water is flowing well in Potrero John Creek, you'll be doing more wading than walking, crossing the creek as much as 20 times on the way to the beautiful falls. A hiking pole, or better yet two of them, can be very useful for this trip. River shoes, which will drain water, aren't a bad idea, either.

Wet feet or no wet feet, this waterfall is worth seeing. The trail starts out just off Highway 33 and makes a 1.5-mile trek alongside (and back-and-forth across) Potrero John Creek to Potrero John Campground. The trail travels along the bottom of a very narrow canyon, with conifers growing precariously on the steep canyon walls. About halfway through this stretch, the trail leaves the creekside and briefly enters a lovely meadow, then quickly returns to the creek. So what does "potrero" mean? It's Spanish for meadow.

Shortly beyond the primitive campground—which consists of a rock-lined fire pit and rusty metal barbecue, plus some stone and log benches—"civilization" ends and the Sespe Wilderness begins. Another 1.2 miles of travel along Potrero John Creek is required to reach the waterfall, and every time I've hiked this stretch, there is a different amount of trail (or to be more exact, "route") accessible. Just keep following the creek and you'll be fine, but figure on at least an hour to traverse the 1.2 miles from the campground to the falls, and maybe double that if the water is high and rocks are slippery.

Potrero John Falls

The increasingly narrow trail proceeds through a fire-scarred area. Most of the conifers are left behind as the forest transitions to oaks. A few more campsites are found along the creek, which becomes increasingly choked with downed trees and more and more rocks. When you come to an eight-foot waterfall, you are very, very close. It's only another 75 yards to Potrero John's 70-foot drop, and your first glimpse a stunner. This sparkling freefall is one of the best waterfalls in Los Padres National Forest, and you're one of the lucky few who has seen it.

Directions

From Ojai, drive north on Highway 33 for 21 miles to where Potrero John Creek crosses the highway. The trailhead is signed on the right (north) side of the road.

Information and Contact

A national forest Adventure Pass is required. Maps of Los Padres National Forest are available for a fee from the National Forest Store (406/329-3024, www.nationalforeststore.com), or can be downloaded for free from www.fs.fed.us/r5/maps/. For more information, contact Los Padres National Forest, Ojai Ranger District, 805/646-4348, www.fs.fed.us/r5/lospadres.

11 SANTA PAULA CANYON FALLS
Los Padres National Forest

Level: Moderate

Best Season: December–May

Distance: 6.0 miles round-trip

Elevation Change: Total gain 800 feet

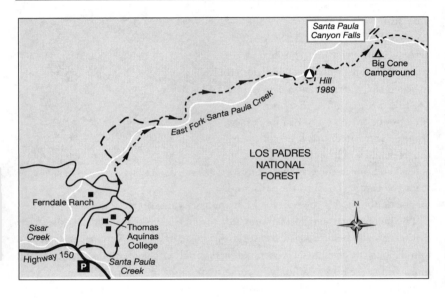

In the last decade, beautiful Santa Paula Canyon has been defiled by graffiti and trash, and although the Forest Service has made efforts to remove the mess, the ingrates who participate in these kinds of activities keep returning to redo their dirty work. It's impossible to imagine why or how anyone would want to spoil such a beautiful spot, but these problems happen here. Before you visit, you might want to check with the Ojai Ranger District (805/646-4348) to find out the current situation in the canyon.

When Santa Paula Canyon is graffiti- and trash-free, it makes a perfect destination for a one-night camping trip. This lovely place has waterfalls, swimming holes, small trout, and a shady campground that's perfectly situated for easy access to fun adventures. You can hike out to the campground late in the afternoon, make a big dinner, get a good night's sleep, and then play all the next day in the river before heading home.

The trail starts out by following an easement around Thomas Aquinas College and Ferndale Ranch, passing school buildings, ranch buildings, oil-drilling grasshoppers, and too much pavement. Posted signs keep hikers on the proper route until, in 0.75 mile, you finally reach the single-track trail along Santa Paula Creek. In spring, streamside wildflowers are plentiful—purple nightshade, purple vetch, lupine, and brodiaea.

In 0.25 mile, you cross the creek and turn right, joining the double-wide Santa Paula Canyon Recreation Trail, which runs level for another mile. After a second creek crossing, the wide trail heads uphill, switchbacking through a tunnel of ceanothus as it curves around Hill 1989. The path moves up and away from the creek, then eventually drops back down. When it descends, you reach a pristine-looking, grassy flat, surrounded by oaks and a few big-cone spruce. This is Big Cone Campground, with a half-dozen sites and fire rings. In late winter and spring, you can hear the sound of nearby waterfalls from the camp, although the creek is a few hundred feet away.

The site on the far left of the camp is set on a bluff above Santa Paula Creek, and from it a spur trail leads to an overlook, where you can glimpse one of the loveliest falls on the stream. The pool above the fall is clearly visible, as well as the top of its narrow 30-foot chute, which is funneled through sandstone. A well-used path leads from the edge of the campground down a single switchback to the creek, where you'll find a narrow sandstone gorge and numerous swimming holes. Small waterfalls are located up and down this stretch, but their accessibility depends on how full the stream is running. If the water level is comfortably low, head downstream a short distance to find them. Many people call this area of Santa Paula Creek "The Punchbowls," but the actual Punchbowls are about a mile farther. Follow the trail from Big Cone Camp for 0.5 mile to Cross Camp and the edge of the Sespe Wilderness. Just beyond the camp, the stream enters a canyon, in the back of which is found a series of sandstone-sculpted cascades. These aptly named Punchbowls, which plummet from one perfectly rounded pool to the next, are even more impressive than the cluster of falls by Big Cone Camp.

Directions

From Ojai at the junction of Highways 33 and 150, drive east on Highway 150 for 11.5 miles to Thomas Aquinas College on the left (look for iron gates and stone buildings). Drive 100 yards farther to the parking pullout on the right side of the road, just beyond the highway bridge over Santa Paula Creek. Park there and walk back across the bridge to the paved road on the right side of the college.

Information and Contact

A national forest Adventure Pass is required. Maps of Los Padres National Forest

Chapter 11

are available for a fee from the National Forest Store (406/329-3024, www.nation-alforeststore.com), or can be downloaded for free from www.fs.fed.us/r5/maps/. For more information, contact Los Padres National Forest, Ojai Ranger District, 805/646-4348, www.fs.fed.us/r5/lospadres.

MORE WATERFALLS IN SANTA BARBARA AND VICINITY

•**Cold Spring Tavern Falls,** on Stagecoach Road off Highway 154 in Santa Barbara. Scramble up the creek alongside Cold Spring Tavern for 0.75 mile to reach a 50-foot waterfall. It only flows in the wettest weather. For more information, phone Los Padres National Forest, Santa Barbara Ranger District, 805/967-3481.

•**Circle Bar B Ranch Waterfall,** near Refugio Beach. See a waterfall by horseback at this privately run ranch. Horse rentals and trail rides are available for a fee. For more information, phone 805/968-1113.

•**Indian Creek Falls, Dick Smith Wilderness.** These falls are accessible via day hike from the Indian Creek Trailhead. For more information, phone Los Padres National Forest, Santa Barbara Ranger District, at 805/967-3481.

•**Sisquoc River Falls, San Rafael Wilderness.** These falls are found near Lower Bear Camp, accessible via a backpacking trip on the Sisquoc River Trail. For more information, phone Los Padres National Forest, Santa Lucia Ranger District, 805/925-9538.

•**Rattlesnake Falls, San Rafael Wilderness.** Located near Cottonwood Camp, these falls are accessible via a backpacking trip on the Sisquoc River Trail. For more information, phone Los Padres National Forest, Santa Lucia Ranger District, 805/925-9538.

LOS ANGELES
AND VICINITY

© ANN MARIE BROWN

BEST WATERFALLS

◀ **Short Backpacking Trips**
Santa Ynez Canyon Falls, **page 416**
Switzer Falls, **page 423**

◀ **Easy Waterfall Walks**
Paradise Falls, **page 409**
Sturtevant Falls, **page 433**
Monrovia Canyon Falls, **page 437**
San Antonio Falls, **page 443**
Holy Jim Falls, **page 457**

◀ **Family Campgrounds**
Millard Falls, **page 429**
Dark Canyon Falls, **page 466**

◀ **Swimming Holes**
Santa Ynez Canyon Falls, **page 416**

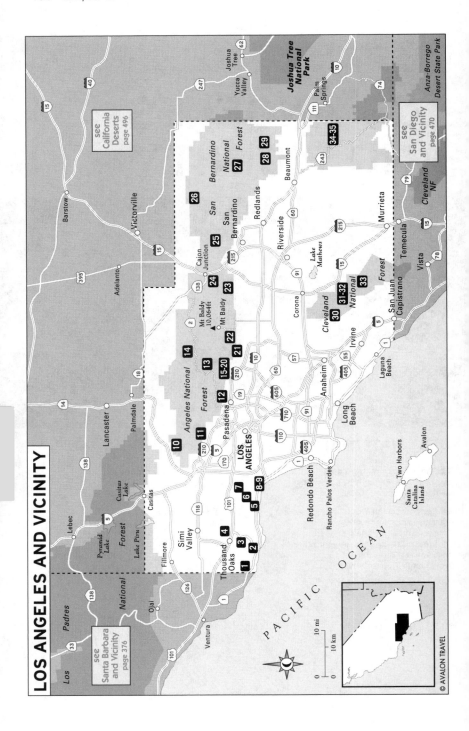

LOS ANGELES AND VICINITY

see California Deserts page 496

see San Diego and Vicinity page 470

see Santa Barbara and Vicinity page 376

PACIFIC OCEAN

10 mi
10 km

© AVALON TRAVEL

TRAIL NAME	LEVEL	DISTANCE	ELEVATION	SEASON	FEATURES	PAGE
1 La Jolla Canyon Falls	Easy	1.6–3.8 mi rt	150 ft	Dec.–May		403
2 The Grotto Falls	Moderate	3.4 mi rt	550 ft	Dec.–May		405
3 Sycamore Canyon Falls	Easy	4.4 mi rt	350 ft	Dec.–May		407
4 Paradise Falls	Easy	2.4 mi rt	260 ft	Dec.–May		409
5 Zuma and Newton Canyon Falls	Moderate	2.4 mi rt	600 ft	Dec.–May		410
6 Escondido Falls	Easy	4.2 mi rt	300 ft	Dec.–May		412
7 Solstice Canyon Falls	Easy	2.0 mi rt	250 ft	Dec.–May		414
8 Santa Ynez Canyon Falls	Moderate	2.4 mi rt	250 ft	Dec.–May		416
9 Temescal Canyon Falls	Easy	2.4 mi rt	300 ft	Dec.–May		418
10 Placerita Creek Falls	Easy	2.4–5.4 mi rt	250 ft	Dec.–May		419
11 Trail Canyon Falls	Moderate	4.0 mi rt	600 ft	Dec.–June		421
12 Switzer Falls	Easy	2.5–5.0 mi rt	600 ft	Dec.–June		423
13 Devil's Canyon Falls	Strenuous	10.0 mi rt	2,000 ft	Dec.–June		426
14 Cooper Canyon Falls	Moderate	4.0 mi rt	850 ft	Apr.–June		427
15 Millard Falls	Easy	1.0 mile rt	200 ft	Dec.–June		429
16 Eaton Canyon Falls	Easy	3.0 mi rt	350 ft	Dec.–June		431
17 Sturtevant Falls	Easy	3.2 mi rt	600 ft	Dec.–June		433

TRAIL NAME	LEVEL	DISTANCE	ELEVATION	SEASON	FEATURES	PAGE
18 Hermit Falls	Easy	3.0 mi rt	700 ft	Dec.–June		435
19 Monrovia Canyon Falls	Easy	1.4 mi rt	100 ft	Dec.–June		437
20 Soldier Creek Falls	Easy	1.25 mi rt	300 ft	Dec.–June		439
21 Fish Canyon Falls	Easy/Strenuous	3.2–9.4 mi rt	2,800 ft	Jan.–May		441
22 San Antonio Falls	Easy	1.5 mi rt	250 ft	Mar.–July		443
23 Etiwanda Falls	Easy	3.0 mi rt	750 ft	Jan.–May		445
24 Bonita Falls	Moderate	1.0 mile rt	3,200 ft	Dec.–May		447
25 Heart Rock Falls	Easy	2.0 mi rt	250 ft	Jan.–June		449
26 Deep Creek Falls	Moderate	2.0 mi rt	200 ft	Apr.–July		451
27 Mill Creek Road Falls	Easy	1.2 mi rt	200 ft	Feb.–May		453
28 Monkeyface and Rim of the World Scenic Byway Falls	Easy	Negligible	3,800–4,800 ft	Feb.–May		454
29 Big Falls	Easy	0.6 mile rt	80 ft	Mar.–Sept.		455
30 Holy Jim Falls	Easy	2.5 mi rt	350 ft	Dec.–June		457
31 San Juan Falls	Easy	1.0 mile rt	100 ft	Dec.–Apr.		459
32 Ortega Falls	Easy	0.5 mile rt	100 ft	Dec.–Apr.		461
33 Tenaja Falls	Easy	1.5 mi rt	300 ft	Jan.–May		462
34 Fuller Mill Creek Falls	Easy	0.5 mile rt	Negligible	Apr.–June		464
35 Dark Canyon Falls	Moderate	2.0 mi rt	300 ft	May–July		466

1 LA JOLLA CANYON FALLS
Point Mugu State Park

Level: Easy

Best Season: December-May

Distance: 1.6-3.8 miles round-trip

Elevation Change: Total gain 150 feet

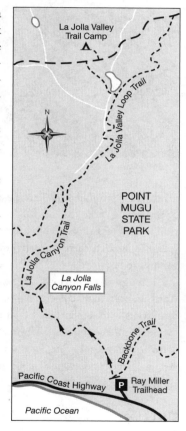

In a beauty contest of all the parks in the Santa Monica Mountains, Point Mugu State Park would win hands down. Maybe it's because Point Mugu is a little farther west on the highway, closer to Oxnard than it is to Los Angeles. Maybe it's the park's wildflowers, waterfall, well-built trails, and serene coastal views. Whatever the reason, Point Mugu always feels more wild and pristine than its eastern neighbors.

Point Mugu has two waterfalls—Sycamore Canyon and La Jolla Canyon. Although the former is better accessed from a Santa Monica Mountains National Recreation Area site near Thousand Oaks (see Sycamore Canyon Falls listing in this chapter), the latter is an easy walk from the state park trailhead on Highway 1, near Thornhill Broome Beach. You can also walk an extra mile and spend the night at the La Jolla Canyon Trail Camp, turning the day hike into a perfect easy backpacking trip.

Start at the Ray Miller Trailhead and follow the wide gated road, which narrows to single-track almost immediately. The trail travels through an open valley that is continually refreshed by ocean breezes blowing up the canyon. In only 0.8 mile, you arrive at La Jolla Canyon's small, two-tiered waterfall. A few railroad-tie stairsteps lead up to the pool between the two cascades.

Although La Jolla Creek flows most of the year, the fall is exciting only shortly after a rain. The rest of the time, it's just a moderate trickle of about 15 feet high. The cascade continues below the trail, but the lower portion is obscured by dense willows and sycamores.

© ANN MARIE BROWN

La Jolla Canyon Falls

But there are other highlights on this trail besides the waterfall. In the early spring months, the canyon walls within a 0.25-mile stretch both before and after the waterfall are blanketed with blooming giant coreopsis. These giant "sunflowers on steroids" are common on the Channel Islands but much less so on the mainland. The bright yellow flower stalks can reach as high as seven feet tall, but in the plant's nonblooming dormant stage, you could easily walk right by them without a second glance.

Since the waterfall isn't much of a destination, you'll probably want to keep heading farther into La Jolla Canyon. As you climb, the canyon gets narrower and rockier, and hidden amid the chaparral you'll see rock caves that were once used by Native Americans. If you're backpacking, take the left fork at the junction with the Mugu Peak Trail. The trail levels and brings you to an area of native grasses. The La Jolla Canyon Trail Camp is located there, shortly beyond a cattail-bordered pond. Water and restrooms are provided.

Although the wildflowers are excellent in La Jolla Canyon in late March and April, an even more colorful happening occurs in January and February: monarch butterflies who winter here begin to mate and leave for their return migration to Canada and the northern United States. The monarchs cluster in both La Jolla Canyon and neighboring Sycamore Canyon in Point Mugu State Park. Each year, generation after generation of butterflies return to these same ancestral sites. If your timing is good, you might see the waterfall and the monarchs in the same trip.

Directions

From U.S. 101 in Camarillo, take the Los Posas Road exit and drive south through Oxnard. Follow Los Posas Road for eight miles to Highway 1, then turn south on Highway 1. Drive five miles to the La Jolla Canyon Trailhead parking area on the left, across from Thornhill Broome State Beach.

Or, from Malibu, drive west on Highway 1 for 22 miles to the La Jolla Canyon Trailhead parking area on the right (one mile west of Big Sycamore Canyon Campground).

Information and Contact

An $8 day-use fee is charged per vehicle at the Ray Miller Trailhead. A park map is available at the entrance kiosk at Sycamore Canyon Campground, one mile south on Highway 1. A detailed map of the Santa Monica Mountains is available from Tom Harrison Maps, 415/456-7940, www.tomharrisonmaps.com. Backpacking campsites are available on a first-come, first-served basis; backpackers must register at the Sycamore Canyon Campground. For more information, contact Point Mugu State Park, 818/880-0363, www.parks.ca.gov.

2 THE GROTTO FALLS
Circle X Ranch

🚶 🐕

Level: Moderate	**Distance:** 3.4 miles round-trip
Best Season: December-May	**Elevation Change:** Total loss 550 feet

Is it a waterfall or a boulder playground? It just depends on when you show up. Circle X Ranch's "The Grotto" is a rugged jumble of volcanic rocks, many bigger than your average Volkswagen, over which the West Fork of Arroyo Sequit tumbles (or sadly dribbles, in summer). Perhaps they should call this rock garden The Playground instead of The Grotto, because in low water you can spend all day climbing around it, making use of millions of possible handholds and toeholds. In high water, don't even attempt exploring; just stand back and listen to the water roar.

Many years ago you could access The Grotto just by driving into the neighboring Happy Hollow Campground,

Botsford Falls near The Grotto

© ANN MARIE BROWN

then walking a few hundred feet through the camp. But that campground and its access road were removed by the National Park Service in 1999. Now you reach The Grotto by following the Grotto Trail 1.7 miles from the group campground near the Circle X Ranch entrance. The trail makes a steep descent with a 550-foot elevation loss that must be gained back on the return trip, so save it for a cool day.

A bonus of hiking rather than driving to The Grotto is that in the rainy season, you'll catch glimpses of a few other waterfalls along the way. The first fall is located in the first 0.5 mile of trail, shortly beyond a fork with Canyon View Trail. This 35-foot-high fall is called Botsford Falls, named by the Boy Scouts who call these parklands home. The trail passes by the top of it, almost at its lip. In another 0.4 mile, you'll pass an overlook with a view of two much higher falls. Neither of these falls is accessible except by a long and nasty bushwhack, and it's not worth the bother. A final 0.8 mile of trail and you've made your way to The Grotto.

If it's your first visit here, you'll notice that Circle X Ranch is a different ball of wax from the coastal parks in the Santa Monica Mountains. Located at a higher elevation, it's much warmer. It also has a tremendous backdrop of rocky peaks looming behind it, including Sandstone Peak, the highest summit in the Santa Monica Mountains at 3,111 feet. But down at The Grotto lies a lush riparian environment, overgrown with oaks, willows, sycamores, and ferns. Even on the hottest days of summer, a pleasant breeze often blows through here. During the wet season, the noise of running water through The Grotto's jumble of boulders can be deafening. The Grotto's many splashing cascades create great echoing sounds as they bounce around the rocks. Even in low water, secret waterfalls are hidden in The Grotto's many caves and recesses. On my June visit, when the water level was dwindling, I stood knee-deep in a pool, the source of which was a cascade concealed behind large boulders.

Directions

From Malibu, drive northwest on Highway 1 for 10 miles to Yerba Buena Road, 1.5 miles past Leo Carrillo State Park. Turn right and drive 5.3 miles up Yerba Buena Road to the entrance to Circle X Ranch on the right. Park at the ranger station and walk about 200 yards to the group campground. The Grotto Trail begins at the group camp.

Information and Contact

There is no fee. A free map/brochure of the Circle X Ranch area is available for free download at www.nps.gov/samo/. A detailed map of the Santa Monica Mountains is available from Tom Harrison Maps, 415/456-7940, www.tomharrison-maps.com. For more information, contact Santa Monica Mountains National Recreation Area, 805/370-2301, www.nps/gov/samo. Or contact Circle X Ranger Station at 310/457-6408.

3 SYCAMORE CANYON FALLS

Santa Monica Mountains National Recreation Area
and Point Mugu State Park

Level: Easy

Best Season: December–May

Distance: 4.4 miles round-trip

Elevation Change: Total loss 350 feet

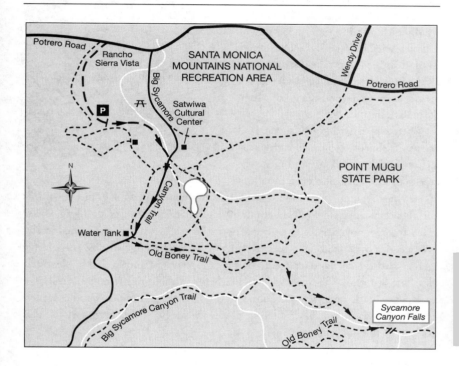

The Santa Monica Mountains National Recreation Area Rancho Sierra Vista/
Satwiwa Site is the very long name for the back door to Point Mugu State Park.
It's a mouthful to say, but all you need to remember is Satwiwa, which means
"the bluffs," the name of the Chumash Indian village that once existed here. Another thing worth remembering is that Point Mugu's back door is only a couple
miles off U.S. 101, so there's no need to drive all the way to the coast to access
these lovely trails.

Start from the trailhead at the junction of Wendy Drive and Potrero Road, following the Wendy Trail as it quickly ascends. (Pick up a trail map at the signboard
before you start; there are multiple junctions to negotiate.) The simplest way to

reach the waterfall is to follow a series of half-dozen "lefts." The route will take you uphill first along Wendy Trail for 0.3 mile, then along the east side of the Satwiwa Loop Trail, past an old windmill and a junction with the Hidden Valley Overlook Trail, and then finally into Point Mugu State Park. Here you finally quit climbing and head downhill on a wide dirt road, the Old Boney Trail. (Canine lovers take note: dogs are allowed on the trails of Satwiwa Site, but are not allowed beyond the Point Mugu State Park boundary.)

Where Upper Sycamore Canyon Trail comes in sharply from the right, stay left on Old Boney Trail and cross the creek (an easy rock-hop even in winter

Sycamore Canyon Falls

and spring). You are now about two miles from your car. Walk about 100 yards and then make one final left. In about 50 yards of easy stream scrambling, you're at Sycamore Canyon Falls. The water pours (or trickles if it hasn't rained lately) over a series of sandstone ledges, artfully accented by huge woodwardia ferns, smaller sword ferns, and an overhanging canopy of sycamores and big-leaf maples. The waterfall isn't huge or particularly forceful but rather more Zen-like in its appeal—dancing its way through a half-dozen miniature pools and cascades. Even in low water, the fall is a serene place, a peaceful shelter from city life and the heat of the Los Angeles sun.

Directions
From U.S. 101 in Thousand Oaks, exit on Wendy Drive and drive north for 2.9 miles to where Wendy Drive ends at Potrero Road. Park here and begin hiking at the signboard.

Information and Contact
There is no fee. A free map/brochure of the Satwiwa Site is available for free download at www.nps.gov/samo/. A detailed map of the Santa Monica Mountains is available from Tom Harrison Maps, 415/456-7940, www.tomharrisonmaps.com. For more information, contact Santa Monica Mountains National Recreation Area, 805/370-2301, www.nps/gov/samo/.

4 PARADISE FALLS
Wildwood Park

BEST (

🏃 🐕

Level: Easy

Distance: 2.4 miles round-trip

Best Season: December-May

Elevation Change: Total loss 260 feet

Paradise Falls

© ANN MARIE BROWN

If you have trouble imagining a 70-foot waterfall in the suburbs of Thousand Oaks, you should lace up your boots and see for yourself. At the parking lot, you may rate this place as "Least Likely Spot for a Great Waterfall," but prepare to be surprised.

One of the best things about Paradise Falls is that it's so easy to reach. Simply drive a few miles off U.S. 101 and take a short walk on fire roads. From Wildwood Park's Arboles parking lot, hike due west on the Mesa Trail for 0.5 mile to the North Tepee Trail, then turn left and head down to the falls. (This is one of several possible routes. Another option is to drive 0.5 mile beyond the Arboles parking lot to a lower lot, which will cut some distance off your hike. Check out the park trail maps at the Arboles lot.)

Shortly, you'll drop into the canyon, where you'll see signs directing you to Paradise Falls, or sometimes Wildwood Falls, the cascade's less imaginative name. The best approach is via the Wildwood Canyon Trail, hiking in from the east so you can see the stream just before it makes its tremendous hurtle over a basalt lip. The trail parallels the creek downhill to the fall's base. A chain-link fence keeps you from tumbling down the hillside at the steepest drop-offs. You might catch a telltale whiff of sulphur, a clue that the waterfall is fed by an underground spring and thus runs year-round, although less enthusiastically in summer and fall. The basalt of the waterfall's cliff was formed by the same volcanic action that created Montclef Ridge, the obvious rock formation looming to the north of the park. These volcanic outcrops remain from a series of eruptions that occurred some 30 million years ago.

Even in low water, Paradise Falls is a frothy white stream, with a startlingly wide pool at the bottom—more like a large pond about 50 yards wide. You can't get directly in front of the fall without getting your feet wet, so most people view it from the side. From this angle, the middle section is obscured by a large rock, but that just makes it look more interesting. The presence of year-round water in Paradise Falls' stream makes this canyon a haven for wildlife; keep on the lookout for mule deer, rabbits, coyotes, and numerous songbirds and raptors. The park's wildlife list includes 60 species of birds, 37 species of mammals, and 22 species of amphibians and reptiles.

Directions

From Thousand Oaks on U.S. 101, take the Lynn Road exit and head north. Drive 2.5 miles to Avenida de los Arboles, then turn left. Drive 0.9 mile and make a U-turn into the Arboles parking lot on the left side of the road.

Information and Contact

There is no fee. Park maps are available at the trailhead. For more information, contact Wildwood Park, Conejo Recreation and Park District, 805/495-2163, www.crpd.org.

5 ZUMA AND NEWTON CANYON FALLS
Santa Monica Mountains National Recreation Area

Level: Moderate   **Distance:** 2.4 miles round-trip
Best Season: December-May   **Elevation Change:** Total loss 600 feet

Waterfalls that are easy to reach are in short supply in Southern California. Many require hours of bushwhacking to spots that aren't on any map. The first waterfall on this trip is ideal for those hiking with small children and water-loving dogs. The second and third falls are, well, more of an adventure.

Winter and spring are ideal for hiking to Newton Canyon Falls, which runs all year but is especially impressive following a good rainy season. The trailhead is along Kanan Dume Road, at a parking pullout with a big Backbone Trail sign. There is also a bus shelter and sign for the National Park Service's Parklink Shuttle (888/734-2323, www.parklinkshuttle.com), which transports hikers and bikers to and from a number of shuttle stops in the Santa Monica Mountains National Recreation Area.

There are two Backbone trailhead signs on opposite sides of the parking lot.

You want the one on the right (north) side, for the Zuma Canyon Trail, which leads to Zuma Ridge Motorway. The other trail goes east on the Backbone, toward Latigo Canyon.

The trail descends immediately into Newton Canyon, a little slice of watery paradise parallel to and just below Kanan Dume Road. The cool and shady canyon is lined with ferns and other lush vegetation, including sunflowers and miner's lettuce.

The trail switchbacks downhill to the left, crosses Newton Canyon Creek, and in only about 10 minutes of walking you'll note a left turnoff. Follow it downhill and you find yourself on top of a 25-foot waterfall, where Newton Creek

the brink of Newton Canyon Falls

© ANN MARIE BROWN

slides down a vertical, moss-covered limestone face. Big boulders above the fall's lip make a nice picnic spot, but watch your footing; it's a two-story drop to the fall's base. To access the base by walking, not falling, descend on one of the spur trails just beyond the waterfall's crest, then head upstream a few yards. The watery scene is set in a rounded rock grotto, where small sandstone caves surround the fall. With all the leafy trees, winding vines, ferns, and thick moss, you might think you are someplace in the tropics, not the near-desert of Los Angeles.

Follow the creek downstream from this upper fall for about 100 yards to the top of Lower Newton Canyon Falls, being careful to avoid ticks and abundant poison oak. You'll have to do some boulder-hopping, which can be easy or difficult, depending on how much water is in the stream. This lower fall is taller than the upper fall, but has less water flowing over it. By late spring, every inch of it is covered with greenery, like a Rose Parade float. You can hardly see the water through the leaves.

Now do some soul-searching. It's up to you and your scrambling abilities whether you want to go any farther. There is considerable risk involved in climbing down to the base of Lower Newton Falls, because the slope is nearly vertical and often muddy, especially after recent rains. Even experienced climbers can slip and fall. If you can safely manage the drop, you'll gain access to Zuma Canyon, at the point were Zuma and Newton Creeks join. Head to the right (east) for five more minutes of stream scrambling to Zuma Canyon Falls. Although it's only 25 feet tall, its setting is a piece of art. The fall drops over a sandstone ledge surrounded by small caves and ferns, and it has a double pool—two basins divided by a rock ledge—at its base. In high water, the waterfall's flow spills from one pool to the next. When the stream warms up, swimming is best in the lower, deeper pool.

Directions
From Highway 1 in Malibu, turn north on Kanan Dume Road and drive 4.3 miles to the Backbone Trail trailhead, which is on the left, just past the tunnel.

Alternatively, from U.S. 101 in Agoura Hills, exit at Kanan Road and drive 7.6 miles south to the trailhead on the right.

Information and Contact
There is no fee. A free map/brochure of Zuma and Trancas Canyons is available for download at www.nps.gov/samo/. A detailed map of the Santa Monica Mountains is available from Tom Harrison Maps, 415/456-7940, www.tomharrison-maps.com. For more information, contact Santa Monica Mountains National Recreation Area, 805/370-2301, www.nps.gov/samo/.

6 ESCONDIDO FALLS
Santa Monica Mountains Conservancy

Level: Easy

Best Season: December-May

Distance: 4.2 miles round-trip

Elevation Change: Total gain 300 feet

This is a strange and wonderful waterfall hike. The strange part? You have to walk a mile just to reach the trailhead, following a paved road through an opulent neighborhood of gargantuan Malibu homes. As you walk by these mansions dressed in your hiking clothes, you half expect a resident to ask if you are looking for a job raking leaves or pulling weeds. But no, they are accustomed to hikers wandering by.

The wonderful part? The payoff is access to a charming sylvan footpath in Escondido Canyon, where a huge, multitiered limestone waterfall awaits—the highest cataract in the Santa Monica Mountains.

Start your trip at the well-signed hikers' parking lot at the start of Winding Way. Walk up the paved road for one mile, gaining ocean views as you climb. Try not to gawk too much at all the affluence. When you reach the trail sign for the Santa Monica Mountains Conservancy lands, veer off to the left, heading into the canyon.

Escondido Falls

Walk upstream, ignoring all trail junctions and keeping close to the creek. You'll cross it a half-dozen times, and if the water is running high, you will have no choice but to get your feet wet. The lush canyon trail is nearly level, extremely well-maintained, and gorgeous to boot. Most of the path is shaded by sycamore trees, but coastal sage scrub and wildflowers make an appearance, too. On a spring day, there isn't a more pleasant walk anywhere in the Los Angeles basin.

In 0.5 mile, you'll catch a glimpse of the big waterfall far ahead, tucked into the back of a high box canyon. One look will be enough to make you quicken your pace. Fifteen minutes later you'll be standing at the base of the lower tier of Escondido Canyon's limestone fall, *oohing* and *aahing* at the 50-foot length of streaming water pouring over a wealth of ferns and moss. Horsetail ferns grow around its base, and a couple of rope swings hang from a sycamore tree. The rotten-egg smell of sulphur, coming from the spring that gives birth to this stream, is often very noticeable here.

If your scrambling skills are good, don't stop here. That big cataract you saw a half mile back is still waiting above this one, and it is accessible by following the use trail on the right side of the fall. This easy stroll through the canyon now becomes an adventure, and it's a good idea to know your limits before you start. Ask yourself a few questions: Is the slope dry? Are you wearing solid lug-soled boots? Are you comfortable with off-trail scrambling? If you answered yes to all of the above, a careful 15-minute ascent using both hands and feet will get you to the upper fall, an immense limestone tier that is 150 feet high. Along the way, you'll pass a middle cascade about 15 feet high. The scrambling becomes more challenging on the final push to the upper fall.

A common remark heard at this spot on one April day was simply "wow." Yes, this is a "wow" waterfall. You'll want to kick off your shoes and wade into its shallow pool. If you do, be careful not to step on the giant Coast Range newts that make their home here. These amphibians, a subspecies of the California newt, are appropriately oversized to match this amazing cataract.

Directions

From Malibu, drive west on Highway 1 for 5.5 miles to Winding Way East on the right and the large sign for the Winding Way Trail. (If you reach Kanan Road, you've gone 1.4 miles too far.) Turn right, then left immediately into the well-signed parking lot.

Information and Contact

There is no fee. A trail map is available by free download at www.lamountains. com. A detailed map of the Santa Monica Mountains is available from Tom Harrison Maps, 415/456-7940, www.tomharrisonmaps.com. For more information, contact the Santa Monica Mountains Conservancy, 310/589-3200, www. lamountains.com.

7 SOLSTICE CANYON FALLS
Santa Monica Mountains National Recreation Area

Level: Easy	Distance: 2.0 miles round-trip
Best Season: December-May	Elevation Change: Total gain 250 feet

© ANN MARIE BROWN

Solstice Canyon Falls on Roberts Ranch

You're tired of getting poison oak. You're tired of scrambling upstream over slippery boulders. Maybe you're just plain tired. You want to see a waterfall in the Santa Monica Mountains and you want an easy walk to get there. If that's your story, show up at Solstice Canyon, where all you have to do is take a one-mile stroll on a paved road.

From the parking area, walk up the paved road, called Solstice Canyon Trail, which parallels Solstice Creek. Where the road reaches a T-junction, bear right, and hike up the canyon to the Roberts Ranch site. Solstice Creek makes fine company along the way, as do the many bunches of orange sticky monkeyflower and sweet hot mustard. The walk is similar to other canyon hikes in the Santa Monica Mountains, but it is made about a million times easier by the wide paved road and nearly level grade.

Pass by the 1865 Keller house, a lovely stone house that's the oldest in Malibu. It's now a private residence, located about halfway to the falls. Continue to the ruins of Tropical Terrace, the 1950s home of the Fred and Florence Roberts family. This beautiful home and its exotic, terraced gardens were destroyed by a fire in 1982, although its foundations, flagstone walkways, and fireplaces remain. Clearly the gardens were once resplendent; even now an array of overgrown palm trees, birds-of-paradise, and other tropical plants thrive among the native sycamores. The Robertses also kept giraffes, camels, and exotic birds on the property.

Walk past the stone ruins of the house, following the stream as it makes a 90-degree turn around the property. First you'll see a small eight-foot-high fall, then on the far side of the house foundation, you'll come face-to-face with 30-foot Solstice Canyon Falls. You can reach the cataract's base fairly easily by following the remains of the stone stairways and paths. There are plenty of rocks to step on, keeping your feet dry and out of the stream.

Solstice Canyon Falls is surprisingly beautiful, often flowing with more volume than other falls in the area. It cascades over huge sandstone boulders, with maidenhair ferns clinging to the rocks around the fall's edges. It's fun to sit by the waterfall and imagine what it was like here when Roberts Ranch was in its splendor.

Solstice Canyon has a few other waterfalls, but most of these are caused by artificial dams on Solstice Creek, so they don't count. There is a notable 100-foot-plus waterfall up in Dry Canyon, which is accessible via the Dry Creek Trail. The trailhead is at the same day-use area where you parked your car for Solstice Canyon Falls. Dry Creek Trail leads 0.6 mile to a decent overlook of the waterfall, but the show only occurs immediately after a rain. This waterfall was completely dry during my May visit, even though the fall at Roberts Ranch was flowing strong. Dry Creek Trail is lovely, however, and only slightly marred by the sight of some monolithic homes high on the hillside above. A use trail continues from the end of the maintained trail, but it gets quickly overgrown with the dreaded poison oak.

Directions
From Malibu, drive northwest on Highway 1 for three miles and turn right on Corral Canyon Road. Drive 0.2 mile to the park entrance on the left. Turn left and drive 0.3 mile to the day-use parking area. Walk up the paved road.

Information and Contact
There is no fee. A free map/brochure of Solstice Canyon is available for free

download at www.nps.gov/samo/. A detailed map of the Santa Monica Mountains is available from Tom Harrison Maps, 415/456-7940, www.tomharrisonmaps.com. For more information, contact Santa Monica Mountains National Recreation Area, 805/370-2301, www.nps/gov/samo/.

⑧ SANTA YNEZ CANYON FALLS   BEST 🄲
Topanga State Park

🚶 🚌

Level: Moderate   **Distance:** 2.4 miles round-trip

Best Season: December–May   **Elevation Change:** Total gain 250 feet

Topanga State Park is a park with nebulous borders, or rather a park with such an odd perimeter surrounding its irregular shape that it's hard to tell where it starts and where it ends. With the exception of the main park entrance at Trippet Ranch on Topanga Canyon Road, the rest of the park seems like a patchwork of wilderness set among continually growing housing developments. You drive through a neighborhood, park your car in front of somebody's house, walk 20 feet, and wham—you're in the state park. It's a bit strange, but you get used to it.

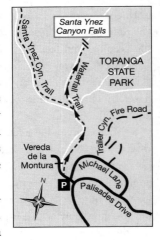

    Don't be put off by the glitzy homes and substantial concrete by the Santa Ynez Canyon Trailhead. You may drive up and wonder if you're going to a waterfall or a cocktail party. But once you're on the hiking trail in the canyon, the world becomes a different place: Santa Ynez Canyon is a natural sanctuary for foliage and wildlife, a swath of dense vegetation bordering a life-giving stream, miraculously encased within the city limits of Los Angeles. Not only that, Santa Ynez Canyon harbors a surprising sandstone waterfall.

    But a caveat is required: sadly, this canyon is often tagged with graffiti. The park rangers have repeatedly gone to great efforts to clean up the mess, and it usually stays clean for a short while, but then some ingrate will go and defile the canyon's beautiful boulders with spray paint. I hope you are lucky enough to see this beautiful place without these ugly markings.

    As the trail drops into the canyon, you'll find the canyon bottom makes remarkably level walking, pleasantly shaded by oaks, willows, and sycamores. In

Santa Ynez Canyon Falls

between the patches of poison oak, look for a wide variety of spring wildflowers, including five-foot-tall tiger lilies. At 0.5 mile from the trailhead, there is a metal gate (it was once across the trail but is now off to the side). Ignore the narrow, unmarked right spur by the gate, and instead bear left and cross the creek. Fifty yards past the creek crossing, there's an unsigned junction. The left fork leads to Trippet Ranch, but head right to stay along the creek.

From here, it's only 15–20 minutes to the falls, which are accessible either by following the route on the right side of the creek or by wading in to it. (During periods of high water, the latter may be easier.) In the last few hundred yards, the sandstone walls squeeze in tightly and you have no choice but to enter the stream. It's great fun walking up the sandstone narrows and climbing over miniature waterfalls. The route ends at a 15-foot fall, dropping over prehistoric-looking sandstone slabs. In summer, a rope is usually in place here for experienced climbers, who scramble up and over this fall to more waterfalls, farther back in the canyon. If you choose to explore them, use extreme caution on the slippery climb.

Directions

From Santa Monica, drive north on Highway 1 and turn right on Sunset Boulevard in Pacific Palisades. Drive 0.5 mile and turn left on Palisades Drive. Drive 2.4 miles, then turn left on Vereda de la Montura. The trailhead is at the intersection of Camino de Yatasto, a private road, and Vereda de la Montura. Park alongside the road.

Information and Contact

There is no fee. For more information and a park brochure/map, contact Topanga State Park, 310/455-2465, www.parks.ca.gov. A detailed map of Topanga State Park is available from Tom Harrison Maps, 415/456-7940, www.tomharrison-maps.com.

9 TEMESCAL CANYON FALLS

Temescal Gateway Park and Topanga State Park

Level: Easy

Best Season: December–May

Distance: 2.4 miles round-trip

Elevation Change: Total gain 300 feet

Even in summer, Temescal Canyon Falls is a sweet little spot, where the sound of tinkling water transports you far from the hustle and bustle of Los Angeles. Okay, so it's not Yosemite Falls. Nonetheless, in the morning, when sunlight hits the cascade's pool, you can watch rippling reflections on the underside of an overhanging maple tree's branches and on the wide face of the rocks beside the pool. If you're lucky, a bright green hummingbird will accompany you in the shade of the grotto or on the trail to reach it.

Begin your trip at the parking area just below the camp store in Temescal Gateway Park. (Sorry, Fido: no dogs are allowed on this trip because the hike leaves

Temescal Canyon Falls

the city park and enters Topanga State Park, where dogs are *ixnay*.) Walk up the asphalt past the store, then bear left and follow the fence line to the trailhead. A signed path directs you up and around the park's youth camp, and in about 50 feet you come to a fork and the start of your loop: Temescal Canyon Trail to the right, Temescal Ridge Trail to the left.

Take the right fork, following Temescal Canyon Trail very gently uphill. In 0.5 mile, at a boardwalk over the wide wash of Temescal Creek, you reach a Topanga State Park boundary sign. Now the trail starts to ascend more seriously, but still on a very manageable grade. The path is lined with small rounded pebbles embedded in conglomerate rock. Bunnies and lizards scurry past. Your trail parallels the stream, shaded by a canopy of big-leaf maples and sycamores. Adding to the mix are a few intriguing rock formations.

Shortly you'll hear the waterfall, which is crossed by a footbridge exactly one mile from the trailhead. If you choose, you can follow a steep spur trail a few yards before the bridge to the fall's base, where you get a close-up view of the waterfall's three separate drops (they are not visible from the trail). Big boulders, clearly volcanic in origin, form the falls. The rocks look like they are made of cobblestones embedded in cement.

You can simply turn around at the falls for a 2.4-mile round-trip. But this park is so lovely and its trails are so well-graded, it's far better to continue hiking, crossing over to the west side of the canyon to climb to an intersection with the Temescal Ridge Trail. Turn left to return to the trailhead. This 3.5-mile loop trip provides lovely views of the coast.

Directions

From Santa Monica, drive north on Highway 1 to Temescal Canyon Road in Pacific Palisades. Turn right (north) and drive 1.1 miles to Sunset Boulevard, then cross it to enter Temescal Gateway Park. Drive up the park road for 0.5 mile to the parking lot just before the camp store.

Information and Contact

A $7 day-use fee is charged per vehicle. A park map is available at the trailhead. A map of Topanga State Park, which includes Temescal Gateway Park, is available from Tom Harrison Maps, 415/456-7940, www.tomharrisonmaps.com. For more information contact Temescal Gateway Park, 310/454-1395, www.lamountains.com.

🔟 PLACERITA CREEK FALLS
Placerita Canyon Natural Area

🚶🏻 🐕

Level: Easy

Best Season: December–May

Distance: 2.4–5.4 miles round-trip

Elevation Change: Total gain 250 feet

Placerita Canyon Natural Area is a perfect destination for a family outing. With plentiful hiking, picnicking, and horseback-riding opportunities, the park is just far enough out of the Los Angeles basin so that going there feels like getting away. And best of all, the park is home to Placerita Creek's waterfall, accessible by an easy hike along the creek.

Start your trip at the Placerita Canyon Nature Center, where you can learn about the flora and fauna of the area. You'll also find out about the short-lived gold rush that began here in 1842, when a cattleman dug up some wild onions

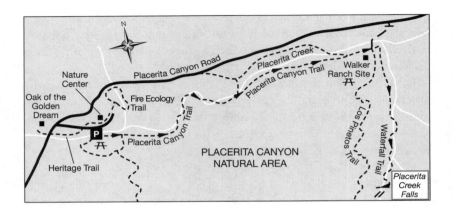

for a snack and found gold flakes attached to their roots. A half-million dollars' worth of gold was taken from this canyon in the 1840s.

Start hiking on the Canyon Trail, which leads from the southeast side of the nature center parking lot and crosses Placerita Creek. The trail winds through Placerita Canyon, passing shady canyon oaks, sycamores, willows, and blackberry bushes, to Walker Ranch, where you'll find the stone remains of settlers' cottages that were built in the early 1900s. Walk through Walker Ranch, then turn right and pick up the path signed as "Waterfall Trail." (Ignore the right turn about 30 yards before this one, which is the Los Piñetos Trail.)

The trail gets more interesting the farther you go, as it narrows and curves its way deeper into Placerita Canyon. Along the way, you can smell the sulphur from underground springs and the springtime fragrance of blooming ceanothus. The edible leaves of miner's lettuce grow near the creek. The path crosses the stream a few times, making it advisable to wear waterproof boots in high water, although plenty of visitors wear everyday shoes. In the final 100 yards before the waterfall, the trail ends and you simply hike up the streambed. When I arrived, I found four happy-looking kids and their mom sitting near the waterfall's base on a fallen tree, chewing on sandwiches.

© ANN MARIE BROWN

Placerita Creek Falls

Placerita Creek Falls is about 25 feet high, with a narrow stream that cascades down its cliff face. It forms a lovely, shaded grotto, with only enough room for a few visitors in its cloister. Did you pack your lunch? Good thinking—the spot clearly suggests a picnic. Some people attempt to climb above the falls, but the cliff face is quite steep and muddy, so it's a bad idea. On my trip, I witnessed a helicopter rescue in progress as paramedics carried out a woman who had broken her shoulder upstream of the falls. It served as a good reminder of the potential dangers of climbing around waterfalls.

If you want to reduce your mileage, you can drive two miles past the park entrance on Placerita Canyon Road to the Walker Ranch gate (a dirt road). Park near the gate; walk around it and into Walker Ranch group campground. From there, head straight on the Waterfall Trail for a round-trip of 2.4 miles instead of 5.5 miles.

Directions

From the San Fernando Valley, drive north on I-5 to Highway 14. Follow Highway 14 northeast for four miles to Newhall, then exit on Placerita Canyon Road. Turn right (east) and drive two miles to the park entrance on the right. Park in the nature center parking lot. (For a shorter hike, drive two miles east of the park entrance on Placerita Canyon Road to the Walker Ranch gate on the right.)

Information and Contact

There is no fee. Park maps are available at the nature center and trailhead, or can be downloaded at www.placerita.org. For more information, contact Placerita Canyon Natural Area, 661/259-7721, www.placerita.org.

11 TRAIL CANYON FALLS
Angeles National Forest

Level: Moderate

Best Season: December–June

Distance: 4.0 miles round-trip

Elevation Change: Total gain 600 feet

You have to hike on the Trail Canyon Trail to reach Trail Canyon Falls. It may sound redundant, but that's what the path is called.

During the wet season, the Trail Canyon Trail begins with a ford, and has several more along the way, so make sure you're wearing good boots or are willing to get your feet wet. Except for the stream crossings, the Trail Canyon Trail is a

Trail Canyon Falls

breeze to follow and rewarding every step of the way. You'll see many wildflowers, gain some far-reaching views, and follow a well-maintained path to a big waterfall. What more could you ask for?

After parking your car in the lot at Trail Canyon, walk on the dirt road into a community of cabins, then follow the road past them, winding around the canyon. At 0.75 mile, where the road makes a hairpin left turn, look for a single-track trail leading off to the right. Follow it and shortly you'll leave the chaparral and cactus, and enter a densely shaded riparian area lined with sycamores, alders, and cottonwoods. Then in turn, you'll leave the shade and climb back out on the sparsely vegetated, exposed slopes. You get a little bit of everything in Trail Canyon.

Although Trail Canyon's stream runs year-round, Trail Canyon Falls can be less than ebullient by early summer. On one May trip, while my hiking partner happily counted wildflowers along the trail (orange paintbrush, purple nightshade, hooker's onion, ceanothus, purple violet), I silently prayed to the waterfall gods. I hiked steeply out of the canyon, turned a sharp left curve in the trail, and suddenly the falls appeared up ahead, about 0.5 mile away. At full flow, they make a stunning show of white as they thunder down the canyon. Few waterfalls look this good from so far away.

The trail, which climbs almost continually up to this point, suddenly levels out here. The last 0.5 mile is an easy stroll to the fall's crest. Trail Canyon Falls spills over a smooth granite precipice in a rectangular block of water. Instead of being funneled through a notch, its stream is given a wide berth over its rounded lip, making it appear much grander than other Los Angeles–area waterfalls. Its breadth can be close to 15 feet when the fall is flowing hard. Spur trails lead to the rocks right above the falls—good spots for picnicking or lying in the sun. The fall's height is 50 feet, but it's impossible to gauge this from the top. To reach the waterfall's base and its big pool, follow the steep spur trail that is found just before the main trail reaches the waterfall's crest. It's slippery and steep, so use caution.

Trail Canyon Trail continues above the falls, crossing its stream and continuing to Tom Lucas Trail Camp. It's worth hiking at least a few hundred feet beyond the falls to a stream crossing where you can examine the colorful granite streambed. The return trip is even better than the hike in. Not only is it downhill all the way, but you also enjoy long-distance views of the canyons below.

Directions

From I-210 in Sunland, take the Sunland Boulevard exit. Cross Sunland Boulevard and head east on Foothill Boulevard for 1.2 miles to Mount Gleason Avenue. Turn left (north), drive 1.4 miles, then turn right on Big Tujunga Canyon Road. Drive 3.4 miles on Big Tujunga Road to a sign for Trail Canyon on the left. Bear left on a dirt road (Road 3N29), drive 0.25 mile to a fork, then bear right and drive 0.25 mile to a large parking lot. The trailhead is on the left side of the lot.

Information and Contact

A national forest Adventure Pass is required. A map of Angeles National Forest is available for a fee from the National Forest Store (406/329-3024, www.nationalforeststore.com), or can be downloaded for free from www.fs.fed.us/r5/maps/. A detailed map of the Angeles Front Country is available from Tom Harrison Maps, 415/456-7940, www.tomharrisonmaps.com. For more information, contact Angeles National Forest, Los Angeles River Ranger District, 818/899-1900, www.fs.fed.us/r5/angeles.

12 SWITZER FALLS   BEST (
Angeles National Forest

Level: Easy	Distance: 2.5–5.0 miles round-trip
Best Season: December–June	Elevation Change: Total loss 600 feet

Your trip to Switzer Falls can be as few as 2.5 miles round-trip or as many as five miles round-trip, and it's a choice that's not entirely up to you. The mileage is partly based on how you decide to view the falls (your choice), and partly based on whether the Forest Service has opened the gate to Switzer picnic area (not your choice). If the gate's closed, you have to park along Highway 2 and hike steeply downhill on pavement for an extra 0.3 mile, then steeply back up on the return trip.

At first, you may curse the holders of the gate key, like I did, but shortly you'll forget all about the inconvenience as you hike deep into Arroyo Seco Canyon along the Gabrielino National Recreation Trail.

© ANN MARIE BROWN

Switzer Falls

Get to Switzer Falls picnic area either by driving or walking, then follow the paved trail that heads gently downhill along the stream. Soon the pavement becomes more sporadic, giving way to a smooth dirt path. It crosses the stream a half-dozen times in the first half mile, forcing you to rock-hop in all but the driest months of the year. The route is pleasantly shaded by willows, alders, oaks, and maples. Less than a mile of trail brings you to Commodore Switzer Trail Camp, a few primitive campsites near the creek. You can't tell from here, but you're perched above 50-foot Switzer Falls.

Cross the creek by the camp and head uphill, climbing above the canyon and following the Gabrielino National Recreation Trail. As you ascend, you'll leave the cool canyon shade and break out into the sunshine. The drop-offs are so steep that a chain-link fence is in place to prevent potential mishaps. Views of the narrow and steep gorge below the trail are impressive, to say the least. The surrounding foliage is of a vastly different ilk from that of the leafy stream canyon. Interspersed among an array of aromatic chaparral are tall oaks, occasional big-cone Douglas fir, and delicate ferns growing out of the cliff sides.

From your vantage point on the trail, Switzer Falls appears through the brushy foliage as a tempting tease, about 50 yards away and impossible to reach because of the steep, deep canyon that separates you from it. The big upper pool above its lip and first 20 feet of its drop are clearly visible, but that is all. The rest is up to your imagination.

The stone building ruins to the right of the falls are the remains of the chapel at

Switzer's Camp, a popular trail resort in the early 1900s. Perry Switzer was called "Commodore" because of his talents in maneuvering his fleet of burros in rocky Arroyo Seco Canyon. Visitors would ride a half day on mules from Pasadena, traveling through eight miles of wild terrain and more than 60 stream crossings to reach the camp. They were treated to a cozy bed, three meals, and plenty of mountain air, all for $1.50 per day. On Sundays, Switzer's guests attended services at the chapel, accompanied by the background music of the waterfall. The scenery probably attracted even the not-so-devout.

A few steps beyond the falls viewpoint is a junction where the Gabrielino Trail heads right and uphill, and the Bear Canyon Trail heads left and downhill. Enjoy the lofty view of Arroyo Seco Canyon from this high point, then take the left fork for Bear Canyon and descend steeply for a 0.25-mile through a couple of switchbacks. When you reach the canyon bottom and a smattering of trail signs, take a 0.3-mile detour upstream (left) to see the lower cascades of Switzer Falls. Resist the temptation to climb over the lower, smaller falls to reach the large drop. There have been too many accidents here.

Should you wish to explore further, more water slides and falls can be found downstream along Bear Canyon Trail. Trout fishing is surprisingly good, and the continual roar and splash of mini-cascades along Arroyo Seco can keep you entertained for hours.

Directions

From I-210 in La Cañada, take Highway 2/Angeles Crest Highway northeast for 9.8 miles to Switzer Picnic Area. It is on the south side of the road, 0.5 mile past Clear Creek Information Station. Turn right, drive down the access road 0.3 mile, and park in the main lot.

Information and Contact

A national forest Adventure Pass is required. A map of Angeles National Forest is available for a fee from the National Forest Store (406/329-3024, www.national-foreststore.com), or can be downloaded for free from www.fs.fed.us/r5/maps/. A detailed map of the Mount Wilson area is available from Tom Harrison Maps, 415/456-7940, www.tomharrisonmaps.com. For more information, contact Angeles National Forest, Los Angeles River Ranger District, 818/899-1900, www.fs.fed.us/r5/angeles.

13 DEVIL'S CANYON FALLS
San Gabriel Wilderness

🚶 🚙 🐕

Level: Strenuous	**Distance:** 10.0 miles round-trip
Best Season: December–June	**Elevation Change:** Total loss 2,000 feet

When you've tired of the frontcountry, it's time to make a trip to the rugged San Gabriel Wilderness. Just be prepared to pay for your pleasure, because this is an upside-down hike—down on the way in and up, up, up on the way out. It's a trail of extremes. There's chaparral on some slopes, then tall pines and big-cone spruce on others. There's sun, then shade. It's dry for the first two miles, then you reach a tributary creek and follow its meander.

The area surrounding Devil's Canyon burned in a wildfire in 1998, causing extensive damage. Miraculously, the trail to Devil's Canyon and the canyon itself were barely touched by the fire. Fortunately, the overstory of big-cone spruce was spared.

It doesn't take long to hike down into the canyon, about an hour and a half for most people. When you come upon an obvious camping area above the creek at 3.5 miles, where there are a few fire rings and flat sleeping spots, you're at the canyon floor and the official end of the trail. From there, you can make your way downstream along Devil's Creek, partly on an anglers' trail and partly rock-hopping, wading, and scrambling. The stream is completely cloaked in alders, and largely choked with willows; occasionally you must bushwhack your way through them. The canyon gets narrower as you go; it's slow travel but not treacherous. Pools are surprisingly deep, and, if you're lucky, you catch sight of little trout. The canyon walls keep squeezing in tighter and steeper until you are in a series of small cascades, two–five feet high. Soon these increase to full-size waterfalls. Some of the best are on side streams pouring into Devil's Creek.

If you can reach it, the highlight of the trip is a 20-foot fall on Devil's Creek at about 1.5 miles from the trail camp. The 1.5 miles can take an hour or more, depending on how high the stream is running, and you'll probably get wet. But the waterfall is a stunner, a well-deserved reward for your hard work, dropping over beautiful light-colored granite. It forms a fine, clear pool, and if you're brave enough, you can wade into it. There are sunny areas around the falls where you can warm up after you get out.

This fall blocks any further travel downstream, so turn around and head back for the long uphill climb to the trailhead. Or better yet, spend the night at the trail camp, maybe invite a few Devil's Creek trout for dinner, then hike back out of the canyon early the next morning. Just remember: the 3.5 miles from the camp back up to the trailhead seems at least twice as long as the trip down.

Directions

From I-210 in La Cañada, take Highway 2/Angeles Crest Highway northeast for 25.5 miles to the Chilao Campground turnoff on the left, then continue past it for 0.75 mile to a parking lot on the left side of the highway. (It is 0.25 mile west of the Chilao Visitor Center turnoff.) The signed Devil's Canyon trailhead is located across the road.

Information and Contact

A national forest Adventure Pass is required. A map of Angeles National Forest is available for a fee from the National Forest Store (406/329-3024, www.nationalforeststore.com), or can be downloaded for free from www.fs.fed.us/r5/maps/. A detailed map of the Angeles High Country is available from Tom Harrison Maps, 415/456-7940, www.tomharrisonmaps.com. For more information, contact Angeles National Forest, Los Angeles River Ranger District, 818/899-1900, www.fs.fed.us/r5/angeles.

14 COOPER CANYON FALLS
Angeles National Forest

Level: Moderate   **Distance:** 4.0 miles round-trip
Best Season: April-June   **Elevation Change:** Total loss 850 feet

Once the snow is gone, most people don't think there's much reason to drive 34 miles to the summit of Mount Waterman. But then again, they probably don't know about Cooper Canyon Falls. The best thing about the waterfall, besides the fact that it's set in a gorgeous 6,000-foot-elevation forest, is that it's just far enough away so that it doesn't get heavily visited. To see it, you have to drive a long way and then you have to hike a couple miles.

Start off from Buckhorn Campground, an hour's drive from La Cañada, at the trailhead for the Burkhardt Trail. Although some campers make use of the swimming holes and small waterfalls in Buckhorn Creek within a few hundred yards of the campground, most of them don't hike the full distance to Cooper Canyon. You'll soon be on your own, wandering through a dense forest of big firs, cedars, and pines. There is almost no undergrowth in these woods, only conifers and big rocks. It feels as if you might be in the southern Sierra Nevada, but no, this is the San Gabriels.

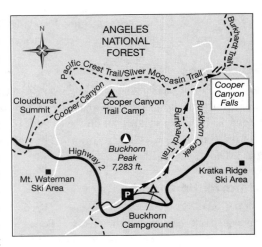

The Burkhardt Trail laterals along the canyon slopes, high above Buckhorn Creek. Just when it seems like you're keeping too high above the stream to be able to see a waterfall, the route makes a left turn into another canyon (Cooper), and traces a long switchback downhill. Look for a group of five young cedar trees, an unusual set of quintuplets, growing together near a tiny stream crossing.

At 1.75 miles from the campground, you'll reach a junction with the Pacific Crest Trail and Silver Moccasin Trail. A sign points left to Cooper Canyon Camp, but you want to head right toward Burkhardt Saddle and Eagle's Roost. It's only

Cooper Canyon Falls

100 yards to the waterfall, which drops just below the trail's edge.

From the top, Cooper Canyon Falls doesn't look like much, but continue another 30 yards to a cutoff trail that leads steeply to the waterfall's base. A rope near the bottom helps you get down (and up) the last few feet. Once you climb down, you can stand in the middle of the stream, on an island of large boulders, for a perfect view. The fall spills into a steep rock bowl with a big pool at its base, which would be perfect for swimming if it wasn't so cold and shady here. The wide main section of the waterfall's drop is 35 feet tall, but there's also a 15-foot cascade above it.

On your return hike, you may want to pay a visit to the small falls that are just 10–15 minutes' walk from Buckhorn

Campground. As you head back on the Burkhardt Trail, look for a huge rock formation across the canyon, 0.5 mile before you reach the camp. Two sets of pools and 10-foot-high falls are found along the stream between the rock outcrop and the camp, accessible via short but steep spur trails. They make great swimming holes in summer.

Directions
From I-210 in La Cañada, take Highway 2 north and drive 35 miles to Buckhorn Camp on the left. (It's 1.5 miles past the Mount Waterman ski lift, just beyond Cloudburst Summit.) The Burkhardt Trail starts at the hiker's parking lot at the far end of the camp, near the restrooms.

Information and Contact
A national forest Adventure Pass is required. A map of Angeles National Forest is available for a fee from the National Forest Store (406/329-3024, www.nationalforeststore.com), or can be downloaded for free from www.fs.fed.us/r5/maps/. A detailed map of the Angeles High Country is available from Tom Harrison Maps, 415/456-7940, www.tomharrisonmaps.com. For more information, contact Angeles National Forest, Los Angeles River Ranger District, 818/899-1900, www.fs.fed.us/r5/angeles.

15 MILLARD FALLS   BEST (
Angeles National Forest
🚶 🐕 ⛰

Level: Easy   **Distance:** 1.0 mile round-trip
Best Season: December–June   **Elevation Change:** Total gain 200 feet

If you want to guarantee your kids a good time, take them to Millard Campground for the short hike and scramble to Millard Falls. If it's winter or spring, make sure they're outfitted with shoes that can get wet, because the trail follows the creekbed and is often immersed in the water. This trip makes a perfect family adventure that is short enough even for little ones to accomplish, but with scenery to impress hikers of any age.

The only minus to a hike in Millard Canyon is the abundance of carvings found on the smooth-barked alder trees. The carvings desecrate almost every tree as high up as human hands can reach. Use this as an opportunity to teach your children never, ever to carve into the trunks of trees. Many people don't realize that over time, this kills the tree. Spread the word.

Start walking at the far edge of the campground, just beyond the camp host's site, where the trail leads to the right past a couple of cabins. After the first few yards, when the stream flow is high, the trail disappears into the creek. Just keep heading upstream, rock-hopping as you go.

Millard Falls

The canyon gets progressively narrower as you travel; finally its walls come together at 60-foot-high Millard Falls. The fall drops over a rugged cliff face; its stream splits in two at the top, forced to detour around two boulders that are stuck in the waterfall's notch. (Those boulders won't last forever; another earthquake or two and Millard Falls will have a whole new look.) The two streams rejoin about two-thirds of the way down, creating a tremendous rush of water in springtime. Pull up a rock, have a seat, and enjoy the spectacle.

If you'd like to see Millard Falls from above, drive your car back up the camp road to the top of Sunset Ridge. Park along the road, and walk eastward on the gated, paved Sunset Ridge Fire Road for 0.2 mile to the left turnoff for Sunset Ridge Trail. Hike about a mile on Sunset Ridge Trail and you'll pass just above the waterfall.

From this same fire road, you can often see another, larger waterfall in Millard Canyon, known to some as Saucer Branch Falls or the Punchbowl. This 75-foot waterfall is located a half-mile upstream from Millard Canyon Falls, but getting to it is much more difficult. From Millard Canyon Falls, you must hike downstream about 100 yards, then follow a narrow path that heads steeply uphill on the south bank of the creek, eventually leading you to the brink of Millard Canyon Falls and the stream above it. Follow the creek upstream, boulder-hopping much of the way, for about 300 yards until the creek forks. The stream coming in from the north is Saucer Branch, and about 100 yards up that stream is the multitiered waterfall known as Saucer Branch Falls. Getting there requires crossing Millard Creek, then crossing Saucer Branch, and this won't be possible if the water is flowing high. But if you manage to get to the base of Saucer Branch Falls, you will be well-rewarded. It's a glorious sight to behold, and much less visited than Millard Canyon Falls.

Directions

From I-210 in Pasadena, exit on Lake Avenue and drive north for 3.5 miles to Loma Alta Drive. Turn west (left) on Loma Alta Drive and drive one mile to Chaney Trail at the flashing yellow light. Turn right and drive 1.5 miles on Chaney Trail, keeping left at the fork, to Millard Campground. Park in the parking lot, then follow the fire road on the right (as you drove in) that leads into the campground.

Information and Contact

A national forest Adventure Pass is required. A map of Angeles National Forest is available for a fee from the National Forest Store (406/329-3024, www.national-foreststore.com), or can be downloaded for free from www.fs.fed.us/r5/maps/. A detailed map of the Mount Wilson area is available from Tom Harrison Maps, 415/456-7940, www.tomharrisonmaps.com. For more information, contact Angeles National Forest, Los Angeles River Ranger District, 818/899-1900, www.fs.fed.us/r5/angeles.

16 EATON CANYON FALLS

Eaton Canyon Natural Area

Level: Easy

Best Season: December-June

Distance: 3.0 miles round-trip

Elevation Change: Total gain 350 feet

How hard this hike is depends entirely on when you go. In the summer, when Eaton Canyon's stream level subsides, this trip is ridiculously easy. In late winter and spring, it can take well over an hour to hike the short 1.5 miles to the falls. You will certainly get your feet wet (and maybe other body parts too), given the umpteen rock-hops that must be accomplished as you crisscross back and forth across the stream. Although this is a great walk for families in the summer and fall months, it is too rugged for children when the water flows hard, with wet boulders to scramble over and deep, cold stream crossings.

© ANN MARIE BROWN

Eaton Canyon Falls

Keep in mind that Eaton Canyon is much more like a desert wash than many other L.A. streams. The predominant foliage is of the xeric variety—chaparral, willows, and low-growing oaks, plus a few chollas and cacti thrown in to keep you on your toes. Wear your sun hat, even in winter, and don't expect to find much shade.

Start hiking at the yellow metal gate at the far end of the parking lot. The trail drops down to the wide wash and travels about 70 yards to a place where you can comfortably cross the stream. On the far side, pick up the wide, level trail and head upstream (left). Some hikers choose not to cross here but instead follow one of several informal paths on the west side of the stream. Sooner or later, though, everyone is forced to cross.

At one mile out, just before the crumbling remains of a white bridge over the wash, the trail splits. A sign points upstream (toward the bridge) to Eaton Canyon Falls; another trail leads right and uphill. Stay low along the stream and continue up the wash, now on a considerably more rugged trail. The wide, straight wash you've been following becomes more channeled, more curvaceous, more wild. You'll see several old check dams and evidence of an aqueduct system—this canyon's water was once tamed for irrigating ranchlands. As the stream's curves get tighter, the canyon walls start to pinch in.

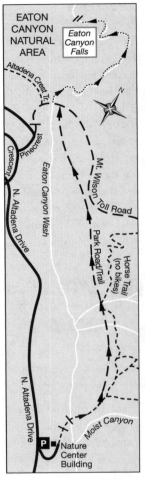

Soon you're in the stream more often than on the trail, crossing it several times as you work your way upcanyon. The route is different each time you hike it, depending on how much water is flowing. Finally, a half mile from the bridge, the canyon makes a sharp left turn, and suddenly you're facing the waterfall.

After a series of good rains, its force and power will surprise you. Eaton Canyon Falls pours over a rock wall that has eroded into a low, jagged V-shape. A large rounded boulder lies perched in its notch. The falls are about 40 feet high, with exceptional flow in springtime. This special spot has been marred by graffiti in the past, but park officials have worked diligently to keep the canyon's rocks and cliffs free of these ugly markings. The great naturalist John Muir, who visited

Eaton Falls in 1877, would surely roll over in his grave at the idea of anyone defiling this spot. Still, on a winter or early spring day, when the water flows with exuberance, nothing could spoil the magnificence of this waterfall.

Directions

From eastbound I-210 in Pasadena, exit at Altadena Drive/Sierra Madre Boulevard and go north for 1.6 miles. Turn right into Eaton Canyon Natural Area.

From westbound I-210 in Pasadena, exit at Sierra Madre Boulevard/San Marino, which turns into Maple Street. Cross Sierra Madre Boulevard and turn right at Altadena Drive. Drive 1.6 miles and turn right into Eaton Canyon Natural Area.

Information and Contact

There is no fee. A park map is available by free download at www.ecna.org, or at the park nature center. A detailed map of the Angeles Front Country is available from Tom Harrison Maps, 415/456-7940, www.tomharrisonmaps.com. For more information, contact Eaton Canyon Natural Area, 626/398-5420, www.ecna.org.

17 STURTEVANT FALLS   BEST (
Angeles National Forest

Level: Easy   **Distance:** 3.2 miles round-trip
Best Season: December–June   **Elevation Change:** Total loss/gain 600 feet

Sturtevant Falls is the crown jewel of Big Santa Anita Canyon, a lushly forested, almost magical gulch just a handful of miles from the Pasadena Freeway. Day hikers in the canyon can't help but covet its small summer cabins, set in the same beautiful ravine where Sturtevant Falls drops. The best kind of life I can imagine in Los Angeles would be to set up house in one of those cabins and take a daily stroll to the waterfall.

The hike is understandably popular. You leave your car at Chantry Flat and hike downhill into the canyon, following the Gabrielino Trail for an easy 3.2-mile round-trip. Since this is a National Recreation Trail, it's open to bikes, horses, and dogs (up to the waterfall cutoff), and you may see a number of each on any spring weekend. In fact, when the falls are flowing strong, get here early if you hope to get a parking spot.

One note of caution: the narrow, winding road that leads to the Chantry Flat trailhead has a long history of washouts and closures. If you are making a long drive to this area, particularly after a series of winter storms, always phone ahead to the Los Angeles River Ranger District (818/899-1900) to make sure the road is open and the trailhead parking area is accessible.

The first 0.6 mile follows a paved road, but once you reach the canyon bottom you cross Roberts Footbridge over Winter Creek, then head right on a wide dirt path, hiking upstream to Sturtevant Falls. (Don't take the left turnoff for Winter Creek Trail.) A sign near the footbridge details the period from 1912–1936 when the confluence of Winter and Big Santa Anita Creeks was the home of Roberts Camp, a popular weekend resort. A stone lodge, dining area, and numerous cabins and tents once stood here—enough buildings to accommodate 180 guests at a time. Some of those old cabins are still standing today.

Gabrielino Trail meanders under the shade of oaks and alders along Big Santa Anita Creek. The stream is tamed somewhat by a series of small check dams, forming oddly pretty artificial waterfalls and glassy pools. At a junction at 1.3 miles, Gabrielino Trail forks left and heads uphill, but you continue straight along the creek for another 0.3 mile to Sturtevant Falls. You cross the creek, the canyon bends to the left, then you cross again. Sturtevant Falls suddenly reveals itself, dropping 60 feet over a granite cliff into a perfectly shaped rock bowl.

Like the Grace Kelly of waterfalls, Sturtevant is an elegant act. Set in the back of this shady canyon, it's gracefully framed by alders and has a large pool at its base. When the water level drops, a pebbly beachlike area around the pool is exposed, where you can sit and compose a few love sonnets or spread out a picnic. If you stand on the right side of the falls, you can see its flow making an S-turn down a chute above the main drop, adding another 15 feet to the falls' total height.

If you want to linger a little longer in Big Santa Anita Canyon after visiting

Sturtevant Falls, you can backtrack to the junction where the Gabrielino Trail heads uphill, then follow it out and back to Cascade picnic area, a shady spot alongside the creek. This will add 2.5 greenery-filled miles to your round-trip.

Directions

From I-210 in Pasadena, drive seven miles east to Arcadia. Exit on Santa Anita Avenue and drive six miles north to the road's end at Chantry Flat. The trail begins across the road from the first parking area as you drive in. (The Chantry Flat Road sometimes closes after severe storms; phone the Los Angeles River Ranger District for an update.)

Sturtevant Falls

Information and Contact

A national forest Adventure Pass is required. A map of Angeles National Forest is available for a fee from the National Forest Store (406/329-3024, www.nationalforeststore.com), or can be downloaded for free from www.fs.fed.us/r5/maps/. A detailed map of the Mount Wilson area is available from Tom Harrison Maps, 415/456-7940, www.tomharrisonmaps.com. For more information, contact Angeles National Forest, Los Angeles River Ranger District, 818/899-1900, www.fs.fed.us/r5/angeles.

18 HERMIT FALLS
Angeles National Forest

Level: Easy

Best Season: December-June

Distance: 3.0 miles round-trip

Elevation Change: Total loss 700 feet

Sturtevant Falls (see listing in this chapter) is the undisputed queen of the waterfalls in Big Santa Anita Canyon, but don't let that dissuade you from making the trip to see nearby Hermit Falls as well. Although your vision of Hermit Falls is hampered by the fact that the trail leads you to its lip rather than its base, you'll be so pleased with the excursion that an impeded view won't matter much.

The trail to Hermit Falls begins on the paved Gabrielino National Recreation Trail, the same route as the trip to Sturtevant Falls. To get to Hermit Falls, however, you must turn off the Gabrielino Trail and onto the First Water Trail, less than 0.25 mile from the parking lot. Don't miss this junction and the right turn on to a narrow, single-track path. This is the forté of the Hermit Falls trip—you get off the pavement, away from the crowds, and on to a lovely single-track dirt trail that switchbacks gently down into Big Santa Anita Canyon, then heads southward along the North Fork of Santa Anita Creek. When you reach the canyon bottom, follow the Horse Trail signs, which point to the right or downstream.

As on the trip to Sturtevant Falls, you'll pass many artificial waterfalls made by small dams on Santa Anita Creek, and dozens of adorable cabins remaining from the area's colorful past as a vacation resort. And just like the trip to Sturtevant, this trail crosses the creek a couple of times. These crossings are easy in summer but can be difficult or even impossible earlier in the year, like when it's pouring rain, you're tired and hungry, and your rain gear has long since given out. (Guess how I know?)

Descend some more as you head downstream through a riparian forest so lush it seems to contain every imaginable type of foliage. In addition to the tall oaks and alders, the ground is covered with huge chain ferns, slender sword ferns, tiny maidenhair ferns, and half a dozen other fern varieties. The constant shade of the narrow canyon, combined with the presence of the year-round stream, makes it possible for every inch of ground to spring forth plant life. Since you're on single-track, the greenery is close enough to touch, and in the morning, dew on the leaves will glance off your skin.

Where your trail meets up with a short spur trail to the top of Hermit Falls (near the metal cylinder of an old gauging station), follow the spur. You can just barely glimpse the top of the falls as it drops over a rounded ledge, then free falls about 25 feet. The stream shoots out from a notch as if from a fire hose, then gets wrested downward by gravity. If you wish, you can very carefully scramble down to the bottom of the falls. Use your hands to help you, and don't try it if the boulders are wet from recent rain. Hermit Falls has an immense pool at its base, which will surely tempt would-be swimmers.

One more note about Hermit Falls: During the wet season (winter or spring) when waterfall lovers are apt to visit, Hermit Falls can seem like an isolated, sylvan sanctuary. But in the summer, this spot turns into a major urban swimming hole, complete with folks cliff-diving, drinking, littering, and—even more unfortunate—"tagging" the rocks with graffiti. Try to pay a visit before the weather is warm enough for swimming. Plus, in cool weather the return trip, which is all uphill, is much more pleasant.

Directions
From I-210 in Pasadena, drive seven miles east to Arcadia. Exit on Santa Anita Avenue and drive six miles north to road's end at Chantry Flat. The trail begins across the road from the first parking area as you drive in. (The Chantry Flat Road sometimes closes after severe storms; phone the Los Angeles River Ranger District for an update.)

Information and Contact
A national forest Adventure Pass is required. A map of Angeles National Forest is available for a fee from the National Forest Store (406/329-3024, www.national-foreststore.com), or can be downloaded for free from www.fs.fed.us/r5/maps/. A detailed map of the Mount Wilson area is available from Tom Harrison Maps, 415/456-7940, www.tomharrisonmaps.com. For more information, contact Angeles National Forest, Los Angeles River Ranger District, 818/899-1900, www.fs.fed.us/r5/angeles.

1 9 MONROVIA CANYON FALLS   BEST (
Monrovia Canyon Park

Level: Easy   **Distance:** 1.4 miles round-trip

Best Season: December-June   **Elevation Change:** Total gain 100 feet

Everything about Monrovia Canyon Falls is a great experience, except if you try to visit it on a Tuesday. That's when the local police have target practice in Monrovia Canyon Park, and they lock the gates and close the whole place down for the day. It's a bummer for waterfall-lovers. Of course, it's better to be safe than be a target.

Time your trip for any day but Tuesday, and get ready for a perfect walk in the woods. The park's Falls Trail is an ideal hike for youngsters because it's nearly level the whole way and less than a mile in length. Start at the picnic area near the park nature center and museum, located at the far end of the park road. Walk through the picnic area and look for the signed single-track trail to Monrovia Canyon Falls. At the first junction, head to the right.

Almost immediately, you pass several check dams, which make small artificial waterfalls of their own. The canyon is lush and shaded, like a smaller version of nearby Big Santa Anita Canyon, crowded with alders, oaks, and ferns. It's the kind of place that would be unforgettable in a light rain.

In less than 30 minutes of gentle climbing, you're at the 40-foot-high falls, which are split in the middle by a granite ledge and framed by oaks and bay trees. Monrovia Canyon Falls is fed by a perennial spring, not just by snow-melt and rainfall, so the waterfall flows year-round. Sun-warmed rocks in front of the cataract make perfect seats for gazing in admiration.

Monrovia Canyon Falls

If you wish to take a longer hike to reach the falls, you can start at the trail-head by the park entrance kiosk. Following the Bill Cull Trail from there, the round-trip to the waterfall is 3.4 miles with a 700-foot elevation change.

Because access is so easy, Monrovia Canyon Falls is a popular place. For the best experience, visit on a weekday (but not Tuesday). Or for a little nature education, show up on Saturday morning, when the park offers free docent-led hikes.

Directions

From I-210 in Monrovia, take the Myrtle Avenue exit and drive north for one mile. Turn right on Foothill Boulevard and drive 0.2 mile to Canyon Boulevard. Turn left and drive 1.6 miles to the park (bear right where the road forks). Park at the far end of the park road, near the picnic area and nature center.

Special note: the entire park is closed on Tuesdays.

Information and Contact

A $5 day-use fee is charged per vehicle. A park map is available by free download at www.cityofmonrovia.org or at the park nature center or entrance station. For more information, contact Monrovia Canyon Park, 626/256-8282, www.cityof-monrovia.org.

20 SOLDIER CREEK FALLS
Angeles National Forest

Level: Easy

Best Season: December–June

Distance: 1.25 miles round-trip

Elevation Change: Total gain 300 feet

Crystal Creek Recreation Area, in the mountains above Azusa, burned in the wildfires of 2002 and has been closed since then, mainly due to severe erosion problems on the access road, Highway 39. Scheduled to reopen in summer 2011 (before attempting to visit, call the San Gabriel River Ranger District at 626/335-1251), this area will be a great place to witness firsthand the processes of fire ecology and see how this landscape heals and regrows after a major burn.

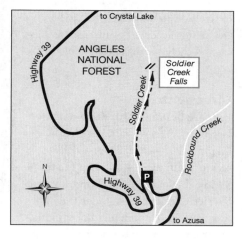

The Crystal Lake Recreation Area has always had a lot to offer, including its alluring 6,000-foot elevation, dense cedar and pine forests, and clean, fresh air. Although it will be some time before these forests return to their previous splendor, it will be fascinating to watch the process take place. Meanwhile, if Highway 39 does open in 2011, you'll want to pay a visit to Soldier Creek Falls (also known as Lewis Falls), which is located just before the entrance gate to Crystal Creek Recreation Area. Although the forested area surrounding the falls was partially burned, it was by no means obliterated, and the waterfall still flows, especially after snowmelt.

Begin by hiking from the parking pullout on Highway 39 at Soldier Creek, walking with the stream on your left. (There's a route on the other side of the creek as well, but it is much rougher and eventually you'll have to cross over.) The start of the trail has some graffiti and often some litter (mutter a few curses at the perpetrators), but as you head back from the road, conditions will improve.

Pass a few cabins and hike upstream under the shade of oaks and firs. When the trail vanishes, start walking up the streambed, rock-hopping over small boulders and climbing over big ones. Your scramble can last anywhere between 200 and 500 yards, depending on how high the water level is and how much of the trail is submerged. Just keep going until you can't go any farther, where the canyon walls close in. There, in a rocky grotto, Soldier Creek Falls pours in from the left. The waterfall holds court in this narrow space, surrounded by big trees and many verdant ferns and mosses. Just to remind you that you're still in Southern California, desert plants, such as yuccas and chollas, cling to the sunnier cliffs above the fall.

Soldier Creek Falls

Directions

From Azusa on I-210, drive north on Highway 39 for 18 miles to Coldbrook Camp on the left. From Coldbrook Camp, continue 2.4 miles up Highway 39 to a dirt pullout on the right, where Soldier Creek crosses under the highway. Park in the pullout and begin hiking from the far right side, heading up the right side of the creek.

Information and Contact

A national forest Adventure Pass is required. A map of Angeles National Forest is available for a fee from the National Forest Store (406/329-3024, www.nationalforeststore.com), or can be downloaded for free from www.fs.fed.us/r5/maps/. A detailed map of the Angeles High Country is available from Tom Harrison Maps, 415/456-7940, www.tomharrisonmaps.com. For more information, contact Angeles National Forest, San Gabriel River Ranger District, 626/335-1251, www.fs.fed.us/r5/angeles.

21 FISH CANYON FALLS
Angeles National Forest

Level: Easy/Strenuous   **Distance:** 3.2-9.4 miles round-trip

Best Season: January-May   **Elevation Change:** Total gain 2,800 feet

Fish Canyon Falls

On most days of the year, if you want to see Fish Canyon Falls, you have to sign up for a difficult hike. Sure, a trail leads all the way to the falls—no off-trail scrambling is required—but this trail has a grade that will leave you begging for mercy.

Public access to the trail to Fish Canyon Falls was closed for most of the 1980s and 1990s. Although the waterfall is on the lands of Angeles National Forest, the popular trail to reach it had been blocked off by the expansion plans of a private quarry, Azusa Rock Company. This caused a fair amount of outrage among local hikers, who for decades had been hiking to the falls via an easy five-mile round-trip trail. To quell the hoopla, Azusa Rock Company and the cities of Duarte and Azusa obtained a grant to build a three-mile-long bypass trail around the quarry. The trail opened in 1998, and Los Angeles–area hikers once again gained access to one of the most beautiful waterfalls in Angeles National Forest.

Except that it was only accessible to the hardiest of hikers. Utilizing the bypass trail, reaching Fish Canyon Falls requires a 9.4-mile commitment with a 2,800-foot elevation gain. Not only that, the trail is poorly constructed, so it is steep, loose, too narrow, riddled with poison oak, and doesn't have nearly enough switchbacks. Oh yes, and it offers unattractive views of the aforementioned quarry. Yikes.

But there is one way to get around the hard work, and that is to plan ahead for the special days of the year when Azusa Rock Company (aka Vulcan Materials) has "open access" days. On these days, the public can ride a shuttle bus through the quarry property to access a much shorter, easier trail to Fish Canyon and its falls (3.2 miles round-trip and with much less ascent). Set yourself up for an easier trip by checking the calendar at www.azusarock.com. Gates open at 7 A.M. and free shuttles run throughout the morning to the trailhead, with the last trip up at 12 P.M. Once the shuttle drops you off at the back of the quarry, you cross a bridge over Fish Creek and are very shortly walking in lovely Fish Canyon.

If you decide to take the longer trail, you can visit on any day you wish. Bring your hiking poles and wear your best-gripping boots. They aren't luxury items on this trail; they are necessities. Also, pick up the Fish Canyon Trail Guide from the signboard near the trail's start; its map will be useful to you as you trudge up (and down) this merciless trail. Start hiking early in the morning. You will ascend south-facing slopes for the first couple miles, so unless it is a gray day, the sun will bake you.

The bypass trail begins at a parking lot just outside the quarry entrance, then climbs steeply up to Van Tassel Ridge via the canyon's west wall. The first part of the ascent doesn't seem too bad, but it quickly gets worse. Spring visitors have the good fortune of passing a spectacular display of wildflowers (lupine, campanula, poppy, larkspur, brodiaea) on this sunny canyon wall, but that is its only redeeming feature. When you stop to catch your breath, you'll see ugly views of the concrete-channeled San Gabriel River Basin below and various industrial enterprises, plus hear the annoying pow-pow-pow from the San Gabriel Valley Gun Club. Boy, this is some fun.

At the ridge top, 1.4 heart-pumping miles later, you join a dirt road and continue the unpleasant ascent for another half-mile. There is a short breather as the trail mellows a bit along the quarry's fence line. Then the trail drops abruptly down the other side of the ridge, losing 1,000 feet in one mile. Thankfully, there are plenty of switchbacks, as well as a bumper crop of poison oak. This brutal up and down on Van Tassel Ridge must be accomplished in both directions of your hike—out and back—and is responsible for almost all of the trail's 2,800-foot elevation gain.

At 3.2 miles from the start, the trail finally joins the old, pleasant Fish Canyon Trail in the canyon bottom (this is where those who have ridden the shuttle through the quarry join the hardcores who hiked the bypass). Your world is suddenly transformed, and your legs won't believe the contrast. This sylvan path meanders gently uphill, sticking closely to Fish Creek, for 1.5 miles. Stone foundations, walkways, and walls of old cabin sites from the early 1900s can be seen, including one belonging to a family made famous by having the only two-seater outhouse. The cabins were destroyed in a fire and flood in the late 1950s, but at one time during the "Great Hiking Era" of the early 1900s, Fish Canyon was one of the premier outdoor recreation destinations in the San Gabriel Valley. More than 50 cabins lined the canyon, along with a dance hall where residents spent their summer evenings.

But it's the greenery that impresses most. The canyon is blessed with an abundance of leafy trees: big-leaf maples, California bays, alders, and live oaks line the streambanks, and nonnative ivy and vinca have covered the ground near the cabin sites. This is one of the most charming canyons in all of the San Gabriel Mountains.

Less then 0.5 mile before you reach the waterfall you'll cross over Fish Creek, then shortly find yourself in a high box canyon, where the waterfall drops. Even at low water, it is an impressive sight: Fish Canyon Falls drops 90 feet in three stairstepped tiers, finally sliding its way into a large and clear pool.

Directions

From I-210 in Duarte, take the Mount Olive Drive exit (one exit east of I-605), drive 0.25 mile and turn right (east) on Huntington Drive. Drive 0.6 mile and turn left on Encanto Parkway. Drive 1.4 miles to the parking area just before the quarry entrance, on your left.

Alternatively, from the I-605 and I-210 split, take I-605 north to its end, then turn right on Huntington Drive and follow it to Encanto Parkway, as above.

Information and Contact

There is no fee. A Fish Canyon Trail Guide, with a topo map, is available from the city of Duarte (and is usually available at a signboard near the trail's start). For more information, contact City of Duarte Parks and Recreation Department, 626/357-7931, www.accessduarte.com.

To find out when the free shuttle bus is available through the quarry, turning this difficult hike into a very easy one, check the Fish Canyon public access calendar at www.azusarock.com.

22 SAN ANTONIO FALLS   BEST (
Angeles National Forest

Level: Easy

Distance: 1.5 miles round-trip

Best Season: March–July

Elevation Change: Total gain 250 feet

When I was a college student in Claremont, wintertime was eagerly awaited, when the Inland Empire air would clear and the first snows would frost the rounded top of 10,064-foot Mount Baldy. From our dormitory rooms in the valley, we could look out our windows and see the wondrous sight of a nearby snowcapped peak—on days when it was 70 degrees and balmy on campus.

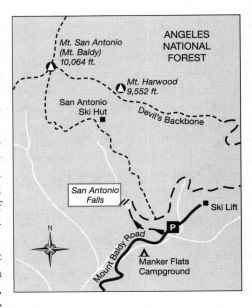

Now I look forward to the cold season on Mount Baldy for another reason: winter snows lead to springtime snowmelt, and that makes an impressive show of water on 80-foot-high San Antonio Falls.

The waterfall's season is short because it has a small drainage area and is fed primarily by snowmelt, so you must time your trip for the first warm days after winter, sometimes as early as March. The hike to the falls follows the Mount Baldy ski lift maintenance road, which is paved and has only a slight uphill grade. If the crews are working on the ski lift, you may share the road with a vehicle or two, but this is a rare occurrence.

At 0.7 mile, you round a sharp curve and see and hear the waterfall. It drops in three tiers; the first is a large free-fall drop and the others are curved cascades over steep granite and talus slopes. If you wish, you can scramble down to its base on a well-worn route. Be careful on the loose gravel, however. A large landslide to the left of the waterfall testifies to the instability of the slope. In a good snow year, white snow patches will frame the waterfall as late as April. The peak of Mount Baldy, high above the falls, can be covered with snow until Memorial Day.

The waterfall's name is derived from its home on the slopes of Mount Baldy, which is really called Mount San Antonio. Few people call the mountain by its formal name; many who live in its shadow aren't even familiar with it. The mountain was named for Saint Anthony of Padua, a Franciscan priest and miracle worker. But the peak's rounded, exposed summit looks more like a baldy than a saint.

You may see other people on the waterfall trail heading up the road carrying ropes and ice axes. They are heading for Baldy's summit, and if there is much snow, they need special equipment to get there. After San Antonio Falls, the maintenance road switchbacks to the right, and most summit hikers follow it to a trail junction at Baldy Notch. From there, they head left to the top of the ski

© ANN MARIE BROWN

San Antonio Falls

lift, then hike along the rather treacherous Devil's Backbone to the south side of Mount Harwood at 9,552 feet and finally to the peak of Mount Baldy at 10,064 feet, a total of six trail miles from San Antonio Falls.

If you opt to make the short return trip to the parking lot instead, check out the great views of the San Gabriel basin far below. On clear days, the hike back to your car is nearly as good as the falls.

Directions

From I-210 in Upland, take the Mountain Avenue/Mount Baldy exit and drive north for 4.3 miles (Mountain Avenue becomes Shinn Road). At a T-junction with Mount Baldy Road, turn right and drive 9 miles to San Antonio Falls Road on the left, 0.3 mile past Manker Flats Campround. Park in the dirt pullouts by San Antonio Falls Road and begin walking on the gated, paved road.

Information and Contact

A national forest Adventure Pass is required. A map of Angeles National Forest is available for a fee from the National Forest Store (406/329-3024, www.nationalforeststore.com), or can be downloaded for free from www.fs.fed.us/r5/maps/. A detailed map of Mount Baldy is available from Tom Harrison Maps, 415/456-7940, www.tomharrisonmaps.com. For more information, contact Angeles National Forest, San Gabriel River Ranger District, 626/335-1251, www.fs.fed.us/r5/angeles.

23 ETIWANDA FALLS
North Etiwanda Preserve

Level: Easy

Best Season: January-May

Distance: 3.0 miles round-trip

Elevation Change: 750 feet

There's a waterfall in Rancho Cucamonga? Why, as a matter of fact, there is. Way out here in the inner Inland Empire, where it is more often hot and dry than wet and watery, lies beautiful Etiwanda Falls, the prize of North Etiwanda Preserve.

The preserve was established in 1998 as mitigation for an improvement project on Highways 30 and 210. Several endangered, threatened, and sensitive species make their home here, including the coastal California gnatcatcher, Southwestern willow flycatcher, least Bell's vireo, San Bernardino kangaroo rat, rufous-crowned sparrow, and San Diego horned lizard. The preserve has all these creatures and a waterfall, too (although technically the waterfall lies outside of the preserve boundary in East Etiwanda Canyon).

Sadly, from 1998, when the preserve was established, until 2008, the land was managed (or more accurately, ignored) by San

Etiwanda Falls

Bernardino County and it became a place for ingrates to shoot off guns and deposit their trash. But in 2008, all that changed when a $1.6 million trails enhancement project went into effect. Now there are benches, restrooms, and interpretive displays along the preserve's four miles of fire roads.

From the preserve trailhead, getting to the falls is easy. Simply hike north, following the main fire road and enjoying fine views of the high peaks above Rancho Cucamonga. At 0.3 mile from the start, you'll reach a fork with a sign pointing right for the picnic area and left for the trail. Don't go left or right; instead, continue straight ahead, hiking around a large metal gate and staying on the fire road. From here it is another 1.2 miles to the falls, heading gently and moderately uphill on the rocky fire road the whole way. Ignore all the side roads and just keep going straight and uphill. In the last 0.5-mile, you'll hike past a second metal gate, this one painted bright yellow.

In teh wet season, there is no mistaking the roar of the 40-foot cascade when you approach it. The falls drop over bright orange–colored rocks in a glorious rush of noisy whitewater. The waterfall has three tiers: the first two are about 10-feet high, with the lower tier the tallest at about 20 feet. Except during very low water in the dry season, it's difficult to get to a spot where you can get a full view of all three tiers. But this is a beautiful and impressive waterfall regardless.

Geocachers have taken to this park, too. Apparently there are more than a half-dozen caches buried in North Etiwanda Preserve, including one or two near the waterfall.

Directions

From the junction of I-210 and I-15, take I-15 south and exit at Baseline Road. Drive 0.5 mile west on Baseline Road, then turn right (north) on Etiwanda Avenue. Drive 2.2 miles north on Etiwanda Avenue to its junction with Wilson Avenue. Bear left (west) on Wilson Avenue for about 100 yards to where it reconnects with Etiwanda Avenue, then turn right and continue on Etiwanda for one more mile until it dead-ends at the parking lot of North Etiwanda Preserve.

Information and Contact

For more information and/or to download a free trail map, contact the San Bernardino County Special Districts Department, 909/387-5940, www.specialdistricts.org/2/nep.

24 BONITA FALLS
San Bernardino National Forest

Level: Moderate

Best Season: December–May

Distance: 1.0 mile round-trip

Elevation Change: 3,200 feet

The San Bernardino National Forest's newspaper proclaimed in large, bold type: "Bonita Falls, a 90-foot waterfall, is visible from Lytle Creek Road in the South Fork area." That intriguing claim was enough to send me heading up I-15 in search of Bonita Falls. I followed the directions exactly, drove up and down Lytle Creek Road about 20 times, stopped at several likely spots and looked around. No waterfall. A visit to the Lytle Creek Ranger Station solved the mystery: there's only one good spot to get a look at Bonita Falls, and it's on South Fork Road, not Lytle Creek Road, directly behind the Bonita Ranch Trailer Park.

The trailer park is on private property, and nonpaying customers may not enter. You have to stop your car before South Fork Road enters the trailer park, but from this vantage point you can look up and plainly see Bonita Falls about halfway up the mountainside. Binoculars will greatly improve your view. From South Fork Road, the waterfall appears as only a white sliver, but its height is obvious and impressive. You can't tell from here, but this is only the top tier of three-tiered Bonita Falls.

If you want to get closer to the falls, you have to be willing to get your feet wet, and you have to be very careful not to stray onto private land. Start from the dirt pullout on Lytle Creek Road (a short distance before its junction with South Fork Road). Look for a safe place to ford the Middle Fork of Lytle Creek. This may not be possible after a period of heavy rain; use good judgment before you cross. With this accomplished, you'll need to cross the South Fork of Lytle Creek next, but this is a much easier feat. Once on the far side of the South Fork, head upstream for about 300 yards, picking your way among the myriad rocks. Keep your eyes peeled for a side stream that will appear on your left. A good trail ("good" being a relative term; the trail is "good" compared to the surface of the rocky wash you've been traveling in) follows that stream about 100 yards to Lower Bonita Falls, which is located in a side canyon that is a tributary to the South Fork.

lower Bonita Falls

This lower tier of Bonita Falls is the 90-foot waterfall the Forest Service boasts about (although it's not the tier that is viewed from the road). At full water, the fall is worthy of bragging rights, but if it hasn't rained in a while, Bonita Falls can be a disappointment. The cataract drops over a fern-covered, near-vertical cliff face, forming what looks like an impasse to further travel in the canyon. For hikers, it is indeed an impasse, but for rock climbers with the proper equipment, this cliff is the route to the upper two tiers of Bonita Falls. The combined height of the falls is reportedly in the neighborhood of 300 feet, but it isn't worth risking your life to find out. This adventure requires about five rappels, plus a one-way shuttle hike beginning at a different trailhead than the one mentioned here. No need to bother with the extremity of this effort: the lower tier is reward enough for your adventure in Lytle Creek.

Directions

From Ontario, drive east on I-10 for seven miles to I-15. Drive north on I-15 for 11 miles and take the Sierra Avenue/Lytle Creek Road exit, then turn left (north) at the stop sign. Drive 6.2 miles (the road becomes Lytle Creek Road). Turn left on South Fork Road and drive to where it intersects with Melody Lane on the right. This is the best spot to view the falls from your car. To hike to the falls' base, park your car in the dirt pullout on Lytle Creek Road, located about 100 yards before its junction with South Fork Road.

Information and Contact

A national forest Adventure Pass is required. A map of San Bernardino National Forest is available for a fee from the National Forest Store (406/329-3024, www.nationalforeststore.com), or can be downloaded for free from www.fs.fed.us/r5/maps/. For more information, contact San Bernardino National Forest, Lytle Creek Ranger Station, 909/382-2851, www.fs.fed.us/ r5/sanbernardino.

25 HEART ROCK FALLS
San Bernardino National Forest

Level: Easy

Distance: 2.0 miles round-trip

Best Season: January-June

Elevation Change: Total loss 250 feet

Heart Rock Falls will steal your heart. The waterfall, which spills on Seeley Creek near Lake Silverwood, is distinguished not by its stream, but rather by the heart-shaped rock sculpture at its crest. This isn't a rock shaped like a heart, but a smooth granite boulder in which nature has carved a perfect heart-shaped bowl, about three feet deep and five feet wide. A 25-foot waterfall spills to the right of the heart, and when Seeley Creek's flow is high, the stream pours into the heart's crown, then flows out the bottom and free falls downward.

The striking thing is that the heart bowl is so perfectly shaped. Plenty of rock formations are named after figures or animals that they roughly resemble,

© ANN MARIE BROWN

Heart Rock Falls

but Heart Rock bears a deep imprint that could be the mold for Valentine candy boxes. With or without water sliding through it, it's unique.

The trail to reach the fall starts out ingloriously, but it gets better. The trailhead is opposite the buildings of Seeley Camp, a Los Angeles Parks and Recreation camp, where there is often a crowd. But once you get past the swimming pool, things quiet down. The forest is thick with cedars and Jeffrey pines, and the trail descends gently to the creek. In a short mile, you near the trail's end, and a right spur leads to granite stairsteps climbing to an overlook above the creek. Peer over the edge and you'll see the top of the waterfall and heart-stopping Heart Rock. This is one of very few waterfalls that is best seen from above—only from a high perspective can you get a full view of the heart and the falls.

Be sure to walk the last few yards of trail, which lead downstream of Heart Rock to a series of waterslides and pools below the falls.

Directions

From the junction of Highways 18 and 138 near Crestline and Lake Gregory, turn north on Highway 138 and drive 2.5 miles to the sign for Camp Seeley, just past the town of Valley of Enchantment. Turn left at the camp sign on Road 2N03, then take the left fork in the road (don't park in the camp parking lot). Cross the creek, which usually flows over the road, then look for the double-track trail on the right, near a sewer pipeline sign. Park alongside the road. (You will be directly across the creek from the main parking lot for Camp Seeley, near the playground area.)

Information and Contact

A national forest Adventure Pass is required. A map of San Bernardino National Forest is available for a fee from the National Forest Store (406/329-3024, www.nationalforeststore.com), or can be downloaded for free from www.fs.fed.us/r5/maps/. For more information, contact San Bernardino National Forest, Mountaintop Ranger District, 909/382-2790, www.fs.fed.us/r5/sanbernardino.

26 DEEP CREEK FALLS
San Bernardino National Forest

Level: Moderate

Best Season: April–July

Distance: 2.0 miles round-trip

Elevation Change: Total gain 200 feet

a Deep Creek cascade

Deep Creek has many personalities. It's a geologically active creek sporting hot springs and pools, where warm-water-lovers flock to bathe. It's a wild trout stream, filled with pockets of moss and algae, the start of a plentiful food chain for the fish. Technically, it's a branch of the Mojave River and eventually it disappears in desert sand. But best of all, it's a year-round creek with many waterfalls, accessible only to those willing to work a little.

First, there's the drive from Lake Arrowhead, mostly on dirt roads. I made it almost all the way to the trailhead in my rental car, but in the final 0.3 mile, the rutted road won and I walked. A ranger told me that sometimes the spot where Deep Creek crosses the road can be as deep as three feet; when I visited in late April, it was only a few inches, but the potholes were deep.

Second, this section of the Deep Creek Trail is vastly different from the downstream section, which is accessed via the well-graded Pacific Crest Trail (and it's where Aztec Falls is found). This upper stretch of creek does not have much of a trail at all, more of an anglers' route, and can be in various states of repair or disrepair depending on the creek's flow.

Whatever it takes, you should make the trip. The falls on Deep Creek are not tall, but they are unusually beautiful, dropping on a pristine stream amid granite, cottonwoods, and conifers. In spring, small trout can be seen in the clear green-yellow waters of Deep Creek. Every turn of the stream seems to be home to a water ouzel flitting among the cascades and pools.

When you reach the trailhead, start hiking upstream on the signed trail. Especially during the high water of spring, you'll be scrambling more than walking.

Take your time, making use of the many good handholds in the rock and admiring the canyon as you go. Big boulders seem to pop up at every turn of Deep Creek. Cottonwood leaves float down from the tree canopy and drift on the surface.

After about 30 minutes of scrambling, you'll get your first peek at Deep Creek's falls as the canyon narrows and the rocks get more massive. The waterfall looks small when you first see it, appearing as a narrow chute of water over big rocks— no big deal. But as you get closer, you start noticing more, and when you're right on top of the fall, you realize that the chute is only part of it. The main fall is a long cascade of ultra-clear water sliding down over granite. It's a 25-foot-long cascade, but with only about 10 feet of height. You can sit right alongside it on the smooth rock and watch the water go by. If you do, you'll be struck by the clarity of the water; it looks like liquid glass.

You may find a cable strung across the stream at this waterfall for people who choose to cross and continue upstream. More falls are above, but they are treacherous to reach when the water runs high. Use caution if you proceed. A better bet is to use the downstream pools as swimming holes; there are dozens of places to wade in and even some small sandy beaches to lie upon.

If swimming is your bag, you might want to pay a visit to another stretch of Deep Creek, where there is a popular swimming hole and waterfall named Aztec Falls (there's a blue and red Aztec Indian painted on one of the boulders). In summer, many people jump off the waterfall's cliffs; there are three obvious jumping platforms of differing heights—approximately 15 feet, 35 feet, and a terrifying 50 feet. These falls were featured in *National Geographic Adventure* magazine, much to the chagrin of the locals, who wanted to keep the place a secret. The easiest way to get to Aztec Falls is to drive to the Splinter's Cabin Trailhead for the Pacific Crest Trail (see *Directions*), then follow the PCT north for 0.5 mile to an obvious made-by-use path that scrambles down the slope to the creek. A crowd is often gathered here on summer weekends, so it's pretty hard to miss.

Directions

From the junction of Highways 18 and 138 near Crestline and Lake Gregory, drive east on Highway 18 for 10 miles to the left turnoff for Highway 173. Drive north on Highway 173 to Lake Arrowhead, then continue 1.5 miles to Hook Creek Road. Turn right on Hook Creek Road and follow it through some residential areas until it turns from pavement to dirt and becomes Road 2N26Y. Continue on Road 2N26Y for one mile, then bear right on Road 3N34. In 0.7 mile, you'll reach T-6 Crossing, where the road crosses Deep Creek. Park before the crossing and begin walking on the anglers' trail upstream.

To head to the Splinter's Cabin Trailhead for Aztec Falls, follow the directions as above to Hook Creek Road and Road 2N26Y, but bear left at the fork with Squint Ranch Road, then turn right almost immediately at the sign for Splinter's Cabin. Drive 0.5 mile to the road's end and the trailhead for the Pacific Crest Trail.

Information and Contact

A national forest Adventure Pass is required. A map of San Bernardino National Forest is available for a fee from the National Forest Store (406/329-3024, www.nationalforeststore.com), or can be downloaded for free from www.fs.fed.us/r5/maps/. For more information, contact San Bernardino National Forest, Mountaintop Ranger District, 909/382-2790, www.fs.fed.us/r5/sanbernardino.

27 MILL CREEK ROAD FALLS
San Bernardino National Forest

Level: Easy

Distance: 1.2 miles round-trip

Best Season: February-May

Elevation Change: Total loss 200 feet

I was staying at Angelus Oaks Lodge in a cute little cabin in San Bernardino National Forest, having a fine time on a research trip. When one of the owners casually mentioned that there was a waterfall about a mile away from the lodge, I couldn't believe my luck. Off I went to see Mill Creek Road Falls.

You can drive to it, but you might as well hike to it, because Mill Creek Road Falls drops along a dirt road that gets very little traffic. In fact, I nicknamed this waterfall "Closed Road Falls" because during my visit, they'd closed the road on both ends so the road grader could smooth out the potholes from winter storms. It turns out the road is usually closed all winter long, because CalTrans doesn't want to be bothered with plowing it. And of course, the best season to admire the waterfall is usually late winter and early spring, during the snowmelt period.

Mill Creek Road Falls is not a showstopper, just a pretty little 30-foot waterfall dropping down a rock face, framed by pines and oaks. If you're heading downhill on Mill Creek Road from Highway 38, you can drive by the waterfall and miss the whole thing, because it's over your right shoulder as you pass. If you're walking, or if you drive back in the other direction, you'll have no trouble finding it. There's a small clearing at the foot of the falls, so you can get off the road while you take a look.

Directions

From I-10 at Redlands, take the Highway 38 exit and drive northeast for 14 miles to the junction with Forest Home Road. Continue past this junction on Highway 38 for five more miles to Angelus Oaks Lodge on the right. Drive past the lodge for 100 yards and look for a dirt road on the left, signed as Mill Creek Road. The waterfall is 0.6 mile down Mill Creek Road, on the right side. (You can walk or drive.)

Information and Contact

A national forest Adventure Pass is required. A map of San Bernardino National Forest is available for a fee from the National Forest Store (406/329-3024, www. nationalforeststore.com), or can be downloaded for free from www.fs.fed.us/r5/ maps/. For more information, contact San Bernardino National Forest, Mill Creek Ranger Station, 909/382-2882, www.fs.fed.us/r5/sanbernardino.

28 MONKEYFACE AND RIM OF THE WORLD SCENIC BYWAY FALLS

San Bernardino National Forest

Level: Easy	**Distance:** Negligible
Best Season: February-May	**Elevation Change:** 3,800-4,800 feet

The Rim of the World Scenic Byway is hands-down the most spectacular drive in Southern California, from its start near Forest Falls to its middle near Big Bear Lake and its end near Cajon Pass. It highlights much of the gorgeous high-mountain scenery of San Bernardino National Forest. If you're going to take a driving tour anywhere, this should be at the top of your list.

If you want to stop along the byway and see a couple waterfalls, you're in luck. Start with Monkeyface Falls; simply turn off Highway 38 toward Forest Falls and you're alongside it in about 100 yards. It's on your left, about 0.25 mile from the road, and there are pullouts where you can stop your car. Unfortunately, the fall is difficult to see unless it's running at full flood because it's set deep in a crevice on the hillside. It drops an estimated 150 feet through a narrow, twisting canyon.

When it does flow, does it look like the face of a monkey? Good question, but the answer's no. It is called Monkeyface Falls simply because it flows on Monkeyface Creek. It's also on private property, so don't make any plans to hike to it. Somebody has his or her own private waterfall and isn't interested in sharing it.

If Monkeyface isn't flowing, don't fret; there's another drive-to waterfall to see. From the junction of Highway 38 and Forest Home Road, set your odometer and drive north on Highway 38 for two miles to a pullout on the left (north) side of the road. The pullout is between mileage markers 17.05 and 17.10 and has a very angular, pointed rock formation right next to it. Park by the rock, then walk to the edge and look down into Mountain Home Canyon below. There you'll see a perfect free-fall cataract, funneled through a narrow 10-foot-wide chute in the rock, then free-leaping about 50 feet into a pool below. It's distant, but very beautiful. A pair of binoculars greatly enhances your view.

The canyon walls are dangerously steep and loose, so don't attempt to climb down to the falls. People have died trying. If you want to see a waterfall from closer up, drive four miles up Forest Home Road to the Falls Recreation Area, where you can walk to or drive by Big Falls (see Big Falls listing in this chapter).

Directions

From I-10 at Redlands, take the Highway 38 exit and drive northeast 14 miles to the junction with Forest Home Road. Bear right and continue about 50 yards. Monkeyface Falls is on the left (north) side of the road.

Information and Contact

A national forest Adventure Pass is required. A map of San Bernardino National Forest is available for a fee from the National Forest Store (406/329-3024, www.nationalforeststore.com), or can be downloaded for free from www.fs.fed.us/r5/maps/. For more information, contact San Bernardino National Forest, Mill Creek Ranger Station, 909/382-2882, www.fs.fed.us/r5/sanbernardino.

29 BIG FALLS
San Bernardino National Forest

Level: Easy

Best Season: March–September

Distance: 0.6 mile round-trip

Elevation Change: Total gain 80 feet

Big Falls has earned its name. At 500 feet, it's the tallest waterfall in the San Bernardino Mountains, and most folks claim it's the largest year-round waterfall in all of Southern California. Big Falls is also the centerpiece of the Falls Recreation Area, just outside of the town of Forest Falls, and get this—it's located on Valley of the Falls Drive. Everything around here is called "falls" this or "falls" that. It's a waterfall-lover's kind of place.

For hardy backpackers, the Falls Recreation Area has plenty to offer. Several trails lead to the San Gorgonio Wilderness, including the shortest and steepest route to the summit of 11,502-foot Mount San Gorgonio on the Vivian Creek Trail. But for the average visitor, Big Falls is the only easily accessible destination in the area, reached by a 10-minute walk from the parking lot.

Big Falls is located northwest of the parking lot, hidden in a side canyon. To reach it, you follow the signed trail from the lot, heading downstream along Mill Creek. In about 200 yards, you reach a couple of cabins and a sign directing you to cross the creek. There is no bridge;

Big Falls

you simply rock-hop across the rounded rocks in the stream. Sturdy shoes or hiking boots are a good idea. On the far side, look for a trail leading uphill on the right side of Falls Creek, which is a feeder stream to Mill Creek. There's a small cascade at the bottom of Falls Creek; hike past it and ascend through an oak and cedar forest for about five minutes to the falls' overlook.

Now for the bad news. From the overlook, you peer uphill at the falls and see very little of it. Much of the waterfall is hidden back in the canyon and out of view; all you can glimpse is the top 40 feet of a very Yosemite Falls–type free fall, complete with what appears to be a hanging valley, and some cascading water down below. The huge middle part of the fall is missing, making it a less impressive sight than you'd expect from the tallest waterfall in Southern California. Don't consider scaling the cliffs for a better perspective, however; many people have died in the attempt.

And a little more bad news: on winter and spring weekends, it can be difficult to find a parking spot at the Falls Recreation Area, which is also a popular snow-play and picnicking area. Visit during the week if you want to avoid a lot of hassle.

Want a better look at Big Falls? The easiest and best view is actually from your car window as you drive up the road between the town of Forest Falls and the Big Falls parking area. Look toward Mill Creek, just east of the last few houses along Forest Home Road/Valley of the Falls Drive, and west of the sign for Falls Recreation Area. In this 300-yard stretch, you get excellent views of almost the entire length of the waterfall. Even though you're almost 0.5 mile from the waterfall, the vista is impressive. This is the view of Big Falls that is depicted on postcards.

Directions

From I-10 at Redlands, take the Highway 38 exit and drive northeast for 14 miles to the junction with Forest Home Road. Bear right and continue 4.4 miles to the Falls Recreation Area, past the town of Forest Falls. (The road's name changes to Valley of the Falls Drive.) Park in the first parking lot on the left, just past the Falls Recreation Area sign.

Information and Contact

A national forest Adventure Pass is required. A map of San Bernardino National Forest is available for a fee from the National Forest Store (406/329-3024, www.nationalforeststore.com), or can be downloaded for free from www.fs.fed.us/r5/maps/. For more information, contact San Bernardino National Forest, Mill Creek Ranger Station, 909/382-2882, www.fs.fed.us/r5/sanbernardino.

30 HOLY JIM FALLS   BEST (

Cleveland National Forest

🏃 🐕

Level: Easy

Distance: 2.5 miles round-trip

Best Season: December–June

Elevation Change: Total gain 350 feet

Holy Jim Falls has one of the most intriguing names and interesting histories of any Southern California waterfall. The fall and its canyon were named for James T. Smith, better known as "Cussin' Jim," a beekeeper who lived here in the 1890s. Apparently, Smith earned his nickname with his bad temper and colorful way with language. Because honey-loving grizzly bears were plentiful in the area in those days, a beekeeper might have plenty of reasons to be angry.

But conservative mapmakers who plotted Trabuco Canyon in the early 1900s found Smith's moniker in bad taste, so they arbitrarily changed it to "Holy Jim." The sanitized name stuck.

The waterfall has made its own name for itself. A favorite destination of Orange County hikers, the Holy Jim Trail is quite busy on winter and spring weekends

when the fall is flowing strong. The drive
to the trailhead can be a bit of a challenge (five miles on a rocky dirt road,
manageable by most passenger cars but
high clearance is recommended), but the
hike is a breeze. It's a 2.5-mile round-trip
stroll through shady oaks, keeping close
company with Holy Jim Creek. The only
tricky part is that the waterfall isn't right
along the main trail; you follow a cutoff trail and then make an easy 0.25-
mile scramble to reach it. A few hops,
skips, and jumps along the streambed
and you're there.

   Start by walking down the dirt road
that leads to some leased cabins, passing big cacti and succulents, until at
0.5 mile you reach the official Holy Jim
Trailhead. Leaving the dirt road for a
narrower trail, you're surrounded by a
lush canyon filled with oaks, vine maples, spring wildflowers, and even a few
ferns, all thriving in the shade alongside
Holy Jim Creek. The trail crosses the
creek several times, passes several small
check dams, and gently gains elevation as it heads upstream.

   After nearly 30 minutes of walking, the trail steepens noticeably. As you pass
a large old oak tree on your left, paths branch off in every direction. Stay on the
main route by continuing upstream for about 40 yards, then cross the creek again
(on your left). Immediately after crossing, follow the trail's right fork, which continues to follow the stream. The left fork switchbacks uphill to the summit of
5,687-foot Santiago Peak, seven miles away.

   Now you have only a 10-minute scramble through the rapidly narrowing canyon to reach Holy Jim Falls. A petite but picturesque 20 feet high, the waterfall
is set in a small, intimate grotto that forms a nearly circular rock amphitheater.
Maidenhair ferns cling to the walls on both sides of the watercourse. You won't
want to leave this special place too quickly.

   A free brochure that describes the Holy Jim Trail is available at the Corona
Forest Service office; it corresponds to numbered guideposts along the route and

provides interesting facts on the natural and human history of the canyon.

Directions

From I-5 at Laguna Hills (north of San Juan Capistrano), exit on El Toro Road and drive six miles east. Turn right on Live Oak Canyon Road and drive about four miles (two miles beyond O'Neill Regional Park). Turn left on Trabuco Canyon Road, a dirt road just past the paved Rose Canyon Road turnoff. (The road is usually suitable for passenger cars, but high clearance is recommended.) Drive five miles to the well-signed parking area for Holy Jim Trail. The trail leads from the parking lot's left side.

Holy Jim Falls

Information and Contact

A national forest Adventure Pass is required. A map of Cleveland National Forest is available for a fee from the National Forest Store (406/329-3024, www.nationalforeststore.com), or can be downloaded for free from www.fs.fed.us/r5/maps/. For more information, contact Cleveland National Forest, Trabuco Ranger District, 909/736-1811, www.fs.fed.us/r5/cleveland.

31 SAN JUAN FALLS
Cleveland National Forest

Level: Easy

Best Season: December–April

Distance: 1.0 mile round-trip

Elevation Change: Total gain 100 feet

San Juan Falls is one of the many fine features of the San Juan Loop Trail, an easy and informative walk that serves as a good introduction to the Santa Ana Mountains. The only stipulation? Make sure you take this walk in winter or early spring. The rest of the year, it's too darn hot, and the waterfall doesn't last long past April.

If you hike the loop trail from its start on the north side of the parking lot, you reach the falls in less than 0.5 mile. Beware of the sign at the trailhead, which warns in doomsday-style of mountain lions, rattlesnakes, poison oak, and rugged terrain. Forge ahead, brave explorers.

You walk slightly uphill, passing a surprising variety of plant life. This lush desert terrain is extremely arid and exposed, but thriving nonetheless. It's filled with chaparral-type wildflowers, including deep-red monkeyflowers, purple nightshades, and tall, spiky yuccas with their silky, milk-white flowers. Many lizards dart among the foliage, including a horned variety that is a member of the iguana family.

San Juan Falls

The trail is sandy but well-maintained. The only downer is the sound of the road, which is a little too close on the first section of trail. As the loop curves to the left, a railing and overlook alert you to the presence of 15-foot San Juan Falls, which is situated below the trail. The view from above is only fair, so take the short spur trail leading from the left side of the railing down into the creek canyon. Standing in the creekbed, looking eye to eye with the falls and its narrow, rock-walled gorge, is your best view. The light gray, polished granite and ultra-clear stream pools invite exploration.

From the waterfall, you can return the way you came (for a one-mile round-trip) or continue hiking the loop, which is a total of 2.2 miles long and ends at the other side of the parking lot. Along the way, you pass the turnoffs for the Chiquito Trail and Upper San Juan Campground, and you walk through a lovely grove of ancient oaks.

Directions

From I-5 at San Juan Capistrano, take the Ortega Highway (Highway 74) exit and drive north. In 21 miles, you'll reach the Country Cottage store on the right (0.75 mile past Upper San Juan Campground). The trailhead is across the road from the store; turn left and park in the large parking lot. Start hiking from the north side of the parking lot.

Information and Contact
A national forest Adventure Pass is required. A map of Cleveland National Forest is available for a fee from the National Forest Store (406/329-3024, www.nationalforeststore.com), or can be downloaded for free from www.fs.fed.us/r5/maps/. For more information, contact Cleveland National Forest, Trabuco Ranger District, 909/736-1811, www.fs.fed.us/r5/cleveland.

32 ORTEGA FALLS
Cleveland National Forest

Level: Easy

Best Season: December–April

Distance: 0.5 mile round-trip

Elevation Change: Total loss 100 feet

Many years ago, *Sunset* magazine ran a story about springtime waterfalls in Orange County, and Ortega Falls was one of their picks. The waterfall is located just off Highway 74 and accessible by an easy walk from a highway turnout, so it's an easy trip that just about anybody can take.

Located in between the small villages of Ortega Oaks and El Caruso on the scenic Ortega Highway, the unsigned parking turnouts for the falls make an inconspicuous beginning to a great waterfall visit. In springtime, as soon as you pull off the highway you can hear the falls roar, and the cascading water is visible from the western turnout. Several short use trails lead from this side of the road down into San Juan Canyon.

Ortega Falls

The easiest way to hike to the falls is to stay to your right along the canyon wall, following a well-worn path as it winds around boulders and brush. As you get closer, you find that there are actually several falls dropping over polished granite, with marvelously clear pools between them. Most people stop by the 35-foot drop, which is only a 15-minute walk from the parking pullout. It's a fascinating study of rock and water: the stream splits into two distinct tongues as it splashes its way over a large, block-shaped granite outcrop, then stills momentarily in a wide and shallow pool at its base. You can also visit the smaller cascades below this fall, where you're certain to find the perfect poolside rock for lounging on.

Intrepid hikers can continue scrambling upstream, heading above the 35-foot fall to more falls and pools. Be forewarned that the route is less well-used and the scrambling gets more challenging the farther you go. If you have children with you, don't climb above the first falls.

Directions
From I-5 at San Juan Capistrano, take the Ortega Highway (Highway 74) exit and drive north. In 21 miles, you'll reach the Ortega Oaks store on the right. Reset your odometer there, and continue 1.6 miles north on Highway 74 to the large, unmarked turnouts on both sides of the highway. There are a few trash cans and usually a few cars parked there. The trail leads from the left (west) side of the highway. (If you are coming from Lake Elsinore, the turnouts are three miles south of the village of El Caruso.)

Information and Contact
A national forest Adventure Pass is required. A map of Cleveland National Forest is available for a fee from the National Forest Store (406/329-3024, www.nationalforeststore.com), or can be downloaded for free from www.fs.fed.us/r5/maps/. For more information, contact Cleveland National Forest, Trabuco Ranger District, 909/736-1811, www.fs.fed.us/r5/cleveland.

33 TENAJA FALLS
San Mateo Canyon Wilderness

Level: Easy   **Distance:** 1.5 miles round-trip
Best Season: January–May   **Elevation Change:** Total gain 300 feet

To me, Tenaja Falls will always be Ha-ha-ha Falls, or maybe Tee-hee-hee Falls. On my first-ever visit to this spectacular waterfall, I parked the car at the trailhead, loaded up my day packs, and set out on the trail, except somehow I managed to miss the trail altogether. I ended up bushwhacking upstream through a veritable forest of poison oak, then scrambling, slipping, and scaling my way to the top of the falls, only to find a pack of teenagers with coolers of beer hanging out there. They had been watching my slow progress up the canyon with great curiosity.

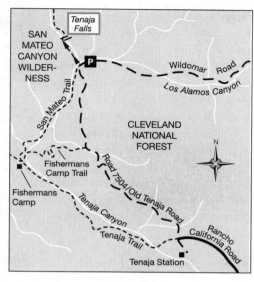

Me: "Hey, how'd you manage to carry a cooler up here?"

Them: "We took the trail."

Me: "Trail? What trail?"

To make a long story short, I took the trail on the way back. It turns out it's not just a trail that leads to Tenaja Falls, but a wide dirt road, easy enough for a three-year-old to walk. I felt like an idiot.

If you do it right, the only hard part in reaching Tenaja Falls is the long drive to the unsigned trailhead. But if you follow the directions exactly, that should be no problem. Then, after parking, head for the metal fence blocking the road/trail into the San Mateo Wilderness to vehicles, and cross the creek on a concrete apron. If it's flooded, as it was on our trip, you can follow a use trail and cross the creek where it's narrower, but be sure to join up with the main trail again. If you stay on the use trails next to the creek, you'll wind up making the same mistake I did and working a lot harder than you have to.

Hike northward, rising out of the canyon and along slopes of sage and chaparral, and in a few minutes you'll round a curve and be treated to a partial view of the waterfall ahead. Keep walking toward it; the trail deposits you at the falls' lip.

Tenaja Falls is surprisingly large compared to other waterfalls in Orange County—it drops 150 feet in five tiers. Unfortunately, you never reach a vantage point where you can see the whole enchilada. Most of the time, you're looking at two tiers, totaling about 80 feet in height. When the water level is low enough, you can cross over the top of the falls to the other side of the creek and gain a different perspective. Some people jump off the rocks and into the waterfall's deep pools, but this is probably only a good idea if you're young and foolhardy. Remember that the granite is even more slippery than it looks.

Tenaja Falls' season is short, so you must visit early in the year. Average annual rainfall in the San Mateo Canyon Wilderness is only 15–20 inches per season, and it's usually all over by March. When I visited the falls in mid-April, the stream's flow was already greatly reduced.

Directions

From Lake Elsinore, drive south on I-15 for about 12 miles to the Clinton Keith Road exit. Drive south on Clinton Keith Road, which will become Tenaja Road, for 4.5 miles. At a signed intersection with Tenaja Road, turn right and drive 4.3 miles west to Cleveland Forest Road. Turn right and drive one mile to the Tenaja Trailhead. Stay right, passing the trailhead parking area. Reset you odometer and drive 4.4 miles on Road 7S04 to a hairpin turn and a parking pullout on the left.

Tenaja Falls

Information and Contact

A national forest Adventure Pass is required. A map of Cleveland National Forest is available for a fee from the National Forest Store (406/329-3024, www.nationalforeststore.com), or can be downloaded for free from www.fs.fed.us/r5/maps/. For more information, contact Cleveland National Forest, Trabuco Ranger District, 909/736-1811, www.fs.fed.us/r5/cleveland.

34 FULLER MILL CREEK FALLS
San Bernardino National Forest

Level: Easy   **Distance:** 0.5 mile round-trip

Best Season: April-June   **Elevation Change:** Negligible

Idyllwild is a fine, unspoiled town in the magnificent San Jacinto Mountains, with easy access to many excellent trailheads. But after you've hiked around a while and worn a few holes in your boots, a laid-back trip to Fuller Mill Creek and its waterfall could be just what you need. Effort required? Almost none. Driving time? Ten minutes from town. Is it good? You bet.

Park your car at the Fuller Mill Creek Picnic Area, a nice place to have a barbecue or to do a little fishing, especially in springtime when the creek is stocked with trout. Then walk across the highway and take the trail that leads along the right (south) side of the stream. Don't take the trail on the left; it's much rougher.

Five minutes of walking upstream brings you to a 10-foot waterfall, but push on for less than 100 yards to a 25-foot fall that is set in a theater of rock and foliage. The creek has cut deeply in granite bedrock to form this perfect slice of white water, surrounded by big boulders and cottonwoods.

If you want more, you get more. Trails continue on both sides of the creek, with more falls continuing up the canyon. I was content to remain by the waterfall in the rock theater, where my hiking partner posed the all-important question: "So, how do you tear yourself away from these places?"

That's always been a hard one to answer.

Fuller Mill Creek Falls

© ANN MARIE BROWN

Directions

From Idyllwild, drive north on Highway 243 for 7.5 miles to the left turnoff for Fuller Mill Creek Picnic Area. Park there and walk across the road to mile marker 12 on Highway 243. A trail leads from the south end of the guardrail alongside Fuller Mill Creek.

Information and Contact

A national forest Adventure Pass is required. A map of San Bernardino National Forest is available for a fee from the National Forest Store (406/329-3024, www.nationalforeststore.com), or can be downloaded for free from www.fs.fed.us/r5/maps/. For more information, contact San Bernardino National Forest, San Jacinto Ranger District, 909/382-2921, www.fs.fed.us/r5/sanbernardino.

35 DARK CANYON FALLS   BEST **C**

San Bernardino National Forest

🚶 🏊 🐴 ⛺

Level: Moderate   **Distance:** 2.0 miles round-trip

Best Season: May-July   **Elevation Change:** Total gain 300 feet

one of Dark Canyon's falls

© ANN MARIE BROWN

You can work as hard or as little as you want when you visit Dark Canyon Falls. The falls are a series of drops and cascades on Dark Canyon Creek, which makes its way through pine and fir forest and over polished granite into the San Jacinto River. It's plain from the state of the use trail that most people only hike 0.5 mile to the first set of falls, then find a rock to sit on and hang out for the afternoon. After that, the trail gets fainter, but the waterfalls continue. How far you go and how much you see is up to you.

Getting to the falls requires an upstream scramble from Dark Canyon Campground, located less than 10 miles from the town of Idyllwild. A use trail starts by the camp restrooms near sites 15 and 16. If you're not staying in the camp, you must park outside its entrance and walk in to access the trail.

Beginning at the far end of the campground loop, follow the obvious route for 0.25 mile along the left (north) side of the stream. When the path ends, you must resort to easy scrambling up the rocky streambed.

The first falls are noisy, but only about 10 feet high—silvery ropes of water splashing against age-old rock. Continue a few yards farther and you reach an impressive 25-foot drop, a narrow chute rushing through granite. Along its entire length, the fall has chiseled a distinct crevice in the rock, as if forming aqueduct walls for its stream. It also has two side cascades that frame the main fall. If you edge closer to the one on the right side, you will find that it conceals a small but deep cave. Inside, moss and tiny ferns grow.

Upstream of this fall, the scrambling gets a little rougher, but it's worth the trouble to continue. I was able to get away from some boisterous campers by simply heading farther upstream. I came across three cascades in the 10–15-foot range, with excellent granite swimming pools at their bases. If you want to go for a dip, be forewarned: this canyon is aptly named. It is dark and shady, and as a result the water is bitterly cold. The icy pools warrant the kind of "swimming" where you jump in, then promptly scramble back out and exclaim, "I'm alive!"

Directions

From Idyllwild, drive north on Highway 243 for 5.5 miles to the right turnoff for Stone Creek, Fern Basin, Marion Mountain, and Dark Canyon Campgrounds. Turn right and drive 0.2 mile, then bear left, following the signs for Dark Canyon Camp. Drive 0.8 mile, turn left and proceed 1.5 miles farther to the campground. If you're not staying in the camp, you must park in the dirt pullouts along the road before the camp entrance.

Information and Contact

A national forest Adventure Pass is required. A map of San Bernardino National Forest is available for a fee from the National Forest Store (406/329-3024, www.nationalforeststore.com), or can be downloaded for free from www.fs.fed.us/r5/maps/. For more information, contact San Bernardino National Forest, San Jacinto Ranger District, 909/382-2921, www.fs.fed.us/r5/sanbernardino.

MORE WATERFALLS IN
LOS ANGELES AND VICINITY

•**Bouquet Canyon Falls, Angeles National Forest.** A 30-foot waterfall called "The Falls" drops right along Bouquet Canyon Road south of Bouquet Reservoir. Unfortunately, this is a popular swimming hole and partying spot. Litter abounds and graffiti covers the rocks. What a pity. For more information, phone the Santa Clara Ranger District, 661/296-9710.

•**Rubio Canyon, Angeles National Forest.** These are the falls that were. The site of the historic Mount Lowe Railway, Rubio Canyon was once filled with waterfalls. A long history of natural landslides destroyed some of them, but an unnatural event likely caused by the Rubio Water Company wiped out the remaining falls in the late 1990s. While the water company was dynamiting a hole to lay water pipe, more than a quarter mile of the canyon was buried under rubble. Local advocates are seeking mitigation and a cleanup of the debris in the canyon. Whether or not this will ever occur is unknown. At present, hiking in Rubio Canyon is dangerous because of extremely unstable conditions; rockslides are a common occurrence. For more information, phone the Angeles National Forest, Los Angeles River Ranger District, 818/899-1900.

•**Emerald Falls, Los Padres National Forest.** This 100-foot-plus waterfall is the locals' "secret" near the town of Fillmore. Access is via a six-mile round-trip hike in the Sespe Wilderness. For more information, contact the Ojai Ranger District at 805/646-4348.

SAN DIEGO AND VICINITY

BEST WATERFALLS

❰ Bicycle
Los Peñasquitos Falls, **page 481**

❰ Most Unusual
Borrego Palm Canyon Falls, **page 477**

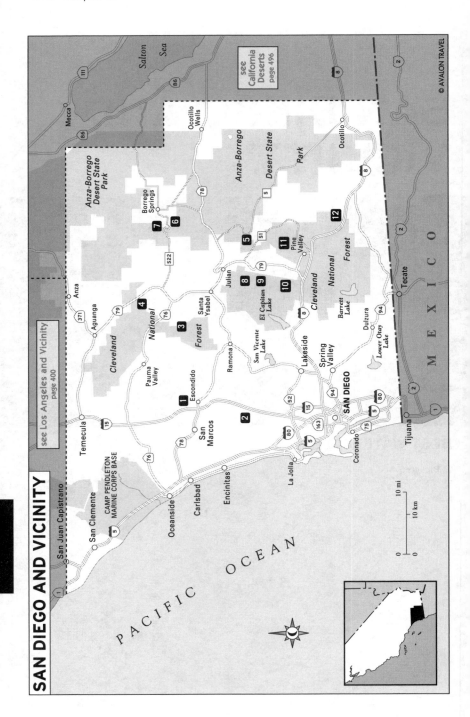

SAN DIEGO AND VICINITY

see Los Angeles and Vicinity
page 400

see California Deserts
page 496

© AVALON TRAVEL

Salton Sea

Mecca

Anza-Borrego Desert State Park

Ocotillo Wells

Borrego Springs

Anza-Borrego Desert State Park

Ocotillo

Anza

Aguanga

Cleveland National Forest

Julian

Santa Ysabel

Pine Valley

Cleveland National Forest

Tecate

MEXICO

El Capitan Lake

Barrett Lake

Dulzura

Lower Otay Lake

San Vicente Lake

Pauma Valley

Ramona

Lakeside

Spring Valley

Escondido

SAN DIEGO

San Marcos

Coronado

Temecula

Camp Pendleton Marine Corps Base

Oceanside

Carlsbad

Encinitas

La Jolla

Tijuana

San Clemente

San Juan Capistrano

PACIFIC OCEAN

10 mi

10 km

TRAIL NAME	LEVEL	DISTANCE	ELEVATION	SEASON	FEATURES	PAGE
1 Jack Creek Falls	Easy	0.5 mile rt	100 ft	Dec.-May	🚶	472
2 Prisoner Creek Falls	Strenuous	3.0 mi rt	400 ft	Dec.-Apr.	🐾 🏕	473
3 Barker Valley Falls	Moderate	8.2 mi rt	1,200 ft	Dec.-June	🚶 🏃 🐾	475
4 Borrego Palm Canyon Falls	Easy	3.0 mi rt	500 ft	Oct.-May	🚶 ◀	477
5 Maidenhair Falls	Moderate	5.0 mi rt	800 ft	Dec.-May	🚶 🐾	479
6 Los Peñasquitos Falls	Moderate	6.5 mi rt	200 ft	Dec.-Apr.	🚶 🏃 🚲	481
7 Cedar Creek Falls	Moderate	4.4 mi rt	1,200 ft	Dec.-May	🚶 🏃 🏕	482
8 Three Sisters Falls	Moderate	4.0 mi rt	1,500 ft	Dec.-May	🚶 🏃 🐾	485
9 Green Valley Falls	Easy	0.5 mile rt	80 ft	Dec.-May	🚶 🏃 ◀	487
10 Oriflamme Canyon Falls	Moderate	2.6 mi rt	400 ft	Dec.-May	🚶	488
11 Cottonwood Creek Falls	Easy	2.0 mi rt	400 ft	Dec.-June	🚶 🏃	490
12 Kitchen Creek Falls	Moderate	4.5 mi rt	500 ft	Dec.-May	🚶 🏃 🏕 ◀	492

⬛ JACK CREEK FALLS

Dixon Lake Recreation Area

Level: Easy	**Distance:** 0.5 mile round-trip
Best Season: December–May	**Elevation Change:** Total loss 100 feet

Several waterfalls in and around San Diego are moderate to challenging to get to, but only a few are just plain easy. Jack Creek Falls, a bouldery cascade in Dixon Lake Recreation Area near Escondido, is a waterfall that's just right for those who have no interest in route-finding, rock-scrambling, or long hikes on hot, exposed slopes. This trip is perfect for children, and likely to turn them into waterfall aficionados at a young age.

Keep in mind that this is San Diego, where more than a foot of rain a year is a big deal, and if it rains for two days straight, people start drawing ark blueprints. Make sure you visit Jack Creek immediately following a wet spell, or better yet, during a wet spell. Otherwise, you could be gazing at a pile of dry (but still fairly interesting) boulders.

First, a few words about Dixon Lake. The reservoir looks more natural than most artificial lakes, set in a deep canyon surrounded by plentiful foliage. Fishing in the lake is fair for largemouth bass, rainbow trout, catfish, and bluegill. If shoreline angling isn't your bag, you can rent a boat or launch your own.

The Jack Creek Nature Trail begins by the park entrance station, and it ends 0.5 mile later at Dixon Lake. It's a self-guided trail, with interpretive brochures you can pick up at the ranger station or Lakeshore picnic area. Start walking by the entrance station, crossing through the Hilltop Picnic Area and passing two large wooden picnic shelters. Head for the shady area behind the shelters, where Jack Creek flows. Cross a small footbridge over the creek and voilà—you're right on top of the waterfall. You can't really see it from here, but when it's running, you can definitely hear it.

Continue down the trail a few yards farther and take the right spur, which leads to the fall's base. If you walk upstream beyond the trail's end for about 30 feet, you'll find the tallest cascade. Huge cattails block some of the view, so scramble around until you find the best spot to sit and admire the falls. The creek drops (sometimes furiously, but most of the time gingerly) over gray- and tan-colored boulders of various sizes. The total length of the cascade is about 20 feet.

If you decide to keep hiking, you'll soon gain a fine view of Dixon Lake, then shortly arrive at the water's edge. At the lake, the Jack Creek Trail connects to the Shoreline Trail and the Grand View Trail, giving you more options for continuing your walk.

Directions

From Escondido, drive north on I-15 and take the El Norte Parkway exit. Drive 3.1 miles east on El Norte Parkway, then turn left (north) on La Honda Drive, and drive 1.3 miles to the Dixon Lake entrance on the right. The trailhead is located directly across from the park entrance. Park by the playground/picnic area to the right of the park entrance, signed as "Hilltop Picnic Area."

Information and Contact

A $5 day-use fee is charged per vehicle (weekends and holidays only). For more information and a map, contact Dixon Lake Ranger Station, 760/839-4680, www.ci.escondido.ca.us.

2 PRISONER CREEK FALLS
Cleveland National Forest

Level: Strenuous

Best Season: December–April

Distance: 3.0 miles round-trip

Elevation Change: Total gain 400 feet

Prisoner Creek Falls is a destination you have to really *want* to reach. It's a terrific waterfall that comes with a big price tag, including a long stream scramble, neck-high poison oak, and the fastest biting ticks I've ever seen.

And also a very short season. If you don't make it here before May, you're likely to miss all the action, unless San Diego has an unusually wet year.

Prisoner Creek Falls is located across the road from a San Diego schools' outdoor learning center, where kids from all over the county come on field trips to learn interesting stuff about their natural world. The creek and waterfall were named years ago, when the outdoor school buildings were part of a prison camp, a place for well-behaved prisoners who worked on road crews. When I visited, the outdoor-school principal told me that this is the only school around where kids can say they are in prison, and it's true.

Start hiking from the wooden railing across the road from the school, where a path leads down to and crosses the San Luis Rey River on a makeshift bridge.

After crossing, walk to your left for about 50 yards, paralleling the river, until you reach Prisoner Creek, which empties into it. Stay on the west (right) side of the creek, and head upstream on the use trail, keeping as close to the creek as possible. (Another trail heads up the east side of the creek, but it rises high above the streambed and then drops steeply back down, only halfway to the waterfall. It's quite steep and overgrown with manzanita. Someday this trail may be extended and maintained, but for now, no such luck.)

When the trail you've been following peters out, you're on your own to make tracks up the streambed. Scramble up and over the millions of rocks, trying not to turn your ankle, and bushwhack through the hanging branches and vines that adorn the creek. You should make it to the waterfall in just under an hour, as long as you keep plodding. If the water is high in the creek, your travel may be slower. Waterproof boots can be an asset.

When you finally arrive, you will find that Prisoner Creek Falls is a 60-foot cascade, dropping in three tiers over dark gray granite. It blocks the back of the canyon, making further travel impossible. A narrow channel of water cuts straight down the middle of the fall's cliff. If you're lucky enough to see this waterfall at full flood, it's a tremendous sight.

After enjoying the falls and resting a while, make your way back down the canyon over the now-familiar route. When you get back to your car, be sure to check for ticks. I neglected to do so, and a few hours later, I was bitten by two of them, escapees from Prisoner Creek.

Directions

From Escondido, drive north on I-15 for 16 miles to the Highway 76 exit. Turn east on Highway 76, and drive approximately 26 miles to the Denver C. Fox Outdoor Education School on the left (north) side of the road. (If you reach Lake Henshaw, you've gone too far.) Park across the road from the school, in the turnout with a wooden railing marked "No trespassing." The trail leads from there.

Information and Contact

A national forest Adventure Pass is required. A map of Cleveland National Forest is available for a fee from the National Forest Store (406/329-3024, www.nationalforeststore.com), or can be downloaded for free from www.fs.fed.us/r5/maps/. For more information, contact Cleveland National Forest, Palomar Ranger District, 760/788-0250, www.fs.fed.us/r5/cleveland.

3 BARKER VALLEY FALLS
Cleveland National Forest

Level: Moderate

Best Season: December-June

Distance: 8.2 miles round-trip

Elevation Change: Total loss 1,200 feet

If the combination of a peaceful valley, soaring hawks and eagles, grazing deer, and a 90-foot waterfall appeal to your hiking sensibilities, you'll love Barker Valley. The hike is a pleasant ramble even in the dry season, but if you go after the Warner Springs area has received a fair amount of rain or snow, Barker Valley Falls is a sight to behold.

The trailhead is 7.9 miles off Highway 79 on Forest Service Road 9S07. This easy-to-miss road is also referred to as Palomar Divide Road. Look for a left (southern) turnoff 6.5 miles west of Warner Springs. The unpaved road doesn't require four-wheel drive, but high clearance is imperative. A gate at 5.7 miles may be locked during and after severe storms, so check with the Forest Service before making this trip in winter and spring. The trailhead is located 2.2 miles beyond the gate.

lower Barker Valley Falls

At the trailhead, you're provided with great views of Lake Henshaw to the southeast and Palomar Observatory just a few miles to the west. Park off the road and follow the trail signs as you descend gradually on switchbacks. The path is a three-mile downhill beginning in chaparral and manzanita and dropping into oak-lined Barker Valley, where the west fork of the San Luis Rey River runs year-round. Keep in mind that downhill is also the way the cold mountain air flows; the coolness may be a comfort in the summer months, but not so in winter. On a winter day that seems warm and sunny at the trailhead, ice can form on the river's more placid stretches.

If you've timed your trip for the wet season, you'll cross a few running creeks as you near the lower part of the trail. No signs direct you to the river's falls, but just before you reach the river you'll notice a few spur trails leading left. Follow any of them along the river's northern bank. The spur trails converge in a pleasant, oak-shaded camping area (backpackers need to obtain a free camping permit from the Forest Service). A rough footpath continues from the campsites for another 0.75 mile downstream along the West Fork San Luis Rey River. (Many hikers get confused here and head upstream in search of the falls. Make sure you go downstream.) Sooner or later, depending on how high the water level is, you'll face a scramble through brush and over smooth and slippery rocks.

Eventually, you'll come out above Barker Valley Falls. If you continue your cautious scramble along the steep northern bank to your left, you'll be rewarded with a terrific view of the 90-foot cataract as it drops to the pools below. Pick a rock to sit on, pull out your picnic lunch, and enjoy the sound of the water pulsing rhythmically through the otherwise silent valley. If you continue downstream, you'll find more waterfalls. On a warm day, you won't need any encouragement to go for a dip in the river's alluring pools.

Of course, after that lovely downhill walk, you'll face a hefty ascent on your way home. Fortunately, the climb is gradual; be sure to reward yourself with frequent stops to admire the scenery.

Directions
From Ramona, drive 15.3 miles east on Highway 78 to Santa Ysabel. Turn left on Highway 79 and drive north for 35 miles. Turn left (west) on Forest Service Road 9S07 (6.5 miles west of Warner Springs) and drive 7.9 miles to the trailhead on the left side of the road.

Information and Contact
A national forest Adventure Pass is required. A map of Cleveland National Forest is available for a fee from the National Forest Store (406/329-3024, www.nationalforeststore.com), or can be downloaded for free from www.fs.fed.us/r5/maps/. For more information, contact Cleveland National Forest, Palomar Ranger District, 760/788-0250, www.fs.fed.us/r5/cleveland.

⁴ BORREGO PALM CANYON FALLS   BEST ◖
Anza-Borrego Desert State Park

🚶🏕

Level: Easy   **Distance:** 3.0 miles round-trip

Best Season: October-May   **Elevation Change:** Total gain 500 feet

The walk from the Anza-Borrego Desert State Park campground to Borrego Palm Canyon is only 1.5 miles in length, but it feels like a trip from the desert to the tropics. You start out in a rocky, sandy, open plain, sweating it out with the cacti and ocotillo plants, and you end up in a shady oasis of fan palms, dipping your feet in the pool of a fern-covered waterfall.

It's incredible but true; water flows from springs most of the year in this part of Anza-Borrego, forming a cool stream and a 15-foot waterfall that drops over big boulders in the back of Borrego Palm Canyon. A large grove of palm trees thrives alongside the life-giving spring, providing shade and an ideal destination for hikers. For true desert rats, more and larger falls lie be-

Borrego Palm Canyon Falls

yond the first fall, but they require climbing skills (and desert survival skills) to reach them. But even families with small children can walk the nearly level route to the palm oasis and first waterfall. Just don't try it during the summer months, when the air temperature is unbearably hot and the stream becomes a mere mirage.

The trip begins on the signed Borrego Palm Canyon Trail from the campground of the same name. The sandy route is marked clearly, so if your water bottles are filled, just start walking. Make sure you bring along an interpretive brochure from the park visitor center, so you can identify the array of desert plants growing along the trail, including cheesebush, brittlebush, catclaw (ouch!), and chuparosa. All these bushes mean one thing—there's no shade anywhere.

In 0.5 mile, after passing interpretive post 20, you're suddenly rewarded with the refreshing sight of hundreds of bright green, leafy palm trees ahead. After walking amid brown bushes, brown sand, and brown rocks, the sight of these palms is more exciting than you might expect. Borrego Palm Canyon has more than 800 mature native palms, the largest of the more than 25 groves in the park. It's one of the largest oases in the United States.

Head toward the palms, and in a few minutes you're nestled in their shade, listening to the desert wind rustle their fronds. Keep heading farther back in the canyon, amid more palms and over and around a few boulders. Another 10 minutes of walking brings you to the waterfall, which streams down over giant boulders framed by palm trees.

Some of the palms are ringed by split-rail fences; this is to protect their delicate seedlings and aid their propagation. Too many heavy footsteps could kill the palm seedlings.

At the fall's base is a marvelously clear pool with a sandy bottom, where you can wade in and cool off your feet. Tiny maidenhair ferns grow around the water's edge. On my trip, a bright green hummingbird flitted about the scene. Sit for a while and listen to the croaking of frogs and the wind in the palms.

Directions

From Julian, drive east on Highway 78 for 19 miles to Highway S3/Yaqui Pass Road. Turn left (north) on Highway S3/Yaqui Pass Road and drive 12 miles to Borrego Springs. Turn left on Highway S22/Palm Canyon Drive, and drive one mile to the signed junction just before the park visitor center. Turn right and drive one mile to Borrego Palm Canyon Campground. The trailhead is at the west end.

Information and Contact

An $8 day-use fee is charged per vehicle. Maps and brochures are available for a small fee at the park visitor center, or by free download at www.parks.ca.gov. For more information, contact Anza-Borrego Desert State Park, 760/767-5311 or 760/767-4205 (visitor center), www.parks.ca.gov.

5 MAIDENHAIR FALLS
Anza-Borrego Desert State Park

Level: Moderate

Best Season: December–May

Distance: 5.0 miles round-trip

Elevation Change: Total gain 800 feet

Stories are told about Maidenhair Falls in Hellhole Canyon in Anza-Borrego Desert State Park. Most of them are along the lines of how the waterfall is darn near impossible to reach and suitable only for experienced desert hikers. So one spring day I got up my courage, filled up my day pack with supplies, and headed for the Hellhole Trailhead, only to find dozens of parked cars and hordes of people hiking up the trail. Hard to reach? Not really. Hard to get away from the crowds? Yes indeed, at least on spring weekends. It turns out this is one of the most popular hikes in Anza-Borrego.

And no wonder. Hellhole Canyon is home to myriad desert foliage—lavender, chuparosa, creosote, ocotillo, teddy bear

Maidenhair Falls

chollas, California fan palms, cottonwood trees, and even ferns and mosses at Maidenhair Falls. Wildlife, too, is prolific—from bighorn sheep and jackrabbits to Costa's hummingbirds, roadrunners, and ladder-back woodpeckers. And best of all, Hellhole Canyon is the site of Maidenhair Falls, a 20-foot-tall waterfall framed by a wall of delicate ferns.

As with most desert hikes, it's wise to wear long pants and long sleeves on this trail, to help avoid the pitfalls of walking among plants with names like "cat-claw acacia." Dress for the terrain, then head for the trailhead on the west side of Highway S22. Hike westward on the wide, obvious trail, heading up a sandy alluvial fan. The canyon mouth is visible straight ahead, and you reach it in one mile of hiking. As you enter Hellhole Canyon, listen for the sound of flowing water. The canyon walls gradually narrow and the hiking slowly transitions to mild scrambling and boulder-hopping. Your feet should follow your ears, which must stay tuned to the cues from the water music. Both Maidenhair Falls and a smaller waterfall called Lower Falls are hidden from the main path. You need to follow the sound of falling water to find them. Lower Falls is only about 10 feet high and located in a secluded grotto on the canyon's left side, amid a stand of fan palms. Maidenhair Falls is about 100 yards beyond, also in a secluded grotto on the canyon's left side.

One not-so-obvious portion of the route may cause some hikers to lose the way. If you don't seem to be finding the falls, here's a tip: beyond the first cluster of fan palms, follow the footpath uphill on the steep right side of the canyon. This will drop you back down to a big stand of a dozen palms and put you back on track to the falls.

What is extraordinary about Maidenhair Falls is not the flow or shape of the cascade, but rather the wall of maidenhair ferns growing alongside it. Who would expect to find this delicate plant growing prolifically in one of the West's hottest deserts? In between the ferns you'll find a variety of mosses soaking up water like sponges.

Directions

From Julian, drive east on Highway 78 for 19 miles to Highway S3/Yaqui Pass Road. Turn left (north) on Highway S3/Yaqui Pass Road and drive 12 miles to Borrego Springs. Turn left on Highway S22/Palm Canyon Drive and drive one mile to the park visitor center. Pick up a map/brochure on Hellhole Canyon and Maidenhair Falls, then drive south on Highway S22 (Montezuma Valley Road) for 0.75 mile to the trailhead on the right side of the road.

Or, from Warner Springs on Highway 79, drive south on Highway 79 four miles to the Highway S2 turnoff. Turn east, drive five miles, then bear left on Highway S22 and drive 18 miles to the trailhead on the left.

Information and Contact

An $8 day-use fee is charged per vehicle. Maps and brochures are available for a small fee at the park visitor center, or by free download at www.parks.ca.gov. For more information, contact Anza-Borrego Desert State Park, 760/767-5311 or 760/767-4205 (visitor center), www.parks.ca.gov.

6 LOS PEÑASQUITOS FALLS   BEST (

Los Peñasquitos Canyon Preserve

Level: Moderate

Best Season: December–April

Distance: 6.5 miles round-trip

Elevation Change: Total loss 200 feet

Even if your Spanish is limited, after you visit this waterfall it will be pretty easy to guess what "Los Peñasquitos" means. If you guessed "big boulders" or "huge chunks of rock," you're pretty close. The exact translation is "little cliffs."

Whether you would call Los Peñasquitos a boulder field or a waterfall depends on when you visit. Although the canyon supports a year-round stream, its level fluctuates wildly, depending on the season. When I visited in May, it was already looking more like a boulder field. But show up in January or February after a good rain, and you'll see a splashy display of white water tumbling over a constricted stretch of tan-colored volcanic rocks.

The hike requires a big leap of faith, because from the trailheads at either end

Los Peñasquitos Falls

© ANN MARIE BROWN

of Los Peñasquitos Canyon Preserve, the landscape appears mostly level and covered with oaks, grasslands, and chaparral. It's unlikely terrain for a waterfall. The preserve is long and narrow, with the waterfall situated practically in the center, so you can hike to it from either side on a dirt road that traverses the park. The road serves as a multiuse path for hikers, bikers, and equestrians. Most people hike from the east end, because it provides more shade along the route. From there, the trek is a nearly level 6.5-mile round-trip.

This is a perfect trail for walking with a friend or even a group of friends—because the path is wide, there's ample opportunity for side-by-side walking and good conversation. But remember not to get so engrossed in your company that you forget what you're looking for. The waterfall isn't clearly visible from the trail; you have to locate and take the spur trails that reach it. Coming from the eastern trailhead, you'll find the right-hand waterfall cutoff located a few hundred yards past mileage marker 3.0. (Coming from the western trailhead, it's past marker 4.0, and on the left.) Look for a long wooden railing, which runs just above the falls. If you're biking, this is where you'd lock up and walk.

A short climb down and over boulders brings you to a 100-yard stretch of *peñasquitos* and pools. Although each cascade is only 5–10 feet tall, the continual series of them is what makes the scene impressive. The "little cliffs" look like a mix of basalt, sandstone, and limestone, giving them unusual colors ranging from pink coral to green to gray. Some are as large as small houses. They are remnants of a volcanic island chain formed underwater 140 million years ago.

In between the largest *peñasquitos* lie limpid pools, reflecting the rocks' polished pastel colors. In the late afternoon light, those colors become richly saturated, making the small cascades look beautiful even with little water in the stream. Have a seat on a boulder near one of the falls' reflecting pools and watch the magic interplay of water, rock, and sunlight.

Directions
From Escondido, drive south on I-15 for 16 miles to the Mercy Road exit. Turn right (west) on Mercy Road and follow it for one mile, crossing Black Mountain Road, to the trailhead parking area.

Information and Contact
There is no fee. A free map is available by download at www.sdparks.org. For more information, contact Los Peñasquitos Canyon Preserve, 858/484-7504 or 858/694-3049, www.sdparks.org.

7 CEDAR CREEK FALLS
Cleveland National Forest

Level: Moderate   **Distance:** 4.4 miles round-trip

Best Season: December–May   **Elevation Change:** Total loss 1,200 feet

One of San Diego's best-loved waterfalls, 90-foot Cedar Creek Falls was nearly obliterated in the massive 2003 Cedar wildfire. The waterfall's pool was filled in with landslide debris, mostly soil and ash, and the surrounding terrain was burned to a crisp. But since that time, Mother Nature has done what she does best—heal, regrow, and beautify. Cedar Creek Falls, tucked back in a tributary of the upper

San Diego River, is once again a favorite destination of San Diego hikers and waterfall lovers.

The trailhead for Cedar Creek Falls is one of the access points for the California Riding and Hiking Trail, a noncontiguous multiuse trail that crisscrosses much of San Diego County. Begin your walk by heading to the right and downhill on the wide fire road. Be sure to look over your right

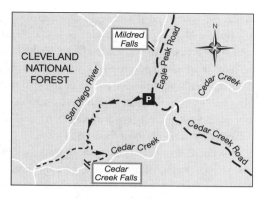

shoulder, to the north, for a view of the largest waterfall in San Diego, Mildred Falls. What? You don't see any water? Right. Almost no one ever does, which is why the fall doesn't get its own listing in this book. Usually you can make out two large sandstone ledges lined with algae and moisture streaks, followed by an S-turn down the back of the canyon, but that's about it. The 120-foot waterfall only runs immediately after a hard rain, and the trailhead access road is not easily passable then.

Keep walking downhill, enjoying the excellent views of the far-off upper San Diego River canyon and the close-up spring wildflowers. The slopes alongside the road are colored with paintbrush, monkeyflower, bush lupine, and huge white morning glory. If you time it right, you may even see the cacti in bloom.

At 1.4 miles, look for a left fork off the main trail. It may be unsigned, but it's the first and only left turnoff you'll see. Follow it southeast, heading up and over a small saddle. When you come down the other side, you'll see two possible trail options: the left fork takes you to the top of the falls; the right fork continues down to the valley, where you turn left and head upstream to Cedar Creek Falls. If it's your first visit, take the left fork so you can see what the waterfall looks like from above.

Beyond that junction, you will soon

© ANN MARIE BROWN

Cedar Creek Falls

reach the water's edge and walk downstream under the shade of oaks and cottonwoods, hopping over the tops of boulders and around crystal-clear pools for about 50 yards until you reach the lip of the falls, where Mother Nature appears to have built an infinity pool. This is where the drama and the danger come in. Whereas all is placid above the lip of the waterfall, its drop is sheer and extremely slippery—a mistake here would have unthinkable consequences. Cedar Creek is one of those edge-of-the-world waterfalls, and because you're at its brink, it's difficult to position yourself for a good view.

It is possible to make your way around the right side of the fall to a rocky ridge where your waterfall picture is more complete, or, if you're very comfortable off-trail, you could scramble down to the 50-foot-wide pool at the waterfall's base, which some call "The Punchbowl"; a rope swing is often in place. If you like to have your feet on solid ground, simply backtrack to the previous junction and take the opposite fork that leads to the valley below Cedar Creek Falls.

Enjoy your time at this special place, but remember that the steep uphill tromp can be quite warm on spring and summer afternoons. Make sure you have plenty of water remaining for this final leg. If you don't like the heat and the summer crowds, and you want to see the waterfall at its best, show up from March to May but no later.

One final suggestion: if you'd like to visit this waterfall without the long drive on a dirt road, it can be accessed via another trailhead in the town of Ramona, off Thornbush Road (take San Vicente Road to Ramona Oaks Road to Cathedral Way to Thornbush Road). The trail from Ramona to Cedar Creek Falls is about five miles round-trip.

Directions

From Julian, drive two miles west on Highway 78/79, then turn left (south) on Pine Hills Road. In 1.5 miles, bear right on Eagle Peak Road. In 1.4 miles, bear right again, staying on Eagle Peak Road. Continue 8.2 miles on this partly paved, partly dirt road to the signed trailhead just beyond mile marker 9, at a four-way junction of roads. (The road gets a bit rough after the first four miles, but it's usually suitable for passenger cars.)

Information and Contact

A national forest Adventure Pass is required. A map of Cleveland National Forest is available for a fee from the National Forest Store (406/329-3024, www.nationalforeststore.com), or can be downloaded for free from www.fs.fed.us/r5/maps/. For more information, contact Cleveland National Forest, Palomar Ranger District, 760/788-0250, www.fs.fed.us/r5/cleveland.

8 THREE SISTERS FALLS
Cleveland National Forest

Level: Moderate

Best Season: December–May

Distance: 4.0 miles round-trip

Elevation Change: Total loss 1,500 feet

Like nearby Cedar Creek Falls, the landscape surrounding Three Sisters Falls was severely burned in the wild-fires of 2003, but it has recovered nicely, and today it's hard to imagine the severity of those not-so-long-ago fires.

Also like Cedar Creek Falls, Three Sisters Falls is a must-see for serious San Diego hikers and waterfall-lovers. In the wet months, when San Diego receives its small allotment of annual rainfall, Three Sisters flows with enthusiasm and puts on an amazing show.

But whereas visiting Cedar Creek Falls is an easy-to-moderate adventure, popular with families and those who haven't necessarily spent much time in the great outdoors, Three Sisters is better left to the more advanced and/or fit hiker. The trail to the falls is a bad choice for beginners or the out of shape, and the drive to the trailhead is also fairly arduous. Whether you start from Julian or Descanso, the dirt access roads are usually passable for passenger cars except immediately after severe storms, but getting to the trailhead requires several miles of bumpy driving.

Start at the signboard for the Cedar Creek Trail, an old ranch road. Follow it for 0.7 mile, heading slightly uphill to a saddle where you can see and hear the falls in springtime, and then switchback down to the left for 0.4 mile until you meet up with tiny Sheep Camp Creek. Cross Sheep Camp Creek and pick up the good trail on its far side, heading right. You'll ascend slightly for 0.3 mile to a second low saddle, where once again you should be able to spot the Three Sisters in the canyon below. This visual incentive is critical, because you're about to face some remarkably steep downhill scrambling, which might be more accurately called "bouldering." Wear your best-gripping boots and bring hiking poles if you have them; the footing is loose and/or nonexistent in places. Some hikers

Three Sisters Falls

have reported that a rope was in place to assist them on their descent; I had no such luck on my trip.

After descending a rugged 500 feet, you'll finally reach Boulder Creek. Hike, rock-hop, or wade upstream for a few hundred yards to get to the base of the falls. Depending on Boulder Creek's flow, there may be several possible routes, but whatever you do, stay off the slick rock as much as possible. If you have to choose between stepping on these rocks and wading through poison oak, choose the poison oak. Really.

When you reach the Three Sisters, all this effort will pay off. A triple set of waterfalls on Boulder Creek, the Three Sisters creates an impressive display of white water on smooth granite. The middle fall is the tallest at about 50 feet. Its flow isn't always wide and full—it depends on recent rainfall—but its setting is spectacular. If the day is warm, its huge pool will beckon you to swim. Just remember to use caution on these ultra-slippery rock slabs.

Remember, too, to save a little energy for the trip back, which, unfortunately, is all uphill, and steep enough to stick in your mind long after your visit.

Directions

From Julian, drive two miles west on Highway 78/79, then turn left (south) on Pine Hills Road. In 1.5 miles, bear right on Eagle Peak Road. In 1.4 miles, bear left (south) on Boulder Creek Road and drive 8.4 miles to a hairpin turn and junction with another dirt road. A Forest Service signboard for Cedar Creek Trail is located there. Park alongside the road and take the trail from the signboard.

Alternatively, from I-8 in downtown San Diego, take Highway 79 north (Descanso exit) for 1.3 miles. Turn left on Riverside Drive and drive 0.6 mile to "downtown" Descanso and its intersection of roads. Follow Oak Grove Drive 1.6 miles to Boulder Creek Road, on the right. Turn north on Boulder Creek Road and drive 13 miles on this part-paved, part-dirt road to a hairpin turn and junction with dirt Cedar Creek Road. Park alongside the road and take the trail from the signboard.

Information and Contact

A national forest Adventure Pass is required. A map of Cleveland National Forest is available for a fee from the National Forest Store (406/329-3024, www.nationalforeststore.com), or can be downloaded for free from www.fs.fed.us/r5/maps/. For more information, contact Cleveland National Forest, Palomar Ranger District, 760/788-0250, www.fs.fed.us/r5/cleveland.

9 GREEN VALLEY FALLS

Cuyamaca Rancho State Park

Level: Easy

Best Season: December–May

Distance: 0.5 mile round-trip

Elevation Change: Total loss 80 feet

Green Valley Falls is accessible via an easy walk from Green Valley Campground, and it's a great place to cool off from the spring and summer heat.

Drive to the Green Valley Falls picnic area and walk 0.25 mile along the Sweetwater River. Campers can walk from their tents, making their trip just over 0.5 mile to the falls. The falls drop on the river, and although they are not tall, they constitute a series of wide cascades with enough ledges and pools to allow plenty of room for everybody. It's the kind of place where you can find your own spot to spread out a blanket or lounge around on a rock.

© ANN MARIE BROWN

a cascading stretch of Green Valley Falls

From the picnic area parking lot, you walk only 100 yards on the Falls Fire Road (also called the Sweetwater River Fire Road) to the Green Valley Falls Trail, then turn left and head downhill to the falls. You reach them in a few hundred yards, then pick your spot and settle in. Because the cascades and boulders are so large, it's difficult to scramble up- or downstream along the river. If you want to explore further, take any of the several spur trails off the fire road to reach the pools above and below the falls.

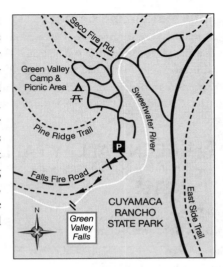

Directions

From San Diego, drive east on I-8 for 40 miles to the Highway 79 exit. Drive north on Highway 79 for seven miles, then turn left (west) at the sign for Green Valley Campground. Follow the signs to the picnic area. One sign points either straight ahead or to the left for the picnic area; continue straight to reach the trailhead.

Information and Contact

An $8 day-use fee is charged per vehicle. Maps and brochures are available for a small fee at the park visitor center, or by free download at www.parks.ca.gov. For more information, contact Cuyamaca Rancho State Park, 760/765-3020 or 760/765-0755, www.parks.ca.gov.

10 ORIFLAMME CANYON FALLS
Anza-Borrego Desert State Park

Level: Moderate   **Distance:** 2.6 miles round-trip

Best Season: December–May   **Elevation Change:** Total gain 400 feet

Oriflamme Canyon is in the desert, but it doesn't look much like the rest of Anza-Borrego. As the crow flies, it's much closer to Lake Cuyamaca and the Laguna Mountains than it is to the main part of Anza-Borrego. Yet it's still within the borders of Anza-Borrego Desert State Park, and set in some lovely terrain that is worth exploring. On the way to the falls, you'll walk through a surprisingly lush riparian environment.

To visit the canyon, begin by parking anywhere near the old primitive camping area in Oriflamme Canyon. Start hiking upstream, following a narrow use trail with the creek on your left. You're hiking under the shade of leafy cottonwoods that grow in profusion along the stream banks. You may notice several use trails; they all converge at an old roadbed on the right side of the stream. Sooner or later, you'll wind up high above the creek, following the old road. This obvious trail makes the first part of the hike quite easy.

After 0.75 mile, you begin to cross and recross the stream repeatedly on a less obvious track. Keep hiking back in

Oriflamme Canyon Falls

the canyon until you reach the falls, which are only a few yards from the trail but hidden below it and completely invisible. Use your ears to guide you. (On my trip, the short spur to the falls was marked with a trail cairn, but I missed it completely. If you hike to the point where the stream becomes very narrow and minimal in its flow, you've passed the waterfall. Turn around and try again.)

The waterfall drops about 20 feet into a large pool that is completely surrounded by willows. It's difficult to work your way to the front of the pool because the foliage is quite dense, but that's the best spot to get the full visual effect.

One caveat: wearing pants and long sleeves is a good idea for this trail. This is a very brushy hike with a ton of vegetation, from chaparral to cactus, such as beavertails, catclaws, and spiky chollas. You can go home with quite a few scratches if you're not dressed right.

Directions

From Julian, drive east on Highway 78 for about 12 miles to Highway S2. Turn right (south) on Highway S2 and drive about nine miles to the Oriflamme Canyon turnoff located one mile past Box Canyon Historic Site. Turn west on the dirt road to Oriflamme Canyon (high-clearance is required). At 0.25 mile, bear right; then at two miles in, bear left. At three miles in, bear left again and continue 0.25

mile to the bright green cottonwood trees near an old primitive camping area. Begin hiking upstream on the right bank of the creek.

Information and Contact

There is no fee at the Oriflamme Canyon Trailhead. Maps and brochures are available for a small fee at the park visitor center, or by free download at www. parks.ca.gov. For more information, contact Anza-Borrego Desert State Park, 760/767-5311 or 760/767-4205 (visitor center), www.parks.ca.gov.

11 COTTONWOOD CREEK FALLS
Cleveland National Forest

Level: Easy   **Distance:** 2.0 miles round-trip

Best Season: December–June   **Elevation Change:** Total loss 400 feet

From the start of the trail, Cottonwood Creek Falls looks like it's going to be a pain in the neck to reach, but don't be fooled. The trail is the steepest, and the brush is the thickest, in its first 100 yards. After that, the trail just keeps getting wider and more level as you descend. It turns out to be an easy hike.

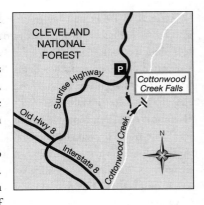

To start things off on the right foot, so to speak, make sure you park in the right spot. You'll often see cars parked in the pullout on the east side of the Sunrise Highway, but if you do this, you have to walk along the road for a few hundred yards to the start of the trail. Instead, park on the west side of the highway, in the turnout with the large rock wall, then just cross the road.

Pick up the unsigned trail at the north end of the guardrail, and make your way steeply downhill through the chaparral. When you reach the bottom of the canyon, which takes about 15 minutes, turn sharply left and walk along Cottonwood Creek, heading upstream. You can't see anything yet, but you're only five minutes from the falls.

The trail gets narrower, passing by many spiny cacti, beautiful rock formations, and a terrific show of spring wildflowers. Shortly beyond a makeshift campsite,

© ANN MARIE BROWN

one of Cottonwood Creek Falls' cascades and pools

you start passing one rock-lined cascade after another. There are three main drops, each about 12 feet high, and several smaller ones. The final fall you reach is a gorgeous free fall, and it's the most impressive of the group. Its pool, which has been dammed by rocks, is just right for swimming.

Directions

From San Diego, drive east on I-8 for 47 miles to the Highway S1/Sunrise Scenic Byway turnoff. Drive north on Highway S1 for about two miles to the large pullout on the west side of the road, between mileposts 15.0 and 15.5. (It has an obvious, graffiti-covered rock wall.) Cross the road on foot, and locate the unmarked trail at the north end of the guardrail.

Information and Contact

A national forest Adventure Pass is required. A map of Cleveland National Forest is available for a fee from the National Forest Store (406/329-3024, www.nationalforeststore.com), or can be downloaded for free from www.fs.fed.us/r5/maps/. For more information, contact Cleveland National Forest, Descanso Ranger District, 619/445-6235, www.fs.fed.us/r5/cleveland.

12 KITCHEN CREEK FALLS
Cleveland National Forest

🚶 🚫 🚣 🐴 ⛺

Level: Moderate

Best Season: December–May

Distance: 4.5 miles round-trip

Elevation Change: Total gain 500 feet

In a word: awesome. That's the only way to sum up Kitchen Creek Falls. Although San Diego and Orange Counties are blessed with many spectacular waterfalls, Kitchen Creek at a strong flow tops them all.

As with many of the streams and falls in the dry and arid Southland, perfect timing is crucial to your visit. Kitchen Creek runs year-round, but the 150-foot fall is a showstopper only from December–May, or when there's wet weather. The trail to reach it is a shadeless two miles through classic chaparral country, and uphill to boot. It's not the kind of place you want to find yourself at high noon in mid-August.

The trailhead is only a few short miles from the Mexican border, so you may see border patrol vehicles and uniformed of-

the base of Kitchen Creek Falls

© ANN MARIE BROWN

ficers near the trailhead. That's just what they do around here. Also, make sure you come with all the supplies you need for your day hike, because the friendly Boulder Oaks Store that used to feed hungry campers and hikers here burned to the ground.

The trail has a rather inglorious start as it crosses underneath I-8, but the views improve as you climb upward. The sight and sound of the highway doesn't stop till you drop down to the falls, but you'll be pleasantly distracted by the colorful ceanothus, paintbrush, and peach-colored monkeyflower along the trail. If you're hiking in the right wind conditions, you may see colorful paragliders soaring high above your head.

It's extremely easy to miss the left-hand spur trail off the Pacific Crest Trail (PCT) to reach the falls. There's no visual indication of a waterfall or even a stream, just the sandy, cactus-lined trail, and your ears can detect water only if it has recently rained. Start paying close attention after about 45 minutes of trail time; keep looking to your left for a side trail. I reached the turnoff in exactly two miles, after a noticeable increase in the sharpness of the grade. On my trip, small rocks were lining the left side of the PCT where three separate spur trails took off within 15 feet of each other. If you follow any of the spurs, you reach a distinctly shaped pointed rock sticking up from the ground, about six feet tall and 25 feet down the trail. This means you're in the right place. From the rock, follow any of several use trails (there's a network of them), descending until you hear the sound of water and reach an overlook with a view of Kitchen Creek.

From the overlook, you'll see some small cascades, but still no big waterfall in sight. That's because you're upstream of the main drop. Cut down the hillside on any of the use trails, heading generally downstream. In a few more minutes you'll be standing at the top of the falls. If you choose to continue to the waterfall's base, use caution. The polished granite is slippery when dry and treacherous when wet. To make your descent, stay off the rock and keep to the dirt routes alongside the falls.

Kitchen Creek's drop is 150 feet of cascading water sliding off slick granite. The tiered cascades twist and turn over an extended series of rounded ledges in the bedrock, creating myriad places to throw down a towel or blanket and listen to the music of the falls.

Directions

From San Diego, drive east on I-8 for 50 miles to the Buckman Springs Road turnoff. Drive south on the frontage road (the old highway) for 2.3 miles to Boulder Oaks Campground. (Make sure you stay on the frontage road; do not turn onto Buckman Springs Road.) Park along the road near the signed trailhead for the Pacific Crest Trail, which is directly opposite the campground.

Information and Contact

A national forest Adventure Pass is required. A map of Cleveland National Forest is available for a fee from the National Forest Store (406/329-3024, www.nationalforeststore.com), or can be downloaded for free from www.fs.fed.us/r5/maps/. For more information, contact Cleveland National Forest, Descanso Ranger District, 619/445-6235, www.fs.fed.us/r5/cleveland.

CALIFORNIA DESERTS

BEST WATERFALLS

◖ Most Unusual
Darwin Falls, **page 498**

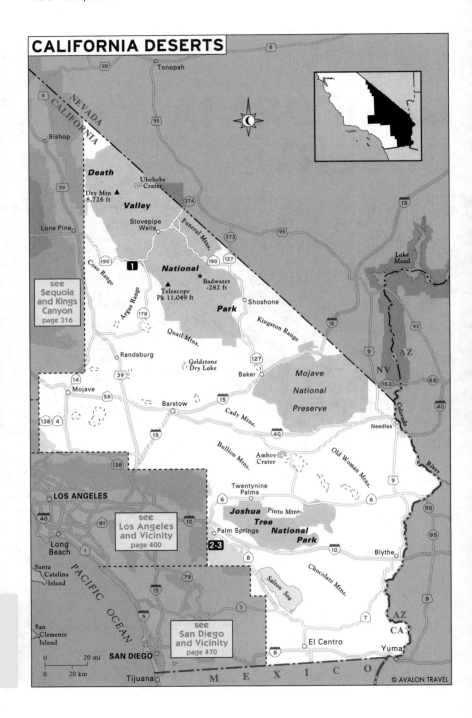

CALIFORNIA DESERTS

Tonopah

NEVADA
CALIFORNIA

Bishop

Death

Ubehebe
Crater

Dry Mtn ▲
8,726 ft

Valley

Stovepipe
Wells

Lone Pine

Coso Range

see
Sequoia
and Kings
Canyon
page 316

National

Funeral Mtns.

★ Badwater
-282 ft

Telescope
Pk 11,049 ft ▲

Argus Range

Park

Shoshone

Kingston Range

Quail Mtns.

Randsburg

Goldstone
Dry Lake

Baker

Mojave

Mojave

National

Preserve

Barstow

Cady Mtns.

Needles

Bullion Mtns.

Amboy
Crater

Old Woman Mtns.

Lake
Mead

AZ

NV

Colorado River

LOS ANGELES

Twentynine
Palms

Joshua

Pinto Mtns.

see
Los Angeles
and Vicinity
page 400

Long
Beach

Palm Springs

Tree

National

Park

Blythe

Santa
Catalina
Island

Chocolate Mtns.

PACIFIC OCEAN

Salton
Sea

AZ

CA

San
Clemente
Island

see
San Diego
and Vicinity
page 470

El Centro

Yuma

0   20 mi
0   20 km

SAN DIEGO

Tijuana

M E X I C O

© AVALON TRAVEL

TRAIL NAME	LEVEL	DISTANCE	TIME	ELEVATION	FEATURES	PAGE
1 Darwin Falls	Easy	2.2 mi rt	120 ft	Feb.-May	🥾	498
2 Murray Canyon Falls	Moderate	4.0 mi rt	300 ft	Oct.-May	🥾	499
3 Tahquitz Canyon Falls	Easy	2.0 mi rt	350 ft	Nov.-May	🥾	501

■ DARWIN FALLS
Death Valley National Park

BEST ◖

🏃

Level: Easy

Best Season: February–May

Distance: 2.2 miles round-trip

Elevation Change: Total gain 120 feet

Darwin Falls is a must-do desert hike. A waterfall in the desert is rare and precious—a miracle of life in a harsh world. On this hike into an arid desert canyon, you follow the trail of a tiny trickle of water as it slowly expands into a fully flowing stream. You trace the stream's path, and at the back of the canyon it drops over a 30-foot-high cliff to create Darwin Falls. The slender waterfall is perfectly showcased in a rock gallery.

© ANDREW SAWADISAVI

Darwin Falls

The hike is just over one mile each way, and except on hot days, it is well-suited for families and beginners. Just be sure to carry plenty of water with you.

At its start, the path is not keenly defined. Its wide dirt track parallels some water pipes through a wash, then slowly transitions into single-track. At several points, you must Darwin Canyon's stream to stay on the route, but rocks are conveniently placed for easy crossing. Route-finding is simple, because you just walk upcanyon, following the stream. Canyon walls on both sides keep you channeled in the proper direction.

The stream flow increases and the canyon walls narrow as you approach the waterfall, requiring some minor scrambling. The amount of vegetation also increases as you near the fall; notice the proliferation of willows, cattails, and reeds jockeying for position next to the running water. If it's spring, you may have some winged companions. More than 80 species of resident and migrating birds have been sighted in this canyon.

You pass a small stream-gauging station right before you reach Darwin Falls, then round a corner and enter a box canyon. The walls around you have become more colorful as you've progressed; now you are completely surrounded by shades of yellow, coral, orange, and crimson. Darwin Falls drops over a rock cliff with a large cottonwood tree growing at its lip. The water pours down and then forks into two separate streams, giving life to ferns and colorful mosses growing alongside the fall.

Some intrepid explorers choose to scramble above Darwin Falls and head farther back in the canyon, where more than a half-dozen small cascades can be found, but this requires advanced scrambling skills. Darwin is the largest and loveliest of the falls, so your best bet is to stay right here and savor the miracle of this desert oasis.

Directions

From Stovepipe Wells Village at Death Valley, drive west on Highway 190 for 28 miles to Panamint Springs Resort. Continue past the resort for one mile to the left (south) turnoff for Darwin Falls. Turn left and drive 2.5 miles on the dirt road to a fork, then bear right and park at the signed trailhead.

Alternatively, from Lone Pine on U.S. 395, drive east on Highway 136 for 18 miles, then continue straight on Highway 190 for 30 miles. The right (south) turnoff for Darwin Falls is exactly one mile before you reach Panamint Springs Resort. Continue as above.

Information and Contact

There is no fee. A park map is available by free download from www.nps.gov/deva, or at any park visitor center. For more information, contact Death Valley National Park, 760/786-3200, www.nps.gov/deva.

2 MURRAY CANYON FALLS
Agua Caliente Indian Reservation

Level: Moderate

Best Season: October–May

Distance: 4.0 miles round-trip

Elevation Change: Total gain 300 feet

If you want to see the "real" Palm Springs, leave behind the shopping malls and swimming pools and head for Murray Canyon. Located on the Agua Caliente Indian Reservation, Murray Canyon is a vestige of what Palm Springs used to be—wide-open vistas of red rock, an oasis of fan palms, a life-giving stream, and an abundance of barrel cactus and other desert flora. You won't find any tennis courts, golf courses, or beauty salons here, but you will find a memorable desert waterfall.

© ANN MARIE BROWN

Murray Canyon Falls

The hike begins from the east side of the picnic grounds between Murray and Andreas Canyons, at a sign reading "Murray Canyon, 20 minutes." It's accurate, more or less. Twenty minutes won't get you to the good stuff, merely to the start of the canyon and the first cluster of palm trees. I passed a guy who had traveled only this far and was clearly disappointed. He told me, "Nothing much down there. Not even much water." Don't make his mistake. Have faith and keep hiking.

The trail is well-packed sand, and it's clearly marked along the way. After an initial stretch through open desert terrain, you soon enter Murray Canyon, which narrows and twists and turns so that you never see where you're going until you come around the next bend. This keeps the anticipation high. Gradually, the stream you've been following begins to show a greater flow of water, and accordingly, the streamside reeds, willows, palms, and wild grapes intensify their growth. The palms are *Washingtonias;* nearly 1,000 of them thrive in Murray Canyon. If you're a fan of red rock, you'll love the 100-foot-tall slanted outcrops that jut out from the earth. They're a photographer's delight. If you enjoy desert flora, you'll be amazed at the hundreds, or perhaps thousands, of barrel cacti that line the canyon's walls.

At 1.5 miles, you'll pass the turnoff for the Coffman Trail on the left, then climb up and over a jumble of boulders. Continue for another 10–15 minutes until you suddenly come upon a delicate waterfall, sculpted out of fine, polished granite. The fall has two 20-foot cascades, each with a mirrorlike pool at its base, set about 50 yards apart. If the day is warm, you'll feel compelled to wade in. A half dozen more cascades await farther back in this canyon, earning these falls the name "Seven Sisters."

Note that in extremely dry years, the reservation sometimes prohibits swimming or any water contact in Murray Canyon. Check with the folks at the entrance kiosk on current conditions and regulations. And one more caveat: the reservation closes its gates at 5 P.M. sharp each day. Make sure you've completed your hike and are driving out by 4:55 P.M. or thereabouts, or your car may be locked in for the night. Guess how I know?

Directions

From Palm Springs, drive south through the center of town on Highway 111/ Palm Canyon Drive, and take the right fork signed for South Palm Canyon Drive. Drive 2.8 miles on South Palm Canyon Drive, bearing right at the sign for Palm Canyon/Andreas Canyon. Stop at the entrance kiosk, then drive about 200 yards, and turn right for Murray Canyon. Drive past the Andreas Canyon Trailhead, and continue to the Murray Canyon picnic area, one mile from the entrance kiosk.

Information and Contact

A $9 day-use fee is charged per adult, $7 for seniors, and $5 for children ages 6–12. A free map/brochure is available at the entrance kiosk. For more information, contact the Indian Canyons Visitor Center, 760/323-6018, www.indian-canyons.com.

3 TAHQUITZ CANYON FALLS
Agua Caliente Indian Reservation

Level: Easy

Best Season: November-May

Distance: 2.0 miles round-trip

Elevation Change: Total gain 350 feet

Just about everything in Palm Springs has a legend behind it, and Tahquitz Canyon (pronounced TAW-quits) is no exception. Named for an Agua Caliente shaman who abused his powers and was banished from his tribe, Tahquitz Canyon is a spectacular outdoor museum of desert flora and fauna. Amid lush stands of desert lavender, mesquite, and creosote, the canyon is home to plentiful bird life, Native American rock art, and a spectacular 60-foot waterfall. Yet the rumored curse of the shaman Tahquitz remains so powerful that even today, local Agua Caliente tribe members refuse to venture into some parts of this rock-studded canyon.

© ANN MARIE BROWN

Tahquitz Canyon Falls

That doesn't keep away the thousands of Palm Springs visitors who have hiked here since the canyon's public opening in 2000. The privately owned canyon had been closed for decades after having been abused by vandals and squatters in the 1960s and 1970s. The Agua Caliente Native Americans launched a massive clean-up effort in Tahquitz Canyon, hauling out tons of debris, garbage, and broken glass, then constructed a beautiful visitor center at the canyon's mouth. Today you can hike on your own or join a group led by a knowledgeable ranger on the one-mile trail through the canyon to the base of its impressive waterfall. Movie buffs will recognize the showering falls as the entrance to the land of Shangri-La in Frank Capra's 1937 film *Lost Horizon*. The waterfall is fed both by snowmelt from Mount San Jacinto and natural springs, so it has more water in it than you would expect. It's a big, happy surprise to see this sparkling cascade in the middle of desert.

If you're new to the wonders of desert flora and fauna, your best bet is to take one of the daily guided hikes. You'll learn a lot about the desert landscape and how the Native Americans used this arid land to their advantage. The trail is easy enough for children, but because this is the desert, don't forget your water bottle—even on cool days.

Directions
From Palm Springs, drive south through the center of town on Highway 111/Palm Canyon Drive and turn right on Mesquite Avenue. Drive 0.5 mile to the Tahquitz Canyon Visitor Center.

Information and Contact
A $12.50 entrance fee is charged per adult; $6 for children 12 and under. Guided hikes are held from October–May at 8 A.M., 10 A.M., noon, and 2 P.M.; you can also hike on your own any time 7:30 A.M.–5 P.M. For more information, contact the Tahquitz Canyon Visitor Center, 760/416-7044, www.tahquitzcanyon.com.

Index

www.moon.com

MOON.COM is ready to help plan your next trip! Filled with fresh trip ideas and strategies, author interviews, informative travel blogs, a detailed map library, and descriptions of all the Moon guidebooks, Moon.com is all you need to get out and explore the world—or even places in your own backyard. While at Moon.com, sign up for our monthly e-newsletter for updates on new releases, travel tips, and expert advice from our on-the-go Moon authors. As always, when you travel with Moon, expect an experience that is uncommon and truly unique.

MOON IS ON FACEBOOK—BECOME A FAN!
JOIN THE MOON PHOTO GROUP ON FLICKR

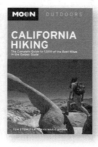

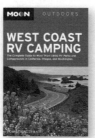

MOON CALIFORNIA WATERFALLS

Avalon Travel
a member of the Perseus Books Group
1700 Fourth Street
Berkeley, CA 94710, USA
www.moon.com

Editor and Series Manager: Sabrina Young
Copy Editor: Kim Runciman
Production and
  Graphics Coordinator: Darren Alessi
Cover Designer: Darren Alessi
Interior Designer: Darren Alessi
Map Editor: Mike Morgenfeld
Cartographer: Mike Morgenfeld

ISBN: 978-1-59880-376-1
ISSN: 1548-2162

Printing History
1st Edition – 1997
4th Edition – May 2011
5 4 3 2 1

Text and Maps © 2011 by Ann Marie Brown.
All rights reserved.

Some photos and illustrations are used by
permission and are the property of the original
copyright owners.

Front cover photo: Vernal Falls, Yosemite
© Reflex Stock
Title page photo: © Ann Marie Brown
Back cover photo: Yosemite Falls © Sabrina
Young

Printed in Canada by Friesens

Keeping Current

We are committed to making this book the most accurate and enjoyable guide to
California waterfalls. You can rest assured that every waterfall in this book has
been carefully reviewed in an effort to keep this book as up-to-date as possible.
However, by the time you read this book, some of the fees listed herein may have
changed and trails or parks may have closed unexpectedly.

   If you have a favorite gem you'd like to see included in the next edition, or
see anything that needs updating, clarification, or correction, please drop us a
line. Send your comments via email to feedback@moon.com, or use the address
above.